School Segregation
in Western North Carolina

CONTRIBUTIONS TO SOUTHERN APPALACHIAN STUDIES

1. *Memoirs of Grassy Creek: Growing Up in the Mountains on the Virginia–North Carolina Line.* Zetta Barker Hamby. 1998

2. *The Pond Mountain Chronicle: Self-Portrait of a Southern Appalachian Community.* Edited by Leland R. Cooper and Mary Lee Cooper. 1998

3. *Traditional Musicians of the Central Blue Ridge: Old Time, Early Country, Folk and Bluegrass Label Recording Artists, with Discographies.* Marty McGee. 2000

4. *W.R. Trivett, Appalachian Pictureman: Photographs of a Bygone Time.* Ralph E. Lentz II. 2001

5. *The People of the New River: Oral Histories from the Ashe, Alleghany and Watauga Counties of North Carolina.* Edited by Leland R. Cooper and Mary Lee Cooper. 2001

6. *John Fox, Jr., Appalachian Author.* Bill York. 2003

7. *The Thistle and the Brier: Historical Links and Cultural Parallels Between Scotland and Appalachia.* Richard Blaustein. 2003

8. *Tales from Sacred Wind: Coming of Age in Appalachia. The Cratis Williams Chronicles.* Cratis D. Williams. Edited by David Cratis Williams and Patricia D. Beaver. 2003

9. *Willard Gayheart, Appalachian Artist.* Willard Gayheart and Donia S. Eley. 2003

10. *The Forest City Lynching of 1900: Populism, Racism, and White Supremacy in Rutherford County, North Carolina.* J. Timothy Cole. 2003

11. *The Brevard Rosenwald School: Black Education and Community Building in a Southern Appalachian Town, 1920–1966.* Betty J. Reed. 2004

12. *The Bristol Sessions: Writings About the Big Bang of Country Music.* Edited by Charles K. Wolfe and Ted Olson. 2005

13. *Community and Change in the North Carolina Mountains: Oral Histories and Profiles of People from Western Watauga County.* Compiled by Nannie Greene and Catherine Stokes Sheppard. 2006

14. *Ashe County: A History; A New Edition.* Arthur Lloyd Fletcher. 2009 [2006]

15. *The New River Controversy; A New Edition.* Thomas J. Schoenbaum. Epilogue by R. Seth Woodard. 2007

16. *The Blue Ridge Parkway by Foot: A Park Ranger's Memoir.* Tim Pegram. 2007

17. *James Still: Critical Essays on the Dean of Appalachian Literature.* Edited by Ted Olson and Kathy H. Olson. 2008

18. *Owsley County, Kentucky, and the Perpetuation of Poverty.* John R. Burch, Jr. 2008

19. *Asheville: A History.* Nan K. Chase. 2007

20. *Southern Appalachian Poetry: An Anthology of Works by 37 Poets.* Edited by Marita Garin. 2008

21. *Ball, Bat and Bitumen: A History of Coalfield Baseball in the Appalachian South.* L.M. Sutter. 2009

22. *The Frontier Nursing Service: America's First Rural Nurse-Midwife Service and School.* Marie Bartlett. 2009

23. *James Still in Interviews, Oral Histories and Memoirs.* Edited by Ted Olson. 2009

24. *The Millstone Quarries of Powell County, Kentucky.* Charles D. Hockensmith. 2009

25. *The Bibliography of Appalachia: More Than 4,700 Books, Articles, Monographs and Dissertations, Topically Arranged and Indexed.* Compiled by John R. Burch, Jr. 2009

26. *Appalachian Children's Literature: An Annotated Bibliography* Compiled by Roberta T. Herrin and Sheila Quinn Oliver. 2009

27. *Southern Appalachian Storytellers: Interviews with Sixteen Keepers of the Oral Tradition.* Edited by Saundra Gerrell Kelley. 2010

28. *Southern West Virginia and the Struggle for Modernity*. Christopher Dorsey. 2011

29. *George Scarbrough, Appalachian Poet: A Biographical and Literary Study with Unpublished Writings*. Randy Mackin. 2011

30. *The Water-Powered Mills of Floyd County, Virginia: Illustrated Histories, 1770–2010*. Franklin F. Webb and Ricky L. Cox. 2011

31. *School Segregation in Western North Carolina: A History, 1860s–1970s*. Betty Jamerson Reed. 2011

School Segregation in Western North Carolina

A History, 1860s–1970s

BETTY JAMERSON REED

CONTRIBUTIONS TO SOUTHERN APPALACHIAN STUDIES, 31

McFarland & Company, Inc., Publishers
Jefferson, North Carolina, and London

Frontispiece: The first public school for colored people in North Carolina, established by Vincent Coyer, 1862 (courtesy the North Carolina Office of Archives and History, Raleigh).

LIBRARY OF CONGRESS CATALOGUING-IN-PUBLICATION DATA

Reed, Betty Jamerson, 1937–
School segregation in western North Carolina : a history, 1860s–1970s / Betty Jamerson Reed.
  p. cm. — (Contributions to Southern Appalachian studies ; 31)
Includes bibliographical references and index.

ISBN 978-0-7864-5965-0
softcover : 50# alkaline paper

1. African Americans—Education—North Carolina, Western—History.
2. African Americans—Education (Secondary)—North Carolina, Western—History.
3. Segregation in education—United States—History.   I. Title.
LC2802.N8.R44 2011   371.829'960730756—dc23   2011030536

BRITISH LIBRARY CATALOGUING DATA ARE AVAILABLE

© 2011 Betty Jamerson Reed. All rights reserved

No part of this book may be reproduced or transmitted in any form or by any means, electronic or mechanical, including photocopying or recording, or by any information storage and retrieval system, without permission in writing from the publisher.

On the cover: *inset* Jackson County Consolidated School in Sylva, North Carolina (photograph courtesy of the North Carolina Office of Archives and History, Raleigh); *foreground* students and teachers outside the Burton Street School, originally named Buffalo Street School, in West Asheville, circa 1925 (photograph courtesy of North Carolina Collection, Pack Memorial Library, Asheville)

Manufactured in the United States of America

McFarland & Company, Inc., Publishers
Box 611, Jefferson, North Carolina 28640
www.mcfarlandpub.com

To all educators who labored
in Appalachian North Carolina's segregated
African American schools, as represented by
J.H. Michael, Oddie J. Cox, Ethel K. Mills,
Bertha Neal, E.L. Cundiff, Gladys Neal Bailey,
Leonidas H. Jones, James T. Sapp, Elma Rai Dennis
and Hortense Potts—role models for entire communities.

In memory of
Floyd and Ella Jamerson, my parents
Earl Leon Jamerson, my brother
William and Ann Jamerson, my brother and his wife
Peggy Jamerson Owens, my sister
E. Allan and Marie Reed, my parents-in-law
and three friends:
Gromer Luther
Randal Aiken
Van Johnson

TABLE OF CONTENTS

Acknowledgments	xi
Preface	1
Introduction	9
1. Roadblocks to Opportunity	17
2. Tracks of African Americans	27
3. Steps to Integration	35
4. Gateway Policies for Education	67
5. Gateway Push to Education	84
6. Conceptual Path to Schools	114
7. Pragmatic Path to Schools	123
8. Leaders in Secondary Education	160
9. Turmoil in Secondary Education	191
10. Reconciliation in Secondary Education	205
11. Expectations of Education	221
Appendix: High Spots in Negro History	235
Bibliography	239
Index	253

Acknowledgments

Howard Spanogle pored over the manuscript of this book, suggested ways to improve it and created an impressive table of contents. Juanita Spanogle pointed out discrepancies and participated in brainstorming activities. Without them this project would have halted long before its culmination.

I appreciate the help and encouragement of my friends and those whom I now count as friends. To those whose personal memories of segregated schools were willingly shared and recorded in the following pages, I am deeply grateful.

Barbara C. Blaine and Charlie Glazener were among those who provided materials, space for research and much encouragement. Patrick Gallegher, author of *The Berkeley Spinners*, read *The Brevard Rosenwald School* (2004) and wrote an encouraging letter of appreciation, sharing his personal disappointment that his alma mater, Hendersonville High School, was deprived of major talent when the Brevard students integrated the high school in Transylvania County. As a sports historian, Gallegher shared much information about the football history of Ninth Avenue which increased my knowledge of other black schools, because no record of sports competition includes only one team. I am grateful for his interest, his generosity in sharing information with me, and his support.

Western Carolina University's Kevin Pennington — encouragement personified — and Beth Coulter and Ted Henson were my cheerleaders who endorsed my project as worthwhile.

Librarians, such as Clifton Sawyerr of Bluford Library at A&T University, often came to my aid, reminding me of a comment made in the past by my then 11-year-old son: "Mom, have you noticed? All librarians are nice." If I had no reason to agree at that time, I surely do today. Marcy Thompson, whose duties are multifold, helped me enormously. Debbie Brewer not only helped but shouldered a great deal of responsibility in gathering information about schools in our northern counties, especially Alleghany. Over the course of the past years, Helen Wykle has assisted me by suggesting sources to investigate and answering questions, some of which dealt with conflicting data. Alex Floyd, extremely skilled in research, answered every query of mine promptly and helpfully and also assisted me with citation issues. Patti Holda came to my rescue on a few occasions. Marie L. Martin of the Wright-Potts Library at Voorhees College graciously offered to prepare a file of information about the achievements of John Potts.

Directors and volunteers at local heritage museums came to my aid over and over again. Stella Mace was the first to offer her assistance and she brought materials for me to examine which otherwise I would never have known existed. John Hawkins shared a wealth of information and patiently allowed me to subject him to question after question. Boyd Cathey assisted me with citation issues related to archival material and answered numerous queries about the North Carolina State Archives. It was my good fortune to gain some assistance for archival documentation from Jeff Petruch-Hume, who, when he was unable to answer, researched the problem. He and Alex Floyd introduced me to *Evidence Explained* (2007), which has been a help. Kay Shoemaker, Jill Jones, and Victoria Howell represent those who generously contributed suggestions and materials. Others, such as Fred J. Hay and Nell Ashworth, shared photographs from their personal collections.

Personal friends and relatives who read and commented on portions of the manuscript showed insight and amazing honesty about its flaws. Among those are Jeannette Nelson Ballew, Peggy McCartney Hay, and my niece Cynthia Nicholson. Peggy Hay e-mailed insightful messages when I was discouraged. My friend and fellow educator Barbara Putnam listened to my complaints about barriers and errors. My nephew John Jamerson gave me frequent pushes by saying such things as, "Hurry up and finish. I want to read that book." My husband, Bill, willingly and often played the devil's advocate, allowing me to see issues from a different perspective, and helped me resolve problems about the conclusion. Floyd and Vanessa encouraged me, and Caleb and Sara-Ann allowed me time off from playing with their children to visit the archives. My son David, whose skills never cease to amaze me, solved many of my technical woes. He also read and commented on portions of the manuscript, as did his colleague Ian Henslee.

And, as in all things, since I frequently called upon God for insight, strength and guidance, I am thankful for being directed to this historical saga and for having drawn a portion of it to a close.

Preface

Western North Carolina is part of the beautiful Southern Appalachian region. Settled by Native Americans who thrived on the land's abundance, the area later attracted the Scots, the Irish and the Welsh. Subsequent migrations brought settlers from the Lowlands of South Carolina. Often excluded from the history of the Southern Appalachian Mountains, African Americans contributed much to the physical and cultural environment of the highland region. More visible were those colonizers of European descent, but black Americans created a unique ethnic culture within the Appalachian territory though details of their early history in the area are elusive. African Americans came to the region in a variety of ways—from accompanying early Spanish explorers to escorting drovers as free men to creating comfort for the wealthy as slaves—but their number was small. However, over time, black communities developed and in a spirit of cooperation, their citizens united to provide places of business, worship and education. Schools were eventually established in small, rural mountain villages and in more populated areas such as Asheville.

The present study targets schools in Alleghany, Alexander, Ashe, Burke, Caldwell, Catawba, Cherokee, Clay, Graham, Henderson, Jackson, Macon, Madison, McDowell, Mitchell, Polk, Rutherford, Stokes, Swain, Transylvania, Watauga, Wilkes, Surry, Yadkin and Yancey Counties, as well as the city school systems such as Asheville, Hendersonville, Lenoir, Morganton, and Glen Alpine. Graham County had few African-American residents during its history, but it is included in the records of the Division of Negro Education of North Carolina's Department of Public Instruction and is discussed in reference to those documents. A few facts are included in regard to schooling in Cleveland and in Gaston County.

The black population established numerous small schools; however, with consolidation the history of those unique institutions has been lost. To include documentation of all small schools cited in school board minutes would accomplish little, but students learned to read, to write, and to cipher, skills valued throughout their lives. Higgins School, located about two miles from downtown Burnsville, offered exciting learning experiences for its students through teachers such as Lois Kearns, Ruby Beard and Charity Hazzard Griffiths. Over time leadership emerged in isolated African American communities in the ranks of educators, ministers, and citizens. For example, J.F. Fox was an educational leader in Wilkes County; Samuel Raper was a minister, a youth advocate, and a civil rights leader in Transylvania County as well as in Cleveland County; and W.S. Nicely was an educational leader in Clay County.

Teachers assumed their roles as instructors of the young in primitive one room school houses across the region. Among that number were Irma Swepson in the school at Fruitland in Henderson County, Elsie J. Osborne at Andrews Colored School, and Stella Hardy in Mitchell County's Altapass Colored School. Leaders supported the move to consolidate the one room schools to establish a more efficient educational system for black students. Such consolidation frequently met strong local opposition but eventually won out. In Caldwell County the elementary schools consolidated in one building at Dulatown. Improved transportation allowed students to enroll in schools outside their home communities. One bus in Caldwell County traveled 78.5 miles daily. In Catawba County, consolidation allowed students from Coulter's Grove, Baker's Mountain, Bandy, and Plateau schools to attend a single school. Catawba Rosenwald School became a model for other high schools in its vocational outreach to adults. Mothers and daughters learned sewing methods in evening class while fathers learned about more up-to-date farming techniques to become self-sufficient with less dependence on debt (Freeze, 2002). An education with practical outcomes inspired rural citizens.

In North Carolina's western counties schools and churches created a strong sense of unity that empowered black citizens to confront the difficulties of living in a predominately white culture with ensuing paternalism, even though within their own communities differing opinions could result in conflict or disagreement. Appalachian school communities played an active role in the desegregation movement.

This study of segregated schools in North Carolina's Appalachian counties developed from an ongoing interest in the educational history and culture of diverse groups. In the 1980s, I searched for the voices of Latino women by probing into the past and present, but my quest found a new direction when I delved into Transylvania County's records of a school for black children in North Carolina. The research resulted in a book: *The Brevard Rosenwald School: Black Education and Community Building in a Southern Appalachian Town, 1920–1966* (McFarland, 2004). The stimulation of that project intensified my craving to learn more about the education of black students in segregated schools.

Beginning the quest of researching school life during segregation, I volunteered to survey historic Rosenwald schools in Western North Carolina for Claudia Brown, architectural survey coordinator at the North Carolina State Historic Preservation Office. As I examined those buildings or what remained of them, my obsession with the past grew. Initially I planned to collect information about the Rosenwald schools in Western North Carolina, but soon I discovered the history of non–Rosenwald schools was equally exciting so my research broadened to include representative schools and to document the struggles and accomplishments of black teachers and students during segregation in part by identifying the hurdles that had to be crossed on the path to integration. Unfortunately, my investigation revealed other barriers to overcome if a path to equal education could be achieved.

As time advanced the Appalachian region became synonymous with poverty and ignorance, thus sparking efforts to educate its population. Whites, blacks, Indians, adults and children all needed to learn, but schools established specifically for African-American students is the focus of this study.

An analysis of schools established in the 1860s through the 1970s reveals the struggles, achievements, and ultimate victory of a unified community intent on achieving an adequate education. The present study identifies the roadblocks confronting African Americans in their journey to provide educational opportunities in remote, rural mountain communities as well as in more urban regions in Western North Carolina. The study examines public, private, formal and informal venues for black schooling and briefly documents events that brought blacks to the region. An early chapter describes the steps to integration — the journey's end — and the achievement of desegregated schools. From there, a look back identifies early community efforts to educate black children and the movement to acquire and to improve schools, with attention to the effect of Rosenwald funding on mountain counties. The movement to provide and to improve secondary education is the focus of three chapters. The conclusion weighs the value and achievement of rural segregated black schools as well as their significance for today's educators. Part of that significance highlights statistics indicating that schools in

North Carolina, particularly in the eastern counties, are experiencing resegregation — an issue to be addressed by modern educators.

Within the years comprising this study, segregation of the races was the law of the land. Early on, race emerged as an educational issue. For example, laws banning miscegenation impacted educational decision makers. Often marriages of African Americans and Caucasians met with violent opposition, especially apparent when inter-racial children of such unions emerged as victims of harsh treatment. Enrolling biracial pupils brought challenges from school officials to produce legal documentation of the student's race with little or no regard for the negative impact such demands produced in the lives of children.

Analysis of the history of segregated schools leads to an examination of the Appalachian communities in which the schools were established, of a number of conditions which brought African Americans to live in those counties and of the strategy parents used to ensure their children's educational well-being. Schools mentioned in official records are identified with an effort to determine the members of the professional staff, the extent of their training, their methodology, and, to a degree, their effectiveness. The study includes architectural considerations as well as academic emphases.

Conclusions surface when the records provide sufficient data. Records document student involvement inside and outside of the classroom.The study, which includes more than 40 schools, presents accounts of extracurricular activities, ranging from music and journalism to sports, including baseball, football and basketball for secondary schools and seasonal programs to playground activities for elementary schools. I examined school board minutes, census data, principal reports, newspaper articles, alumni records, reports by superintendents, theses and dissertations as well as scholarly articles and books. I also scrutinized online documents. When possible, I have interviewed former students, parents, and teachers to gain their perspective about educational opportunities available in segregated schools. More than 100 individuals were interviewed, and those interviews elicited additional telephone conversations, as well as exchanges of e-mails or letters, and questionnaires. The documentation of randomly chosen former students reflects an effort to determine the degree to which segregated education effectively prepared alumni for the challenges of adult life. While prominent accomplishments of alumni are noted, I made a deliberate effort to target a wide range of people and their contributions to society. Occasionally, segregated schools for the white population have been included for comparative purposes.

Three scholars have published in-depth studies about segregated schools in North Carolina. David C. Cecelski (1994) presented case studies of integrated schools in Hyde County, North Carolina, in *Along Freedom Road*; Vanessa Siddle Walker (1996) addressed the merits of a segregated school in *Their Highest Potential: An African American School Community in the Segregated South*; Sherick A. Hughes (2006) researched the educational experiences of families in Northeastern Albemarle in *Black Hands in the Biscuits Not in the Classrooms*. Civil rights historian Adam Fairclough has completed an impressive study — *A Class of Their Own: Black Teachers in the Segregated South* (2007) — of African-American educators in the southern states. The current study differs in that it addresses another geographic region and presents a survey of schools serving black students in areas with a minimal black population.

I found the reoccurrence of segregation in modern classrooms startling. Even though it is occurring to a lesser degree in Western North Carolina, where the black population is small, there are patterns of segregation in school data in the western counties. That information evokes a number of questions: Is history repeating itself? Has ignoring past mistakes led to a recurrence of transgressions from policymakers? Are minority students again suffering from discriminatory practices in their schools? Is majority privilege reverberating in academic halls? Perhaps a fresh look at the history of segregated education may create echoes in the present that will ensure a brighter outlook for today's students of all races.

The decision to research the segregated schools of Western North Carolina developed by stages. While probing into the history of the Rosenwald School in Brevard, North Carolina, I discovered there were Rosenwald buildings in two adjoining counties: Shiloh in Buncombe County and East Flat Rock in Henderson County. Then, as happens with any research, my knowledge expanded to include schools such as Stephens-Lee, Allen and Ninth Avenue. I decided to do an intensive study of education for black students in all the schools within those two counties. Records showed that students were bused from Madison, Yancey, Transylvania and Polk to schools outside their districts, and the busing factor led to widening the scope of my research to include all of Western North Carolina's segregated schools. Limiting the study to a single geographical region was difficult.

The saga of segregated schools developed through numerous alterations resulting in a survey of elementary and high schools and the black communities they served. The process involved gathering information, sorting it by various methods—from geographic to thematic—identifying conflicting data, attempting to resolve conflict through triangulation, incorporating diverse techniques to organize the material, altering outlines for a book and persuading interested individuals to give me their reaction to various segments. Like other researchers, I found discarding information was painful but necessary (Bogdan and Biklen, 1992).

African Americans enriched my investigation by revealing the past interaction and cohesive network embedded in local black communities. I learned about neighborhoods such as Stumptown and Boozer Town in Buncombe County; Peacock, Brooklyn and West End in Henderson County; Bobtown and The Hill in Catawba County; Frog Bottom in Transylvania County; and Texana in Cherokee County. As I ascertained a great deal by reading scholarly accounts about the education of black citizens, my investigation targeted local communities—their relationships with one another in homes, churches and schools as well as with their white neighbors.

Segregated schools played a dual role by providing a haven and also by functioning as a hotbed of conflict. While individuals had a great deal in common and formed strong alliances, they also had disagreements that required mediation and resolution. Confirming factual data based on memory was challenging.

I searched local records, newspapers and public documents. In addition, interviewing parents, principals, teachers and students provided an especially satisfying aspect of the study. As referenced by Marshall and Rossman (1995), research is an attempt to gain insight into the "complexities of human interaction" (p. 15) through a process often disorganized, complex and definitely nonlinear. Their description aptly describes the process as I experienced it.

My objective was to revisit segregation in the black schools in the mountains of North Carolina, to gather details about their histories by examining school board minutes, county heritage documentation and newspaper articles, to identify leaders in those schools and to contact any living persons who taught or studied at the schools. The population of interest, while chiefly the black community, included white school board members and public officials. When possible, I met with those parties and used a semi-structured interview protocol to glean information about their school experiences and their evaluation of education in segregated and, when appropriate, integrated environments. At other times, individuals communicated through telephone conversations, letters and e-mail messages.

Marshall and Rossman (1995) identified qualitative research stages, such as firsthand observation, in-depth interviewing, personal involvement in the setting and document review. I traveled hundreds of miles to locate many of the schools and spent hours talking with individuals. I read memoirs, newspaper accounts, contacted knowledgeable individuals via e-mail, explored offerings at libraries, school board offices, heritage museums and spent days, perhaps weeks, at the North Carolina State Archives. Exploring county heritage publications, I found little material about black communities but the minimal information discovered required care in evaluating due to sparse documentation.

My study evolved into units of historical narrative, which Marshall & Rossman (1995) regard as the most appropriate method to convey the unique quality of human experiences and their relationships as a vital part of history. The research explored the investment of family in education and the extended community, which was a strong component of support for schools. For example, childless couples were often involved in local schools. Former students referred to the school community as "family." Their memories provide a record of relationships among people: parents and children, teachers and pupils, administrators and community, children and community.

Oral history demands careful scrutiny as a research tool because with the passing of time, human memory distorts certain aspects of earlier events. The tendency to paint past experiences with the human longing to emphasize the positive and perhaps to overlook the negative requires careful scrutiny. Nostalgia is a factor that cannot be ignored (Walker, 1996). One technique to deal with that tendency is to compare accounts of related events—a method I used. As I collected oral histories, I attempted to align facts based on human recall with data from minutes of school board proceedings or in newspaper accounts. But more important than determining the day-by-day accuracy of those oral histories was the goal of providing an avenue of expression for the voices of those who had firsthand experience with segregated education and with civil rights restrictions and who had lived under the harsh oppression of Jim Crow traditions.

My historical inquiry led to archival files in homes as well as in institutions. Former educators and students treasured school memorabilia and records. These people shared personal papers, scrapbooks and newspaper clippings. Sylvia D. Blakley was one who shared personal collections as well as stories about her father, John Davis, a school administrator. Roles within the schools varied and shifted.

As I pondered the condition of helplessness in light of legal oppression of black citizens, I concluded that, far from being helpless, communities were citadels of empowerment. I admired the strength developed by cohesive groups of citizens determined to fight for their rights. Similar to those under attack who fight mightily to defend homes, the black population united in a mighty way to demand their right to an adequate education. Their solidarity resulted in success.

Although, as indicated by Klotter (1980), the white Appalachians matched their black counterparts in poverty and deprivation, this study was not designed to compare the schools and communities of rural whites and blacks. However, occasionally comparative issues emerged. Educator William Darity's denunciation of the contrast of science laboratories in black and white schools of Hendersonville focused on two "town" schools. White rural schools also lacked up-to-date equipment, or if equipment were available, lack of materials or of a qualified instructor curtailed any use of the science lab.

My study highlighted a consideration of community and home influences. The schools reflected community values, and students responded to the educational concerns of their parents. In fact, what Hughes (2006) identifies as the pedagogy of struggle and of hope is rooted in the family and taught in the home. Respect for learning was an important element taught within the family circle. Other values impacted daily living.

One research challenge involved the use of archival material, not only at the North Carolina State Archives, Raleigh, but within collections of letters and articles in the archives of libraries and local history museums as well as in the collections maintained at offices of city and county boards of education and within the personal files of former teachers and students. For example, Victoria Howell has a personal archival collection of Freedman School in Lenoir while Wilbur and LaTiece Eggleston have a collection related to Reynolds School in Canton. Sylvia D. Blakley compiles information about the Jackson County Consolidated School. Blakley, Howell and the Egglestons generously allowed access to their documents. Such material was rich in information but often challenging due to a lack of sufficient documentation — a problem that created questions about proper citation details. *Evidence Explained* by Elizabeth S. Mills became a vital addition to my library. The information was clear, but identifying elements of the exact source continued to be a challenge.

Another difficulty was winning the trust of those I interviewed. I had no privileged access. Often, I was granted immediate support only to have it withdrawn. Expressions of appreciation for my project and a willingness to share suddenly changed to "Sorry, I have decided to write my own book"— a valid reason in my judgment but nevertheless disheartening. Also, information that was promised often never arrived. On a few occasions I invested time and money to keep an appointment, only to have the appointment suddenly canceled. For instance, I drove more than 100 miles to find a note posted on the door saying: "Sorry — will have to talk another day." Once, after traveling 60 miles I waited for an extensive time, but the gentleman who chose that time and place never arrived, nor did he call. On another occasion I traveled to Washington, D.C., to conduct an interview and to do additional research. The interview went well, but a major storm blocked further investigation in the area so I drove to Raleigh, excited to spend time at the North Carolina State Archives, only to learn that the archives had closed due to plumbing problems. Such disappointments were rare, and I searched out other ways to make my time profitable when they happened.

Other problems wreaked havoc on my efforts. Shortly after my arrival at Caldwell County Public Library, patrons were asked to leave because it was time for an annual dinner for the staff — an event that occurs only once a year. The unanticipated complication led me to call Leatrice R. Pearson, who immediately invited me to her home, where she shared information about her family, her schooling and her career as an educator. Subsequent telephone calls and letters allowed me to acquire treasured information from this knowledgeable woman. Others also opened the doors of their homes and received me warmly. I am grateful for the gift of their experiences and of their insights.

Use of an interview protocol gave me a sense of knowing where I was going, but usually the person being interviewed prompted other questions. My final question allowed the other party to suggest questions omitted that should have been asked. As a result, relevant issues came to my attention in several instances. For example, interviews with Gladys Russell Freeman and Leon Anderson were conducted exclusively by telephone, but their interest in and enthusiasm for my project were exhilarating. By telephone, Freeman, a woman advanced in years, directed me to sketch the Edneyville community and to show the proximity of homes to school and church as she described events along the way. I am grateful that Freeman's niece Betty J. Payne, suggested I contact her aunt; our conversations were amazing.

Occasionally I resorted to mailing questionnaires to individuals who were willing to respond, but that technique, although fruitful, was not as satisfying or as rewarding as the "in-person" interviews. One woman in advanced years answered my questions through her care provider. Her mind was clear, and she pointed out elementary school teaching challenges that would otherwise have eluded me. Attempts to identify recurring motifs eventually produced satisfaction. Schools dealt with obvious challenges: leadership, curricula, classroom procedure, celebrations and landmark events. Others illuminated issues of race. Another factor spotlighted the difficulty of evaluating one's own education. A number of themes concerning the community and the school revealed an extension of the home and of the church. Ownership of children — a psychological phenomenon — pervaded relationships among neighbors. The solidarity and the power of community, evident as delegations confronted city and county officials to improve their schools, brought about desegregation. The result, which required tremendous commitment and determination, was awe-inspiring as this study substantiates.

Introduction

When Buncombe County teenagers intimidated Henry Logan, no one stepped up to protect the young student. Logan assumed personal responsibility for his well-being by avoiding contact with his tormenters. White teenagers would show up near Henry's school to terrorize the youngster. Pulling a .45 bullet from his pocket, one of the white boys would show it to Logan and say, "Kid, this has got your name on it. If you show up here again, you're going to get it" (Burrell, 1992, p. 32). Fearful, he would stay out of school for weeks.

The older boys' taunts and the limitations prevalent in a segregated school robbed a future record-setting athlete of a sound basic education. Eventually Henry Logan would be chosen to represent his nation abroad and win great acclaim, but his lack of a "sound basic education" created persistent, unrelenting difficulties. Other African-American students also rejected the educational process, but black families pushed youngsters to learn all they could. However, the obstacles were numerous. The history of black education is accented by white indifference, underfunding, lack of adequate materials, and frequent postponement of needed improvements, but it also showcases the power of community.

Schools—a building furnished with desks, chalkboards, and books—plus teachers plus students equals hope. The educational setting itself may seem dreary, but the conviction that learning guarantees brighter futures enables students and their parents to look beyond the immediate setting to achievements that will promote prosperity and happiness. Hope bolstered by the promise of an education is not relegated to a single race or a single segment of a population. All cultures share the belief that to learn can bring positive changes. Past generations believed an opportunity to learn was worth any price. While most adult populations prize education—or at least they pay lip service to the concept—those who have been denied an education often earnestly seek it as a treasure to be cherished. The enslaved population of the American South, finding the path to learning closed to them, earnestly sought forbidden "book learning" and as freedmen established schools as their fortresses of learning. Anderson (1988) depicts the passion of former slaves for schooling by citing a remark of Harriet Beecher Stowe: "They rushed not to the grog-shop but to the schoolroom—they cried for the spelling-book as bread, and pleaded for teachers as a necessity of life" (p. 5).

However, their opportunity to learn would not continue to have the support of powerful whites. With the end of Reconstruction more roadblocks would be erected, a condition that damaged both races because trapping the Negro in a web of inferiority harmed the entire nation. In *An American Dilemma*, a classic published in 1944, Gunnar Myrdal earmarked as unreasonable the practice of proclaiming all Americans equal while denying equal rights to Negroes. The boldness with which this foreigner condemned discrimination to Americans by Americans was unprecedented, but that boldness stirred leaders to revisit the arena of human rights as it affected black citizens.

Much earlier than Myrdal's denunciation, two renowned black Americans realized that their country must eventually address the problem of its Negro citizens. In 1892, Anna Julia Cooper, an educator, addressed the dilemma: "In the clash and clatter of our American Conflict, it has been said that the South remains Silent. Like the sphinx, she inspires vociferous disputation but herself takes little part in the noisy controversy. One muffled strain in the Silent South, a jarring chord and a vague and uncomprehended cadenza has been and still is the Negro" [p. i].

Cooper, an important member of the black intelligentsia, apparently saw a need for the South to enter into the national dialogue to solve the race problem. She dedicated her life to education, assuming an active role in a number of reform movements, but her beginnings in Raleigh, North Carolina, were quite humble. The daughter of a slave named Hannah and Hannah's white owner, Cooper was acclaimed for academic achievement. Her life modeled the pursuit and the advancement of education. She called for black women to act on their own behalf and on behalf of their race, explaining that formal education would empower them as individuals and would strengthen their race and their nation.

Another highly educated Negro, W.E.B. Du Bois, said of the racial mindset of the South, there exists

> the sincere and passionate belief that somewhere between men and cattle God created a *tertium quid* and called it a Negro—a clownish, simple creature, at times even lovable within its limitations, but straightly foreordained to walk within the Veil. To be sure, behind the thought lurks the afterthought [that] some of them with ... chance might become men, but in sheer self-defense we dare not let them and build about them walls so high ... between them and the light a veil so thick that they shall not even think of breaking through" ["The Training of Black Men" in the *Atlantic Monthly*, September 1902. Cited by Leah Hammond in "A Tale of Two Schools," doctoral project, Fall 1999].

The Southern white view that the black man or woman was an inferior being because God had ordained his role as that of a simpleton fostered widespread belief that such a person should be educated in a minimal fashion. Southerners, convinced that the light of learning should be withheld from the Negro, prevailed, but in the 1950s law would replace the ignorance of that segment of the South's population, and the black population would own the right to be educated, a right that their ancestors could merely dream of.

Nevertheless, analysis of current school data indicates that modern educational practices may victimize persons of color as well as persons of lower economic status. In the segregated schools of the nineteenth and twentieth century instructors for black students frequently lacked adequate training, their students were from poor families, and white school officials displayed minimal interest in the achievements of either black students or their teachers. Analysis of past failures may trigger renewed concern for protecting the modern black student from discriminatory practices and may inspire efforts to insure that steps are taken to prevent injustice in local school policies and practices so that the failures of the past will not be repeated.

This book is an effort to memorialize black Appalachian communities, and the students and educators with an investment in segregated mountain schools. American icons Carter G. Woodson and David McCullough accentuated the importance of African Americans being personally involved in preserving their rich heritage. In an article analyzing the political victory of Barack Obama in his bid to become the 44th president, Leatrice R. Pearson (February 2009) cites the following remark by Woodson: "If a race has no history, if it has no worthwhile tradition, it becomes a negligible factor in the thought of the world and it stands in danger of being exterminated." In the same article, Pearson also quoted David McCullough, author of *History and Knowing Who We Are,* who wrote: "We must communicate to younger generations that Americans ... cannot truly know who we are or where we are going unless we know where we have been."

The history of everyday people is often more intriguing than the exploits and the accomplishments of those who become famous. By focusing exclusively on men and women who attain glory and recognition, historians bow to the need for efficiency in creating a written chronicle, but in many ways their records are weakened by omission of the activities of the so-called average person, who often toils in the midst of adversity, poverty, illiteracy and a myriad of other struggles. Universal loss occurs when recorded history is limited to one culture.

"If you believe that a man has no history worth mentioning, it's easy to assume that he has no humanity worth defending," cites an anonymous source. Gaining a true sense of the past may be enhanced by participating vicariously with the men and women who created the movements and achievements of the past. James Agee, a Pulitzer Prize winning novelist, described history as an exercise of the imagination during which individuals identify vicariously with the humanity of the past in order to determine the reasons for their actions (Hoopes, 1979).

The history of North Carolina is filled with exciting events, amusing ones, conflicting accounts, tragic episodes and much that is merely humdrum. As historians focus on the mainstreams of history, the behind-the-scenes minutiae are of necessity often relegated to oblivion. However, obscure events were frequently responsible for triggering mainstream movements. Behind each of history's worthy episodes, the common individual was there reacting to affairs in his or her daily existence. An individual's response often sets in motion a chain reaction prompting larger social consequences. So it was with segregation and the Civil Rights Movement of the twentieth century. The role of the ordinary man, whose name has escaped the historical records, was major in fostering civil liberties and in fighting segregation.

Earning the right to an education was especially significant for a population handicapped through enslavement. Beginning with the Emancipation Proclamation of 1862, popular support advocated universal public education for all, black and white. In 1875 North Carolina added the following to its constitution: "And the children of the white race and the children of the colored race shall be taught in separate schools; but there shall be no discrimination in favor of or to the prejudice of either race" (Section 2, Article IX, cited by Newbold, 1928). In the same article Newbold posts a comment by State Superintendent J.Y. Joyner, who said, "The State's obligation for the education of the child is the same whether the child is wrapped in a white skin or a black one" (Joyner Report, 1902, cited by Newbold). However, decades of struggle were required to make a sound education available to the African American population. Advocacy for educating the black race brought its members no immediate widespread opportunity to learn because the obstacles resulting from enslavement persisted in the South and prevailed in Western North Carolina.

Mistreatment of the black race was ingrained in the Southern mind and practices. That mindset evolved from the days of slavery when dealing with the temperament of owners resulted in the slave's involvement in "games" which allowed him or her to maintain a sense of self-worth. The Negro's proprietor might be subject to frequent mood swings, which could result in a variety of humiliating experiences, including beatings and harsh demands. Even family life was haunted by uncertainty for slaves whose spouses and children could be placed on the auction block, sold to strangers and transported far away. In such situations slaves were forced to search for an inner source of empowerment to preserve their dignity and self-esteem while surviving relentlessly brutal circumstances. For a few fortunate ones, book learning created a reservoir of strength through enlightenment. But empowerment by the written word was reserved for only a small number.

All slaves learned to practice the fine art of duplicity, a clever way to appear dumb when circumstances made that a desirable front. It was a survival technique not dependent upon formal education. Litwack (1979) describes the art of subtle taunting: "The education acquired by each slave was remarkably uniform, consisting largely of lessons in survival and accommodation — the uses of humility, the virtues of ignorance, the arts of evasion, the subtleties of verbal intonation, the techniques by which feelings and emotions were masked and the occasions that demanded the flattering of white egos and the placating of white fears" ("Preface," p. xi).

After having lost the War Between the States, Southerners, including those residing in Western North Carolina, displayed relentless resistance to equalizing the status of the Negro with their own. D.R. Goldfield (1990) provides this explanation for the delay:

> The racial etiquette governing encounters between black and white produced a "stage Negro" ... but from this etiquette flowed an array of assumptions held about blacks that reinforced the inferior role of black southerners. Blacks were childlike; they were prone to steal and prone to violence; they were oversexed, stupid, lethargic, dependent on whites, and, above all, happy. And when blacks confirmed these assumptions, they were generally rewarded — with employment, a good word at the bank, food, or even money [p. 3].

The black citizen found that patronizing the "superior" white man could bring personal satisfaction and physical comfort. Although the strategy to win rewards by manipulating the outcome may have reaped short term rewards, it postponed more permanent gains. Although lessons necessary for survival were mastered, for many the thirst for a more formal education created a persistent craving for additional knowledge. In spite of this, as history shows, the much sought right to an education would eventually empower the race and alter their fortunes in positive ways.

Building on the conventional attitudes of the late nineteenth century, members of the black race in the twentieth century were haunted by fear that defying or infringing on designated racial boundaries — social or economic or geographic — would result in vicious mistreatment. After the Civil War, adoption of the disparaging "Jim Crow" lifestyle led to a widespread practice of white supremacy. That practice was well established and widely applied in twentieth century America and reared its ugly face in Western North Carolina. The development of Jim Crow-ism, often traced to a skit popularized by Thomas Dartmouth Rice in the mid–nineteenth century, grew out of the iconic Jim Crow character (Emmerich, 1998). The skit, presented to white audiences, popularized stereotypes of an intellectually inferior African American, inherently unable to relate to white society. Eventually, the "Jim Crow" epithet became the acceptable characterization of all African Americans and rationalized prejudicial treatment of the Negro. In its 1896 ruling *Plessy v. Ferguson*, the Supreme Court validated Jim Crow customs by mandating the "separate but equal" principle dominating the South.

Efforts to attain legal segregation of the races can be traced to the Black Codes established after the Civil War. According to Leon F. Litwack (1979), Southern states enacted legislation to regulate the activities of newly freed slaves. Such laws codified the civil liberties of Negroes, which included freedom to marry and to own property. Black codes used the white man's rhetoric to retain white supremacy by downplaying the prevalent bias that blacks were useful only for working in the agriculture arena as farm hands or as owners of farms. Other economic opportunities were not easily open to black citizens. However, after only a short period, federal

Opposite: Henry Logan, known as the "Asheville Flash," was the first African-American collegiate athlete in North Carolina. A graduate of Stephens-Lee High School, Logan and his fellow Stephens-Lee athletes won the 1962 State Negro 4-A Basketball Tournament by defeating Atkins High of Winston-Salem, 66–59. Along with Bennie Lake, who later played for the Harlem Globetrotters, Logan was named an All-State player (courtesy Western Carolina University, Cullowhee, NC).

agents declared war on black codes, by having those laws suspended or by persuading legislatures to either repeal or reverse them. Attempts to relegate the former slaves to near serfdom was short-lived as a result of the passage of the Fourteenth and the Fifteenth Amendments, the Civil Rights Acts of 1866 and 1875, as well as the Enforcement Acts of 1870 and 1871.

Vigilante terrorism swept through the South in attempts to destroy the prospect of equal civil rights for African Americans, who were frequently subjected to vile treatment as punishment for infringing on the white man's turf. Lynching did occur and went unpunished. Hangings by vigilantes occurred throughout the South, including Western North Carolina. Blacks had reason to fear reprisal by whites. Heated racial relations boiled over in Clay County when a seventeen-year-old black boy was charged with the attempted assault of a thirteen-year-old white girl (Murray, 2002). The *Jackson County Journal* covered the story in its March 17, 1922, issue with the headline "Lynching is Barely Averted." As reported by Murray (2002), the news item about the Clay County "incident" indicated that if the angry white mob "had had its way," the boy would have been executed, his body "riddled with bullets." Murray points out that the sheriff did not intervene; it was the boy's father who managed to persuade the mob to spare his son's life. Blacks could relax only in their section of town, but even there they were fearful of angry whites showing up at their front doors.

In some instances, segregation offered protection for the black race, but the *Plessy v. Ferguson* decision of 1896 established segregation as the accepted manner of life—the norm—in all southern states, including North Carolina. That practice dictated separate service for the races in the educational system. Indeed, at great expense dual systems of public schools were maintained regardless of the number of students to be served. Although economically unsound for each race, segregated schools were regarded as educationally sound and as necessary.

Relegated to an inferior station in life, members of the black race seized upon education in the twentieth century as a panacea offering a cure for social and economic deprivation. African Americans viewed knowledge acquired in the classroom as the path both to prosperity and to freedom from mistreatment. Ignorance had contributed to disempowering African Americans. Minds crammed with grammar, history, geography, mathematics and literature coupled with vocational training provided the means to drastically alter their lifestyles and to ensure a brighter future. However, their hope for a better life focused not on themselves, but on their children and grandchildren.

This book includes an analysis of the African-American journey to integrated schools, a consideration of representative decisions and goals which initiated that journey, and the achievements along the way which filled the travelers with a sense of anticipation and hope. The educational dilemma of those residing in the western counties of Appalachian North Carolina is addressed in Chapters 1 and 2 by identifying roadblocks hindering the way to educational equity, representative accounts of black-white relationships, and characteristics of the region in which black citizens settled. Chapter 3 has a more in-depth account of major events in the desegregation of mountain schools, which symbolizes the journey's end. Chapters 4 through 7 outline community efforts to improve and expand elementary education and the problems hindering those efforts. Chapters 8, 9, and 10 relate attempts to establish accessible high schools. Chapter 11 provides a backward glance at the total journey and references current roadblocks for black learners while showcasing a few success stories.

Henry Logan's "bullet" experience symbolizes the fear tactics experienced by many African Americans that negatively impacted their educational triumphs. Even in a region not celebrated for slavery and with only a sparse black population, white efforts to degrade African-American achievement occurred frequently. Logan, as a young child, could not have foreseen the changes that would eventually earmark a better educational experience for blacks, at least in theory. However, it would require a decade before his graduation from Stephens-Lee High School would coincide with his accepting an invitation to attend a college that historically served only whites.

While Appalachian students received support and motivation from their parents, family and neighbors, often the key to their success in the classroom lay in the hands of their instructors. Although black educators were often undertrained and frequently performed in a mediocre manner, their achievements deserve praise. Laboring in ramshackle buildings with classrooms that were poorly lighted, poorly heated, and poorly equipped, those men and women made a noteworthy contribution toward improving life for their students and for their communities. Viewing their service from a 21st century perspective, however, should persuade the general public that as pioneers in a difficult educational arena, they deserve a place of honor in the educational history of the previous two centuries. However, arriving at the educational journey's end required cooperation and diligence from the total community; from Ashe County to Cherokee to Polk to Rutherford and Catawba and up to Alexander, over to Stokes and back to Alleghany and in all the counties in between were groups of African Americans determined to gain access to educational opportunities equal to those in white schools, and for their vision and sacrifice they deserve applause while their schools merit documentation in the annals of educational history.

1

ROADBLOCKS TO OPPORTUNITY

Americans take pride in an oft-repeated adage: The United States of America is a land of equal opportunity. In response, citizens believe that all children born within the national boundaries can expect to achieve their dreams. The expectation comes as a privilege of American citizenship.

Adults, especially parents, wonder, "Is there truth in this saying?" In education, the axiom is not true, neither in the educational practices of the past nor in those of the present. According to statesman Adlai Stevenson, considered "a voice of conscience," free public education is the right of all children and is the "most American thing." Stevenson delivered the comment when speaking to the Citizens' School Committee in Chicago in 1948 (John Hawkins, Personal Communication, November 24, 2009). While there is truth in his claim, the idea leads to another question: Are segregated or unequal educational opportunities un-American?

The use of learning as a vehicle to success in life's undertakings is ongoing. Study today; succeed tomorrow. The challenge is constant. However, from the 1860s to the 1970s, black citizens achieved remarkable victories in the educational journey to integrated schools. Moving forward required a century of heroic efforts to hurdle immense roadblocks, especially formidable for black citizens in the Appalachian region of North Carolina.

Roadblocks that prevented black children from acquiring an education equal to their white counterparts are many. Conditions of slavery, legalized by acts of legislative bodies, had barred any opportunity to learn the basics of reading, writing, and arithmetic. Despite victories that came with the conclusion of the Civil War which led to creating and conducting schools for former slaves, the black population residing in remote rural areas in Appalachian North Carolina received comparatively little attention. The geography which had allowed escape from the demands of prior obligations proved a hindrance in capitalizing on new routes to learning.

In Western North Carolina, early pioneers included indentured servants, runaway slaves, and free men of color. Often desperate for a fresh start, the needy pioneers claimed both European and African ancestors. Without access to wealth, the new settlers lived off the land. Of course, as settlements expanded, more prosperous individuals moved into the region.

Nevertheless, those first settlers, regardless of the color of their skin, were usually poor and usually established homes in secluded mountain coves to ensure a barrier against discovery by oppressors who might be searching for them. They needed homes that guaranteed security (Montell, 1970). Appalachian blacks relished a sense of place that allowed independence despite the challenges of survival. Experiences of the formerly enslaved had hindered their opportunity to be educated. As time passed, the prospect of learning for the black Appalachian faded as the white majority increased and yielded to the vice of racism. Benevolent protectors had returned to their homes, and the white leaders frequently ignored the needs of the black population. Scholar Maryam I. Moses (1989) said it well: "Gone were the Yankees who inspired a resistance to discrimination, a feeling of equality and who planted the hope of equal status among the Freedmen.... In their wake lay the hornets of racial prejudice that would sting the conscience of this country for generations to come" (p. 47). With few exceptions, those outsiders who had invested in establishing mountain schools left the region or united their efforts with the public school system.

In *The Mind of the South* (1941), W.J. Cash said the mountaineer "had acquired a hatred and contempt for the Negro even more violent than that of the common white of the lowlands, a dislike so rabid that it was a black man's life to venture into many mountain sections" (p. 219, and cited in Turner and Cabbell, 1985, p. xix). The white hill people, while generally religious, could shift to sudden acts of violence and create unrest among the black highlanders.

Dictates of Slavery

Slavery, its rites and traditions, was the original barrier to education for black people. During the ante-bellum period slaves courageous enough to seek lessons in reading or writing faced severe penalties. The black scholar Carter Woodson (1919) addressed the history of educating slaves and attributed their education to two main motives: white masters wanting to increase the economic value of their servants and Christians wanting to enable them to read the Bible to grasp principles of Christianity. The Bible and prayer books were their primers. Reading and writing, which enlightened slaves, created dissatisfaction with their lack of liberty. Empowered with learning, they were able to forge passes and to read inflammatory literature. Responding to the spread of anti-slavery pamphlets, states passed Slave Codes to prevent dissemination of literature and to outlaw assembling (Moses, 1989).

Whites developed distrust and fear of knowledgeable black men and women. In North Carolina that suspicion resulted in an 1831 state law that made educating a slave a criminal offense. In 1838, the legislature repealed a 1762 law mandating education for free black apprentices (Moses, 1989). Breaking the law resulted in lashes, fines, or imprisonment for those found guilty. Thus begins a tradition demanding that any African American seeking literacy must cope with staggering odds to achieve success. Exceptions existed, but in secret. Masters continued to allow slaves to learn to read, to write, and to do arithmetic. If such learning added to their bankrolls or freed the masters from tedious business responsibilities, it was acceptable but not advertised. Slaves trained to assist their masters with responsibilities requiring literacy could in turn teach others, but in secret. Eager pupils found isolated spots in orchards or in cornfields where a literate black created a primer by marking letters of the alphabet in the soil.

Many slave masters had forbidden slaves to learn to read. Close analysis of oral histories of former North Carolina slaves and their children — gathered by the Federal Writers' Project of the depression era of the 1930s — confirms reluctance by white owners to allow slaves to be educated. In *My Folks Don't Want Me to Talk About Slavery,* edited by Belinda Hurmence (1995), a recurring theme of unfair treatment documents the resentment by black parents that their children had been denied an education. Learning to read and to write was highly esteemed by illiterate or educationally deprived adults. In their own words, the men and women who were interviewed in this federal project reveal the educational hardships that were part and parcel of their lives as slaves.

Parker Pool, age 91 at the time of his interview, expressed that situation in this manner: "No, sirree, they wouldn't let us have no books. They would not let none of the chilluns tell us anything about a book. I can't read and write, not a bit.... No nigger was allowed to preach.

They was allowed to pray and shout sometimes, but they better not be catched with a book" (Hurmence, p. 84).

W. L. Bost, who was interviewed at age 87 in Asheville on September 27, 1937, had been a slave on a plantation in Catawba County near Newton, North Carolina. Explaining that Negroes were never given the opportunity to attend school because the whites feared their being educated, he stated: "Us poor niggers never allowed to learn anything. All the reading they ever hear was when they was carried through the big Bible. The massa say that keep the slaves in they places. They was one nigger boy in Newton who was terrible smart. He learn to read and write. He take other colored children out in the fields and teach them about the Bible" (p. 94).

Isaac Johnson, 82, who was interviewed in Harnett County, confirmed that whites prohibited slaves from learning to read or write, but he remembered that such ignorance was also prevalent among poor white folks. Hannah Crasson, 84, mentioned slaves being treated well by her owners and identified enjoyable times that came in the midst of their chores. Among those happy occasions were times of candy pulling, corn shucking, quilting and dancing, but the white rule forbade having anything to do with books. According to Crasson, "You better not be found trying to learn to read.... You better not be catched with a book" (p. 18).

Humiliation of Illiteracy

War was waged; battles were fought and won before slaves became free and legally entitled to an education. At the close of the Civil War, only from 5 to 10 percent of the nation's entire black population could read or write (Long, 1932). Without the economic support supplied by their former owners, black men and women sought an avenue to self-sufficiency, and achievement of that status required ownership of literacy. Convinced that the road to economic success depended on being educated, the freedman, from day one, looked for a school where an instructor would open the door to learning. Following Lincoln's Emancipation Proclamation on January 1, 1863, efforts to educate the recently freed slaves came with the establishment of the Freedmen's Bureau and the involvement of religious groups, such as the Society of Friends (Quakers) and the American Missionary Society (Moses, 1989).

In 1864, a major change occurred offering annihilation of the barrier between blacks and an education. The Union's Secretary of War Edwin Stanton commissioned the superintendent of freedmen to begin organizing schools in the South. Most freedmen had never entered a schoolhouse (Litwack, 1979). Compassionate individuals, church businessmen, and others, including unlikely sources, offered goodwill donations to give impetus to the education project and to provide the means to ensure its having a measure of success. Unfortunately, on many home fronts, opponents blocked the fruition of the project. Because the Freedmen's Bureau concentrated on areas inhabited by a black population of significant numbers, such as North Carolina's coastal and Piedmont regions, black mountaineers received negligible benefit from the project (Pollitt, 1993). In the early twentieth century, the same group for the same reason — because they were small in number and resided in scattered, rural communities — received marginal assistance from philanthropists, with one major exception: Julius Rosenwald. However, mountaineers benefited indirectly from philanthropic donations to the state — the director of Negro education received his salary from the general education board and Jeanes supervisors were supported by the Anna T. Jeanes Foundation.

Newly freed slaves startled their supporters by the extent to which they clamored for an education. Litwack (1979) documented the strength of the school textbook by citing the efforts of Henry McNeal Turner, a minister in the Israel Bethel Church of Washington, D.C. Serving

A family portrait records five generations of black mountaineers near Asheville, North Carolina, in the early twentieth century (North Carolina Office of Archives and History, Raleigh).

as the chaplain of the U.S. Colored Troops, First Regiment, Turner expressed pride in his race and suggested freed individuals had a right to claim greatness. As schools were opened up for the freedmen, their joy prompted them to dream of accomplishing major changes in their lifestyles and in their communities. The power gained by newly acquired skills of reading and writing was intoxicating.

Reconstruction, though, brought a setback to the joy of newly acquired freedom. Black Codes provided a temporary barrier by attempting to create segregation of the races based on law (Litwack, 1979). Such laws, similar to the earlier Slave Codes, were passed in Northern and Southern states during President Andrew Johnson's term, 1865–1869. Their content included restrictions on the rights to vote, to take part in jury duty, to testify against white men, to carry weapons, and to work in certain occupations. Fortunately, by the time the 14th and 15th Amendments to the Constitution passed, those acts had been declared null and void. Nevertheless disfranchisement came to black North Carolinians with the enforcement of "the grandfather clause" requiring literacy or descent from a grandfather who could vote. Furthermore, bands of vigilantes promoted terrorism as a means to deny civil rights to black Americans. Even though black children and black adults had a legal right to attend school, there were few schools available or accessible in the mountains.

Tests of Reconstruction

In his 1869 report, S.S. Ashley, North Carolina's first superintendent of education during Reconstruction, established the graded school system, identified the curriculum for each grade, and provided information about textbooks and teacher certification. He also included a letter from Assistant Superintendent J.W. (James Walker) Hood, a black minister — a carpetbagger — from the North who had been asked to prepare a report on the number and condition of schools for "colored youth." Hood's letter recognized the work of the American Missionary Association (AMA), the American Freedmen's Commission, the Friends Schools, the Episcopalian Parish Schools, and the Presbyterian Parish Schools. Concerning a final category he simply called "Private Schools," Ashley said, "I have not yet found a single day school beyond the Blue Ridge" (p. 24).

The AMA provided teachers, erected buildings, and collaborated on projects with the American Freedman's Commission. The Johnson School in Raleigh, under the supervision of the AMA, had been leased to the Deaf and Blind and Dumb Institution to house 75 colored students. Hood summarized the number of schools established by each group. There were 82 private schools, 29 Friends schools, 16 Presbyterian Parochial schools, and six Episcopalian Parish schools. In all he reported that there were 152 schools, 224 teachers, and 11,826 students.

Hood's letter, appended to Ashley's report, does not identify schools located in the western counties, but Ashley's account includes a state school census for 23 western counties. The pupil population, those between ages 6 and 21, range from 60 in Clay County to 827 in Rutherford. Burke had 784; and Wilkes, 726. Cherokee County included only 120, but that number seems large compared to 65 in Watauga, 74 in Mitchell and Yancey, 89 in Madison, and 90 in Jackson. Other western counties include a range from 117 in Alleghany to 609 in Yadkin ("Report of the Superintendent of Public Instruction for the year 1869," retrieved from http://docsouth.unc.edu/nc/report 1869/report1869.html).

From 1868 until 1871, Hood continued to safeguard the interests of his people, African Americans, as in his role as the state's assistant superintendent. Hood's principal responsibility was to found and to supervise schools for black students. His success is mirrored in the increase of attendance in black schools. By 1871, there were 49,000 black students attending school. It was a daunting task because of white hostility, which at times erupted into arson. The assistant superintendent expressed satisfaction at the interest freedmen had in attending schools and described their delight in creating an impromptu schoolhouse by piling up logs and covering them with boards, only to have it burned down by vicious whites. Hood was hampered even further by the lack of black teachers available to conduct classes. Hood strongly advocated that black teachers provide instruction for black students, and he favored segregated schools, but not to be mandated by law (Fairclough, 2007). He felt white teachers effectively convinced black students that they were inferior. He disliked being obligated to white teachers due to the shortage of black teachers. By 1900, black teachers had replaced almost all white teachers in North Carolina's black schools largely due to Hood's efforts.

Ashley documented these statistics in his September 30, 1870 report: There were 229,000 whites and 113,000 blacks eligible to enroll in public schools, but 31,093 children were actually attending school. Of those, Ashley found that 75 percent were black students (Moses, 1989, and "Report of the Superintendent of Public Instruction for the year 1869," retrieved from http://docsouth.unc.edu/nc/report1869/report1869.html). Such statistics reflect the mindset of blacks who longed to take advantage of learning options.

In the mountains those options were often lacking. The triumphs that were birthed during Reconstruction were short-lived. Prejudice and hostility, which became ingrained in the white population, wrecked many attempts to educate black students. As legislators became more convinced that the denial of an equal education to an important part of its citizens was unconstitutional, the tedious, but necessary, process of change erected still another roadblock.

Acts of Repression

During Reconstruction, benevolent groups commissioned educators to head south to support black education. Both men and women responded to the call, but their attempts to establish schools rarely elicited white approval. The mission of white Yankees to educate the black population aroused resentment and created hostility targeting the Caucasian teachers themselves. Finding a place to live proved to be a challenge for idealistic instructors, as white innkeepers denied their applications and forced teachers to seek living quarters with the black families they served (Litwak, 1979). Mountaineers intimidated white educators such as Emily Prudden (Pollitt, 1993). Violence hindered the establishment and services at the Salem Orphanage and School in Elk Park (Inscoe, 2001).

In 1892 teachers at the Allen Home and Industrial School in Asheville received a threat late at night from a crowd of white citizens who told them "if they didn't clear out in two days, they would swing on the tree where the nigger was lynched" (letter from Edward Stephens dated January 20, 1892 to Charles McNamee, Biltmore House Collection. Retrieved from http://www.ymicc.org/unmarked_trail/board14.html). Stephens writes that an appeal to the mayor and to the chief of police failed to elicit support for the white missionary teachers, who packed their bags and prepared to leave. However, a few citizens urged them to remain and the threat was ignored. Alsie B. Dole, principal of the school, shared this and other instances of white abuse that resulted from her staff's persistent efforts to educate black children and adults in Asheville.

Previously, by the end of the Reconstruction era in 1877, whites feared that education for blacks would impel them to seek equal status. With few exceptions, benevolent Northerners had returned to their homes and left the responsibility for providing schools for black students in the hands of the state government (Moses, 1989). In essence, mountain African Americans had to fend for themselves.

The segregation roadblock in Appalachian North Carolina developed according to regulations requiring separate facilities for the races and was a result of the establishment of private schools within western counties. State laws and judicial rulings about public schools played a major role in establishing guidelines for segregated black schools. Also, there was the impact of federal laws such as *Plessy v. Ferguson* (1896), which riveted attention on mandating separate but equal educational facilities. North Carolina had already passed laws in 1869 to maintain separation of the races in public schools (Moses, 1989).

By 1900 there was optimism for advancing the cause of public education. Charles Brantley Aycock, inaugurated as governor on January 15, 1901, immediately launched a school-improvement campaign. In response to his critics' focus on the need to invest in other government-sponsored projects and responsibilities, Aycock asserted that the citizens of North Carolina were far too poor not to invest in the education of their children. Superintendent E.C. Brooks later described that era as marked by the public's unwillingness to support public education. Ample evidence substantiated Brooks' remark (Ferguson, 1962).

Dearth of Dollars

During that time period, according to Ferguson (1962), North Carolina had only 30 school districts that levied a local school tax. Not one of those districts was rural. County school superintendents earned less than $1 per day. Public school teachers averaged a salary of $91.20 for the school term. Schoolhouse and equipment maintenance was rare. At least 950 districts did not have a single building, and 1,132 districts used log houses chinked with clay. Schools operated for 73 days of the year with fewer than one-third of eligible students attending them (Connor and Poe, 1912). White supremacist Aycock, with a wisdom often lacking in political practice, appealed to the people to support public education and to leave the development of public policy in the hands of professional educators. The governor's earnestness, sincerity and eloquence eventually won support.

Promoting the dual system of segregated schools was a financial nightmare. There were squabbles about whose tax dollars should be invested in which schools. Black communities sponsored fundraisers to purchase materials and equipment that should have been provided by the state. Using the excuse that the black school served a reduced student population, most money designated for schools was invested in white schools. Although white citizens who made their homes in rural Appalachian communities were also poor, their schools received a larger portion of the state's allotment for schools simply because of the color of their skin.

Townspeople were not easily persuaded that a local tax should be levied for schools (Ferguson, 1962). Individuals simply failed to comprehend why their hard earned money should be used to support another family's children. In the arena of miscomprehension, the ugliness of the race problem inflamed opponents. A large number of North Carolinians felt a duty to provide support for white children but no compulsion to educate the Negro. Fearlessly, Governor Aycock affirmed the innate right of each child to have an opportunity to learn and to claim that opportunity (Ferguson, 1962). From the highest office in the state came support for universal education. The support, philosophically bound into the state's educational practices, encompassed both urban and rural schools, as well as both white and black schools.

In 1913, State Superintendent J. Y. Joyner requested funds from the General Education Board of New York to hire two rural agents. Upon confirmation of his request, Joyner hired N.C. Newbold as an agent to supervise state schools for Negro children. Choosing Newbold as the Negro agent proved to be a major victory for black education in North Carolina. His sense of duty and fairness led to the removal of a number of roadblocks, such as funding irregularities, building restrictions, and limitations related to secondary education, but advancement occurred slowly. It seemed each victory for African-American schools brought still another setback.

Newbold's goals, such as providing a secondary school program and further preparation for future teachers in county training schools, focused on improving black education throughout the state. Once again, though, with a limited mountain population to serve and the gradual unfolding of school improvements, black highlanders had few triumphs in their educational experiences. Advancement came slowly.

Superintendent Joyner's action resulted in a new focus on educating Negro children. Within seven years, Superintendent E. C. Brooks, supported by the state legislature, reorganized the Department of Public Instruction by creating the Division of Negro Education. Brooks promoted Newbold to be its director. G.H. Ferguson served as assistant director and was designated as the leader responsible for teacher training. Two members of this division — W.F. Credle and G.E. Davis — were assigned to oversee the Rosenwald Fund and the Rosenwald buildings. Credle was an Euro-American and former school superintendent while Davis was an African American and former college professor. Davis successfully raised vast funds to improve school plants for black Americans. Together Credle and Davis proved to be a highly effective team. Organization at the state level created the threshold for the golden years — 1921 to 1927 — in black education (Cooke, 1935; Moses, 1989).

The Brooks team developed a graduated salary schedule for Negro teachers and improved the quality of teacher training through approved summer school programs for teachers holding certificates that were below state standards. The team also established county training schools and consolidated services to include several counties (H.V. Brown, 1964). For the first time, leaders were removing annoying roadblocks.

An early task of the Division of Negro Education was a survey to determine the status of schools providing for black children. Ferguson (1962) summarized the findings: Fewer than 50 percent of school age children were enrolled. Of that number, fewer than 50 percent attended daily. Even fewer children came to school during the opening and closing months. Instruction was largely unsupervised. More than half of the total students enrolled, particularly in rural schools, were assigned to the first grade. Their ages ranged from 5 to more than 15. Only seven high schools had any accredited rating. According to Ferguson, approximately 18 private high schools existed and, although not accredited, were doing their jobs well. Challenging conditions confronted students residing in the mountain region. One was the lack of well-maintained roads. Winding roads with no guardrails, no pavement, and no upkeep hindered school attendance.

Blemish of Bloodline

Another problem affecting schools revolved around bloodlines, which determined race. Between 1873 and 1957 North Carolina legislators passed numerous Jim Crow laws ("Jim Crow Laws: North Carolina," retrieved from http://www.jimcrowhistory.org). At least seven concerned school segregation and four outlawed miscegenation. North Carolina law prohibited marriage of Indians and whites and of African Americans and whites.

A 1903 North Carolina asserted that "no child with Negro blood in its veins, however remote the strain, shall attend a school for the white race.'" (Ibid.). That decision impacted families in Western North Carolina, especially the Anderson clan in Buncombe County, and created challenges for white school officials. School board members often became embroiled in public disputes about the bloodline of students enrolled in white schools or seeking enrollment. Each claim consumed enormous time and scarce money for the investigation. Families were directly affected by such publicity, and the arguments posting a stigma to having black blood in one's veins strengthened the feeling of inferiority held by African Americans and the sense of superiority ingrained in many white Americans.

In one urban area of Appalachian North Carolina, a landmark case acquired coast-to-coast attention in 1905. The case, dated September 26, 1905, was *Sylvia Gilliland, et al. v. Buncombe County Board of Education and School Committee of Avery's Creek*. The decree affirmed that the Gilliland children were not black. Instead, according to the decree, they were of Portuguese descent. Widespread attention focused on the possibility that the descendants of Jeffrey and Lewis Grimes (name later changed to Graham), Wilkes County natives who had relocated to Buncombe County, "were tainted" with Negro blood. Federal census records indicate they were free men of color who owned land along the French Broad River, but the court ruled in 1905 that their skin color derived from Portuguese ancestry. The court record does not label the Grimes/Graham family Melungeon but does recognize a darker skin and hair. A November 26, 1905, *Asheville Citizen* headline proclaimed: "Not One Drop of Negro Blood in Grahams" and announced the verdict that the Gillilands had been decreed "pure" white.

The decision applied to several hundred descendants in Asheville and in Western North Carolina. The Buncombe County Board of Education, assuming that the Grimes' ancestor was African, had set up a separate school for the children in the Avery's Creek community

(Gary McElroy, Compiler, "*Sylvia Gilliland, et al. vs. Buncombe County Board of Education, 1905,*" and other papers. Asheville, NC: Old Buncombe County Genealogical Society, on file in Special Collections, D. Hyden Ramsey Library, University of North Carolina at Asheville). The judicial decision allowed the Gilliland children to enroll in the white Avery's Creek school, but it further hindered the children of African-American descent by strengthening the laws and attitudes that Negro blood was so polluted that those afflicted should not be allowed to share a classroom with classmates blessed with "pure white blood," as if such a person existed.

In the present, blacks look back with heightened nostalgia at segregated schools as places of security and of learning, but, in the 1950s and 1960s, the black population focused on the inferior aspects of their education as compared with the education of white students. Stories of one-room black schools cramped with 42 students and one teacher and functioning with few texts and little chalk surface documents the reality of so-called separate but equal educational opportunities. A comparison of the educational training of black and white teachers indicates a higher degree of preparation for teaching in the white society. Other statistics related to acreage, size of buildings, provision of maintenance, and money further accents the gap between educational opportunities for blacks and for whites. The 1954 decision in the case of *Linda Brown v. the Board of Education of Topeka, Kansas* reversed the *Plessy v. Ferguson* decision of 1896, which had created the legal concept of "separate but equal."

Conditions of Neglect

Once the *Brown v. Board of Education* (1954) decision declared schools segregated on the basis of race unconstitutional, efforts to desegregate became the focus of black communities and of all those supporting equal educational opportunity. Opponents of desegregation argued that separate schools should be maintained for the good of the state. The voting public required further convincing following the *Brown* verdict.

The roadblocks were so formidable that they caused serious problems for parents and children throughout Western North Carolina. Strong proof is apparent in a prepared speech, marked confidential, by William Bagwell, director of American Friends Service Committee's School Program. He delivered a list of scathing facts to the Asheville Area Human Relations Executive Committee on February 20, 1962. Following is a summary of Bagwell's remarks:

1. Thirteen Alleghany County children make a 100-mile round trip each day to attend school—leaving before daylight and often returning after dark (and) passing other schools (2 or 3) along the way.

2. Avery County's Negro high school students attend a one-teacher school with six students while a large, modern school with several hundred students is located nearby.

3. Five counties in WNC have one-teacher high schools of 6–16 students for Negro students, but each county has a fairly adequate high school for white students.

4. Two counties have no schools for Negroes—each has only a few Negro students.

5. Six counties and 16 school districts have no Negro high schools, but all have students of high school age.

6. Two counties and four school districts have no elementary schools for blacks, but all have black elementary students.

7. There is one county that has no Negroes.

8. It is true that many poor school facilities exist for white children.

9. Apathy, lack of leadership, lack of vision and of planning for the future, and excessive concern about political implications seem to be the basis for lack of effort to provide equal opportunities.

10. Larger communities (Asheville, Morganton, Rutherfordton, Lenoir, Marion, and Hendersonville) have facilities fairly comparable to whites but serve two or three counties.

11. Continuing the operation of unequal and inadequate schools for Negroes promotes inferior education for all students, encourages lawsuits, costs an enormous amount of money unnecessarily spent, creates bitterness, and hampers economic, spiritual, intellectual, and moral development.

Bagwell's speech, delivered about five decades ago, shows that educational conditions for black students in Western North Carolina were in what he labeled a "pitiful state" in 1962. If such were the case in the early '60s, what was the state of black schooling in earlier decades? While his assessment signals the need for improvements, more facts could have been included. For example, students from other Appalachian communities crossed over county lines to attend high school in Wilkes, Surry, and Catawba and across state lines to schools in South Carolina, Georgia and Tennessee.

Roadblocks to equality in education resulted from demographics, geographic features, settlement patterns, limited funding, and an emphasis on separation with little concern for equality. However, forces had been at work for decades to challenge the system that downgraded black citizens to second-class status while elevating white citizens to a superior level — all based on the color of skin. In the 1950s and 1960s, those efforts triumphantly challenged and defeated the practice of segregated schools. The journey reached a high point though descendants have found they must keep ascending to maintain equal opportunity for education.

2

TRACKS OF AFRICAN AMERICANS

Long before other travelers invaded their domain, Native Americans explored the region which was to become Appalachian North Carolina. Their eyes beheld towering mountains layered with walls of granite, deep valleys thick with laurel and rhododendron, rushing streams difficult to ford, and dense forests. Other attractions were bountiful — abundant game, streams plentiful with fish, and untouched natural resources. By the time Europeans made their appearance, the Eastern Woodland tribes, according to Schwarzkopt (1985), had established a centuries-old claim to the area. The Warren Wilson College site in Swannanoa, North Carolina, offers archeological evidence of Native American cultures dating as far back as 5,000 B.C. Before the Europeans arrived, the Cherokee Nation, with rich traditions and a strong heritage linking their tribe to the land, had laid claim to the Southern Appalachians (Schwarzkopt, 1985). Surprisingly, blacks left their footprints well before Europeans established settlements in the region.

Benjamin Quarles (1964), eminent scholar and author, writes, "Except for the Indian, the Negro is America's oldest ethnic minority.... Afro-Americans helped to make America what it was and what it is today" (p. 170). Theda Perdue (1985) writes, "The first black Appalachians did not live under the control of white planters, railroad builders, lumber companies, or mine operators; instead, they lived within the domain of the Cherokee Indians" (p. 23). In Surry County on the Virginia border, according to Martha Rowe Vaughn (Thompson, 2005, p. 8), the first permanent black settlers in that region arrived in the 1580s. Sir Francis Drake had freed his "shipment" of slaves when he landed in Virginia, and many of them put distance between themselves and Virginia.

Information about the white man's first appearance during the 1770s in Appalachian territory, which includes Western North Carolina and regions to the north and south, is easier to unearth than information about the first footprints of blacks in the area. During the spring of 1774, Samuel Davidson, who owned slaves, came to the area with his family to establish a homestead. Davidson died in a skirmish with the Indians, but his wife, his baby, and a black servant girl escaped. In the 1780s, William and Eleanor Mills settled in what would become Henderson County. In 1817, two white settlers, Jacob Siler and William Britton, built a trading post in what would become Macon County (C. Richards and K. Richards, 2008). While the post seems to be a sign of progress, details about its history are meager and difficult to confirm.

Facts about the arrival of black pioneers are elusive. Turner (1985) summarizes perspectives about the early arrival of blacks in the Appalachian region in the introduction to *Blacks in Appalachia*. He references blacks accompanying explorers of the Mississippi Valley. They deserted their French and Spanish leaders to live among the Cherokee and the Chickasaw in the early 1500s. Turner also contends that a black man recorded the first trek by Daniel Boone through the Cumberland Gap.

While blacks journeyed with European explorers, the history of black mountaineers has its roots in a time period that began nearly two centuries before the major influx of white settlers in the region, according to Turner and Cabbell (1985). Their individual stories left distinctive and memorable marks on history. Spanish explorers also left a number of their entourage behind when they returned to the coast after exploring inland regions. For example, blacks were a part of Hernando de Soto's 1539–43 expedition that crossed into the Catawba River valley and turned west to explore regions in the valleys of the Blue Ridge and Great Smoky Mountains (Williams, 2002). In 1566–67, Juan Pardo explored the region in search of gold and other precious metals. His party included African Americans. Blacks in unfamiliar territory encountered what must have seemed like overwhelming weather conditions—blustery winds, drenching rainstorms and heavy snowstorms of the kind that can still paralyze mountain counties, though today's citizens have four-wheel-drive automobiles, heavy-duty trucks and paved highways and interstates. What seems like a vast and remote 27-county region now must have been enormous and imposing to people who traveled by foot or by horse-drawn wagons.

Perdue, in her essay "Red and Black in Southern Appalachians," verifies that one of de Soto's most prized Indian prisoners, perhaps a Cherokee, Lady of Cofitachequi, managed to escape her captors with a black slave who was fleeing to the Cherokee village at Xuala. There the two established a home as husband and wife (T. Perdue, 1985, and C. Richards and K. Richards, 2008). Their co-habitation suggests that Cherokees viewed blacks as equals, not as second-class citizens. Purdue asserts that Cherokees met blacks prior to meeting Europeans, perhaps even before the arrival of Spanish explorers in their settlements. In 1526, a number of blacks rebelled in Lucas Vásquez de Ayllón's ill-fated outpost on the Pee Dee River and sought refuge in Indian territory, a detail that leads Perdue to entertain the likelihood that the Cherokee saw either those escapees or their offspring.

Eventually the English enslaved Cherokees, but their desirability as slaves waned. As a result, however, both the American Indian and the black man shared a common experience of bondage until the viewpoint of the Cherokees changed. From as early as the sixteenth century, the Cherokees owned black slaves and eventually, lured by the prospect of economic profit, became involved in the slave trade (Roethler, 1964). Cherokee warriors captured black men not for their personal use but to sell as contraband. In that way they gained revenue. Slavery was widespread in the Eastern Woodland cultural area, and Cherokees also enslaved other Native Americans.

In the 1800s, though, Negroes living in an American Indian territory apparently enjoyed a normal life without burdensome restrictions. Runaway slaves sought refuge with the Cherokee. Plantation owners in South Carolina feared a conspiracy between the blacks and the Native Americans would bring trouble. However, a conspiracy did not materialize because blacks were denied the right to take part in Cherokee governing bodies after the formation of the Cherokee nation and were barred from establishing residence (T. Perdue, 1985).

Though blacks lived in the region throughout colonial history, black Appalachians have been marked with a "cloak of invisibility" that sets them apart from black slaves who toiled on plantations. The "melting pot" that merged other Americans did not include the blacks (Turner and Cabbell, 1985). However, an increasing number of interracial marriages in modern times is altering that fact.

In the 1730s, Cherokees, while exploring the area now within the boundaries of Henderson County, brought both slaves and free blacks. In the 1830s, however, the influx of black settlers increased markedly with the growth of employment opportunities spawned by the opening of the Buncombe toll road. Two additional waves of black migration coincided with the coming of the railroad in the 1880s and in the opening decades of the twentieth century with the region's developing tourist industry (Ready, 1986).

Western North Carolina's natural geography forced first the Native Americans and later mountain highlanders, both blacks and whites, to rely on their own ingenuity to survive. Challenged to find and to build shelter, to gather food, and to fend against wild animals and hostile weather, those who lived to see other days became strong, self-reliant people who developed justifiable pride in the skill, the pluck, and the determination that enabled them to survive. Living independently without the ease of luxuries, they created an Appalachian spirit of survival. Geographically isolated, Appalachian Native Americans, African Americans, and Euro-Americans ardently sought personal liberty free from dependence on outside support.

In the isolated and remote region, travel by canoe, by foot, or by horseback was common. As paths became worn and widened, yokes of oxen were used to pull wagons, but clearing a path and building the most rudimentary road to facilitate transportation required backbreaking work.

The settlers found that mountains greeted them with ranges that include spectacular peaks such as Mt. Mitchell (originally known as Stepp Mountain), the highest at 6,684 feet above sea level, and Clingman's Dome, second highest at 6,643 feet above sea level. Grandfather Mountain continues to be a major regional attraction. Ashe County's folklore suggests that Mount Jefferson, prior to the Civil War, provided sanctuary in its coves and hiding places for runaway slaves. For that reason local citizens originally called the peak "Negro Mountain," but by 1952, the community had changed that name to Mount Jefferson (W.G. Lord, 1981). (During the Revolutionary War, Europeans also sought hideouts in caves and mountain valleys, as did the Cherokees in a desperate move to avoid removal to Oklahoma.)

The fourth highest summit in the Appalachians, Mount Guyot in the eastern Great Smokies, forms the border between Sevier County, Tennessee, and Haywood County, North Carolina. Pilot Mountain, located to the east, is 2,421 feet above sea level and is most unique in its formation. Though exceeded in height by many other mountains, none is more distinctive nor more prone to stimulate the imagination. Its unusual shape is carved from highly durable quartzite. To the Native American, Pilot was the Great Guide and to early Christian settlers, another Mount Ararat (W.G. Lord, 1981).

Elevation coupled with thick vegetation on the mountains delayed accessibility by groups interested in relocating and retarded widespread settlement. Rivers and waterfalls add to the spectacular features of the region. The French Broad, New, Yadkin, Tuckaseigee, Watauga, Cane, Nolichucky, Toe, and Catawba are a few that create white water rapids, cascades, waterfalls, and scenes of remarkable beauty. Linville Falls and Bridal Veil Falls, with drops of 45 feet and 120 feet respectively, are two of the best-known waterfalls.

Modern mountain hikers often find the physical tests of nature formidable, especially if they arrive from less rugged terrain. Though modern hikers have the advantages of thermal clothing and high-tech equipment, both refined by extensive scientific research, every year individuals submit to nature when they find it is still too strong a force to battle. Those realities lead to questions about how earlier explorers managed to survive as they stepped on new territory and fought their way through the highland wilderness.

The challenges confronting the region's original travelers continued to create hazardous travel in the late nineteenth century and on into the twenty-first century. School founder and missionary teacher Emily C. Prudden discovered the harshness of travel firsthand when she made a trip in 1891 to Altamont in what later became Avery County, formed in 1911. After sunset she and her entourage arrived by wagon at the Linville River. Her driver was unable to locate the crossing ford, so Prudden waded across to the other side. There she climbed up the bank, and searched in darkness through the tangled growth. Eventually she located the road, descended the bank and signaled the driver where to cross over. Then in the wagon loaded with supplies, Prudden, her entourage of teachers and the driver made their way to Altamont, but Prudden's discomfort had not ended. She wrote, "Snow through a thousand holes sifted down on our papers as we wrote and moistened our bed" (cited by Thomson, March 1984, p. 10). Her words and experiences disclose the hardships of travel in nineteenth century Western North Carolina.

A changing array of counties identified Western North Carolina's geographical boundaries. At the onset of the Civil War, 20 counties— some of which, such as Burke County, were especially large — had comprised the western portion of the state (Blackmun, 1977). In the mid–1880s, 32 counties were listed as "western" ones, but by the late 1930s that number had been reduced to 27 (Department of Public Instruction [DPI], Division of Negro Education [DNE] 1921–1960, Special Subjects, Box 11, North Carolina State Archives, Raleigh). County boundaries as they currently exist had not yet been determined, but the modern county list more clearly defines the Western North Carolina area. Traditionally the region's southern borders extend from today's Cherokee County in the extreme western portion of North Carolina to Rutherford County in the eastern segment; from Ashe County on the northern Virginia and Tennessee border to Surry County — and in certain time frames to Stokes County; from Alleghany southwest through Wilkes, Caldwell, Burke, Rutherford and Polk. The region is a part of Appalachia, where blacks were obscure among a people not well known to their fellow Americans.

In Western North Carolina, white mountaineers typically owned few slaves. Their slaves made up the work force on small farms, helped operate businesses, kept house for white owners, or participated in logging and mining enterprises. Records document the inclusion of slaves as a part of their owners' estates in wills. A slave might be presented as a gift to honor a major event in a white person's life. For example, in 1843, Grace Gates Smith, a black woman, was presented as a wedding gift to conjoined twin Eng Bunker and his wife Sallie. Smith fulfilled the duties of a nursemaid for the couple's 22 children (Thompson, 2005). According to Milton Ready (1986), few blacks actually established homes in Western North Carolina prior to the 1830s.

However, both slaves and free blacks resided in Henderson County. Slaves accompanied their owners to look after their needs in an area with refreshing mountain air that granted relief from the oppressive heat of the lowlands. In particular, wealthy Charlestonians— in a pattern made famous by the 1997 historical fiction novel *Cold Mountain* by Charles Frazier — sought respite from heat-induced diseases in what they regarded as a healthier climate. Of course, their slaves, often being sent ahead to clean houses and to stock larders, accompanied them. In the mountains, slaves continued to serve their masters in aristocratic style, by providing personal care, by maintaining gracious homes, by overseeing extensive grounds, and by serving lavish meals to many distinguished guests. Charleston's lifestyle, made possible by the labor of its slave population, had simply been relocated to the more refreshing climate of Western North Carolina.

In the 1830s, the completion of the Buncombe Turnpike toll road opened up the way for more blacks to come into Western North Carolina sometimes accompanying drovers who herded huge numbers of cattle, chickens, geese, other poultry, and sheep to market. Gaggles of cackling geese or herds of noisy sheep or cows stirred up dust and provided excitement as well as the chance to earn money and to hear news from other places for folks living along the turnpike.

Among the wealthy Charlestonians who built summer residences of quarters in Flat Rock was Mitchell King, who in 1830 built his mansion "Argyle" to provide a healthy retreat for his family. So many affluent South Carolinians moved there that the community became known as "Little Charleston." In 1841, King donated 50 acres for a county seat. King's slaves were responsible for laying out the main street in Hendersonville (C. Marsh and K. Marsh, 1961). King, an immigrant from Scotland, specified the width of Hendersonville's Main Street and later allotted one and three quarter acres of land to be used for schools (Patton, 1947).

Unfortunately, the shots fired at Fort Sumter in 1861 drastically altered the lifestyles of Flat Rock's resident Charlestonians—the Barings, the Kings, the Memmingers, and the Trenholms. War devastated the fortunes of wealthy Southerners and wreaked havoc on their ability to earn a living. Their lives of luxury had ended. The homes of the formerly wealthy Charlestonians were ravaged and became the headquarters for government officials or schools for former slaves (C. Marsh and K. Marsh, 1961).

Uprooted families of blacks and whites sought refuge in Flat Rock as they returned to homes that had once provided enormous pleasure. Freedmen with happy memories of life in the mountains returned to seek work and to establish homes. However, the problems of war did not subside, for the lavish lifestyle of the past had ended. Havoc also invaded mountain communities with the presence of bushwhackers and night-riders.

Both black and white communities throughout Western North Carolina lost loved ones among the vast casualties of the battlefields. In fact, Trotter (1988) designates the state's Appalachian region as the site of extremely high casualty rates, largely underappreciated since no major battles were fought in the area. During the early period of Reconstruction families continued to grieve for their losses and yearned for times of normalcy to enjoy family and to pursue learning and establish schools. Out of one tragedy comes an example of a black slave's faithfulness and devotion to duty. Owned by William Bryson, George Mills served as the personal valet of his master's son, Walter Bryson, who enlisted in 1861 and was deployed to serve on the battle front, accompanied by the eighteen year old slave George. Moving from battlefield to battlefield, George carried supplies for his young master, provided personal services, and, at times, even took part in the fighting. At Antietam (Sharpsburg), Maryland, on September 17, 1862, Walter was killed in the bloodiest one-day battle in American history. George transported the body back to the Bryson family in Henderson County. The trip to Hendersonville from Maryland was an arduous journey as George vigilantly safeguarded the corpse. His journey to Fletcher, North Carolina, permitted William Bryson to claim his son's body. George then helped dig his master's grave, but the young black man did not remain there; he enlisted in the Home Guards and served until the end of the war (Sadie D. Patton, May 7, 1960, *Times-News*, "Faithful Servant to Be Honored Here Saturday"). George Mills exemplifies loyalty and a sense of duty; other black Appalachians shared those qualities.

The restrictive, but normally adequate, care provided for Negroes by their white "families" as valued slaves also became a casualty of the war. Black families, though reveling in newly acquired freedom, found adversity a frequent companion. That was true not only in the "Little Charleston" of Flat Rock but also throughout North Carolina and throughout the South. To convert freedom into a comfortable condition required that the black man be able to earn a living, and to do so mandated acquiring new skills and additional education. Much opportunity existed, but finding a way to take advantage of it was an almost insurmountable social and economic challenge. Adults realized that the fruition of their dreams rested in the future of their children.

As the black work force expanded in the region which was becoming increasingly more hospitable, the need for educational opportunities for black children became urgent. Prior to the Civil War, education was limited to occasional instruction, some of it in secret. Ready (1986) states: "Education for blacks in Western North Carolina was clandestine at best, usually little more than infrequent meetings in fields, homes, and cellars" (p. 53). Schools were more easily achieved in areas with a greater black population, such as Asheville, but every family pursued educational options for its children.

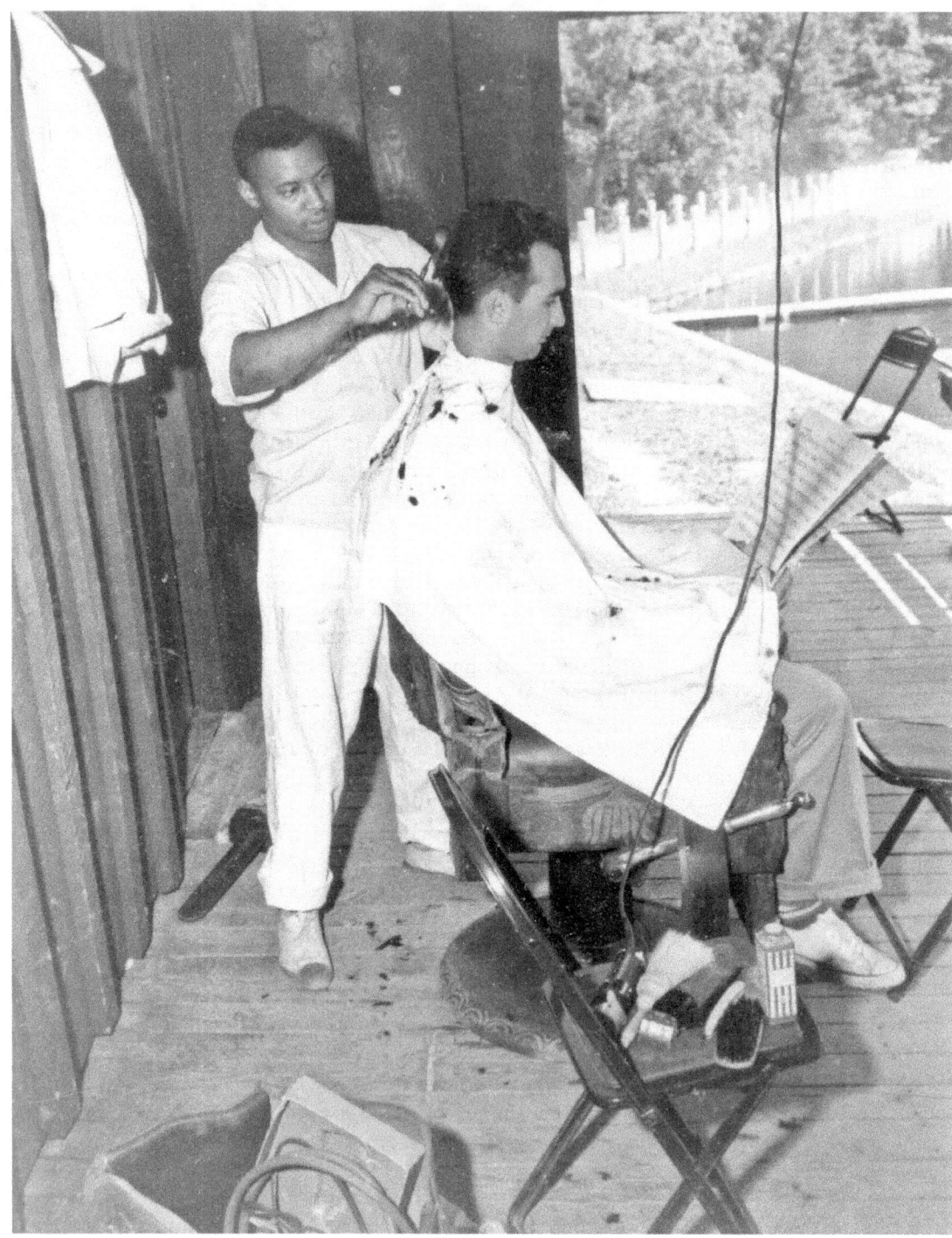

Job prospects related to mining, lumbering, tanning, tourism, and employment in medical sanitariums lured blacks to the mountains. Here a barber finds summer employment at the Brevard Music Center in the early 1960s (North Carolina Office of Archives and History, Raleigh).

Additional job opportunities developed. As the years passed, employment came through schools and universities, such as the teachers colleges in Jackson County and in Watauga County. Tourism also provided widespread employment for black workers. Tourism began to develop in Watauga County as early as the mid-nineteenth century. For example, tourist enterprises in Blowing Rock provided summer employment for from 200 to 300 African Americans (Horton, 1942). Black workers also found employment in construction.

Blacks were also involved in mining enterprises wrestling mica, iron, gold, and other ores from the earth. Early exploration, road building, mining, agriculture, industry and tourism attracted black families to the region. Again, the growing presence of black families increased the demand for schools to be established.

Those transitions during the 1800s stamped an imprint on the roads to success, the compelling need to go forward, in Western North Carolina. Despite decades and eventually centuries of prejudice, there was no turning back. Individuals and families would keep knocking on the doors of education. However, they could not foresee the years it would require as well as the turns and curves they would need to smooth out to achieve an adequate and equal education.

Relief for the area's economic problems that influenced educational issues came when political efforts—long after black slaves and runaways had arrived in the area—mandated action to deal with the region's poverty. By creating the Appalachian Regional Commission in 1965, Congress identified Alexander, Alleghany, Ashe, Avery, Buncombe, Burke, Caldwell, Cherokee, Clay, Davie, Forsyth, Graham, Haywood, Henderson, Jackson, Macon, Madison, McDowell, Mitchell, Polk, Rutherford, Stokes, Surry, Swain, Transylvania, Watauga, Wilkes, Yadkin, and Yancey counties as part of Appalachia. The area traditionally known as Western North Carolina boasted one main urban center: Asheville, which now exceeds 76,000 residents, of which approximately 14,000 are African Americans. However, by 2000 the populations of Boone, Hendersonville, Lenoir, and Morganton had grown substantially. Boone had a total population of 13,472 with 461 blacks; Lenoir, 16,793 with 2,470 blacks; Morganton, 17,310 with 2,208 blacks ("2000 Census," U.S. Census Bureau. Retrieved from http://factfinder.census.gov).

The statistics demonstrate that within the neglected white population of Appalachia was an even more neglected minority group—the black Appalachians. As the realization grew that blacks were more severely challenged economically than poor whites, leaders considered ways to improve their lives. The awareness led to establishment of the Black Appalachian Commission in 1969 with Carl Johnson of Asheville as its chairman (Turner and Cabbell, 1985).

In 1965, Western North Carolina, along with the rest of Appalachia, was considered a region apart from mainstream America, and that included both its white and its black residents. The region's poverty and its lack of progress impacted its schools, with widespread results. Residents without an adequate education lose not only as individuals but also as communities because outsiders take advantage of them.

In sharp contrast to its economic deprivation was its abundance of natural resources, often "stolen" from the natives when greedy business-smart absentee proprietors used questionable methods to wrest marketable materials, such as timber and minerals, from their original owners. However, despite depression of monetary resources and lack of adequate educational opportunities, stunning natural beauty—accented by mountains, streams, and waterfalls—continues to characterize the region.

During the 1970s, Appalachian blacks had a higher percentage of poverty than did blacks on the national level, and during that time frame the black median income amounted to almost half that of white families (J. Guillebeaux, 1985). The economic plight of Black

Appalachians remained an issue in need of a solution, one that required radical educational changes.

Those first black settlers faced harsh physical obstacles to survive. A small group came with the protection of wealthy white landowners. However, that protection disappeared fast as the chains of slavery left its marks within families and within the social status. While they dreamed of physical freedom and valued it as a human right, they struggled for decades to experience educational freedom.

Their original footprints on the paths marked physical experiences in the beautiful geography of Western North Carolina. The trails set them on a journey that took them more than 100 years to achieve—finding the path of education that would guarantee equal privileges and unlimited opportunities. First, they needed a building for education; then, access to the same building as whites for education; and now, the same cyberspace opportunities and wireless connections from the mountains to the world for education.

As the journey continued, blacks discovered the need to awaken humanity to the need for a clear path to their destination: integrated schools.

3

Steps to Integration

African Americans demonstrated remarkable determination as they trudged unmarked trails that led centuries later to ideological trails. Little did they know that justice and equality would be more difficult to achieve than crossing the highest mountains. The result was another kind of mountain-top experience, one for hundreds to test and for thousands to claim as their right and their privilege. First came recognition of the turmoil. Next came courage to open the door to integration for all.

Court Prequel: Judicial Decisions

A charge of discrimination arose at last in the late 1940s. The accusation sent waves of alarm through members of the State Board of Education. Facing threats of looming lawsuits, a troubled board sought not one but two opinions from State Attorney General Harry McMullan and ordered the state controller to notify all school districts to expect careful scrutiny of their use of local funds, especially those provided by the state. The equality issue as it related to North Carolina's black schools, especially to the salary of educators, spurred the board to immediate action. Controller Paul A. Reid, State Board of Education, mailed a letter dated May 3, 1949, to every school superintendent in the state. Reid announced that no irregularities would be tolerated in racially unequal disbursement of state school funds on the local level.

Armed with the attorney general's legal opinions, the controller advised each school superintendent that the state board would meet its responsibility by examining all local budgets to ensure that no racial discrimination had occurred. Though concerns about equal treatment were minor, they may have alerted school officials to the state board's zero toleration of discrimination (letter on file with Marion City and McDowell School Board minutes from Paul Reid, controller, State Board of Education).

In the 1930s and 1940s, there were court challenges to *Plessy v. Ferguson*'s (1896) declaration that separate and equal facilities did not create unfair — and therefore unlawful — treatment. When confronted with charges of unequal city and county distribution of funds based on race, the state board acted to protect itself. Subsequent acts in Raleigh reversed responsibility for enforcing court decisions. The intention was to remove responsibility for financial appropriations from the state and to transfer responsibility to cities, small towns, and counties. The decision may have prepared state officials, to a small extent, to deal with civil rights victories that would lead to heated debates about educational equality within the next decade.

Understanding the efforts to sidestep civil rights laws in Western North Carolina requires consideration of the impact of federal and state laws, of enforcement issues on state and local levels, of models of integration crises, and of desegregation complexity throughout a region with unforgiving transportation challenges and with a widely-scattered black population.

Educators and students who experienced first-hand racial desegregation of schools found themselves caught in a dilemma: the advantages of better facilities and curriculum in integrated schools vs. the attachment to schools that had become valued cultural centers, untainted by white interference.

Representative cases of desegregation add insights into the complexity of desegregating lives, not just buildings, complicated by adherence to the law or noncompliance to the law. The Old Fort challenge (the first in the state), the integration challenge in Buncombe County and in Henderson County, reoccurring violence at Asheville High School, and 80-mile journeys required by Yancey County are microcosms of the intense struggle. When violence erupted, it inflamed passions of civil rights advocates. While history records past discord, it also predicts future solutions as evident in examples that pre-date *Brown*. In retrospect, they give clues about tensions and solutions to come.

Though integration was already inching its way into educational institutions in Western North Carolina, 17 Southern and border states were reluctant to enforce the *Brown v. Board of Education* directives to do away with segregated schools. Southern states were immediately up in arms. Faced with the groundbreaking law, states such as North Carolina, Georgia, and Virginia detested the move to integrated schools and worked vigorously to find legal ways to maintain their segregated systems.

State laws mandating segregated schools obviously violated the national Constitution and ultimately met defeat, but such laws did create postponement of compliance with federal laws. Like its bordering states, North Carolina was not eager to endorse public school integration. Governor William B. Umstead appointed a special committee to develop a plan of action, but Umstead's untimely death brought Luther Hodges to the helm of state government. The Governor's Special Advisory Committee on Education included three black members and 12 whites. Following the *Brown II* decision, in which the Supreme Court delegated the task of desegregation to district courts with orders to complete it with deliberate speed, Charles F. Carroll, the state superintendent of education, acknowledged the noble cause embedded as the foundation of *Brown II*. Nevertheless, he asserted that abrupt changes should be avoided to prevent "grave repercussions" and to preserve North Carolina's system of public education (Brown, 1964, and cited by Fryar, 2003).

To delay the transfer of blacks to white schools, the General Assembly then enacted the 1955 Pupil Assignment Act, which delivered responsibility for school transfers or assignments into the hands of local school boards throughout the state (A. Dunne, 2010,"Pearsall Plan," North Carolina History Project, Raleigh: John Locke Foundation; retrieved from http://www.northcarolinahistory.org/commentary/318/entry). By deliberately omitting any reference to race and by specifying that local boards take into account the best interest of the child as well as the safety and health of school children, the plan provided a means to circumvent desegregation.

State Prequel: Regional Resistance

In August 1955, Governor Luther H. Hodges appointed a committee headed by Thomas J. Pearsall to devise a state program of desegregation. In July 1956, Governor Hodges called a special session of the General Assembly to analyze the recommendations of the Pearsall Committee. The legislature approved the Pearsall Plan, which stalled integration but not in a manner as defiant as in other states. Delay tactics inherent in the Pearsall Plan, adopted in 1956, and complicated application forms to enroll in schools of choice were attempts to undermine the Constitution. The idea was to transfer authority over public schools to local boards of education; placing the decision primarily in the hands of local officials would allow an individual community to integrate at a time of its own choosing. Should a student be assigned to an undesirable public school, state or local government was authorized to provide vouchers to underwrite the expense of a private education rather than to enforce compliance with the Supreme Court decision (A. Dunne, 2010).

Although the verdict deeming segregated schools unconstitutional was handed down in 1954, for many communities integration was delayed until the 1960s and into the 1970s. Following the merger of black and white schools, opponents continued to oppose mixed groups sharing a common classroom. The Pearsall Plan paved the way for delay. Using telling rhetoric that clearly suggested the need to keep African Americans in "their place" as second-class citizens, the Advisory Committee on Education contended that an integrated student body would destroy the state's public school system.

Adherence to the Pearsall Plan was unconscionable because even its supporters realized that the concept was a devious tactic that would eventually be declared illegal. Foremost in this shameful strategy were the government leaders who were ethically bound to uphold the law of the land.

Admittedly courts had held that the pupil assignment act and the Pearsall Plan were "not unconstitutional on their face," but lawyers and state officials, after studying the 1955 and 1956 legislation, were convinced that token desegregation was essential to avoid the possibility of having the statutes declared unconstitutional in administration, with resulting court-enforced desegregation.

In a 1956 address to the North Carolina Bar Association, Raleigh attorney W.T. Joyner, vice chairman of the Pearsall Committee, announced that the Pearsall Plan assumed there would be some racial mixing in the schools (Bagwell, 1972).

Joyner admitted that, in his personal opinion, the admission of less than one percent (for example, one-tenth of one percent) of Negro children to white schools was a small price to pay for the ability to keep the mixing within the bounds of reasonable control. Joyner also said he had nightmares about ending up in a federal court trying to defend a school board that had rejected transfers by Negro students in a state that had never had a single Negro student admitted to any one of the approximately 2,000 white schools in North Carolina (Bagwell, 1972).

Joyner's fears were likely alleviated in 1957 when the state's three largest cities assigned a total of 12 Negroes to previously all-white schools. The limited assignment, which occurred simultaneously without open discussion on July 23, 1957, in Charlotte, Greensboro, and Winston-Salem, marked the state's first official integration. Charlotte admitted five Negro children and rejected about 40; Greensboro admitted six and rejected seven; Winston-Salem admitted one and rejected three.

The three boards had met secretly for joint sessions in hotels and restaurants at which they discussed mutual school problems, according to Bagwell (1972). Later local newspaper and other media leaders attended joint meetings before the three school boards officially adopted a desegregation plan. The purpose of inviting select media representatives was to solicit their advice and cooperation.

The tone of editorials preceding the action created a favorable climate for the boards' announcements. Editorials following the action were also complimentary. The general reaction to this initial token integration was that it was a step forward in preserving the segregated school system throughout the state.

In an editorial that spoke favorably of token desegregation, *The Raleigh Times* wrote, "[What the boards] have done will make it possible for schools and areas where integration is surely not possible or even feasible to continue completely separate schools. This action has been taken for the benefit of the whole school system of the state, not just for the benefit of the 12 Negro children involved" (cited on p. 73 of 1962 *Staff Reports to United States Commission on Civil Rights,* retrieved from www.law.umaryland.edu/marshall). North Carolina felt it was in step with the times as neighboring states partnered for protection. Georgia made crystal clear its stance on fighting integration by putting legislative power behind the opposition in February 1955 as the General Assembly approved the following action: "No state or local funds derived from taxation or otherwise, shall be appropriated, paid out, used, or in any wise expended, directly or indirectly for ... support of any public school district or system in this state which does not provide separate schools for white and colored children ... in which all the white and colored children attending public schools do not attend separate schools" (Cited by T. Barnwell, Fall 2004, "Public School Integration in Georgia and Gwinnett County," retrieved from www.mgagnon.myweb.uga.edu/students/3090/04TA3090-barnwell.htm).

In similar fashion, Virginia, under the political leadership of Senator Harry F. Byrd, Sr., promoted opposition to integrating public schools by a set of laws known collectively as Massive Resistance, which was approved in 1958 and designed to halt school integration. The law allowed the state to withhold funds and to close schools not in compliance with state law ("Massive Resistance," The Civil Rights Movement in Virginia, June 2004, retrieved from www.vahistorical.org/civilrights/massiveresistance.htm).

The governor of South Carolina won admiration from the supporters of civil rights legislation by calling for racial integration of public schools. In South Carolina, hostility to desegregation triggered a number of violent events, but most of their schools were integrated with a minimum of such fights, largely due to the leadership of Governor Robert E. McNair, who courageously counseled the public to accept the inevitable with grace and to avoid hostile confrontations. McNair was one of only a few Southern politicians who publicly denounced rejecting *Brown v. Board of Education* ("The Challenge of Civil Rights," http://www.sc.edu/library). However, the 1968 Orangeburg massacre shortened the fair-minded McNair's promising political career.

Mixing the races in a school would upset the basis of southern ideals. Though disguised with subtle language, the dominant white view maintained that black citizens needed to remain second-class citizens. In the view of the majority, it would be better to continue white supremacy and allow black schools to decay rather than to integrate schools. Vocal opposition to desegregation echoed from state to state and from county to county in a last-ditch effort to strengthen state laws to oppose federal mandates.

Class Prequel: Integration Experiments

Meanwhile, the tide of history was making waves in remote classrooms. Minimally integrated schools existed in the Western counties prior to the compulsory integration of North Carolina's public schools in both public school extensions and in private colleges. Their existence, though, documents how remarkable the achievement was during the well-established practice of segregation in Western North Carolina. Alma Lee Shippy, a Buncombe County resident, experienced a unique role at Warren Wilson College in the integration process.

In 1952, Warren Wilson College enrolled a young man from nearby Buckeye Cove in Buncombe County's Swannanoa community. Two years before the *Brown v. Board of Education* decision, Shippy became the first African-American student to attend what was then Warren Wilson Vocational Junior College — and perhaps he was the earliest black to enroll in any private Southern college during the era controlled by Jim Crow. According to journalist LeeAnn

Peake, historians endorse Shippy as the first black student to remain enrolled in a private Southern college during segregation ("Breaking a Barrier," February 2, 1994, *Asheville Citizen-Times*).

Warren Wilson officials, however, felt compelled to secure approval from the students prior to accepting Shippy's application. "I attended Warren Wilson College because Marvin Lail and Dean [Henry] Jensen invited me to go there," Shippy explained. "The students voted, accepting me 54–1. I never did know who the one was who voted against me" (personal communication, January 31, 2006). Shippy discovered that a family spirit prevailed on campus and felt at home among the predominantly white students. Peake quotes Shippy, initially viewed with curiosity by his fellow classmates, as feeling a bit conspicuous: "Shippy recalls thinking, 'I am the only fly in the buttermilk with all these white folks'" (Peake, February 2, 1994).

A record of the vote to accept Shippy appeared in the September 2007 edition of Warren Wilson's *Owl and Spade*. An article titled "East Meets West — Jimmy Ning & Alma Shippy" (p. 27) narrated insights about a special friendship. Ning, who was born and raised in China, is identified as one who voted in favor of accepting Shippy. Puzzled by the need for a vote approving the young black American's enrollment, Ning inquired, "Did you guys vote on whether I could live here, too?" It was inevitable that the young man from China and the black student would become friends, a friendship based on mutual respect that resulted in a lifelong association. During their college days, Shippy invited Ning to his home in Swannanoa for the Chinese fellow's first taste of pan-fried chicken, collards, grits, and biscuits — an intercultural culinary gift from a native of Western North Carolina to his Chinese friend, a gift made possible by an integrated student population.

Although welcomed by fellow students, Shippy found doors to off-campus restaurants and theaters closed to his business as a paying customer. On one occasion when he and his white friends sought a break from their studies by venturing away from school, he was confronted with the standard rule "for whites only," which barred his entry into an Asheville theater, though his friends had notified the management with an advance telephone call. The young man, unwilling for his friends to relinquish the evening's entertainment, spent the time window-shopping as he pondered his feelings of rejection. On another off-campus excursion, the manager of an ice cream parlor explained that, although Shippy could make a "to go" purchase, it would be impossible for him to sit with his friends and be served (personal communication, January 31, 2006). His money was welcome, but his presence was not.

That time, Warren Wilson students took their business elsewhere. Although Shippy dropped out before completing his program of studies, the Stephens-Lee graduate paved the way for other black students to enter Warren Wilson College. A business opportunity offering an attractive salary lured Shippy to another state before he graduated. However, Shippy regarded his time at Warren Wilson as personally beneficial.

Warren Wilson College also accepted non–Caucasian students in its junior and senior high school program. In the "High School ... Principal's Preliminary Report" filed by Dean Henry W. Jensen for the 1955-56 scholastic term, the request for "race" is completed by "white and yellow." In the school's 1956-57 High School Annual Report, Arthur H. Bannerman indicated that students in the school's secondary program included members of the white, Negro, and Oriental races. Integration also existed at a small church-related school. In a report for Asheville Catholic High School in 1957-58, Sister Mary Inez confirmed that the 48 students were racially integrated. (High School Principal's Annual Report, Box 26.)

Much later than Shippy's hurdle over racial barriers, a young athlete, another graduate of Stephens-Lee, enrolled at Western Carolina University as a much sought-after addition to the school's athletic program. In 1965, Henry Logan integrated Western Carolina College's basketball team. A four-time all–American athlete, Logan attracted more than capacity crowds to the college games, as he had when playing for Stephens-Lee High School. Dagan Lamont Burrell, a Western Carolina University alumnus who researched Logan's experiences as part of his master's degree thesis (1993), documented the athlete's impressive collegiate record, but Burrell also addressed the lack of preparation Logan received in his segregated elementary and secondary schools. Logan's inadequate training made personal tutoring necessary for him to earn academic success.

Black Mountain College was also open to blacks under the direction of John Andrew Rice, founder and first rector. He encouraged blacks to enroll, but that did not happen until after World War II, when one black teacher and one black student joined. Neither stayed long, according to Swannanoa Valley Museum volunteer Harriet Styles (personal communication, August 7, 2007).

Another path to integrating the races in school settings occurred in hospital facilities in Buncombe County. The need for medical treatment to address health issues related to tuberculosis and polio also opened the door for racially mixed classes. High school instructors at the Western North Carolina Sanatorium, managed by the county administrative staff, taught eight black students and six white students at the Black Mountain facility during 1955-56. According to her High School Principal's Annual Report, Ann Coleman Dickerson served as acting principal and offered six hours of instruction daily sponsored by Buncombe County Public Schools (Box 26).

As acting principal for the high school program at the Polio Convalescent Center, Ruby Crayton Bowman filed a principal's 1955-56 preliminary report, in which she listed nine students, some of whom were white and some "colored." Bowman's high school annual report for the same year indicated an additional three students had enrolled and that the racial makeup of the students remained the same. However, enrollment on the final school day in 1956 included only two students, a number suggesting that either their health improved so they were discharged or their health worsened so they were transferred to another facility (Department of Public Instruction, Division of Negro Archives, Annual Report, Box 26).

Legal Prequel: Congressional Action

Previously, personal dilemmas such as contracting tuberculosis or polio had led to establishment of small interracial student populations in Asheville to avoid contact with carriers of disease. Eventually a wave of demands for civil rights by a persistent black population brought about laws recognizing injustices inherent in maintaining segregated schools and created an urgent demand from civil rights supporters for integration in all of Western North Carolina's public schools. It is true that limited progress marked the educational offerings for black students during the century prior to the historic *Brown v. Board of Education*, but courts in other regions of the United States paved the way for solutions to unequal educational opportunities.

During this era, as complex injustices took center stage in the national spotlight, not only in Appalachia but also throughout the United States, political influences led to laws that opened the doors to equal educational access. The delaying tactics of the Pearsall Plan were declared unconstitutional, and the power of an important and long overdue piece of legislation at last toppled the practice that prevented equal schools for blacks in Western North Carolina.

The key piece of legislation, the Civil Rights Law of 1964, resulted from courageous leadership on the national level by Senators Hubert Humphrey of Minnesota and Everett Dirksen

Governor Terry Sanford — North Carolina's Education Governor — visited Marion and Brevard in 1962. In September Sanford addressed students in Marion, challenging them to rise to meet the demand of the "fastest moving scientific age the world has ever known." Black students were not invited to the event (North Carolina Office of Archives and History, Raleigh).

of Illinois. Their dual effort was bolstered by staunch support from President Lyndon B. Johnson, who was carrying on the ideals initiated by his predecessor, President John F. Kennedy. The monumental legislation provided means to enforce desegregation in its Title VI, which prohibited any use of federal funds to finance segregated schools ("Title VI of the Civil Rights Act of 1964," retrieved from http://www.justice.gov).

The Civil Rights Law of 1964 effectively rendered North Carolina's Pearsall Plan unconstitutional. Though token integration edged its way into the state school system, the plan continued to delay total school integration until the 1969 case of *Godwin v. Johnston County Board of Education* was resolved ("Pearsall Plan," North Carolina History Project, http://www.northcarolinahistory.org). The landmark law of 1964 provided standards that eventually influenced every county in the nation.

Eventually the public, despite words of hatred and resistance, realized that legislative keys were not simply unlocking a few doors in big cities or rural counties with large black student populations. Instead, citizens, informed by media efforts to increase national awareness of injustice and to publicize public marches and demonstrations, gradually recognized that the legal process had invented master keys to open the doors to public schools in every county throughout the United States. Western North Carolina, with inadequate resources for its black schools, was in need of such legislation. It was the time for blacks to use those legal keys to experience equal access to schools and to all educational opportunities.

Act 1: Delays of Reluctant Leaders

Throughout North Carolina's Appalachian region, school boards designated plans to gradually integrate public schools and to begin with the practice of token integration. Once the Civil Rights Act of 1964 and the decision to withhold federal funds from any school system not in compliance were in force, the school boards reluctantly made plans for total desegregation. However, a number of challenges preceded that victory. An Old Fort case was already on center stage to challenge the status quo, based on *Brown*, for Old Fort citizens had filed a lawsuit in 1953 to force the McDowell County Board of Education to allow their students to bypass the ride to Marion to attend the city-county consolidated school for blacks.

Disenchanted blacks living in Old Fort sought justice in the courts, but first the group filed a petition with the McDowell County Board of Education to request that black students be allowed to attend the white school in Old Fort.

The lack of an Old Fort school for black children happened because county-city consolidation of black schools centered on their attending the newly constructed Mountain View School (formerly Hudgins School) in Marion. The black community's efforts to reopen the Old Fort school for blacks or to compel officials to build a new one by means of court action failed when Judge Wilson Warlick struck down the 1953 suit and declared it had been rendered "moot" due to the Supreme Court decision making construction of segregated schools illegal, as cited in an article in *The McDowell News*, dated July 7, 1955, 59/50, "Suit Against Board of Education Is Dismissed by Judge Warlick" (African American Scrapbook of News Clippings, Vertical File, McDowell County Public Library, Marion, NC). His decision came in 1955, two years after the case was filed. To avoid the trek to a Marion school, Old Fort Negroes then sought admission to the white school, an action that drew attention throughout the region and throughout the state (B. Connelly, "Hearing Opens in Old Fort School Desegregation Appeal," March 1, 1956, *The Charlotte Observer*, p. 2A).

The action tested the state Pupil Assignment Law of 1955 for the first time since its enactment and provided more than ample opportunities for the local school board to develop alternative solutions. The initial attempt to gain admittance for black students at Old Fort's all-white school unrolled in a peaceable manner even though the five black students accompanied by Albert Joyner were turned away. However, Joyner and the husband of a black teacher were attacked a short time later on the streets of Old Fort ("Affray Case Is Continued," September 6, 1955, *The Charlotte Observer*, p. 8B, African American Scrapbook, Vertical File, McDowell Public Library, Marion, NC). Joyner was beaten by a white man, W.W. Arney, Jr., who pleaded guilty to the assault. Another white man struck William C. Brittain because he suspected Brittain sent Joyner to enroll black students at the white school in an effort to win a teaching position for Brittain's wife. Attorneys for the black community, Herman L. Taylor and Samuel S. Mitchell of Raleigh, persevered on behalf of their clients for years. Eventually the attorneys presented their case to Superior Court with Judge George B. Patton presiding. ("Five Negro Children Attempt Admittance at Old Fort School," August 25, 1955, *The McDow-*

ell News, 60/5 and "Hearing on Affray in Old Fort to Be September 19," September 8, 1955, In African American Scrapbook, Vertical File, McDowell Public Library, Marion, NC).

Judge Patton upheld the 1955 legislative act empowering local boards to handle student assignments and transfers by rejecting the suit because it was based on claims for a group and not for individuals wishing to enroll. Later Chief Judge John J. Parker of the Fourth Circuit Court of Appeals upheld the ruling that refused Lionel C. Carson and other black children admission to McDowell County's white school because they had not exhausted all remedies at their disposal. Parker affirmed the right of the children to be admitted without racial discrimination but affirmed that being allowed to attend the white schools had to be determined individual by individual, not as a group ("McDowell School Case Stymied," November 15, 1956, *The McDowell News*. In African American Scrapbook, Vertical File, McDowell County Public Library, Marion, NC). Such was the law, slow and steady. Subsequently, Taylor and Mitchell filed a writ of certiorari asking that the decision be reviewed.

In reference to Ashe County, Cooper (1964) stated: "The decision of the United States Supreme Court relative to the integration in the schools has not yet (1956) brought about any changes in the county school system, and a new modern physical plant for Negro pupils, fewer than 30 in the county, is being planned for construction near Plumtree as the present schoolhouse at Cranberry is both obsolete and too far removed from the homes of most of the Negro families" (p. 64). Ashe was not the only Western county that elected to invest funds in school construction for black students after the Brown decision became law, as a way of presenting a "separate but equal" challenge to integrating schools. Ultimately, however, the law prevailed. In Ashe County and throughout the United States, segregated schools ceased to exist, at least in theory.

University of North Carolina's Richard E. Day completed a report on the state of school desegregation in the state of North Carolina for the United States Commission on Civil Rights in 1962 (www.law.umaryland.edu/marshall). In that report, he included information about Asheville. For example, in 1962 Asheville's school enrollment included 9,825 students, of whom 2,809 were black. Within the city's dual system were two high schools, Lee H. Edwards for whites and Stephens-Lee for blacks. There were also two white junior high schools, but no black junior high, seven white elementary schools and four black elementary schools. A new senior high school for the black community was under construction and was to be available for the 1963-64 term with the possibility of converting Stephens-Lee into a junior high school.

Asheville's school board received 11 requests for transfers to all-white schools for the 1961-62 term, of which five were approved for grades 1 and 2 at Newton Elementary School. All other requests were rejected because the board had determined to desegregate only the first three grades. Day (1962) cited as unusual the near total blackout of news coverage for the first steps toward desegregating Asheville's schools and explained that school officials asked managers of the local television station and their representatives in New York City to avoid brandishing the spotlight on local desegregation through pictures or on-site reports.

Day describes the school day as developing with no press lurking to talk to students, teachers, or parents and no cameras documenting the event. He writes: "There was no trouble, no crowd, or anything unusual. Police were alerted, drove by, and generally remained ready — but inconspicuous. Desegregation was smooth and uneventful" (p. 85). As a result of the success of its initial step toward integration, the Asheville City School Board resolved to continue with grades 1–3 and to extend that perhaps at the rate of three each year — with grades 1–6 on schedule for the 1962-63 year — until total integration was achieved. Pupil assignments for grades 1–3 would be based strictly on area of residence, with the prospect that approximately 30 black pupils would be eligible to attend formerly white schools.

Students lead a silent tribute to slain civil rights leader Martin Luther King, Jr., on April 9, 1968, walking from South French Broad High School to Asheville City Hall and back. Blacks and whites, students and adults, marched in solemnity to honor the advocate of non-violence, who had visited Asheville in January of 1964 and in August of 1965 (courtesy *Asheville Citizen-Times* and Citizen-times.com/historic).

Day emphasized that Asheville's approach was token integration and that any student of a minority race in the school to which he or she was assigned could choose to attend a school in which his or her race was in the majority. According to Day, the plan offered white students living in a largely black residential area a way out. He introduced his report, written before any of the later disturbances, with a comment about Asheville experiencing the quietest and least disruptive integration in the state. Day's initial report appeared in 1962, seven years before violent events erupted in 1969. Soon, however, the silence disappeared, and the publicity absent on that first day at Newton Elementary School could not be quelled.

The Asheville City Schools received support for its effort to integrate schools from the Asheville Area Council on Human Relations, which had been founded as an interracial body to keep open lines of communication between the two races and therefore achieve desegregation in a harmonious way. The council had success in desegregating Asheville businesses and, having accomplished that undertaking without a major problem, stood ready to assist school communities ("Human Relations Project Is Highly Encouraging Development; Asheville Uproar Area Council on All Interracial Problems," April 14, 1960, *The Asheville Citizen*). UNCA senior Daniel Maddelena (2000) described Asheville's Council on Human Relations as a 75-member bi-racial group with a 14-member executive committee whose aim was to improve alliances between blacks and whites. They were willing to help in school desegregation if needed.

Act 2: Fervency of Assertive Students

Peaceful demonstrations protesting segregated facilities spread throughout the state. On February 10, 1960, black students took part in a "sit-in" at Asheville's Woolworth Store. Trained by civil rights activist William Roland in the back room of his jewelry store, students resisted reaction to mistreatment and ended their demonstration quietly (G. Roland, personal communication, July 11, 2007). That night, though, white students painted a giant Confederate flag on the sidewalk in front of Woolworth's. Civil Rights had moved from the wings into center stage.

In 1965, historic Stephens-Lee High School was abandoned so black students began to attend their new South French Broad High School, which was built to meet the "separate but equal" requirement for segregated schools, according to O.L. Sherrill (personal communication, September 3, 2010). Subsequently, the board developed plans for the consolidation of the black South French Broad School with the white Lee Edwards High School. Representatives from each school agreed that the name would be changed to Asheville High School, which all students in grades 10–12 would attend. All ninth grade students would enroll at South French Broad School before attending the high school (Buncombe County Board of Education minutes, January 1965 to December 1969).

Violence erupts at Asheville High School on the morning of September 29, 1969, just days after desegregating South French Broad and Lee Edwards High Schools. After presenting a list of grievances to Principal Clark Pennell and battling with police for about fifteen minutes, two hundred students wreaked violence on the campus as they fled. Violence would occur there once again in 1972 (courtesy *Asheville Citizen-Times* and Citizen-times.com/historic).

Despite previously published plans, the Asheville City Schools did not achieve total school desegregation until the fall of 1969. School board members invested years planning the event, which would finally bring the system into full compliance with the law. Any reference to desegregation issues was absent from *The Asheville Citizen*'s report on the opening day of school so apparently no problems surfaced. Its headline on August 23, 1969, stated "20,698 Students Register in Buncombe County Schools." No disruptions marred routine classroom procedures during the closing days of August or during the early days of September. Apparently all was calm, but it would prove to be the calm before the storm, for violence erupted on the Asheville High School campus the morning of September 29, 1969.

A group of black students staged a walkout to protest their grievances and refused Principal Clark Pennell's repeated requests that they either return to class or leave campus. Despite Pennell's assurance their list of grievances would be considered, protesters ignored his requests. Fearing escalation of disorder, officials called the police. Students responded to the police demand that they disburse with "singing and clapping and obscene language" (Mary Cowles, "Police Action Is Described," October 4, 1969, *The Asheville Citizen*).

Mounting tensions culminated in a clash between students and police officers that morning. Brick and rock throwing and baton swinging injured students and police officers. As violence damaged the building, broken glass threatened persons inside the school. An Asheville high alumnus stated that he and friends watched the unfolding scene and observed a dozen police cars arrive with officers in full riot gear that included helmets, shields, and lengthy batons ("Asheville High Riot," retrieved from http://www.facebook.com/topic). A riot, a three day curfew, and additional safeguards marked the following weeks.

That day Asheville city policeman John Pipitone observed windows being shattered in the vocational training nursery so children wedged themselves under desks to escape harm. One teacher covered infants with her body. Injuries were reported as minimal, but on a nearby street James Dorn was dragged from the cab of his truck and suffered a beating that culminated in a fractured nose. Alfred Fulton Weaver was struck on the head with a bottle. A few businesses reported windows broken by bricks and bullets (Jay Hensley, "City Police Arrest Two Militant Leaders," October 1, 1969, *Asheville Citizen*). A state of emergency was declared, and Mayor Wayne Montgomery proclaimed a curfew for Asheville, with Buncombe County following suit by order of Commissioner Chairman Gordon Greenwood. Montgomery also asked assistance from Governor Robert W. Scott's office.

Governor Scott asked State Highway Patrol troopers in the Asheville area to assess the situation and to remain on alert. After receiving their report, he ordered 27 riot-trained troopers to the region. All available county and city police officers were put on standby. Arrests were made for curfew violations and for possession of explosives and firearms. The events of September 29 ended the smooth transition to desegregation.

Charles Wykle, an Asheville High School history teacher during that time period, said he is still aghast at the number of police officers who showed up at the high school:

> When the riot broke out, I was amazed at the amount of police on campus— FBI, SBI, State Highway Patrol, Asheville City Police, Buncombe County Police. It was unsettling, and on the day school reopened, there was a policeman every 20 feet in the building. Amazing!
>
> Of course, I was young and had no sense, but I never felt threatened. The rioters targeted the building, the trophy case, and unfortunately they threw rocks at the Vocational Building, where a day-care training center was located. The African American lady in charge [Lucille Burton] literally protected the children with her body, and she was so angry she was ready to take on the world to fight the culprits who endangered her charges [personal communication, September 3, 2010].

Then Co-principal O.L. Sherrill explained the circumstances. The vocational building, he said, had recently been completed and the contractors had not yet moved a lot of the debris so students "unloaded the rocks on the building," which had a lot of glass. Sherrill also said that for 30 days no one was allowed to enter or leave the school except students— and teachers were deputized to help (personal communication, September 3, 2010). Typewriters were tossed through second story windows (S. Reese, September 3, 2010). Tension ran high and parents, white and black, were disappointed and terrified.

Wykle added, "Because of segregation, people of the two races had a lack of knowledge of one another. It was a sad time, a bitter experience for the young, but thank goodness it came to an end.... There had been a lot of preparation with high hopes of avoiding violence, but some things went unattended" (personal communication, September 3, 2010).

"Some things went unattended"— that remark aptly condenses the underlying causes of the riot. Rather than citizens and board members congratulating themselves about what a good job they had done in the transition to an integrated school, now it was time to ask serious questions: What efforts had school leaders made to make black students welcome in a white school community? Why did black students stage a walkout? How should the school address black concerns?

Community leaders spent the next days investigating the cause of the confrontation and developing a plan of action to forestall additional violence. A newspaper report said students were allowed to voice their grievances at a September 30 meeting of the Buncombe County Community Relations Council. Leo Gaines, the student whose expulsion (because he refused to wear socks) was rumored to have triggered the walkout, expressed his view that violence resulted from excessive police force and that "Asheville will continue to have hell until we get what we want" ("Open Meeting Is Scheduled in High School Disturbance," 1969 September 30, *The Asheville Citizen*, and cited by Fryar, 2003).

Subsequent meetings of the Asheville School Board resulted in efforts to respect the demands of the black students. A major resentment resulted from the absence of any Stephens-Lee/South French Broad trophies on display alongside those exhibited touting Lee Edwards High School's achievements. Students also objected to a portrait of Lee Edwards being displayed in the school's lobby and stated that portraits of their principals should have been on display in the Asheville High lobby. Restraining orders for violating the curfew were issued for three black leaders: Victor Chalk, Jr., James McDowell, and Shirley Brown (Ed Seitz, "Schools to Reopen; Militants Enjoined," October 2, 1969, *The Asheville Citizen*).

Chalk, a young adult who organized the students to list their grievances, to stick together, and to protest by walking out, was jailed and later convicted for breaking curfew and violating the firearms control laws. McDowell and Brown were Asheville High School students who spoke in public meetings in support of the young people who had committed acts of violence on school property (Department of Public Instruction, Division of Negro Education, Special Subjects File, Box 11). An editorial, "The City Is Now Faced with a Test of Reason," called for the city to respond to the unsettling demonstrations at the high school with reverence for the law. School officials received severe criticism from numerous sources for not having the foresight to include mementos from the black South French Broad High School.

Meeting on September 30 and again on October 1, 1969, members of the school board examined the grievances presented by the black students. The board affirmed its commitment to give every child an equal educational opportunity and to continue to study racial problems affecting the instructional program, and agreed to some student demands, including immediately hiring a black cosmetology teacher, doing away with the requirement that majorettes be musicians, deferring the issues of requiring haircuts as well as socks to a dress code committee, removing Lee Edwards insignia from all band and other uniforms, displaying memorials of principals of Stephens-Lee and of South French Broad schools, exhibiting trophies of both schools, practicing a more lenient policy toward "tardies" until the transportation system could be improved, and encouraging discipline methods other than corporal punishment. The board reacted to the emergency with common sense, but greater foresight might have curtailed enormous ill will and great damage.

Other demands would be studied in more depth, including those concerning the black history program. Students were convinced that a white faculty member should not be teaching black history (Wykle and Sherrill, personal communication, September 3, 2010). The board voiced high praise for the actions of Principals Clark Pennell and James Penley at their respective schools—Asheville High and South French Broad—during the disturbance ("Principals Praised," October 3, 1969, *The Asheville Citizen*).

The board also mandated the reopening of school on October 2. Attorney William C. Morris reviewed with the board the court injunction issued to restrain all persons from interfering with the operation of the schools. Superior Court Judge Harry C. Martin signed the document ordering all enrolled students to return to class at the regular time and banning individuals who had been named as instigators of violence.

School resumed on the following Monday. Mary Cowles ("Asheville Schools Open as Police Stand Guard," *Asheville Citizen*, October 3, 1969) reported that police stood guard at the school and that, although absenteeism was high, no serious incidents occurred. On Saturday, October 4, officials declared an end to the city-county state of emergency. The move toward normalcy was underway. Media coverage of the event seems one-sided — opposition to reactions of blacks but praise for actions of whites. However, black students succeeded in increasing public awareness of their educational heritage in all–Negro schools.

Following the riots, the Rev. Wesley Grant, Sr., quietly sat on the steps of Asheville High, simply sat there, most likely with permission. He was a reminder of expectations the black community had of student behavior. Others described his presence as a calming influence ("Black History Month," February 18, 2005, *Asheville Citizen-Times*, p. 1B).

Outsiders were involved in the melee, according to a story by Bill Mebane in the October 3 issue of *The Asheville Citizen*. Mebane reports that Sgt. J.E. Fleming, a black police officer, observed "outsiders" who had no association with the school present at Asheville High School on the morning of the walkout. City Manager Phin Horton claimed responsibility for sending police to the scene but refuted the statement that he ordered officers to "double step." Horton also assured the public at various times that everything possible was being done to ensure public safety.

During the second semester of that first year of total integration, a city school board meeting deteriorated into violence ("Protesters Turn Destructive," *The Asheville Citizen*, February 3, 1970). On February 2, 1970, demonstrators strongly objected to the closing of Livingston Street and Herring (Mountain Street) Schools. The Board of Education meeting erupted into disorder and a rampage followed. Windows and windshields were smashed. City Council members' blazers were stuffed into the commode. Members of the board sought refuge in the offices of the Public Works Department. A few hours later all was quiet. No disruption of school took place.

However, another riot occurred on the Asheville High School campus in 1972. On the morning of October 18, fighting broke out at the school as issues surfaced about the National Honor Society selection process. Fist fights and rock throwing forced officials to close the school. Students adjourned to South French Broad School where clashes erupted and forced that school to close. Windows were broken, and books and papers were scattered on the floors (Mike Boyd, "Fracas Closes City Schools," October 18, 1972, *The Asheville Citizen*, p. 1).

Authorities dispatched all available ambulances and police officers to Asheville High. Ambulances transported injured students to Memorial Mission Hospital for treatment. Police officers quickly established order, but some teenagers looted downtown stores. About 15 students invaded the G.I. Outlet on Biltmore Avenue. Resisting attempts by employees to restrain them, the students left with seven short leather coats, worth $100 each. The Dollar General Store on Haywood Street reported a loss of 16 Timex watches, valued at $150 each. Fain's Thrift Store was the site of a broken window, caused by a rock. S.H. Kress and Co. reported three incursions resulting in the theft of umbrellas, cookies, and cakes as well as toys and bracelets. The manager also noted that a gumball machine had been broken and several counters were overturned ("Businesses Are Targets of Students," October 19, 1972, *Asheville Citizen*).

A second outbreak at the high school the next day resulted in three arrests but not before damages estimated at $2,000 occurred. Fleeing students hurled rocks through windows in the still new Vocational Education building, a $1.3 million structure. The school superintendent closed city schools until the following Monday (Mike Boyd, "Closes City Schools," October 18, 1972, *The Asheville Citizen*).

Hearing that "all hell will break loose," Principal William H. Stanley had alerted the police. Fewer than 25 students were involved in the fracas. Stanley explained that dissatisfaction over the basis for selecting National Honor Society members appeared to be the root of the problem. Adult leaders had apparently overlooked how racially diverse students might perceive the decision process. He assured the public that the complaint would be checked out and that any inequities would be addressed ("Three Arrested in Second Outbreak at High School," October 20, 1972, *The Asheville Citizen*). Once more order was restored.

Act 3: Expectations of Persistent Parents

Assuring the public of the board's interest in promoting the educational interests of all students, the Buncombe County Board of Education adopted its policy regarding desegregation in 1956. The board also appointed a committee to study the problems of desegregation and advise them of their findings. Advisory Committee members, led by chair Sam Dixon, were Mrs. Robert Russell, J. Fred Hall, C.U. James, Miller Ramsey, Robert R. Barnes, Gordon Greenwood, J.C. Daniels, Ben Clark, and Ben Davis (Buncombe County School Board minutes, June 20, 1956).

The interracial committee laid the groundwork for adopting a complicated policy for student assignments. Such action resulted from the Pupil Assignment Act passed in 1955 by the North Carolina General Assembly and the accompanying Pearsall Plan, two tactics that allowed local school boards to determine their own plans for desegregating public schools. Such measures delayed school integration. And that was the intent of enforcing the plan — to localize decisions on integration issues and avoid dictates from the Raleigh offices of state government (Earp, 1979).

The Buncombe County procedure required an interview process and completed application forms. The complicated procedure enabled the board to refuse permission with some ease. Buncombe County's procedure was later challenged, but on June 20, 1956, the board affirmed that any parent wishing a change in a child's school assignment must apply in writing 60 days prior to the opening date of school, complete an application in full, have the application notarized or signed by an individual duly authorized to administer oaths, and submit both to the board.

Any omission of information on the application or any tardiness would render the application invalid. However, the board confirmed its intent to act with reasonable speed to render a final decision on the parents' requests (Buncombe County School Board minutes, June 20, 1956).

In 1963, two years after the city of Asheville began complying with the law of the land, the county schools also initiated a gradual approach to desegregation. Leonard P. Miller, in his *Education in Buncombe County 1793–1965* (1965), documents the integration of the county schools.

At its May 6, 1963, meeting, the board recognized attorney Ruben J. Dailey to speak on behalf of a delegation of visitors. Dailey explained that approximately 18 students, ranging in grade level from the first through the seventh, wished to enroll at Haw Creek Elementary School for the 1963-1964 year. Dailey and other visitors were told that applications for admission would be available at the superintendent's office on May 15, 1963.

As a result, on August 12, 1963, the formerly all-white Haw Creek Elementary School admitted 12 Negro children who lived in the Haw Creek community. Miller (1965) points out that this event launched the first implementation of the U.S. Supreme Court's 1954 decision within the Buncombe County school system. However, eight applications for the upper grades were denied due to lack of space. The explanation attributed the denial to the committee's unwillingness to jeopardize accreditation by the Southern Association of Schools and Colleges because of overcrowding. As a result, those eight students were assigned to schools outside the district with the county paying tuition for their classes.

Attorney Dailey, on behalf of his clients, requested further consideration be given to assigning the other pupils so desiring to the Haw Creek School, but the county board assured Dailey that existing space was too crowded to allow other students to enroll. However, the board agreed to take a student population census to confirm overcrowding and to share the results with Dailey and his clients. In addition, John Hamilton of Black Mountain requested that Linda Dale Dillingham be admitted to the Buncombe County Administrative unit (Buncombe County School Board minutes, August 13, 1963), but the board rejected the application on the grounds that it did not comply with the assignment procedure. The tedious process for making such applications allowed rejections to occur with comparative ease.

The practice of token integration at Haw Creek did not appease the county's black residents, so they sought further action through their lawyer. Dailey contended that county schools had been in violation of the Supreme Court decision of 1954 by operating on a strictly racial basis for nearly a decade.

Miller (1965) identified two Buncombe County elementary schools for black children, Carver Elementary School at Black Mountain and Shiloh in Biltmore, that had been in existence for a long time. Five teachers had been assigned to Carver Elementary and 10 to Shiloh. Approximately 20 percent of the county's elementary school children were enrolled in the Asheville City Schools, and every black high school student residing in the county was compelled to attend secondary school within the city system.

Parents of 10 Buncombe County families representing 32 students filed a petition on November 20, 1963. The petition prompted the board to finalize its intent to end segregation. On January 7, 1964, the Buncombe County Board of Education adopted a four-year plan for integration. The plan earmarked the 1967-1968 school year as the terminal date to end segregation. Its provisions included assigning first graders to schools in their residential districts and the right of parents or guardians whose children in grades 1–4 were assigned to schools outside their districts for the 1964-65 school year to request reassignment to a school within the pupil's residential district. It also provided a comparable arrangement for pupils in grades 1–3 for 1965-66 and for grades 1–12 for the 1967-68 school year (Miller, 1965).

Gradual desegregation provided an unacceptable alternative for black parents in part because of the tedious application for transfer process and the obvious delay tactics.

Referring to Buncombe County's plan as "antiquated," Dailey filed a suit in District Court on January 23, 1964, on behalf of parents who wanted their children to be sent to the school nearest their homes. He called for the complete integration of county schools beginning with the 1964-65 school year. Defendants in the case included the Buncombe County Board of Education, its chair J.G. Northcott, and Superintendent T.C. Roberson. Attorney Lawrence C. Stokes filed the case, which was tried on July 14 and 15, for the defendants. The court ruled that the proposed plan was reasonable but in need of modifications with Step 1 integrating grades 1–8; Step 2, grades 9–10; and Step 3, grades 11–12. Complete integration was to be in place by September 1966 (Miller, 1965).

Students at Carver Elementary School in Black Mountain were assigned to Black Mountain Elementary School in 1966. Board member Morris L. McGough moved to close Carver School as a step toward compliance with civil rights legislation, but the board suspended the motion temporarily, pending an investigation by Superintendent Roberson ("County Board Approves Carver School Closing," August 10, 1966, *The Asheville Citizen*). Following desegregation, Carver School became the site of Carver Optional School (*The Asheville Citizen*, June 29, 1976), which closed in 1987 at the end of the school year.

Superintendent T.C. Roberson faced a dilemma with the merger of Carver Colored School with Black Mountain Elementary School and the appointment of two principals to head the French Broad School. The court order, which related to county schools' compliance with the 1964 Civil Rights Act, demanded that the schools merge. Superintendent Roberson, after conferring with local school committees and personnel, announced that the Carver School would be closed, at least temporarily. The principal mix-up resulted when the French Broad school committee elected Robert Young to be principal and Roberson selected Jerry M. Plemmons. Roberson interpreted state law as designating the local school superintendent to select principals. Facing down the French Broad community's representatives who claimed turmoil had erupted over the possibility that Young would not be principal, the board unanimously supported Roberson in his appointment.

In her article "Livingston Street School Fate to Be Known by May 1," published in the April 11, 1972 *Asheville Citizen,* Mary Cowles explored the fate of the Livingstone Street School. Hope existed that the building would once again house a school. The article cited Superintendent W.P. Griffin's concern about causing a hardship on other schools by reopening Livingstone as a school. Griffin pointed out that busing would be necessary to establish racial balance if a school were to be located in the Livingstone Street structure. In a September 13, 1973, follow-up story, Cowles, staff writer for the *Asheville Citizen,* wrote about the $100,000 purchase of the Livingstone Street School, which was to be converted into a multi-purpose community center by the city of Asheville. Since closing, the former all-black elementary school had served as the headquarters of the Opportunity Corporation of Madison-Buncombe Counties. Plans for the newly purchased building included constructing a gymnasium for intramural sports.

In the August 19, 1964, *Asheville Citizen*, Bruce Gourlay reported that 54 Negroes had been assigned to 10 county schools. A court order issued by Federal Judge J. Braxton Craven compelled that action by the school board. Black students were assigned to three high schools: Owen, Reynolds, and Erwin. Blacks would also attend Valley Springs, Swannanoa, Fairview, Black Mountain, Leicester, and Weaverville schools. Six additional students were assigned to the already integrated Haw Creek School. Black enrollment at those schools was sparse. For example, at Erwin High School and at Weaverville Elementary School, only a single back student was assigned. At Reynolds High School as well as at Black Mountain and Leicester Elementary Schools, four were assigned. The largest numbers assigned to a single school was 15 at Valley Springs and 11 at Swannanoa. Fourteen black students were to attend Haw Creek that year.

The colored school at Weaverville was moved to a new location and continues to be used as a community center. Shiloh School, although the building contains little that was a part of the Rosenwald construction, functions as a community and recreational center. Some neighborhood schools were not lost but used as centers for community business. Others, such as the historic Stephens-Lee High School, were razed. After five decades, black education in Asheville and in Buncombe County continues in an integrated environment that has grown more and more diverse. However, segregation would probably have endured much longer had it not been for Title VI of the 1964 Civil Rights Act. Change, even in Western North Carolina's largest communities, happened only with the push of national decisions—and that was often at an extremely slow pace.

A number of individuals, when approached to share their personal experiences with integration in Western counties, indicated that the entire process was seamless and that the transition flowed smoothly. Such was the report that came from Cherokee County when the two races entered the same school one morning and no conflict occurred. Perhaps because only a small number of black residents made their homes in the area, violent episodes did not occur. However, there were subtle barriers erected. According to a Murphy High School white alumna, black students were more sophisticated because they had attended high school in other locales and had a wider experience than the mountain students who had limited opportunities to travel to nearby cities such as Asheville and Hickory or out of state to Atlanta, Knoxville or Greenville, South Carolina.

The day before the integration change at Murphy, parents and teenagers met at Zion Baptist Church, according to Pat and Gwyn Kincaid. Students were told to mind their p's and q's, that they had heard the word N----r before. On integration day, two deputies and two city police drove by, but all was peaceful. Citizens felt police were mainly creating a presence.

At times blacks were called names, but usually they ignored the incidents. Six months later, however, a male student kicked another guy from behind. The "guy" swirled around with a punch that broke the receiver's jaw and the thrower's hand. The white student who kicked was reprimanded. The black student who responded was suspended (personal communication, Pat and Gwyn Kincaid, brother and sister; June 22, 2009).

Act 4: Extension of Integration Process

Hugh Randall, Hendersonville's superintendent of schools, transferred white coach James (Jim) H. Laughter to Ninth Avenue School for a trial integration year in 1964–65. Students were allowed freedom of choice, but, according to Laughter, no whites went to the black school. He recalled the powerful football magnet of his assignment:

> I was sent to teach PE and to coach. About 29 students chose to attend Hendersonville.... Before the year ended, all or about all came back.... Athletes were Walter McIlwean and Joe Greene. They played for Harold Clyde at Hendersonville High until Christmas. The next year, 1965–66, there was full integration.... At Ninth Avenue — there were no records, but we played our games at the high school [the white Hendersonville High School's football field], usually on Thursday nights. Marable was an outstanding coach.... Ours was the dominant black football program in the state.... We traveled a lot just to get a schedule ... played in Hickory, Shelby, and in South Carolina — really outstanding football. Two of the best players were brothers: Willie Mitchum (running back) and Shag Mitchum (quarterback). Our local radio station, WHKP, broadcast the Ninth Avenue Tigers' games (personal communication, March 10, 2009).

Laughter, describing Ninth Avenue's Principal Marable as a strict disciplinarian, said, "During our 'trial year,' there were no problems. He ran a really tight ship. The worst thing was using the old, dilapidated Hendersonville High School gym.... It was in really bad shape. Originally Sixth Avenue School was Ninth Avenue. The school colors were blue and gold. Lemuel Jones replaced me at Hendersonville Junior High. He was a real disciplinarian ... no foolishness. In 1968, a new gym was built, and another later on. Sam Gash's dad played there" (personal communication). Sam Gash, a native of Hendersonville, is a former professional football player and now a college coach.

"Integration's going to be a struggle," Hendersonville Superintendent Hugh Randall said when he reassigned Laughter to Ninth Avenue School, "You won't see a difference for 13 years, after a group has gone through kindergarten and 12 years of school, but it will get better all the time."

Recalling the conversation, Laughter said, "Randall was never as far off base as when he said that. Our black kids were well guided at home."

Laughter continued his 32-year career in education until his 1991 retirement. Laughter, who remains active and helps coach, thinks of his interim at Ninth Avenue as being one of his best experiences, in part because of the support of outstanding black parents. Sharing one experience related to the difficulty of being the male physical education teacher for girls, Laughter explained that it was awkward.

He found it especially difficult to discipline young female students. "A young girl kept getting out of hand," Laughter said. "I was at my wit's end." When Laughter took his problem to the principal, it seemed the solution involved consulting the girl's grandmother, who was raising her. Marable summoned the lady to school and explained that her granddaughter Darlene refused to do as she was asked. Hearing that the principal and the girl's teacher found it difficult to discipline a girl, the grandmother inquired, "Do you wear a belt? Then take it off and use it on her." Both men expressed reluctance to use a belt on the girl, whereupon the grandmother demanded the principal remove his belt and hand it to her.

Laughter described what followed: "Right there, she lit into Darlene with that belt and wore her out. Then she said: 'Coach, I'm a busy woman. I can't be running up here all the time. Now you use that belt on that child or I'll come up here and use it on you and wear you out'" (personal communication, March 10, 2009). Involving the girl's grandmother brought the matter to its conclusion.

Henderson County's move to integrate was instigated by a request. Grace Ledbetter, executive assistant to Henderson County's superintendent J. M. Foster, explained that a striking woman came to the central office and said, "We want the schools integrated." Libby Payne presented her request to Superintendent Foster, and desegregation became the focus. Ledbetter said that such a request was expected, but that suddenly fear descended on the school offices — that bad things were going to happen. Seeking guidance throughout the process, the school board approached three respected black gentlemen: George E. Weaver, James Pilgrim, and Sam Mills. "Glen C. Marlow approached Sam Mills to get his 'feel' for the situation. We wanted things to go smoothly ... no explosives! And integration went very, very smoothly. It was handled quietly and with dignity. We called the board together for a lot of private meetings" (personal communication, February 1, 2003).

Although the memory is difficult to retrieve after 50 years have passed, conflict did occur in the Hendersonville City Schools, as John Sholar reported in "Negro School Applicants in Final Steps Prior to Court" in the *Times-News* on September 27, 1963. Five parents requested a transfer for their children to the white schools to provide them with better learning options. The parents, bringing a suit in Asheville's District Federal Court, named the members of the school board — Keith Arledge, H.C. Livingston, L.B. Prince, J.D. Lutz, and John Gregory — as defendants. The use of the courts was modeled after the action taken by a group of Transylvania County parents, who won their battle to enroll their children in Brevard High School. Dailey, who had been active in integration cases, served as attorney for both counties — and for other Western counties as well.

When county integration occurred, Ledbetter said that some black teachers taught in the formerly all-white schools. Hortense Potts was at West Henderson High School, and Thelma Gash taught at Balfour. Hannah Logan Edwards described herself as a "pioneer teacher" at Hendersonville High School in 1965. "I got to work in my field, business education," she said. "I taught 11 years at Ninth Avenue and 25 years at HHS. My job was interesting, and I liked the administrators, the teachers, and the students."

Edwards recalled learning in the "hot 60s" that Stokely Carmichael and Rap Brown were bringing a bus to Hendersonville. "Mr. Stikies, who worked at the A&P, asked if I knew what bus was coming to town. He was scared to death. He said, 'It will tear this town up.' But somebody turned back the Freedom Bus" (personal communication, November 16, 2004). Eddie Young, another Ninth Avenue teacher, sought a position at Brevard High School, but unsuccessfully. Eventually Young moved his family to Bridgeport, Connecticut, where he found work with a good salary (personal communication, October 31, 2006).

Of course, Henderson County simply represented what happened with assignments of black teachers. Black professionals spoke out to retain fairness in the teacher assignment process. However, they themselves had been victims of lifelong segregation. No matter how scholarly, most never had the opportunity to attend colleges and universities with the highest academic ratings. Also, they had taught with inadequate equipment and had been required to use outdated textbooks. Daily they had endured classrooms and buildings that were often in poor condition. Dedication and commitment helped them perform valiantly, but everyone knew that the odds were against them. All of those factors stacked the odds against being assigned to formerly white schools that housed better students. It would take more decades to achieve progress in developing integrated faculties. In the 21st century the role has reversed. Ironically, high-paying business jobs attract African Americans so schools are searching for qualified minorities to teach integrated students. The situation represents an unusual way to turn back the clock.

After Libby Payne enrolled sons Carlos and Curtis in Etowah Elementary School, the process was underway. Although not accepted by all their schoolmates, they were well received by the faculty. Etowah teacher Lucy Sitton, while grading papers after school, heard a disturbing sound well after the dismissal bell had rung. Walking to her window, she saw boys peppering the Payne brothers with rocks. To stop the harassment, Sitton raised the window and shouted, "Stop!" The white boys ran off. She then invited the two lads into her classroom to help them deal with their experience. The boys explained that their presence, caused by an

Friends since before Henderson County's school integration, Lucy Sitton and Libby Payne visit on March 5, 2005. The school board, on July 27, 1964, granted Payne's petition to allow her two young sons, Carlos and Curtis, to transfer from Ninth Avenue School to Etowah Elementary, where Sitton taught (photograph by B.J. Reed).

impulsive decision to return to school to play, had triggered hostility on the playground (personal communication, February 23, 2005). According to Sitton, the Payne children had enrolled before Henderson County established total integration. Their mother, Payne, and their teacher, Sitton, established a friendship during the integration process that lasted down through the years.

The Rivers family also broke the color barrier in the city schools. Gary Rivers, director of Minority Affairs at Blue Ridge Community College, described his part in Henderson County's integration process:

> My family was one of the first to opt for integration because Mother [Ruby Rivers] was a progressive thinker. I attended Ninth Avenue, which was as good as any school could be at that time, for the first grade. In second, I had Miss Sousanman at Bruce Drysdale. We walked in, and the school was integrated. It was an optional thing. The transition was really good with no problems at the schoolhouse door. George Wilkins was principal. I vividly recall racial instances, but Miss Sousanman took me under her wing.

Rivers confirmed that it was difficult entering a totally unknown environment with the expectation that hatred was on the other side, but his mother impressed upon her son that he was just "as worthy and as capable as any other person" [personal communication, December 1, 2005].

Rivers, recounting some of the firsts for members of his family, said, "My family was in the right place at the right time." Rivers was the first African American in baseball at the University of Tennessee. His sisters also were among the first individuals to make inroads on the traditions of segregation. Cathy Rivers Turner was the first black student to become a member of student government at Hendersonville High School. Deborah Rivers was the school's first black cheerleader, and the oldest sister, Rosalind Rivers Evans, was a National Merit student and a finalist for the esteemed Morehead Scholarship (personal communication, December 1, 2005).

Leon H. Anderson, principal of Ninth Avenue School in its final days as a segregated institution, told students that the ticket they needed to punch for success was education. Taking seriously his role to prepare them to face integrated classrooms, Anderson, an Airborne Ranger who turned in his military gear to become a freedom fighter, recommended that students reach beyond the mediocre and strive to excel. Students should establish goals and strive to attain them. Anderson also encouraged them to remember who they were, not to sacrifice their identity, but to be confident that success was within their grasp. He recommended that they seek more education beyond high school, which he described as "the tip of the ice berg." Anderson also related attempts by Ninth Avenue teachers to train students for comfort in integrated classes. "Younger children," Anderson said, "were above all integration issues ... not overly concerned.... Older ones didn't know what to expect. Their teachers prepared them by telling them 'History is history, no matter who is sitting in the room. You are as good as anyone. Just do your best'" (personal communication, April 7, 2009). Anderson drew on personal experience, as he had participated in lunch counter sit-ins and had marched with Martin Luther King, Jr. He worked to create an integrated society and prepared his students to assume their rightful place there.

Students received advice from other professional educators to focus on learning the subject matter within integrated classrooms and to put forth a strong effort to excel to the best of their abilities. One young lady who took their advice to heart was Gwen Lucas nee Simmons, who explained that she inflicted herself with stress because she was determined to do as well academically as any white student. Her quest for perfection took her from Henderson County schools through law school at Boston University, where she was always striving to excel (personal communication, May 19, 2005). Simmons' accomplishments are the envy of former white classmates.

Act 5: Influence of Legal Crusaders

Delay works against the clock to prevent upcoming change. However, momentum is a powerful force. Momentum jumps over county lines. In Western North Carolina, it eventually affected all corners. In the 1960s, local media and national media, which included vivid television newscasts, supplied information that escalated the momentum of integration. Conversations with friends and relatives also motivated parents.

Reports about integration spread quickly. There was no longer any validity questioning how many blacks were residents or how distant they were from schools. Instead, the Civil Rights law made those excuses irrelevant. Equality was achievable because the roadblocks had been shattered. However, it takes leaders to maximize the value of momentum as a force of change. Usually the leaders were conscientious attorneys and activists doing their utmost to protect the rights of deprived students.

In county after county, the struggle for integration was a difficult battle. Blacks refused to be silent. As blacks in other counties found breakthroughs, their plight seemed more serious and more frustrating. Sometimes school boards and dominant racial populations acted as though they could whitewash the problem. However, parents and protestors were stronger than long-time leaders had imagined.

Inevitably information reached the masses. Appeals could be ignored once, twice or more. However, later there was another appeal. Sometimes publicity, which appeared in North Carolina media or in distant media such as the *New York Times*, brought awareness. Eventually there was no county too small to ignore the requirements of the 1964 Civil Right law and the needs of all students, no matter their race. The steps to reconciliation took years and required diligence. It also required social influence — by black parents, by county residents, and by outside supporters, especially those providing essential legal assistance to overcome the obstacles racists continued to erect.

In county after county, attorney Ruben J. Dailey confronted school boards who were trying to find ways to ignore the law and to overlook students with black skin. Dailey never gave up. He went where needed, as the historical records demonstrate. He found no case too small and no county too poor or insignificant to ignore. In county case after case — Buncombe, Henderson, Madison, Polk, Transylvania, Yancey, and more — he surfaces as a force that brought reconciliation to the forefront. Of course, other individuals, such as Samuel L. Mitchell and Herman S. Taylor from Raleigh, Harold Epps in Asheville, and Judge Wilson Warlick, emerge too. In Western North Carolina, though, Dailey endures as a leader to applaud because his efforts dramatically changed and improved the educational opportunities for all students wherever they lived.

Yancey County provides a prototype of the typical mountain county's inability to deal with desegregation — a mindset that declares the races belonged in separate schools. In the early 1960s, with a total county population of slightly more than 14,000, of whom fewer than 150 were African Americans, Yancey County showcased the prevalent Appalachian opposition to desegregation as one of attitude rather than of black-white ratios. In the county system, which included 4,000 students, fewer than 30 students were African American. However, serving the small black student population created a dilemma for school officials without resorting to desegregating its schools. Yancey bused high school students to Asheville to attend Stephens-Lee School. A remote dilapidated building with no plumbing served elementary black students.

Immediately prior to desegregation, Yancey County erected a new black elementary school, Oak Crest School, which had only four students ("High Schools Must Integrate in 30 Days in Yancey Co.," September 1, 1960, *The Times News*). Oak Crest replaced what had been

Lincoln Park, which may have also been called Burnsville Colored School. Later Judge Wilson Warlick noted that the county had made no offer to provide a new Negro high school and that Negroes had complied fully so they must be allowed to attend a white school.

In 1953, African American families had requested a new school, and the county had purchased a construction site, but the site did not meet the approval of the black community, so plans were in limbo. In 1958, the black school was condemned after a report stating the conditions were unsafe and unsanitary. As a result, the district found it impossible to justify operating the school for only seven students, so the State Board of Education closed its doors.

According to its July 1, 1959, minutes, the Yancey County School Board met with attorney Dailey, who explained that the county's black citizens had given him the power of attorney to address the board regarding their desire that the long ride to Asheville end and that their children be allowed to enroll in white schools. Dailey recommended that the board, for its own protection, enroll the elementary children in Burnsville Elementary School and continue sending high school students to Asheville.

The minutes for July 6 document the board's discussion of a letter from Dailey prepared on behalf of the parents of 17 students asking for assignment to local schools. However, the board resolved to petition the Asheville City Schools to allow the students to enroll at Hill Street School and Stephens-Lee High School. As an alternative in case their request was refused, the board developed a backup plan to approach Madison County School Board. The board instructed Superintendent Hubert D. Justice to write Charles F. Carroll "for advice and help on the colored situation." However, Asheville City Schools agreed. During its August 10 meeting the board formally assigned all students represented by Dailey to the same school attended during the 1958-59 term. As a result, the elementary students and older teenagers continued their 80-mile round trip daily to attend classes in Asheville. At other times Yancey black students traveled to Marion or to Mars Hill.

Parents responded with an unsuccessful boycott to object to their children's 11-hour absence from home. The parents succeeded in negotiating a promise from the board that a new school would be provided by the next school term. The agreement became a broken promise due in part to the hefty debt incurred by constructing two new white high schools at a total cost of $850,000. The broken promise plus the substantial investment in the two new buildings changed the attitude of black parents. No longer did they waste energy demanding a new school. They shifted their position and demanded that their children be enrolled in all-white schools. The school board refused and made arrangements for continued transportation of black students to Asheville. Another boycott ensued, but this time a volunteer group launched a private elementary school in a church basement with two teachers for 24 students. Seven high school students, four boys and two girls, were enrolled in Asheville's Allen Home School (Day, 1962).

Dissatisfaction persisted while temporary solutions continued. The press focused national attention on the Burnsville battle. The dramatic situation appealed to the National Association for the Advancement of Colored People, which entered the confrontation by financing a lawsuit and sponsoring an advertisement in *The New York Times*. The ad featured a photo of a sleeping child on a school bus with the caption: "Eighty miles in 11 hours— that's a long day for a 6-year-old."

In response, *The New York Times* published an editorial comment on December 4, 1959, entitled "The Long, Long Road." Using persuasive language, the writer explained that the 6-year-old's daily journey showed to what lengths Southerners would go to avoid righting a wrong. Faced with a lawsuit, the Yancey County commissioners and school board decided Burnsville needed a new school for its black students. With a state loan of $30,000, the county constructed a building with a large classroom that could be divided by partitions to accommodate two teachers. The building had indoor plumbing with two restrooms and a kitchen sink. All black students, both high school and elementary, were assigned to the new school. However, only four of the 24 (17 elementary and eight high school students) enrolled, an action taken by their parents to put teeth into their objection to an assignment based solely on race.

Again the volunteer group re-established a private elementary school and enrolled the high school students in boarding schools. However, in 1960 Judge Warlick decreed that the eight black high school students should be admitted to Yancey County's public schools, a first in the Western counties. The board complied by assigning four students to Cane River and four to East Yancey High School. However, in part due to overcrowded conditions at the white elementary schools, the black elementary children were assigned to a segregated school (Day, 1962). Convinced they were right in turning down a second-rate education for their children, parents persisted in confronting the local authorities until the board desegregated its schools.

Courageous parents of Yancey County students filed suit in federal court: *Griffith v. Robinson* (Civ. No. 1881, W.D.N.C., Oct. 28, 1963, 8 Race, Rel. L. Rep. 1433) in their persistent efforts to avoid long bus rides and inferior education. According to the staff report of 1964 to the United State Civil Rights Commission, Yancey County's Board of Education received a mandate on September 26, 1963, to desegregate all its schools. In 1960, the county had been ordered to admit black students to its white high school. The decree by the federal court allowed white students to enroll in the recently constructed two-room elementary school for black students or to assign black students to the all-white elementary school. The court demanded action by the second semester of the 1963-64 school year (*Griffith v. Robinson*, 1963, retrieved from http://www.law.umaryland.edu/). However, the decision represents an extension of the court order.

In Marion, councilman Billy Martin, one of 11 students to integrate Marion High School, described his experience as calm and peaceful. He learned that there is not much difference between whites and blacks once they get acquainted. Now in the political arena, he has earned the support of many white Marion residents.

Martin described the transition to integration as a smooth one. When he and 10 other black students reported to class at the opening of school in 1965 at the white Marion High School, there was a calm atmosphere, with no commotion of any kind. He recalls no racial incidents (personal communication, June 18, 2010). Reporter Mike Conley (February 26, 1996) quotes Martin: "I had the best of both worlds. I had a good experience in Mountain View ... and a good experience at Marion High. We ran into no hostility that I can remember.... It's just an ongoing example of what kind of people we have here in Marion and McDowell County" ("Before Integration Black Students Attended Hudgins, Mountain View," February 21, 1996, *The McDowell News*).

Ten years after the Brown ruling on April 6, 1964, the Madison County Board of Education received a delegation from Asheville to discuss school integration. A large crowd had convened at the county courthouse. The minutes record that Mr. Day, a prominent Asheville attorney, was one member of the delegation. That gentleman was no doubt Ruben J. Dailey, who had been widely engaged in court litigation to desegregate schools in Western North Carolina, one of which was the Rosenwald School in Brevard.

Another visitor was William Roland, who had trained the Stephens-Lee students to demonstrate peacefully. Day (Dailey) explained that he represented the "NWACP" (NAACP) and had been successful in winning suits to establish integration in public schools through the courts. Manual Briscoe, chairman of the Black School Committee, made a "triple-barreled" recommendation: The board should build a new school for the black community, provide additional black teachers, and allow Geraldine Griffin's child to attend the white Mars Hill School as requested. The school board responded by suggesting the representatives return on the first Monday in June with a reasonable request.

On June 1, 1964, the board minutes record the following: A black delegation made up of the local colored school committee and Asheville businessmen William Roland and Jesse Ray attended the meeting along with reporters from area newspapers and the board's attorney, A. Eldridge Leake. They supported ASCORE, the Asheville Student Committee on Racial Equality, whose student members were later called Peaceful Warriors in a *Mountain Express* investigative story by Lisa Waters ("Peaceful Warriors," Oct. 26, 2005, retrieved from www.mountainx.com).

Again at this meeting, Geraldine Griffin presented a written request that her child be assigned to the white Mars Hill School.

Learning that others had a similar request, Chairman Zeno Ponder adjourned the meeting until 9:30 P.M., at which time Briscoe was to return with additional written requests. Two hours later the board met with a black delegation, which was accompanied by Ray and Roland of Asheville. The board granted five of the requests for reassignment. Geraldine Griffin, who was employed by board member W.O. Duck, received notice that her daughter Vickie Louise could attend the white school. Others allowed to integrate Mars Hill School were first grader Jean Dobbins, seventh grader Phillip M. Ervin, and fifth graders Betty and Anne McDowell.

Denying other requests, the board declared that their decision rested on the black community's inability to make an all-out effort to integrate Anderson School (formerly Mars Hill Colored School and Long Ridge School). The possibility that the black school might integrate was suggested in the July 6, 1964, minutes. In the August 19, 1965, minutes, the board denied Gibby Briscoe's request to send her black students to Mars Hill School, as another county was involved. According to the board records on April 3, 1967, it appears that the conflict over desegregating Madison County schools had been resolved. Board members listened to an explanation of Elementary and Secondary Education Act, Titles I, II, and III, discussed a mini-grant for summer school, the benefits of the Neighborhood Youth Corps, and the professional rights of teachers.

Other counties took action locally to integrate their schools. In 1963, forward-looking Catawba County created the Community Relations Council in response to the civil rights movement (Hartsoe, 2001). The council was composed of four white and five black members. The intent was that the council would lay the groundwork for desegregating the schools. In 1964, E.T. Moore, assistant principal of Ridgeview School and later principal of East Hickory School, spoke to the group about dissatisfaction with separate schools for the races. He pointed out that students walked a long distance on the side of the road to reach a segregated school rather than attend the one nearest their homes.

As the 1965-66 school year approached, Drusilla S. Hartsoe received a "chilly reception" when she approached the school superintendent about enrolling her daughter at Hickory High School. In a time when the Russian satellite *Sputnik* had spurred increased emphasis on science in the curriculum, black students were forced to use outdated books and to share frogs for dissection. The school board allowed the rising ninth grader to enroll. Then others sought the same privilege. When the 1966-67 school term began, a large number of blacks enrolled at Hickory High School, and, according to Hartsoe (2001), "all hell broke loose." Parents and police were summoned to the campus, but integration took place.

Earlier in the decade, providing for Polk County black students had been difficult. The county board of education resolved, in May 1960 and in May 1961, to assign all Negro high school students living in the Cobb area to Carver High School in Spindale in Rutherford County, all elementary students in that residential area to Cobb Elementary School, and all black students in Saluda to the Hendersonville school. However, by April 1964, Polk County parents had enlisted the services of attorney Dailey, who mailed a certified letter to Superintendent David Cromer asking for the immediate integration of all Polk County schools. With the letter on the table, the board entertained Transylvania County Superintendent C.W. Bradburn and Brevard High School Principal N.A. Miller and their own attorney, J.T. Arledge. After lengthy discussion, it was determined that Dailey be notified to expect an answer in 30 days.

The May 20, 1964, minutes recorded the decision reassigning all students to the schools they had attended the previous year. However, a change occurred. A July 3, 1964, letter attached to the minutes and addressed to Dailey from Superintendent Cromer explained that nine high school students had been assigned at their request to transfer from black Carver High School to white Polk Central High School. At the board's May 26, 1965, meeting, all black students from Saluda, who had been attending school in Hendersonville, were assigned to Saluda School. The board also approved a Plan of Intent for the Civil Rights Law. Then followed, on March 6, 1967, the adoption and announcement of a Freedom of Choice policy (Polk County Board of Education minutes, 1960–1964).

Tryon, the county seat, became the site of heated opposition to continued school segregation. Two news articles in the June 26, 1965, issue of Tryon's *Herald Journal* centered attention on Edmund Embury School for blacks. The Tryon City Board of Education's decision to fire dietititian Sarah Shields because of her complaint to the school board that Embury School had been assigned to step-child status and forced to use "hand-me-down" equipment launched a student boycott of the school lunchroom.

A follow-up article by James Bryan, "Parents rally behind NAACP," said the "paper-sack" protest had entered its second week with only five students eating in the school lunchroom. The dispute had prompted parents and other supporters to join in the fray and resulted in a substantial increase — 32 new members—for the NAACP. The group demanded immediate desegregation and had enlisted the services of Ruben J. Dailey (*Tryon News, Washington Afro-American Newspaper,* March 31, 1964, retrieved from http://news.google.com/newspapers). Desegregation did not happen overnight. The Edmund Embury School closed in 1967 when schools were integrated. In 1968 a brand new Tryon High School was built, and in 1969, the city and county systems consolidated (Conner, 2008).

In a northern section of Western North Carolina, J.J. Jones, formerly Mount Airy Colored School, had a student population that periodically included pupils from Surry, Stokes, and Yadkin counties in North Carolina and from Patrick County, Virginia. Evelyn Scales Thompson reported that on the surface integration proceeded smoothly in Surry County, but displeasure was expressed behind closed doors (personal communication, July 29–30, 2010). One disappointment was the post-integration transfer of teachers to other counties and the assignment of a few to positions for which they were overqualified. Questions used by interviewers were frequently insulting. For example, black teachers were asked, "Do you know how to teach white children?" The local NAACP, under the leadership of Surry resident John Lovell, provided support and direction to deal with the complexities of racial injustices.

Black professionals often faced the loss of their jobs once their students were accepted at white schools. Following integration in Jackson County, Frank Davis, the black school's principal, began working as an instructor at the Job Corps in Macon County. Naomi L. Brown began teaching special education in Spartanburg, South Carolina, and Alberta C. Hunter moved to Shiloh Elementary School in Buncombe County.

Effley Howell, a black native of Wilkesboro and an expert in black history, maintains an archive and is the winner of numerous awards, such as the Nancy Susan Reynolds Award for improving race relations. He shares artifacts and lectures by taking his traveling museum throughout the state. Director of the Thankful Heritage and called "The Great Storyteller," Howell was raised in the Boomer community of Wilkes County and started his education at the Boomer school for blacks. However, when he was 9 years old, the black and white schools in Boomer community integrated for the 1966-67 school term. Howell refers to his experience as "tough." "I call myself a product of integration," he explained. "I remember the ... N word. There were fights and overall tension everywhere. It was a change." However, by the time he entered high school, conditions had improved with blacks and whites getting along despite underlying tension (Jerry Lankford, "Exhibit to Showcase Black History," February 18, 2004, *The Record*, North Wilkesboro, http://therecordofwilkes.com).

When Transylvania County integrated its high school, one county resident found more distress in the rural-urban conflict among blacks than in being outnumbered by white students while sitting in class. William Hemphill, Sr., grew up in the rural area of Hudlin Gap Road, where he had daily chores after school. It came as a relief when he was finally able to attend high school within his residential area. "We had no trouble in Transylvania when the schools desegregated.... People knew ... the black people as good, hard-working families, and I think that's why we didn't have many problems."

He explained that city blacks were more sophisticated than those who lived in the country, and in his youth a trip to Brevard was considered a distance. Although Hemphill did not experience deep racial tensions that ruled in most of the South, he recalls standing at back doors of restaurants to be served, not having the use of public restrooms at filling stations, and being confronted with delay in getting a driver's license. Hemphill, like Fred Logan in Henderson County, also remembers that Rosman was a sundown town — "blacks better not show up after the sun goes down or else"— so any trip to that section of Transylvania County had to be a real necessity, like completing a job with his father (C.K. Knight, February 1, 2007, "Family's History Resonates with Hard Work," *Transylvania Times*). Logan's father's gift for healing animals won him respect in Rosman. Rural people were willing to over look race to get help for sick animals but only during daylight hours.

However, Morris Young believes that integration may have hurt as much as it helped African Americans. Black teachers lost their jobs, and the one-on-one practice so prevalent in small black schools, where teachers took a personal interest in each pupil, went out the window. Young does not mean that white teachers showed no interest in their students, but their approach was less personal. He found the integrated classroom hard to deal with, but being an athlete helped because that brought recognition and appreciation for skill (personal communication, October 31, 2006).

However, there was one bit of drama when he de-boarded the school bus and found his way blocked by two brothers, one in front of him and the other behind him. Hearing one say, "Let's get him now," Young knew they intended to fight, so he turned and swung a punch at the teenager behind him. Principal William Stanley called him to the office and upset him by saying, "If you weren't playing ball and running track, I'd expel you." Young found that hard to understand. He had been accosted by two students, but he would have been expelled had he not been an athlete (personal communication, October 31, 2006).

In Watauga County, the school board approved five students being reassigned from the Watauga Consolidated School to the white Appalachian High School at its September 8, 1964, meeting. The group included one freshman, two sophomores, and two seniors. The board's topic of discussion on February 4, 1965, concerned the relationship of Watauga Consolidated School to the 1964 Civil Rights Act. The issue, as board members saw it, was the overcrowded condition at Appalachian Elementary School. To assign black students there would complicate the issue.

However, the Watauga board realized that to be eligible for federal funds, it had to develop

Watauga Consolidated School, Boone, North Carolina, 1960–1965. During its final year as a functioning school, 49 students were enrolled. Compliance with the Civil Rights Act of 1964 allowed its students to enroll in the white Appalachian High School. The building is now occupied by Western Youth Network (courtesy Fred J. Hay).

a satisfactory plan of compliance for school desegregation. The March 30, 1965 minutes document further grappling with the issues of student assignment and developing a plan of compliance with the Civil Rights Act. The board assigned 27 students to Appalachian Elementary School. However, the board's "Plan for Compliance with Title VI of the Civil Rights Act of 1964" documented that as of April 14, 1965, 51 black students attended Appalachian High School along with 651 white students. Also, 49 students attended the black Watauga Consolidated School. Eleven county schools were listed, but there were only three black faculty members, all of whom were assigned to Watauga Consolidated. The board maintained that, effective with the closing to the 1964-65 term, Watauga Consolidated would be closed and all students would attend schools in their residential areas (Watauga County Board of Education minutes, March 30 and April 14, 1965).

Each county's plan of compliance was sent to Raleigh and from there to Washington, D.C. Acceptance of their plans was far from routine. Many were disapproved and returned. The United States Office of Education postponed approval of Marion City Schools' compliance until an addendum could be created. The addendum included inserting comments like "and each year thereafter," "without regard to race, color or national origin." One statement had to be revised to read: "All facilities, activities and programs, of all schools will be available to all students without regard to race, color, or national origin." Other changes involved protecting student choice and job security of black teachers (Marion City Board of Education minutes, July 2, 1965). Adherence to the law and assurance that local officials would protect its black citizens involved a painstaking study of each county and city unit's plan, a monumental task.

In 1975, a federal judge ordered that 29 North Carolina school districts be investigated for possible civil rights violations. Four were in Western North Carolina (Burke, Polk, Swain, Wilkes) which was targeted for alleged racial disproportions. Although no fault was found, such actions kept local school officials aware that their policies were under scrutiny by the federal government. Individuals advocating moderation faced reactions. Attorney Max F. Ferree, who served as a member of the North Wilkesboro School Board, advocated the common sense of desegregation. In the next election, he lost his seat (E. Ferree, October 27, 2010).

A 1975 Associated Press story ("WNC Schools in Civil Rights Probe") documented details about the federal judge's order. He called for enforcement proceedings against Kings Mountain City system and the Cherokee County system and a so-called Swann school district for alleged racial discrimination. The news article cites a Swain County decision, which referred to the court case to bus students to achieve racial balance as a decision in violation because one or more schools had a racial makeup at least 20 percent in disproportion of the district's entire white-black ratio. Also, in a document stamped "Saturday, March 15, 1975," the judge ordered investigations of Stanly County and Wilkes County for alleged racial disproportions.

In Graham County, the process, if it can be called that, went by effortlessly, for there were no black students to enroll. One morning Tom Carpenter, then associate superintendent of Graham County schools, took a call from Washington, D.C., regarding the demographics in a report he had submitted to the Department of Education. Carpenter assured them that the report was correct. His answer resulted in an education official flying to Knoxville, Tennessee, renting a car and driving to Robbinsville, in the westernmost part of the state, to confirm that there were no black students in Graham County's public schools (personal communication, May 7, 2010). It took an investment of taxpayers' dollars to persuade those in Washington that Carpenter's report was correct.

A research appendix, compiled by Elliot Jaspin (2007), cites statistics that support the minimal black population in Graham County. Jaspin's chart records a zero percent change in the black population in 1890 and again in 1920. In 1900, there was a 512 percent increase from 25 to 153 blacks. By 1910, there was a 100 percent decrease. By 2000, however, out of a total population of 7,993 individuals, 15 were blacks—a figure that represents a 1,400 percent growth from 1930's one black resident.

Educational Sequel: Transformative Changes

Early on, the decision was to use delaying tactics but to remain within the law in response to the 1954 federal mandate that segregated schools were unconstitutional and therefore illegal. Throughout Appalachian North Carolina, school officials held secret meetings to ensure that desegregation would be delayed. More than 50 years later, can Western North Carolina residents say that integration has occurred? Though there may be gaps or backward steps to ignore the intent of Civil Rights legislation, certainly blacks have taken major leaps forward in educational environments. The contrast is striking: From the furtive hush-hush lessons of pre-emancipation days to the post-war and Reconstruction efforts to provide authentic learning opportunities for the newly unshackled black men and women to the surge of emphasis on universal education, children and adults have found encouragement to hone the basic skills of learning.

The move to create secondary schools was slow, but efforts on the state and local levels increased the number of high schools for black students in the western counties. Other counties opted to pay a limited amount of money, similar to a modern voucher, so students could enroll in private schools or to board to attend public high schools. Tremendous pride emerged from the schools and throughout the communities they served, so it comes as no surprise that, as Asheville City Schools assistant Janice Gibson Weaver (personal communication, April 4, 2007) said, communities wanted to keep their schools. They preferred to integrate schools by transferring white students to black schools rather than by sending black students to the white schools.

North Carolina's state school board had evened the playing field for distribution of funds to African American educators in 1949, but the legislative acts that tossed the total responsibility for pupil assignment to local boards prolonged discrimination. In community after community, persistent parents, adamant attorneys, and civil rights advocates conquered resistance to integrated schools. Although the battle had not ended, the door had been opened. Blacks knew there was a new room, one they were about to decorate with new standards, inside the door. Now their image of learning could be the same as for everyone else.

Integration sparked the closing of black schools, which had served not only as educational institutions but also as community centers. Buildings which once stood as the heartbeat of black neighborhoods were abandoned. Others were sold or torn down. Marion resident Billy Martin explained that it sickened him to see Mountain View School converted into a chair manufacturing facility. "You look over there and know that a baseball field used to be there and a basketball court. It's pitiful" (Conley, February 26, 1996).

The Stephens-Lee building, valued as an architectural wonder, became home to the Opportunity Corporation of Buncombe and Madison Counties and to Handi-Skills, Inc. When alumni of the Stephens-Lee School failed in their efforts to purchase the property, all but the gymnasium was razed in 1975. The destruction of their "Castle on the Hill" erupted into a never-ending resentment within the black community.

"Nobody really cared for integration," Hendersonville educator Frank Wilson said. "Blacks were against integration. Parents were afraid for their kids ... didn't trust white teachers to treat their kids fairly. It was an end to an era that wanted to preserve and maintain our identity" (personal communication, March 10, 2009). Haywood County resident Janice Weaver echoed his sentiment, indicating that Reynolds High's students and staff wanted to remain in their school, that it was like home to them (April 4, 2007).

Virginia Daniels, who taught most of four decades in segregated schools, remembered parents commenting that they wanted their children taught by white teachers. "Those black teachers are going to have to get on the ball now," she said. "Now when these people see ... the old teachers ... they'll tell you they wish it was like it used to be and what a good job we did" (Henry Robinson, "Looking Back: A Former Educator Remembers Earlier Times, Values," March 31, 1993, *Asheville Citizen-Times*). Despite the hardships of segregation, in retrospect former students and teachers recalled with appreciation the community schools where they felt valued by the teacher and by the community.

School integration clearly provided expanding curricula, especially for high school students, more elaborate support services, and equal access to all available educational opportunities. However, in the 21st century the loss of historic black schools remains a source of resentment for the black community, even though some small black schools were less than effective. Educator Wanda Butler of College of Staten Island, New York, described the students attending the small Leicester Colored School — of which she was one — as having been "short changed" in their segregated educational opportunities (personal communication, April 24, 2009).

As integration began in earnest, black individuals remained vulnerable to hurtful words and to violent acts. Henry Logan, who gained fame as the Asheville Flash in basketball, experienced the extremes of public treatment simply because the young Stephens-Lee graduate became the first African American to break through the color barrier in Western Carolina University's athletic program in 1965. Sports, the arena of democracy, offered the talented athlete a position on the team and in the classroom. Decades later no one blinks when black athletes lead teams to prestige on the field or on the court. Rather than being victims of derogatory name-calling, often they are heroes or heroines who increase the status of the school and rally the enthusiasm of students and alumni. The current educational scene is a different world from the one that D.L. Burrell, a graduate student, alluded to in his 1992 master's thesis when writing about Logan. Burrell included Logan as one of three examples of blacks crossing the color line at Western Carolina University — a professor, another student, and Logan, an athlete.

Despite the widespread admiration for Logan's prowess on the basketball court and the loyalty of his fans, he had to ignore many racial slurs. Burrell recounts the following conversation by two long-time Catamount fans as they watched Logan rack up 30 points with little effort: "Look at that nigger go," says one. "That," replies the second, "is a black gentleman" (p. 25). In the span of seconds, the old attitude was confronted with the new, and the confrontation would occur over and over again as Western Carolina's athletic department continued to welcome African Americans.

"Perhaps the most insidious scar Logan bore as a result of racism," Burrell said, "was the poor education he received before reaching WCU" (p. 26). The segregated schools he attended failed to prepare him adequately to meet the academic demands of the university. Western Carolina English Department chair Mable Crum tutored Logan so he could maintain eligibility standards. She regarded him as an intelligent and likable student. However, he did not graduate. Much sought after, Logan joined the ranks of professional basketball, but old injuries shortened his career. Today the Asheville resident wishes he had done some things differently, but he has a strong faith in God and is thankful for the success he experienced at a previously all-white institution and is proud of the Stephens-Lee tradition.

Logan paved the way by providing four years of spectacular performances, but racial discrimination persisted even in the wake of an athletic career that created records not yet broken. Displaying courage, ability, and poise, Logan won friends and admirers, but not everyone was on his side. Unfortunately, just as Alma Shippy did, Henry Logan dropped out and never returned to earn a degree.

As recently as the 2008 political campaign, a Western Carolina University incident made national news. Seven students, later arrested, dumped the carcass of a black bear cub wrapped in political posters of the Obama-Biden campaign in front of the administration building. Subsequent notoriety embarrassed staff and students at the university. Confusion about what kind of political statement was made caused widespread negative publicity for the university. The fact that then-candidate Obama was the first African American with a strong possibility of winning the White House added to public speculation that using a black bear wrapped in political posters was a racial as well as a political statement. The incident publicly suggested that anti-black attitudes still prevail ("Dead Bear Found Wrapped in Obama Signs Carcass Found on Western Carolina University Campus," retrieved from http://www.wyffa.com/). However, such may not have been the case.

The journey's end had a measurable goal: integration. Of course, achievement depends on the definition of the ideological goal. In the Smoky Mountains, sometimes climbers reach a peak and think that they are at the top. When clouds shift, however, the climbers discover there are still peaks to conquer and maybe miles to ascend. Always, though, the goal is upward. Progress has challenged black and white students the past five decades as integration lurched from expectation to expansion. First came the achievements of "one school for all," but there were additional struggles, as obvious in such places as Asheville and Hendersonville, involving the need for more guarantees. Also, climbers have learned that there are new places where they need a foothold so they can take the next step upward. So do citizens seeking to defend further denial of civil rights in educational venues.

The way up, though, benefits from an overview of the paths that led to the integration success. The earliest paths, requiring simply a building for a rudimentary education for all blacks, cleared more quickly with the help of the historic Rosenwald Fund, which supplied thousands of dollars for school buildings in black communities. Then came journeys to what was perceived as better schools, separate buildings for elementary schools and later for high schools.

Earning high school diplomas turned out to be a small dream when compared with the goal of receiving diplomas at an integrated school, where both blacks and whites could use the same labs, the same books, and the same gyms and athletic fields as they played on the same teams against other integrated schools. Like those who climbed high peaks, appreciation multiplies as climbers look back at obstacles previous generations overcame to make the educational progress possible.

The dramatic process presents portraits of successful African Americans, achievers who enlighten those anticipating future roadblocks to overcome. Now trusting sojourners ask what maneuvers prevented integration and why did it take so long.

4

GATEWAY POLICIES FOR EDUCATION

After the Civil War blacks had a simple goal: an elementary school in their community. In post–1870, an elementary school meant simple structures, from a makeshift operation in a home or a church to a one-room or multi-room building. Achieving the goal, though, was not simple. It required the same qualities that sustained blacks a century afterward during the Civil Rights struggle of the 1950s, '60s, and '70s.

During the late nineteenth and early twentieth centuries, white communities typically spurned permitting their black neighbors access to educational equality. Keeping the black man ignorant enabled white people to nourish their feelings of superiority, to reserve higher paying jobs for whites only, and to ensure doors to prosperity would open exclusively to their kind: Euro-Americans. Observing a slave or former slave exhibit signs of intelligence or waves of wisdom enflamed white citizens who hurled insults at members of the black race. Such behavior had a long history in white-black relationships.

Pulitzer Prize–winning historian William S. McFeely, in his biography *Frederick Douglass* (1991), reveals this harsh diatribe spoken by Hugh Auld, Douglass' master, to reprimand his wife Sophia Auld for daring to educate their young slave:

> If you give a nigger an inch, he will take an ell [about 45 inches]; he should know nothing but the will of his master and learn to obey it. Learning would spoil the best nigger in the world; if you teach that nigger how to read the Bible, there will be no keeping him; it would forever unfit him for the duties of a slave; and ... learning would make him no good — making him disconsolate and unhappy. If you learn him how to read, he'll want to know how to write; and this accomplished he'll be running away with himself [p.30].

Douglass' Baltimore master would have considered the black community's pride in its triumphal accomplishment of mastering the 3 R's as evidence of their "running away" with themselves. However, Hugh Auld had unwittingly taught Douglass a vital lesson. By refusing to allow his slave to learn to read, he inadvertently identified education as a power tool for the enslaved. That tool would become Douglass' weapon.

Prodded by Freedom

Freedmen believed freedom would forever elude them unless they acquired education. As they were able, former slaves began teaching one another. Because learning to read and to write was no longer outlawed for the South's black children, parents eagerly sought schooling for themselves and for their youngsters. Before laws could be passed and enforced to promote education, black communities introduced primitive schools in havens whose names, like Beulah Land and Happy Land, suggested a place far removed from their previous neighborhoods that had allowed mistreatment to be the normal pattern of life. Always freedmen pursued education, and education guaranteed freedom.

Former slaves, fleeing the prospect of prolonged economic failure, settled in Henderson County and established a tradition of schooling in their unique commune. Except for a deed recorded in 1882, few sources document their community. However, relics and architectural remains, verified by stories passed from one generation to another, confirm its existence.

Half a century after its demise, Sadie Smathers Patton, in the 1950s, compiled a saga of the band's pilgrimage and colony. Remnants of the community exist on site and have been documented in articles in the Hendersonville *Times News*. Staff writer Harrison Metzger located vestiges of the compound while researching an article used for a black history feature in the February 22, 2004, issue. While preparing "Former Slaves Founded Kingdom of Happy Land," Metzger discovered piles of rocks, remains of a chimney, and periwinkle — a plant believed to have been propagated by the original settlers — on the Kingdom land, which has been owned since 1910 by Joseph Oscar Bell and his descendants.

Why such a community was established and why it ceased to exist has aroused speculation. William Judson King, whose grandparents resided in the Kingdom of the Happy Land, asserted that the "kingdom" was an attempt to revive African traditions by establishing a new tribe and by preserving elements of their ancestral roots. King, whose view was shared by East Flat Rock native Ernest Mims, attributed the commune's dissolution to an economic crunch caused by introduction of new technology that eliminated the need for their skills from the marketplace, so they sought employment elsewhere (Greene, 1996). Frank FitzSimons (1976), Henderson County historian, attributed their push to find a site for the "kingdom" as the result of their human longing to live as they pleased, with few restrictions, a kind of utopia.

The displaced slaves founded their Kingdom of the Happy Land along the North Carolina and South Carolina border area in southern Henderson County. Though liberated by the Emancipation Proclamation of 1863, which had essentially robbed them of their homes, slaves were shackled by bondage to fear and poverty. With no place to call home, perhaps as early as 1864, the band of impoverished men and women searched for a place of refuge, a place where whites would respect them.

Oral tradition indicates the former slaves assembled first at a plantation in or near Mississippi and chose a leader. Elders interviewed by Sadie Smathers Patton (1947) indicated their leader's young mother, impregnated by her master, had been freed prior to her son's birth and that her little boy, due to his father's generosity, had received more education than the other freedmen in his community. As a young adult, the son owned his own piece of land and a few slaves.

The group invested their loyalty and confidence in their leader. With no treasures left and no masters to provide for them, the group analyzed their options. Relocation provided hope for a better future. Driven by the idea of a utopian community governed by the concept of "one for all and all for one," they journeyed across Alabama, Georgia, and South Carolina and picked up other hopefuls all along the way. In upstate South Carolina, the itinerant group may have heard of vast stretches of uninhabited mountain land to the north and decided to seek their fortune there. For whatever reason, they trekked to the mountains and eventually provided homes and a school for their children.

Following the Buncombe Turnpike into North Carolina, they arrived at Oakland, an estate owned by Serepta Merritt Davis, widow of Col. John Davis, whose family had operated a stagecoach stop. The aging lady offered them safe haven, perhaps in exchange for labor. There, on land extending across the South Carolina and North Carolina border, the roving group founded their Kingdom of the Happy Land. In the tradition of their African ancestors, they chose a king and a queen to lead them. The name of only one king, Robert Montgomery, has survived, and the unmarried king designated his brother's wife, Luella, to serve as queen (Patton, 1947).

In 1882, Montgomery purchased 180 acres of the Davis property at $1 per acre to provide an estate for the Happy Land commune, which placed all its money (derived from individual members) in a common treasury. The deed identifies both Robert and Luella Montgomery as the legal owners of the newly acquired property.

The extension across state lines proved to be a wise choice because trouble in one state might be avoided simply by assembling on the section of property located in the other state. Ed Bell of Blue Ridge Community College laughingly told reporter Harrison Metzger that legend suggested the Happy Landers' moonshine production invited raids from law enforcement. By simply retreating across the state line, citizens of the Kingdom were able to avoid arrest ("Former Slaves Founded Kingdom of Happy Land," *Times-News*, February 22, 2004), an alternative to which their white bootlegging competitors had no access.

Whether true or not, such tales lend credence to the community's existence. The Happy Land residents discovered a welcome at St. John's in the Wilderness, an Episcopal church originally constructed as the chapel on the Charles Baring Estate in Flat Rock, where members of Kingdom of the Happy Land occupied the back pew. The Rev. William King ministered to their spiritual needs (Louise Bailey, personal communication, January 18, 2006). East Flat Rock native William Darity recalls both his grandmother and his mother mentioning the Happy Land community. Retired educator Hortense Potts also heard accounts about the Kingdom shared by her father and by other members of the East Flat Rock community. Descendant William Judson King documented his family connections with the Kingdom during interviews with members of Henderson County's Black Research Committee and Gary Franklin Greene (1996). King's grandparents, the Perry Williamses, joined the Kingdom after it had established roots in Henderson County and threw in their lot with the band of freed slaves. After the turn of the century, they resumed residence in Hendersonville, but their grandson recalled easily their chronicle of living in the kingdom.

Having at last realized their dream, the community made educating their children a priority. In the 1880s and 1890s, Luella Montgomery taught the Happy Land children reading and writing by using stories from the Bible and songs (Greene, 1996). Mary Couch Russell shared memories of Montgomery's lessons with Sadie Smathers Patton (1947). As a small child playing in her yard on the hillside, Russell could see Montgomery beckoning the children to assemble for their lessons. Russell would race down the hill to join the other students. There Montgomery would instruct them and lead them in singing spirituals and other songs. Her "field trips" included taking the children to sing at the homes of white people living nearby, where they received an enthusiastic welcome. Her lessons also focused on religious instruction.

Mary Couch Russell and her brother Ezel Couch recalled that after reaching a certain age, they, along with other older students, were sent to a school conducted by the Reverend Walter Allen at a place known as Possum Hollow. Allen, a former slave, gained his reputation by teaching and preaching at various sites in Henderson County (Patton, 1947). In Henderson County, evidence exists of education for black children in one form or another from the time of the Civil War. The Happy Land Kingdom lasted from approximately 1864 until shortly before 1900.

Other more formal schools emerged. No doubt legal restrictions that had denied slaves instruction in basic reading simply strengthened the resolve of the black community to acquire that skill. Acting upon their post–Civil War right to be educated, parents petitioned local white school boards to provide schools for black children. White leaders grudgingly provided elementary schools that offered basic classes in reading, writing, arithmetic, spelling, geography, history, and vocational subjects.

Shaped by Legal Racism

1868: In North Carolina, the Constitutional Convention of 1868 proved successful in creating improvements to the original constitution, first drafted in 1776 and then amended in 1836. Surprisingly a politically inexperienced group of delegates—Negroes and carpetbaggers—were responsible for that success story. The black delegates had little or no political experience, and the carpetbaggers had little knowledge of the needs of North Carolina's citizens. Despite those limitations, the delegates established a basis for future progress.

The state provided a system of public education by establishing schools with open enrollment for every young person between 6 and 21, and such schools were to be in partnership with the University of North Carolina. Especially noteworthy was the stipulation that public schools were to be available equally to both African-American and Caucasian youth (*Journal of the Constitutional Convention of the State of North-Carolina, at Its Session 1868*, electronic edition retrieved from http://docsouth.unc.edu/nc/conv1868.html#p338).

1869: With the amended constitution, the right of the Negro to a basic education was firmly entrenched in the law of North Carolina. The School Law of 1869, written by Superintendent of Public Instruction Samuel S. Ashley to implement the provisions of the new constitution, included specifications for reopening the state's public schools and created separate schools for the "white and colored races" to operate for a four-month school term (Van Noppen and Van Noppen, 1973).

Contributing their share of funds to support public schools challenged citizens residing in poor mountain counties. White poverty coupled with the developing attitude that only white schools should receive white dollars established what would be a long tradition of economic barriers hindering educational advancement for black learners. The attitude decreed there should be no mixing of black and white revenues. During the period of Reconstruction, both black and white students attended the same schools in Henderson County (Greene, 1996). However, increasing hostility toward that arrangement throughout the state brought about change. Soon school statistics confirmed that a dual education system was the practice in Henderson County, too.

1877: Henderson County's Black History Research Committee cites Kirsten Mullen's research. Her findings indicate that about 483 black students were enrolled in public schools by the mid–1870s. In 1877, committeemen for black schools had been appointed for eight townships: Blue Ridge, Clear Creek, Crab Creek, Edneyville, Green River, Hendersonville, Hooper's Creek, and Mills River—an indication of the establishment of community schools under black supervision (Greene, 1996). According to Patton (1947), in 1890 the average attendance in North Carolina schools numbered 134,108 white and 68,992 black pupils. More than 6,800 schools were in operation. School property was valued at $1 million, and North Carolina was investing more than $500,000 in its schools annually (Patton, 1947). State support of education strengthened the segregated schools established in Henderson County.

However, the guarantee of community schools did not reach every area. In August 1879, Jackson Halback, George Potts, and Allen Williams formed a school committee for District 5 of Flat Rock. The school's exact site is unknown. It may have been in a private home or in a brush arbor. Private instruction for black children occurred from time to time. Tradition attributes South Carolina native Mary Foules with providing schooling for black children at her summer estate on Glassy Mountain near Flat Rock (Culpepper, 2002).

1901: Later, the Act of 1901 strengthened the demand for dual educational systems throughout North Carolina and impacted Henderson County. Again law mandated the establishment of separate schools for black and white students based solely on race. Patton (1947) summarized the following information about the public schools of Hendersonville and Henderson County during the early years of the 20th century. In 1913, the average school term was six months. As a result of legislation mandating a minimum six-month term, school personnel expected a longer semester would soon be the norm.

School taxes provided by a 25-cent tax on each $100 value of real and personal property and a $1.50 poll tax accrued a total of $16,278.15. Of the county's 60 school districts, only five were for blacks, as contrasted with 55 for whites. The length of the school term varied from four to eight months. While R.M. Ivins served as Hendersonville's superintendent of schools, the number of colored students enrolled in the city schools increased from 98 to 185, and of whites from 226 to 236. During 1915-1916 the white enrollment was 596 while the colored was 175. At the same time there were 17 white teachers and two colored employees in Hendersonville.

During Superintendent George W. Bradshaw's tenure (1917–1919), the number of white students increased from 596 to 627 while the Negro student population was 166. A decade later there were 1,139 white pupils and 334 black students. Superintendent A.W. Honeycutt's report for 1919-20 indicates the total enrollment was 805 white and 217 black. There were 23 white teachers and four black instructors.

1931: In 1931, the school for Negroes had acquired several hundred books, donated by friends and catalogued with the help of the city's librarians. In contrast, the library of the white elementary school contained 2,669 books, and the white high school contained 2,000 volumes. The dramatic difference between the number of volumes available to the two communities, white and black, seems noteworthy — only a few hundred for blacks as contrasted with nearly five thousand for whites. The inadequate state laws made it easy to deprive part of the student population of equal opportunities.

The principle of "separate but equal" was incorporated through the Act of 1901 by the North Carolina legislature. The General Assembly provided for the appropriation of taxes for public schools—$100,000 each year of the biennium. The assembly established the Henderson County School District with authorization to provide schools for both white and colored students. A board of trustees was appointed to oversee schools and to provide tuition-free education for students age 6 to 21. The district was instructed to maintain a classroom and a teacher for each grade. The board, however, failed to set up graded classrooms for black schools until the 1950s (Greene, 1996).

Having a dual system of schools for the two races required qualified instructors be employed for each school. The dual city and county school systems further complicated budget matters. In 1901, the Hendersonville Board of Education hired a Howard University graduate from Buncombe County to conduct workshops with a curriculum that could lead to state certification for black teachers. John Wesley Neill conducted the classes and then accepted the position as principal of the school for black children located at Ninth Avenue West. He served there from 1902 to 1909. His administrative duties extended to cutting wood, building fires, sweeping and other janitorial duties, as well as teaching. An activist, he advocated to state officials that each grade have a self-contained classroom in a formal school setting. Neill lobbied successfully to include classes for high school students. However, the secondary curriculum was soon abandoned, thus denying black students a chance for an education beyond the elementary school or compelling them to attend private schools or to live with friends or relatives outside the county (Greene, 1996).

The concept of "separate but equal" did not apply to secondary education in the real world, and that void created hardships for families intent on pursuing the dream of improving their status in society through education. The concept of separate schools— which took young people from their homes in Hendersonville and Henderson County to Allen School in Asheville; to Tuskegee Institute, Tuskegee, Alabama; to Voorhees College, Denmark, South

Carolina; to Barber Scotia Seminary, Concord, North Carolina; to Lincoln Academy, Kings Mountain, North Carolina; or wherever relatives were willing to take them in — defies the concept of equality on any level.

1951: During the era of segregation each system, city and county, had its own administrative staff with separate budgets and separate offices. However, with the 1951 opening of the Ninth Avenue Union School, Henderson County students were awarded access to the city's new facility, thus combining the efforts of the city and county systems to educate their Negro students.

Though whites chose to ignore the realities, legal requirements of "separate but equal" bred unnecessary financial obligations for communities. The economic tailspin which kept districts impoverished hurt both black and white students for more than a century.

During the early 20th century, problems increased while progress came slowly. For Catawba's black citizens, gradual improvements in their schools increased their optimism that better days were coming. Instead, racial conflicts occurred, and white dissidents were jailed for violence. In 1919, there had been a near lynching outside Newton when a black mob attempted to grab a man accused of killing a white woman (Freeze, 2002). Responding to a growing sense that blacks did not receive fair treatment, the county's first interracial discussion, in 1923, filled the civic auditorium to overflow capacity.

P.M. Smith, a black physician, presided and allowed the audience to air grievances and ask that more be done for colored citizens. Things went well that night, but soon the Ku Klux Klan made its presence known by burning a cross. Ironically, the black hope for progress lay in their segregated schools. Writer and scholar Gary Freeze (2002) cites a remark by W.T. Abernethy that demonstrated the white perspective: "It is a common error to believe that education will not make a Negro a better farmer, drayman, cook, or nurse" (p. 342).

White patrons in Snow Hill helped improve the black school in that community. The New Deal brought hope to citizens in Catawba, as well as throughout the country, and resulted in improvements in racial relationships, which Freeze (2002) suggests may have resulted from having federal officials present in greater numbers than at any time since Reconstruction. Caucasian citizens began recognizing the extent to which black citizens had contributed to the county's history.

One example of improved status occurred in May 1934 at the county's Heritage Celebration. A.W. Booker, principal of Central High School, accepted an invitation to speak about the Negro heritage. A descendant of a slave, Booker planted a weeping willow tree to honor the memory of the first blacks in the county. White participants planted a white oak sapling to honor early white pioneers. The incident showed that prosperity had encouraging results. A pocketful of coins, not a restrictive law, precipitated a positive outlook for both races.

Sensitive citizens realized they needed to step beyond the destructive effect of the North Carolina constitutional guidelines.

Another moment of light happened in Mitchell County, which had been the sight of an ethnic cleansing in 1923. There, 27 years later, an official of the State Department of Public Instruction found a few black students in the region. In January 1950 (almost a century after the Emancipation Proclamation), M. Ruth Lawrence, state supervisor of Negro Elementary Schools, found seven boys and girls "learning their lessons" in a church at the foot of an unidentified mountain in Mitchell County (Department of Public Instruction, Division of Negro Education, General Correspondence of the Director, Box 18). According to Lawrence, that space provided the only black school in the entire county and operated for only six months of the year. The legal decisions of 1868, 1877, and 1901 continued to cast a long shadow over young learners.

Though Lawrence knew the makeshift school would shut its doors in February, she provided new library books for the children. During the director's visits to other Western North Carolina schools, Lawrence had discussed principles of Resource-Use Education with the teachers.

Also, she recognized that the Mitchell County quarters were inadequate — students were in a room, not in an elementary school. Later, in her monthly report she commented on Brevard's black school building, a new structure replacing a Rosenwald school: "I was so very pleased to see a well constructed granite stone and brick building for the boys and girls in Transylvania County. There is no auditorium, but there is a very nice lunchroom. The high school students are transported to Hendersonville" (DPI, DNE, Special Subjects File, Box 11).

Limited by Community Finances

North Carolina "separate but equal" regulations rolled a boulder-size roadblock on the road to basic education for blacks. "Separate" was a physical structure, easy to identify. The "equal" standard, always more complex, led to a question: "Where's the money?" History sounds the disconcerting answer: "Missing."

The white majority, recognizing they could retain power by preventing others from learning, was unwilling to pay taxes that would benefit the educational system for blacks. As Caucasians, they voiced opposition to improving the social status of poor African Americans. In the twenty-first century, it is alarming to observe a resurgence of similar attitudes about financial investments in students.

Throughout the century-long journey to integrated schools, Negroes assumed an important role in developing North Carolina's system of education. Never passive, they struggled to maximize educational opportunities for their race. Mission groups and enlightened white citizens supported efforts of blacks to establish schools (Chujo, 1988). Statewide efforts by blacks and whites, in both public and private domains, enabled western counties to take small steps to improve education for black children. The quality of school facilities, equipment, educators, and enrichment options was helpful in areas with historically larger African-American populations, such as Asheville, Hendersonville, Hickory, Morganton, or Rutherfordton. In more rural areas, expenditures for public education of black students ranged from zero to minimal.

Beginning in the 1860s, mission groups or missionary-minded individuals stepped in to address educational needs of African Americans. To compensate for the dearth of public financing, philanthropists funded projects by providing resources to meet specific needs. Based on the lack of inclusion in public records of school business, educating black pupils was rarely addressed unless community leaders confronted school boards about the needs of their children. The failure to spend money on black children built a strong case against "separate but equal."

Mountaineers battled poverty and viewed survival as a major success. White highlanders typically rejected any notion that they were their black brother's keeper. Rare exceptions show a white person reaching out to assist black children. A survey of Appalachian schools in North Carolina revealed an investment in black education by Methodists, Baptists, Congregationalists, Quakers, and Mennonites among others (Pollitt, 1993). While adequate facilities were often hauntingly absent, impromptu quarters permitted learning to take place.

On the trail to integration, landmark dates surface as bookmarks to show how black schools earned the right to financial support in communities trying to sidestep state statutes.

Church leaders such as Charles B. Dusenbury, who established Calvary Presbyterian Church in 1881, stepped to the front among supporters of classroom education for black adults and children. Supported by the northern Freedmen's Board, Dusenbury began church services in the former Catholic Hill church. In 1884, he organized a parochial school that met in its basement. Dusenbury, an advocate of "a soap and water gospel," included instruction in hygiene and gardening as well as in the basic skills of reading and writing. Dusenbury's Asheville school, which closed in 1927, outlasted its founder, who died in 1920 (Ready, 1986).

1879: Education received a boost in Asheville when a black man served on the City Board of Education — a way to have financial influence. Though not elected to that position, the black man won a political favor because Asheville's black citizens exercised their right to cast a vote. In 1879, the state legislature enacted a charter that led eventually to an election for public schools. Asheville voters went to the polls to decide whether taxes would be allowed to establish a school district — an issue with racial inferences. School supporters narrowly won the July 28, 1887, election, an event delayed eight years after the 1879 legislative decision allowed such action (Brown, 1940). At first the measure, opposed by vocal whites reluctant to support another man's children, seemed doomed, but the black man helped a white man who was championing education, so soon a black served on the board.

1887: Remarkably, it was the Negro vote that helped carry the election. Richmond Pearson, former member of the United States House of Representatives and future ambassador to Persia, aggressively campaigned in the Negro community to win support for the establishment of public schools. Pearson assured Negroes that if voters approved public schools there would be little impact on taxes, only a negligible increase. Furthermore, the astute politician promised Asheville's black voters that one of their race would serve on the school committee — equivalent to a school board — if the proposal won acceptance. Pearson succeeded, for the measure passed by two votes when the final ballot was counted. Out of 1,440 votes, 722 voted in favor of the measure — one more vote than the needed majority. The win allowed Asheville to have its own tax-supported school district. The election provided a tax of $16^{2/3}$ cents on $100 of property value and a 50 cent poll tax (Brown, 1940). The Negro vote had determined the outcome.

Victory for public schools coincided with technological advancements on the local scene. Julia Capps (June 2, 1983) writes: "In the year that public schools were approved ... Asheville was on the verge of a new era. During that year, the first electric lights had been turned on and the first public railway, linking what is now known as Pack Square with the railroad station had been put into operation. Few streets were paved, and most of them were stone." Such progress probably stimulated classroom discussion.

The new era placed Asheville in a period of educational growth during the next 46 years. Education could develop from a system with minimal opportunities to one of the more progressive school systems in North Carolina. W.H. Plemmons (1983) affirms that educational leaders succeeded in establishing a solid foundation during this initial period of public education.

1887: Isaac Dickson (Dixon), a colored businessman, soon found himself on the first Asheville City School Board, formally organized on August 9, 1887. Other members were W.W. West, chairman; W.F. Randolph, secretary; H.A. Gudger; D.T. Millard; and S.R. Kepler. Pearson had kept his promise. Dickson conscientiously represented needs of the black community and contributed to decisions affecting white schools. He was successful as a businessman, as a community leader, and as a school leader (Brown, 1940).

On the school committee, Dickson found himself challenged daily to assist in putting together the "nuts and bolts" of a public school system. He added input on numerous financial decisions: purchasing land, renovating buildings, buying furniture and school materials, and hiring teachers and workmen — a rare opportunity for a black man in that era.

Official 1887–1892 minutes of the Asheville School Committee reveal Dickson assuming a strong leadership role in providing schools and instructors for both the white and the black community. In its meeting on August 16, 1887, the committee appointed David T. Millard, S.R. Kepler, and Isaac Dickson to determine the best available location for a white graded school and to evaluate the condition of Beaumont Academy. On August 19, less than two weeks after its organization, the committee appointed Randolph and Dickson to receive contracts for improving the "colored school building" by adding a basement and outfitting a room below the school, rather than using the upper story. On August 26, Dickson was asked to find a site for a colored school building. Obviously, the decision had financial implications. But so did other board projects involving Dickson: receiving bids for repairs to Beaumont Academy, employing two men to teach colored pupils—E.H. Lipscomb and D.C. Suggs—(Asheville School Committee minutes, November 15, 1887), textbook choices, examinations for prospective primary teachers in the black schools, advertising a system for naming black and white schools, visiting colored schools, inspecting other sites for a proposed colored schoolhouse, hiring a census taker as well as two additional colored teachers (H.R. Brown and Mrs. Hester Ford), and arranging janitorial services for the colored schools. As the committee's sole black member, Dickson also worked with the school committee to establish a set of rules applicable to all schools, white and colored.

East of Asheville in Black Mountain, a community formerly known as Grey Eagle, another African American joined the ranks of such men as Isaac Dickson by serving on the school board. During childhood and early adolescence, John Myra Stepp resided on the Stepp Farm where his mother worked. Mrs. Stepp, his white owner, took an interest in the lad and taught him to read and to write. A favored servant, he was never a field hand and in adulthood served as a member of the school board in Black Mountain for 30 years. The father of seven children, Stepp, who died in 1955 at age 105, saw six of his children earn college degrees. Education was his personal priority (Hootman, "John Myra Stepp Has Important Place in Black Mountain History," *Black Mountain News*, March 3, 2005).

In September the Asheville school committee hired Philander P. Claxton as superintendent. Claxton, who later served as United States commissioner of education, 1911–21, worked with Isaac Dickson during his 1886–88 tenure in Asheville. The contact was a special start for a black man learning the ropes about coordinating a school system in a city.

Dickson's personal history is equally interesting. A businessman as well as a civic leader, Dickson was born into slavery in 1839 and died as a highly respected citizen in 1918. Dickson's father was his mother's owner, a Dutchman. The slave owner presented his enslaved son, Isaac, to his daughter by his legal wife, as a gift. Later Dickson's half-sister honored her half-brother by granting his freedom. Afterward he relocated. Arriving in Asheville from Cleveland County with a letter of recommendation, Dickson quickly established himself as a prominent and prosperous black citizen.

The letter of recommendation—on file in the Black Highlanders Collection at the D. Hiden Ramsey Library at UNC–Asheville—states: "We the undersigned citizens have bin acquainted with Isaac Dixon for years past and have ever found him to be an honest and upright man." Those signing the document were E.M. Dixon, Sheriff J.Z. Halls, Mr. Wells, M. Putnam, and I.A. Botts. Dickson earned local fame as an entrepreneur who owned a business, a grocery, a wood shop, a dray service and numerous other business interests. In addition to serving on Asheville's first board of education, Dickson was the moving force behind the early organization of schools for black children in Asheville.

1888: Dickson participated in decisions about expenditures for new buildings. He led efforts to provide the first school for Negroes in a building on Beaumont Street (Ready, 1986). Asheville's voters ushered in a bond issue of $25,000 on May 4, 1891, in response to Superintendent Claxton's recommendation that four well lighted, well ventilated and well heated

schools, including one for "the colored children," be built (Brown, 1940). A sub-committee investigated suitable sites and recommended a colored school on Catholic Hill.

1892: The contract for the Catholic Hill building was finalized on May 15, 1892, for $7,390. In the first hint of education beyond an elementary school for blacks, Catholic Hill School included high school classes and is recognized as Asheville's first public high school for African Americans. Dickson's involvement in the school committee's actions to build schools is well documented, though his name does not appear on the roster of the second school committee. Nevertheless, Dickson may have been the first Negro to serve on a school board in North Carolina or perhaps in the South.

1905–1906: The average length of school term for local tax districts in Henderson County was six months. The school term in non-local tax districts averaged 3.93 months. The average term length for black schools was 10 days less than that for white schools (Superintendent McD. Ray's 1906 Report of Henderson County Superintendent of Schools, July 1, 1906). Fewer days or months justified budgeting less money for black schools and their teachers.

Slightly more than 10 years later, plans to provide a new school building for black students were being developed. In a bold headline, a Hendersonville news article, on file at the offices of Henderson County Historical and Genealogical Society, for July 1915 announced: "*Movement on Foot for New School House for Colored.*" Trustees for the Hendersonville graded school confronted the need to provide a new building for the colored children. According to the article, sites for the school were being explored and a loan application had been sent to the North Carolina Department of Education.

The Henderson County board also mandated enforcement of the school attendance law that called for compulsory education of children age 8 to 12. The board went on record as opposing broken school terms. All members agreed that from that time on, school terms would be continuous with no school dismissals for fodder pulling, which was an activity that reinforced the need to support a family's prosperity but played havoc with school attendance. In most rural communities from the time that public schools were established till the 1960s, students were excused from attending school when they needed to help on the family farm. Often that meant closing the school to accommodate widespread harvesting. When daily attendance became the basis for teacher allotment, school boards carefully weighed permitting students to miss school when they were needed at home. In essence, leaders wondered whether finances should trump family traditions.

1906: On July 1, Henderson County Superintendent McD. Ray presented an update to the board of education and to the public regarding finances and statistics about black and white schools in 1905-06. Private donations for school buildings and for lengthening the school term amounted to $2,884.70. Additional sources of revenue included poll taxes, property taxes (both rural and city), fines, forfeitures, and penalties as well as $1,260 from the State Loan Fund and the State Library Fund. Ray's report cited $50 from the Peabody Fund. The total charged to the treasurer for the 1905-06 amounted to $16,335.94. Ray recorded expenditures of $18,261.39, with the treasurer having paid $15,376.69, leaving on hand a total of

Opposite, top: The Clearview Colored School in Black Mountain was built in 1917 and continued in use until Carver School opened in 1954. Since no high school classes were available at Clearview, the community purchased a bus to transport black students to Stephens-Lee High School in Asheville. Students at Clearview School in the 1940s: Sitting: Charles Daugherty; standing (left to right): Inez Daugherty, Sunny Featherstone, Joanna Gross, Lee Roy Lytle, Gertrude Lytle, and Clarence Moorehead (courtesy Swannanoa Valley Museum). *Bottom:* A rhythm band practices at Asheville's Hill Street School in the early 1950s. Instructors also taught students to play chimes and emphasized musical activities in its curriculum. Later Hill Street students had an opportunity to join Stephens-Lee's acclaimed marching band (courtesy Asheville City Schools).

$959.25. Expenditures for the salaries of white teachers amounted to $7,872.70, and those for colored teachers equaled $737.20.

Records disclose numerous inequities. The details speak with historical authority. The county had invested $1,049.24 in new schools and sites for the white race. Repairs for buildings servicing white students equaled $340.90. Repairs for old school houses for the colored race amounted to $36.90. Little had been provided for black education, but conducting a census of the rural school population had cost $13.02 and may have included both black and white students. Provision of such items as institute expenses, fuel, postage and libraries were not designated according to race. However, in Ray's general statistics in his 1906 report, every entry is designated as either white or colored.

Grade levels were included for both races through the sixth grade, but only white students were enrolled in seventh and eighth grades. The lack of black students in those grades is a clear indictment of the county system. Ray's report contains typographical mistakes, since the average age for a colored child enrolled in the first grade is listed as .9, an obvious error. On each grade level in which both races are enrolled, the Negro student's average age is higher. There was apparently no wholesale promotion in any of Henderson County's schools, white or black, for according to the report 335 pupils were numbered in grades 1–6 with 45 being the "Number Promoted." Therefore, most children were required to repeat their grade. No doubt the superintendent listed the number of non-promotions by mistake. Such a small percentage of promotions startles the mind.

The remainder of Superintendent Ray's 1906 report includes district and township reports. Information about Negro schools is detailed: the value of school property, the number of children, the percentage enrolled, the percent of those enrolled attending, and the percent of all school children attending. The Clear Creek Township had one colored school with a value of $50, and there were 29 children, of whom 90 percent were enrolled. Half of those enrolled were attending and 45 percent of eligible children were in attendance. The Crab Creek Township had one school building, valued at $50, for colored students. However, with only five students, no classes had been taught. The building in the Edneyville Township was valued at $150. Of the 41 students, 83 percent had enrolled — a statistic that brought the total percentage of all potential students attending to 50 percent. In Green River Township, 76 percent of its 39 students had enrolled and 86 percent of those were attending.

Four Hendersonville Township schools were listed. Hendersonville Graded School for colored students had a value of $1,000 and 260 students, with 42 percent of those enrolled and 42 percent of enrollees attending class. The total amounted to 19 percent of those eligible attending. The sharp contrast between Hendersonville Graded School and its counterpart spotlights inequality in educational funding.

The Hendersonville Graded School for whites, valued at $10,000, had a school age population of 376, of which 72 percent were enrolled and 72 percent of enrollees were attending. The school was serving 51 percent of those eligible. Other colored schools were in Districts 1, 2, and 3, with a total of 228 children of school age. The District 1 building was valued at $300; District 2, at $150; and District 3, at $250. The percentage of all resident school-age children attending was 61 percent for District 1; 37 percent for District 2, and 13 percent for District 3. District 1 students numbered 101; District 2, 82; and District 3, 45.

One school for colored children existed in the Hooper's Creek District 1 Township. District 2 provided classes but no school building. In the "houseless" school, 59 percent of its 51 eligible students had enrolled, with 58 percent of those enrollees attending classes. The value of the building in District 1 was cited as $125, with 62 percent of those enrolled attending. Two school buildings in Mills River's Districts 1 and 2 townships were collectively valued at $250. In District 1, 71 percent of the 42 eligible students had enrolled, and 54 percent were attending; in District 2, 20 students were of school age, and 60 percent of them were attending school.

1900: On May 31, the Asheville school committee decided to purchase a house on Hill Street near Maiden Lane. The committee assigned two teachers to the Hill Street School and appointed a third one to join them in January 1902. School officials then negotiated plans for the construction of a brick building on that site (Brown, 1940). By 1905, the school occupied the entire house, with so many first graders that it was necessary to have both a morning session and an afternoon session.

1907: Divisive issues developed in response to efforts to construct an elementary school on Hill Street in Asheville. On June 1, the *Asheville Citizen* reported that the local school committee unanimously approved the construction of a new school for colored children on Hill Street. The article praised the site as less expensive and more desirable than others being considered. In an earlier article on May 24, the reporter had indicated that the new school planned for the Negro community might be comparable to the modern school for white children on Park Avenue. The school being replaced had been condemned by the building inspector, but, with makeshift improvements, had continued to be used long after the inspector's recommendation. However, safety concerns prevailed, and plans were underway to replace the condemned building.

The white community responded with increasingly hostile objections to having a new black school built on Hill Street. Citizens insisted that all residents there would be white and that a black school would be inappropriate in such a community. Even though Hill Street's white residents voiced mounting dissent, the majority of its residents were Negroes, so plans for the school's construction moved forward with great effort. City aldermen refused to grant a building permit, and school officials hired an attorney to secure one. Judge T.A. Jones accused the aldermen of misusing their authority. Turmoil ruled the day among the white ranks. Beneath the emotional reactions there were concerns about finances, both the funding and the effect on property value.

Appearing in court as a private citizen, white attorney Frank Carter spoke in support of the construction of a school for black children on Hill Street. However, aldermen affirmed their conviction that the school should be located on Catholic Hill in the building formerly used as a home for orphaned or deprived black children. They asserted that such a solution would save money and that expenditures would be far less than the cost of erecting a brand new building.

Aldermen pointed out that in the past Negro families had purchased property in the vicinity of Hill Street to be near their children's school and had objected to their offspring being transported clear to the other side of Asheville. Court observers were members of the white population who expressed apprehension about having a large Negro population live near their residences ("Negroes Will Fight Hill Street School Action," *Asheville Citizen*, June 18, 1907).

An article appearing in the June 15 *Asheville Citizen* carried the headline: "To Segregate Negroes is a Minor Objective." Community leaders protesting the establishment of a school for black children suggested there was merit in relocating Negroes into a single neighborhood so one school could serve the needs of a single black "village." Aldermen argued that the accommodations available at Catholic Hill would be a money-saving solution. They reasoned that the expenditure of $14,500 for one Negro school was excessive because other schools were badly needed. Highlighting the timing of closing the former Negro reformatory, city leaders declared the availability of a 20-room building as a godsend to the black community. No longer the property of the Colored Children's Home, but that of Captain T.W. Patton, the site would be, in the opinion of the white opposition, a perfect solution to the black community's need for a school.

Though the school committee insisted that additional rooms would be required to accommodate all black students, the aldermen focused on what amounted to a $5,000 savings for the city if the Catholic Hill building were renovated. Again, finances told a story of prejudice. They stressed operational expenses would be far less if one school served the entire black student population. Property, it was pointed out, was available nearby for Negro families to purchase to establish residences near the site. Aldermen insisted such a move would benefit the black community because property values in the Catholic Hill vicinity were low.

However, financial considerations expanded to social and personal concerns. Montford Street residents claimed they would be handicapped in finding suitable servants if black domestic workers moved farther away. Those involved were unable to reach an agreement. Though a contract had been let to construct a brick building for $13,985 on Hill Street, the project was abandoned and the committee elected to reopen the school on Mountain Street (Plemmons, 1983). The situation forced a compromise, one that did not meet the so-called "equal" standard.

1910: Because the Catholic Hill School was overcrowded, discussion about erecting an eight-room building on Hill Street resurfaced. The need for additional space for black students at Catholic Hill and in the expanded Hill Street School House, coupled with the need for additional classrooms in the white schools, would total $75,000. In 1911, the aldermen, facing financial needs, arranged to introduce a bill for $50,000 into the general assembly. The school bond issue, combined with the opportunity to change city government from the aldermanic to the commission pattern, was defeated. However, in 1912, the electorate voted in favor of the school bonds. At that time, the school committee included the new building on Hill Street in its bond-sponsored projects. They selected William H. Lord as its architect.

1915: Finally a financial investment achieved a major improvement. Despite all previous arguments, the school was erected. The local newspaper announced the near completion of Hill Street School on January 18, 1915, eight years after the initial efforts to build in that location ("New Colored School Nearing Completion," *Asheville Citizen*). Need triumphed over concerns about expenditures. Principal, J.H. (John Henry) Michael wrote a letter extending thanks to the community, to the school superintendent, to the school committee, and to private citizens for supporting the bond issue, for paying taxes, and for praying with the result that a modern building on three acres with a spacious play area, with good ventilation and lighting, steam heat and wires for four electric lights had been provided for the children.

Architect William H. Lord earned acclaim for designing a splendid brick building with banks of windows flooding the interior with light. The school's three acres provided a magnificent view of the surrounding mountains and showcased a park of oak trees with plenty of room to expand. Judge George A. Shuford, a member of the school board, called it the finest school building in Asheville and praised its safety features ("Hill Street School Dedicated," *Asheville Citizen*, February 23, 1915).

The Hill Street School, which had enrolled 240 students, was dedicated on February 23, 1915, at the YMI center, and the event was featured in the *Asheville Citizen*. Dignitaries participating in the event included board President W.B. Northup, Judge George A. Shuford, Congressman J.J. Britt, Zeb F. Curtis, and Otis Green. Representing the black community were Principal Michael, Principal W.S. Lee of Catholic Hill School, and the Rev. C.K. Brown. The chorus from Allen Industrial Home School sang "The Negro National Anthem." Congressman Britt's speech praised the cooperative spirit and the pleasant relations between the white and the colored communities. The public appeared to have forgotten previous hostility and dissension.

Two state dignitaries, who had attended a conference in nearby Tennessee, visited the Asheville area one week later on their return trip to Raleigh. When James H. Dillard, director

Hill Street School held its first classes in a two-story house with Walter Lee as principal and moved to this building, constructed in 1917 and torn down in 1953. Architectural plans for a new replacement building were drawn up in 1952; the new Hill Street School was dedicated on March 29, 1953, and was later renamed to honor Isaac Dickson, a black member of Asheville's first school board. During its history as a segregated school, three other principals guided its development: J.H. Michael until 1940, and Paul Dusenbury until 1949; then Rita H. Lee until 1966 (North Carolina Office of Archives and History, Raleigh).

of both the Slater and the Jeanes funds, and N.C. Newbold arrived, they requested an inspection tour of the new Hill Street School and afterward expressed delight with the new building.

1949: The Asheville and Buncombe County school boards, recognizing the growing financial pressures, united on February 10 to enact a resolution establishing a building program for new construction as well as for remodeling and enlarging existing buildings and for purchasing equipment and expanding sites. An estimated cost for the project was $4.61 million, of which the State of North Carolina would provide $609,000. The boards requested that the board of county commissioners provide a bond because no public funds were available for the building program. Therefore, a special election was called on April 18 for bonds not to exceed $5.5 million to be issued. Acreage in Black Mountain marked the site of the consolidated school. Carver Elementary School in Black Mountain opened in 1951 and provided educational opportunities for local black children until integration closed its doors 15 years later.

Though segregation was both the priority and the practice, decisions revealed the complexity of the growing financial squeeze.

A major recommendation, and perhaps the state school survey committee's most urgent, was that Asheville City Schools and Buncombe County Schools consolidate (p. 7). However, the consolidation did not occur, and the two administrative districts continued to operate separately in 2010 (State School Survey Panel's Report, December 6, 1949, on file at Asheville City Schools Offices). The survey stated:

> Because of financial exigencies which developed in Asheville and Buncombe County about 20 years ago, the county and the city found their credit destroyed and their ability to meet the needs of the schools as to capital outlay and maintenance depleted almost to the vanishing point. As a remedy for this situation, special taxing units (not school districts) were created by a special act of the legislature.
> The districts, by popular referendum, were thus able to vote special taxes, float bonds, and thus provide buildings, maintenance, and extra services in some of the schools (p. 1).

The two systems were experiencing rapid changes: brisk growth of the school population, decreases in numbers of elementary students in the city, two city buildings being condemned causing city schools to become overcrowded, and all county schools becoming overcrowded. The result was numerous inequalities.

Still pressing for consolidation to equalize educational opportunities for the students, the survey committee stated that rejecting consolidation would mean the capital outlay program for the two administrative units should be placed on a county unit basis. The report, without references to segregation, implies that the county setup was making education expensive. Based on its three day on site study, the committee determined that the county contained too many high school centers (for white students—there was no high school for Negroes) and a new building project should include consolidation; small elementary schools lacked an adequate educational program, and the program developed for the county's black students indicated undue neglect.

1953: After 1950, in Yancey County there was one small union school for black pupils with an impressive name, Lincoln Park School. Located in a barely accessible gully and described as unsuitable to house stray dogs, the building had fallen into disrepair. It was condemned by a grand jury. While the all-white school board budgeted $350,000 to build a new white school, it closed Lincoln Park and petitioned Asheville City Schools and Allen School in Asheville to allow its black students to study in Buncombe County, a distance of 40 miles each way. During winter the trip required carrying flashlights to the bus stop at 6:20 A.M. and not returning home until 5:30 P.M. If the bus were cold, children huddled together under a blanket (A. Poinsett, October, 1959. "N.C. Students Who Refuse to Go 80 Miles to School Seek to Integrate White Schools in Yancey County." *Jet*, 16 [24], 22–25. Retrieved from http://books.google.com).

Yancey County parents were furious, but their protests provoked threats. A cross was burned at the edge of their community, an act which one white claimed was the black citizens' attempt to stir up trouble. As a temporary solution, Pearl J. Oliver tutored pupils in a church (Poinsett, October 8, 1959). Among the black community's residents, Celesta and John B. Griffith and Hubert Young and his wife actively sought a better education for black children. They influenced the board's decision to purchase property and build a new school (Yancey County Board of Education minutes, July 6, 1952).

The building project moved forward. In the November 2, 1953, minutes, board members recognized the need to persuade the State Highway Commission to build a road to the proposed site for the new school (Yancey County Board of Education minutes). In 1964, 11 years later, the board approved employing Cora J. Jackson to teach its African-American children (Yancey County Board of Education minutes, May 26, 1964).

By 1950, Lincoln Park School, a union school, was the only site for black pupils to receive a formal education. The rural Higgins School had been discontinued.

In the meantime, parents who wanted better high school offerings purchased a small van and transported students to Stephens-Lee in Asheville and at other times to Hudgins School in Marion. In addition, they transported elementary students to Hill Street School in Asheville or to Long Ridge in Madison County.

In 1958, the board built a new school for grades 1–8 and changed the school name to Oak Crest. Most students boycotted the new school. Plans were underway for desegregation, and the courts ruled in 1962 that Yancey County's black students were not receiving an adequate education. The last one-teacher school closed, and elementary school students were assigned to white schools. Despite the extensive efforts to subvert integration and to avoid paying thousands for adequate buildings for black students, the record suggests an intriguing question: Was Yancey County the first school system in the state to be integrated?

Counties had to overcome prejudices, but they had to solve shortcomings that the prejudice had established. Financial decisions, which signaled restrictions for black students, had begun more than a century before the court decisions and legislative actions of the 1950s and the 1960s. More than five decades after the court decisions, educational leaders are still working to even the classroom "playing field" for blacks and for students from lower social-economic families. Affluent taxpayers may look at their tax bills, but eager learners do not. Most children begin school with awe. Those with more opportunities, provided by higher salaries for teachers and modern buildings and high-tech access, have a better chance of sustaining the enthusiasm and traveling the road to education with fewer obstacles.

5

Gateway Push to Education

Long before wired classrooms promoted high-tech learning, Western North Carolina teachers responded to complex challenges. Daily routine involved occasional treats, recess and games, classroom drills in spelling and penmanship, discipline as required, and a myriad of unexpected demands requiring immediate attention. For sure, lunch duty was more inviting than dealing with non-existent toilets. Students carried lunches that included beans or milk and cornbread in a jar; biscuits with jelly, apple butter, or brown sugar. Classroom teachers knew their students' chores at home also built character though sometimes the chores interfered with completing homework in front of the fire or at the kitchen table.

To compete with daunting educational complications imposed by financial limitations, teachers had an invaluable resource: willpower and determination. In classrooms where teachers used the resource daily, students responded.

Teachers followed the standards of the day. They typically stressed penmanship, and parents took pride in having offspring who could write "a good hand." In the late nineteenth century and early twentieth century, teachers emphasized the elegant Spencerian style. Later the Palmer method became popular. Teachers found writing in block letters, the manuscript style, was a speedier approach more quickly mastered by their pupils. They taught all three styles to young pupils who struggled to hold a quill, a pen or pencil. Also, teachers routinely required left-handed students—a minority population—to write with their right hands.

Teachers also had to find ways to deal with classroom conflicts. In the years devoted to initiating public education, young teachers, with experience limited to their front yards, asserted their authority by reacting to the challenge of disobedient students by enforcing standard rules. In their classrooms visitors could see an assortment of discipline methods: a wayward student standing in a corner; a student copying sentences to reinforce correct behavior; and a culprit guilty of a devious stunt being publicly humiliated. Frequently more experienced educators resorted to corporal punishment and administered a spanking or a whipping. If other measures failed, the disciplinarian administered a certain number of lashes depending upon the nature of the mischief. Scuffling or calling one another names might merit four lashes while not paying attention or speaking out of turn might require only two to impress the importance of obeying the teacher or of avoiding mischievous actions. Teachers also had to pay attention to long lists of rules for safety precautions, such as "no climbing trees" and "no playing too near the stream."

More important than the discipline was the three R's of education: "Reading, wRiting, and aRithmetic." Also, spelling was a popular subject regarded as a way to strengthen both reading and writing skills, but its mastery did not guarantee that a pupil could either read or write. Emphasis on rote memory ensured that students might know answers to specific questions but did not guarantee mastery of the subject matter. Educational expectations were difficult to meet because black highlanders lacked access to a decent school building, an ade-

Vivian Cooper's students practice manuscript writing at Hill Street School. Manuscript writing was taught in all 1–3 grades in Asheville City Schools. Instruction in cursive writing commenced in the latter part of each third grade class. Vivian Cline Cooper taught first grade for 43 years at the school (Black Highlanders Collection) (P77.10.2.1.9. Hiden Ramsey Library Special Collections, University of North Carolina at Asheville).

quate playground, qualified teachers, a well-developed curriculum, lunchroom facilities, indoor toilets, textbooks, and enrichment activities.

Empowered by Resourceful Teachers

Teachers themselves personify the strengths and the dignity that eventually led to the achievement of integrated schools in the twentieth and twenty-first centuries. In the early days slaves, poverty-stricken parents, white men and women, black men and women, and devoted religious missionaries made up a diverse and evolving staff in the widespread and multi-challenged Western North Carolina schools. They recognized the need for education and moved forward step by step. Only in the twentieth century did they address more philosophical questions: When does ignorance begin? How and why does it continue? What are the dangers of being uninformed about any subject, whether science, history, or language? What is the potential of a society in which everyone has an equal opportunity to learn? How can efforts to initiate and to multiply schools move communities closer to that goal? Educators in the past and in the present waged war against ignorance and dedicated themselves to providing each pupil with a knowledge base and personal confidence in basic skills.

Catholic Hill School: A major emphasis in black education emerged when Catholic Hill School, a three-story brick structure, was erected in Asheville. The all-black school, located adjacent to South Charlotte Street close to the traditionally designated site of an "arbor school" for slaves, opened in 1892. Philanthropist George Vanderbilt persuaded Edward Stephens of Raleigh, North Carolina, to become its first principal. Stephens was a native of the British West Indies who had studied at Cambridge University in England, as well as at universities in France and Switzerland. Catholic Hill School, designated as the first public high school for blacks in Asheville, was established with the vigorous support of committee member Isaac Dickson (Ready, 1986).

Stephens, who was well liked by his peers, modeled the pursuit of learning. In addition to English, he was fluent in six other languages. Acknowledged as the visionary who conceived of an institute for the young men of Asheville, he won the support of Vanderbilt, who was instrumental in financing the construction of the Young Men's Institute (YMI), which was erected during 1892 and 1893. The institute provided a gathering place for members of the black community and a venue for various businesses serving Asheville's black population.

Black and white schools established a basic education for Asheville's pupils from the early 1890s until the arrival of the twentieth century. A long delay ensued during which the school system added the tenth grade in 1903, extended the school year from 172 to 190 days and added domestic science to the white curriculum in 1904, and in 1906 added classical and sci-

Catholic Hill School opened in 1891. Here teacher Agnes Knuckles Gallego poses with a group of Catholic Hill students in 1916. After fire destroyed the facility on November 17, 1917, teachers held classes in a variety of vacant places as near to the original school site as possible until the construction of Stephens-Lee School was completed in 1921–22 and it opened in 1923 (North Carolina Office of Archives and History, Raleigh).

entific programs to the white high school's course of study in addition to hiring five additional white teachers. In 1906, Catholic Hill School added domestic science to its curriculum.

Stephens and his faculty faced numerous challenges as suggested by developing state standards. In 1906, compulsory attendance reform mandated school enrollment for students between the ages of eight and 14, and for those between 14 and 16 who were unemployed. The city limits of Asheville were extended, and a 1907 law allowed the city to assume responsibility for the formerly private kindergarten system (Plemmons, 1983).

From its opening in 1892, Catholic Hill School served its black pupils well, creating confidence that local students were involved in lessons that would lead to an adequate education, but 25 years later the school became the scene of what may have been Asheville's worst tragedy. On November 16, 1917, fire broke out in the school's furnace room and quickly spread throughout the building. The flames dealt both death and destruction. Initially Mamie Martin, whose classroom was located on the third floor, became concerned and, upon investigating, saw smoke escaping through the walls of the furnace room. She rushed back to her students warning other teachers along the way. Martin called for the fire escape plan to be executed, and teachers maintained order as students exited the building. The fire killed seven children: Henry Thompson, Elsie Thompson, Mary Jamison, Hazel Harris, Inez Davis, Hannah Simulton, and Daisy Dobbins. Henry Thompson went back into the building to look for his younger sister, who ran back inside because she remembered her new coat had been left behind. The loss of young, innocent lives was devastating.

The public praised teachers for the orderly manner in which they led their pupils to evacuate the building. An article in the *Asheville Citizen* dated November 17, 1917, featured this headline: "Death Toll at Catholic Hill School May Be 8 Children." According to the article, flames destroyed the school and a contributing factor may have been delay in turning in the alarm. So much was going on that nearly 20 minutes elapsed before anyone called the Asheville Fire Department. Residents had rushed to ensure the safety of the children and to fight the blaze, but by the time help arrived the building was fully engulfed.

The report documents death, destruction and discipline: "In what has been the most disastrous fire ... in the history of Asheville, the Catholic Hill School, an institution given over to the education of colored children, was totally destroyed yesterday, and from five to eight of the children were burned to death.... Splendid discipline was responsible for the saving of the majority of the children in the school at the time, the teachers coolly guiding their children out, and only one serious case of panic being reported." The inquiry showed that all teachers had stood with backs to the doors and kept their pupils orderly, and in doing so saved many lives that day. The report strongly commended their handling of the situation, without exception.

Twenty years later on November 16, 1937, the headline featured in the Asheville Citizen was "Fire Which Took the Lives of 7 Was 20 Years Ago." The reporter documents that firemen used 3,500 feet of hose, which proved to be useless, as the entire building was ablaze. Fire Chief J.H. Wood and his assistant, A.1. Duckett, directed futile efforts to save the three-story brick school.

A temporary school was set up nearby at an abandoned sanitarium, which in 1894 had housed the Calvary Presbyterian Church. Classes continued in makeshift circumstances in various churches and buildings throughout the city from that time until 1922. In the early 1920s, a new high school was built for black students on the site of the Catholic Hill School.

Hill Street School: An outstanding educational leader in Asheville and in the Western part of the state, J.H. Michael served not only as Hill Street's principal but also as its fifth and sixth grade teacher. His dual involvement and development as an educational leader is typical of how teachers led the way toward improvement and integrated schools that happened decades later. In addition, he served as the county's supervisor of black teachers and was the originator and director of a summer school for teachers and worked tirelessly to have recreational facilities provided for the community. Michael's contribution to black education was impressive. Assigned to Asheville as its first Jeanes supervisor, a training position supported by money from philanthropist Anna Jeanes, Michael influenced numerous local teachers, such as those on his staff: Hattie V. Swann, first grade; L.B. Michael, second grade; and Rosa Rhume and C.V. Thomas, fourth grade. His influence extended beyond Asheville and Buncombe County throughout the western region and into Raleigh.

In 1916, Michael was successful in obtaining funding to hire L.C. Davis of Tuskegee, Alabama, to take charge of the Home Makers Club activities in Buncombe County. Part of her responsibility in that role was to provide assistance in teaching housewives how to sew and how to maintain sanitary methods of cooking and housekeeping, as well as how to preserve fruits and vegetables. Davis was responsible for teaching girls and women to cultivate gardens, to sell produce, and to can food used by Negro families during the winter months when money was short in black households (Department of Public Instruction, Division of Negro Education, General Correspondence of the Director, Box 2).

Davis's influence also affected Black Mountain because N.C. Newbold, director of Negro education, suggested that she organize the first club in that community. Newbold was confident that Willis D. Weatherford, president of the Blue Ridge Assembly, would be interested in purchasing fresh fruits and vegetables for use at the YMCA facility. Having a ready market was no doubt an encouragement to Davis's students. The multiple efforts show how a teacher's influence spreads like concentric circles on a pond.

Under Michael's leadership, Hill Street School, where he taught, became the site of summer programs designed to help teachers to improve their skills. His plan to bring university opportunities to the community allowed rural teachers to earn additional college credits without incurring the expenses of traveling far from home. The proximity of classes proved to be a godsend for teachers in Asheville and in surrounding communities. Respected educator Ethel Kennedy Mills, who was educated in Franklin, North Carolina, and taught in both Buncombe and Transylvania Counties, expressed appreciation for Michael's establishment of the summer school and for encouragement of teachers enrolled in the summer school classes. Mills acquired her teacher certification by taking advantage of the summer school Michael directed (personal communication, June 17, 1999).

Michael fulfilled multiple roles: teacher, principal, supervisor, director of summer school for teachers, civic leader, county leader, and liaison with Raleigh. Because his interest in students created a desire to help teachers advance in their professional education, he devoted hours to planning and to teaching workshops. However, he was also a "human figure" in his community. He knew classmates walking to Hill Street School were sometimes "lolly gagged," yielding to the early morning temptation to delay reaching the campus to socialize en route. However, the school principal dutifully rang bells to speed reluctant students on their way. "Mr. Michael was very strict about time. He rang the bells, more than one. He would hang out the window, swinging that bell in his hand ... sometimes one in each hand" (Patricia Roland, personal communication, May 23, 2007). Hearing the bell, students, remembering the consequence of being tardy, made haste.

His Hill Street School, which had opened in 1915, was leveled in December 1952 and replaced by a new facility, which opened with 30 classrooms and specialized areas to a burgeoning student population in 1953. By 1958, the school had an expansion program to add four classrooms. Nine members of the teaching staff held master's degrees, and each faculty member had completed study beyond their bachelor's degrees. The Asheville City Schools administration had cultivated essential improvements in its black facilities. Lindsey M. Gudger,

Students and teachers gather outside the Burton Street School, originally named Buffalo Street School, in West Asheville, circa 1925. In 1920-21 Hattie Hardin and Regina Fortune taught at Buffalo Street School for a salary of $99 and $70 respectively. The original frame structure was replaced with an eight-room brick building in 1928. One hundred and forty children were enrolled in 1940-41 with an average daily attendance of 109. The abandoned school was turned into a community center (North Carolina Collection, Pack Memorial Public Library, Asheville).

architect, designed a new Hill Street school. The builder was James Miller. Its completion coincided with the 65th Anniversary Celebration of Asheville City Schools, 1888–1953. J.W. Byers was the superintendent at that time and Rita Hendrick Lee became the school principal (*Asheville Citizen*: "Workmen Raze Hill St. School," December 20, 1952; March 29, 1953, "New Hill Street School").

Eventually the school's name was changed. Citizens noted that Isaac Dickson had served with two white citizens—William Randolph, a school board secretary, and P.P. Claxton, Asheville's first superintendent—each of whom had been honored by having an elementary school called by his name ("Hill Street Name Changed," *Asheville Citizen-Times*, June 21, 1991). In response, the Asheville City Board of Education honored the first black member of the Asheville school council by changing the Hill Street School name to Isaac Dickson Elementary School. Also, Mountain School was named Lucy Herring Elementary School in 1962 in honor of Principal Lucy Herring, an African American career educator.

Though Michael's professional growth and contributions were pace-setting, leaders in other counties moved at a slower gait.

Burton Street School operated first as a county school and then as part of the city school system. It is indirectly linked to the remarkable E.W. Pearson. Known as the black mayor of West Asheville, he established a settlement near Asheville in 1912 and as the population grew, perhaps in response to Pearson's energy and vitality, Buffalo Street School was organized, but the name was changed in the 1920s to honor one of Asheville's founders, John Burton.

The history of the school's administration is well documented. J.E. Young of Memphis,

Tennessee, was the school's first principal. U.S. Reynolds became principal in 1917 and employed Ellen Sorrell as his assistant. In 1918 Hattie Love replaced Sorrell, becoming principal in 1918 and serving until 1945. Other principals were Nellie Clinkscale, Gertrude Dixon Jones, and Alsie Y. Bovian.

At its beginning, Burton Street, formerly Buffalo Street, School was a two room facility which soon required more space. In 1928 an eight-room brick building with four classrooms, an auditorium, a lunchroom, a library, and a principal's office replaced the original frame structure. Classes were offered to approximately 200 pupils in grades one through seven. A major change occurred in 1937 when the board of education mandated that all seventh graders be sent from Burton Street to Asheland Avenue Junior High School. The board made that decision to reduce elementary class size and to cut back on the range of grade levels per teacher.

Citizen-Times journalist and local historian Rob Neufeld interviewed Burton Street elders on October 11, 1991, one of whom was Gertrude Jones, who had reluctantly accepted a teaching position in 1927 at the three-room Burton Street School, at a time when a new building was under construction. Jones initially taught third graders in the old building. Jones served under principals Love and Clinkscale; then Jones became principal but was later transferred to Herring School on Mountain Street.

The old school had a long porch located street-side. A pump provided drinking water and there was an outdoor toilet. Desks provided double seats so each pupil had a partner to study with or to whisper to. However, discipline also punctuated classroom activities as teachers challenged their young pupils to master their lessons. When Jones worked at Mountain Street, she taught the older students black history, and that was somewhat rare on the elementary level. Music offered an outlet to a child's need to give voice to gladness. Once or twice a week, Annie Mae Clark Bolden came from Emma to teach vocal music and piano. She also led in group singing, practicing do-re-mi exercises and giving the children a break from desk work. Another event broke the monotony of routine as occasionally there would be a movie, an event the children enjoyed immensely.

Almost every black family in West Asheville convened for the school's annual closing program, during which students presented recitations from memory, the length ranging from four lines to a couple of pages. Students who memorized easily were given longer presentations. At times teachers and their pupils combined efforts to write a play. Occasionally, the play was a means of enriching academic study. For example, if pupils were studying Japan, they might write a play centered on Japanese customs or history. Teachers also assigned roles in plays and operettas, making sure each child had a part. There was no stage, but sheets were hung to form stage curtains. It was a happy time, according to the former students interviewed by Neufeld (October 11, 1991).

Edna Ford — responding to Neufeld's question, What were the hopes of parents and teachers for students?— said, "One of my parents finished sixth grade at Leceister School and the other finished fourth at Weaverville.... My parents were very anxious for us to have a better education because that meant better living and better enjoyment of life."

During school recess boys and girls used separate play grounds. Once in a while the children crossed over to the opposite play area for competitive games between boys and girls. Strict rules governed their exiting and entering the schoolhouse for the mid-day and afternoon break. Marching in and out, pupils moved in straight lines, always separated by their gender. Games at home and school included a wide variety. Children enjoyed seesawing on a device constructed on the playground by one of the fathers, a seesaw that went high in the air; the boys often made their own wagons with skates or old wheels and brought them to the playground to try out. Swings were suspended from trees. Burton Street became the site of skate races. In the spring students made kites to test the wind and their skill. Some playground pastimes included "lost my handkerchief," "hide and go seek," "ring around the rosie," "red rover," and "farmer in the dell."

After school there were required chores on the home front, such as looking after cows and chickens. After school or on Saturdays students might return to the playground to compete with teams from other communities. The games stirred up spirits and it was not unusual for fights to break out between boys from West Asheville and those from Shiloh, Hill Street, Southside, Mountain Street. The town versus rural competition may have stirred up rivalry that required fists to prove worth. First, the fellows played ball and then fought.

Knowing that high marks and good citizenship could win recognition and commendation contributed to diligence in study and in obeying the rules. One of the aging Edna Ford's fond memories of school days was receiving a good conduct award from Hattie Love. Douglas Horn, whose family's musical talent amazed the community, won academic awards. Haywood Horn could play the classical music of Beethoven and Bach by ear. The gifted musician attended Julliard. School alumnus Edward Pearson became a professional photographer who did public relations work in California and photographed state politicians including Ronald Reagan and Pat Brown. Pearson pointed out that it was not always easy for a black photographer to gain entry to a political event, but he developed a strategy for dealing with the closed door. Another exceptional Burton Street scholar was Nathaniel Felder, who earned his Ph.D.

Discipline was maintained at the school, but it was not viewed as effective by every parent. Once a year the Williams family prepared a big dinner for all the Burton Street staff. Former principal Jones told Neufeld that at that meal, Mrs. Williams would bring out a strap and inquire, "Do any of these children need a whipping? Have they been giving you any trouble? If they do, I will deal with it because you teachers don't know how to whip." Mountain parents traditionally provided at-home support for teachers' decisions, and often a whipping at school ensured a double measure of discipline because the school event mandated an additional whipping at home. Infrequently mothers assumed the role of home disciplinarian, because fathers often traveled from site to site for extended periods due to their jobs. For employees of the Southern Railroad Company, assignments could mean a journey of several days. The Burton Street faculty knew the families of their students and were able to support their personal and educational needs (Neufeld, 1991).

In 1963 the school's faculty completed a self-study report for the Southern Association of Colleges and Schools. The report documented an enrollment of 108 children and a parent-teacher organization that included 90 percent of the parents, indicating a high interest index by school families. Typically Burton Street parents were employed in domestic and custodial work; however, 80 percent owned their own homes. Sixty percent of the parents had graduated from high school and ten percent had completed at least one year of college. As was the norm in African American homes, parents pushed their children to achieve academically in order to ensure brighter futures (Self-Study Report, March 1963). Davidson indicated that having your teachers as neighbors reinforced learning and discipline, while creating an enduring awareness that what happens at school really matters (personal communication, June 3, 2008)

Livingstone Street School: Another community school commenced its service in 1920. Livingstone Street School began in a four room frame building which housed grades 1 through 3. At one time its faculty consisted of Principal Rachel S. Battle, Mayme E. Johnson, Janet Battle Kebe, and Pearl Jordan Oliver. Because of the large number of students enrolled, double sessions became necessary. To alleviate that burden, two additional rooms were attached. However, the burgeoning population in South Asheville required adding seven more rooms by 1927. A fourth grade was added in 1932, and four years later the fifth grade. By 1932 the number of faculty members had increased to twelve. ("History of Livingston Street School,

1920–1957"). The school was developed "piece-meal," increasing the cost of major improvements.

A Parent Teacher Association was formed during the school's first year. Soon Livingston Street School was also used as a center for adult education with evening classes in reading and writing. A Reading Circle met in the afternoons. Instruction and activities were directed toward increasing the community's awareness of the duties of citizens and of the value of education.

During the depression the school physician, Dr. Margery Lord, shared her concern about children with Mamie Hudson. Many did not receive hot meals because of their parents' work schedules. So Hudson moved her personal kitchen equipment to the school and provided hot soup and sandwiches at a minimal cost, another example of looking out for the neighbors' children.

In 1943 the school was remodeled with a lunchroom, auditorium, and recreational area housed in the former furnace room. Four years later the county recreational program began using the building for evening activities and later summer programs became a valuable addition. The school functioned as a community center.

Continued crowded conditions led to the construction of a new Livingston Street School, which opened for the school year 1952-53. The modern building contained classrooms, a lunchroom, a spacious auditorium which seated 475, and a library. Shortly, however, crowded conditions developed again, and in 1956 a six room addition was begun, and on January 23, 1957, the fifth and sixth grades occupied the new annex ("History of Livingston Street School").

One former student of the Livingston Street School is retired journalist Henry T. Robinson, who became the first African American to break the color barrier at *The Asheville Citizen-Times*. Robinson (personal communication, April 8, 2009) affirmed the high quality of the Livingstone Street faculty's professional training: "Livingstone Street had the finest teachers ... so strict! Many of them had graduate degrees, some from Columbia University. A.S. Reynolds succeeded Rachel Battle as principal. Battle was a staunch disciplinarian. Teachers were excellent, excellent! I mean they laid a foundation, a strong foundation.

"One of the oldest teachers was Mrs. Janie Few. She probably finished high school in 1913, but she was *good*.... Principal Arthur Edington went from Livingston Street to Hill Street School and retired there."

Robinson also testified to the impact that non-professional personnel had on students. "Mrs. Hudson, an exciting woman, ran the cafeteria. She served the best food. Those smells would float throughout the building, all through the schoolhouse. Man — that was good!"

Robinson voiced excitement as he recalled the fun of break time at Livingstone Street School: "At recess I would shoot marbles. We had a 'thumper' and a 'buster.' We used the big one to bust up the marbles and then we'd shoot and work around the center. It was fun!"

When integration struck the death blow to the school, the community grieved. "It was a sad time when the school closed, and, when I reflect on it I think of the stupidity of mankind. Kids should have been trained to join together and work together. Then they closed the school and the reasons were (1) The School Board claimed that the streets were too narrow to get the buses there safely, and (2) The 'majority culture'—I'll just word it that way — was afraid to enter a predominantly black neighborhood. Of course, because of economic reasons, there was a touch of a slum element, but it was safe. That was just an excuse. Good people lived there, but the school closed" (personal communication, April 8, 2009). Integration was responsible for the demise of the Livingstone Street School.

Watauga County: In Watauga, a northwestern county, educational developments ensured that an opportunity to learn, though limited, existed for black students. Existing statistics verify that Watauga County was in desperate need of educating its white as well as its black

The former Watauga Consolidated School, 1937–1959, is currently a private residence in Boone, North Carolina. After 1937, with a new five-room building, better equipment, more teachers, and a 500 volume library, the consolidated school, initially boycotted by county students, offered two years of secondary work, after which students could enter other high schools in the state (courtesy Fred J. Hay).

population. In 1870, there were 1,415 individuals aged 10 and above who were illiterate. Among the county's adult population, 216 white males, 439 white females, 38 colored males, and 29 colored females were unable to write. A courthouse fire in 1873 destroyed early school records, but later documents provide a record of actions taken to educate black children. In 1882, the public paid $5 for one acre of land as the site for a colored school in Laurel Creek (Corbitt).

Because no black teachers were available in Watauga County, its first instructors for black students were local white men: Charlie Cullars, Mark Holesclaw, and Ben Tester. The three men taught respectively in the rural communities of Boone, Cove Creek, and Sugar Grove, also known as Beaver Dam. Terms were brief because the teachers condensed their learning programs to be completed in only a few short weeks during the year, often providing the same curriculum for a limited time at more than one locale. They established a pattern of moving from one village to another.

Watauga schools succeeded in enrolling only a few pupils for each session, perhaps seven or eight. As time passed, schools were housed in buildings and had a fixed locale that resulted in regular terms of instruction, but Watauga County never had more than six black schools at one time. In 1887, there were three school buildings for African Americans. Two were made of rough-hewn logs. Seats were rough logs, and the teacher's desk was usually a discarded box. Students wrote on slates with slate pencils and commonly studied Webster's *Blue Back Spellers* (Horton, 1942). Vigilance was required, for on more than one occasion the timber of the chimney ignited, and the teacher and students hustled to extinguish the flames.

An early black teacher was Boone native Emory H. Hennessee, who was raised by the white Jim Hardin. Hennessee received his early education in Boone, but Hardin enrolled his young protégé at Warner's Institute in Jonesborough, Tennessee. Upon returning to Boone in 1885, one year short of completing his training, Hennessee embarked on a teaching career at Boone and Cove Creek, earning the reputation of being an able and effective teacher. His career in education appeared secure, but he also had a back-up career as a barber. If he found himself short of funds, he offered haircuts to the public (Horton, 1942). After moving to Morganton, Hennessee earned his living with his barbering skills.

In 1886, the Watauga Board of Education compiled a census of school children in Elk Creek Township to justify establishing a school. The board amassed $8.75 for the new school for blacks, which enrolled eight students, and hired Zetta Mathes, a young woman from Yadkin County, as the instructor. After completing eighth grade in Sugar Grove, North Carolina, Mathes began to teach for a monthly salary of $8. Joining the education ranks was a Negro teacher named Webb Moore, a native of Caldwell County, who had attended school in Greensboro, Tennessee. Moore taught successfully for 35 years at Boone and Beaver Dam in North Carolina and at Butler, Tennessee (Horton, 1942).

Retired educator and Caldwell County resident Leatrice R. Pearson shares information about her elementary school experience in the 1930s:

> My journey in education began in Cleveland County at the New House Elementary School. It was a house ... used as a school for blacks. It was dilapidated with no outhouse so there was a wooded area with one section designated for boys and another for girls. Two teachers came from Shelby: Miss Christine Abernathy and Mr. W.J. Rogers. Teachers were beloved. We ran to meet them, had them on a pedestal.
>
> In grade one there was newspaper stuffed around the walls to make the room warmer.... One morning those papers caught fire, and it spread.... We got pails to dip in water, but someone said, "Let it burn." I suspect it was Mr. Rogers. We let it burn and we got another school ... an elongated room with a partition. There were grades 1–8. Children learned. There was a split term with time off for cotton picking. Folks forget about that.... There were always books around [personal communication, November 16, 2009].

Population growth added to struggles within the educational arena. Schools and churches frequently used the same facilities. State support for public schools came to the aid of struggling rural communities such as Watauga. School board minutes document that Superintendent J.W. Thomas received a salary of $2 per working day. Thomas was responsible for "numbering"—an expression for counting eligible pupils living in the area. Thomas also dispensed teacher salaries, which were $17 a month for white teachers and $15 a month for black teachers. Poll taxes, property taxes, and fines provided funds for schooling.

In 1900, three of 81 teachers in Watauga County were Negroes. Each teacher was required to earn a certificate, which was granted after making an acceptable score on test administered by an examiner, who was sometimes the superintendent of schools. In 1900, Superintendent B.B. Dougherty examined 30 white and two black teachers. In 1901, he conducted a weeklong teacher's institute. Anyone planning to teach was required to attend and to take an examination. Not to do so resulted in unemployment (Corbitt). In such ways local efforts emphasized professional development, not only in Watauga County but also throughout Western North Carolina. White superintendents, however, did not always expect black instructors to take advantage of training provided in local workshops.

Hendersonville: Faculty member Odell Mitchum Rouse began teaching at Sixth Avenue School in 1926. A native of South Carolina, Rouse herself had been a student at Sixth Avenue. She attended Benedict College and earned a degree from Winston-Salem State Teachers' College. During a career spanning 44 years, Rouse contributed to Henderson County's education for black students. At times Rouse directed learning activities for as many as 65 students in a single room. According to her (Greene, 1996), "It wasn't hard if you knew how to organize your work and give them something to do (p. 17).

Starting at Sixth Avenue School in 1926 and then transferring to the new Ninth Avenue School, Rouse taught first grade for 39 years. She taught until the school closed in 1965 when integration began. Following that, she taught special education at Bruce Drysdale until 1970.

Louise Bailey shared personal recollections of Rouse (1905–1991): "Odell Rouse was a remarkable woman. She served hot soup to her students to thaw them out. She did a nursemaid's job as well as a teacher's. If a child's feet were cold, she'd rub them until they got warm" (personal communication, January 18, 2006).

Gary Rivers, another former student, said, "She didn't just teach. She made sure her students had food to eat and clothes on their backs. She was firm, but she truly cared about her students" (personal communication, December 1, 2005). Such remarks by former students illustrate why Rouse was nominated for the Henderson County Hall of Fame for Educators. Henry "Tippy" Cresswell described Rouse as a compassionate and much loved teacher, who adjusted her instructional style to the needs of her students. The Hall of Fame Committee quotes Richard Morris, a journalist: "Odell Rouse has washed away more tears, fed and clothed more children who might otherwise have gone hungry and cold, and brought more smiles and laughter than anyone imagined possible" (Henderson County Hall of Fame for Educators Acceptance Information, in personal files of Gary Rivers, Blue Ridge Community College, Hendersonville, NC).

Boone to Brevard: Like the self-grown talent and the professionally trained pedagogues, religious leaders committed themselves to improving education. Both males and females committed themselves to make education happen, often with few financial resources as devotion outweighed the limitations of dollars.

In 1885, a teacher from the North, Emily Prudden, opted to vacation in the Blowing Rock area. Ever alert to the needs of those around her and finding no schools in Blowing Rock, Prudden returned the next year to purchase land for a school site (Emily Prudden, 1832–1917 in Blowing Rock, retrieved from www.stoppingpoints.com.) She built a dormitory and opened Skyland Institute in September 1887 for white mountain girls and their smaller brothers. In 1884, she founded a school for white girls in Gaston County, North Carolina. The earlier experience in Blowing Rock allowed her to embark on a second school project with her eyes wide open.

Soon Prudden, called the "Yankee Schoolmarm," was a visionary who wanted to educate black children beyond one room school houses. In 1886, despite attempts to intimidate her, Prudden, whose resources were limited to an annual income of $500, founded Lincoln Academy for African Americans. Her white neighbors were vocal in their disapproval. Prudden described the challenges of that experience: "The white people protested ... my doing this: 'Miss Prudden, you can make nothing out of these lying, good for nothing Negroes.... I trembled for the safety of the new Home [Prudden's term for boarding school], and I gave it to the Lord with absolute trust that he would guard and bless it'" (Pollitt, P. "Learning Freely," *Then and Now*, Summer 1993, pp. 31–32). A short time later Lincoln Academy guaranteed its own success by enrolling 300 day and boarding students.

The Gaston County academy was the first of seven that Prudden built for African American students. Subsequently, Prudden moved forward to establish 12 schools: Connelly Springs, Burke County; Elk Park and Altamont, Avery County (then Mitchell County); Big Lick and Hudson, Stanly County; Mill Springs, Saluda, and Tryon, Polk County; Cedar Valley and Lenoir, Caldwell County; Lawndale, Cleveland County, and Brevard, Transylvania County. Prudden kept her schools segregated, not because of personal conviction but because white enmity dictated that black pupils could not be schooled alongside whites (Pollitt, 1993).

The Prudden School in Avery County grew out of her being invited to establish a school for white mountaineer children. After launching the Elk Park Academy, Prudden felt guilt ridden as she observed the poverty and the doors closed to the few African Americans in Avery County, so she purchased four acres of land in a prime location and built a school. At the time of the purchase, those who sold it did not realize she intended to build a school for black children. Despite warnings not to, Prudden moved forward and began a school for African Americans. Jealousy and hostility swept through the Elk Park community, creating enormous hardships for black students and their teachers. Fear drove the first students and teachers away.

Unable to recruit teachers, Prudden called in help from the Mennonite Church, which sent a young couple, Henry and Elizabeth Wiebe. At first, the Wiebes attempted an integrated school, but a note threatening any white man who would stoop to teach a person of color persuaded Henry to limit student enrollment to African Americans. The school found so many homeless waifs at its door begging entry that the Mennonites established Salem Orphanage. As a result, the couple needed to acquire more acreage and embark on farming to support the children. Reinforcements arrived with the Rev. Jacob Tschetter and his family, and in order to accommodate the new workers, a large addition was necessary. Two local black women, Alice Garrett and Gertrude Sapp, joined the staff as teachers. Threats remained constant, but the orphanage lasted until 1912. Then Garrett and Sapp began teaching in the Avery County segregated public school (Inscoe, 2001).

Overcoming her slim resources, Prudden developed a strategy to ensure financial backing for her schools. She established a school and stayed with it long enough to get it on a firm footing. Then she transferred ownership to a Protestant mission society. For example, the American Missionary Association of the Congregational Church accepted responsibility for Lincoln Academy and Skyland Institute (Corbitt; Pollitt, 1993). Prudden, who became deaf at age 17, built schools for both white and black students in North Carolina and South Carolina (Corbitt). She was also instrumental in enabling Wilkie Carpenter Johnstone to establish a school for blacks in Brevard, North Carolina.

The new construction in Brevard stimulated many questions about the black community's windfall that allowed building a new school. How local blacks obtained funding was a mystery to local whites (Reed, 2004), but financial support came from Prudden's resources. Johnstone, who had graduated from Lincoln Academy and had taught and served as principal at Lovejoy Academy in Saluda, moved to Brevard with her husband and two children only to discover there was neither a public nor a private school for her youngsters to attend, so she sought help from Emily Prudden. At age 77 in 1909, Prudden founded Mount Herman Academy, her last school.

The Brevard academy was the sole school Prudden did not place under the wings of a denominational group. Mount Herman was built in the center of Brevard's black community, and students from rural clusters rented or lived with their "city" relatives to attend. Perhaps due to Johnstone's influence, the school stressed academic achievement and assigned a lesser role to vocational or industrial education because the teachings of intellectual leader W.E.B. Du Bois had influenced Johnstone.

St. Anthony of Padua School: In 1936, Catholic nuns traveled from New York to Asheville, North Carolina, to establish an elementary school for black children in grades 1–6. Frederick Necker of New York, with input from Father Ronald Scott, designed the school, and A.J. Durner and Son built the church-school for $30,000, with construction commencing in June and ending in September. That first semester the school enrolled 120 students. Only six were Catholic, as religion was not a requirement. The curriculum followed the standard North Carolina plan with nuns providing instruction in arithmetic, geography, spelling, history, nature study, physical education, English, writing, reading, word-building, drawing, recitation and games. Sister De Paul provided instruction in music and led students in singing religious and folk songs. Mass was a daily occurrence, as were devotions. In Volume 5 of *The Community Improver*, an announcement of graduation exercises was posted for Saint Anthony of Padua School. Father Joseph L. Howze presented diplomas to eight graduates. Robert Dorn delivered the valedictory address, and school alumnus Dr. Otis B. Michael was the guest speaker. The writer praised the quality of education provided by the staff of Saint Anthony ("Toward a Better Christian Education and Building of Character," July 1966, retrieved from http://toto.lib.unca.edu/findingaids/mss/housing_authority_city_asheville/boxes_001_admin.com).

According to Father Scott, discipline emphasized respect for others, especially for the teachers. Students stood in unison when a teacher or older person entered the room, and marched in order from class to playground and back. John Williams (personal communication, February 2, 2008) remembered well that the nuns enforced discipline by using paddles. Alumnus Lonnie Gilliam recalls, as reported in *The Community Improver*, "Failure was not an option. Even though all the students in the school were poor, our families wanted us to have this great education."

Architecturally, the church-school was laid out in the form of a cross and was finished with yellow tapestry brick. Centered above the arched doorway was an emblem depicting the crossed hands of St. Anthony with his palms displaying the stigmata, marks suggesting the wounds on the crucified body of Christ. Large corridors and a modern lighting system allowed light to create a sunny, cheerful atmosphere. The school installed regulation desks throughout the classrooms and made use of a steam radiator system ("120 Enrolled in Catholic Negro School," *Asheville Times*, November 27, 1936).

Asheville resident Henry Robinson claimed teachers at St. Anthony's had to be superb professionals because their students entered Stephens-Lee with knowledge that was two or three grades ahead of the other students (personal communication, April 8, 2009). At a reunion in 1999 as quoted in the black history month column in the *Asheville Citizen-Times*, February 2, 2004, Lonnie Gilliam said, "I think every single one of us would say ... that the education we got here was superior to any school in the ... state of North Carolina." By the late 1960s, administrators faced an increasing challenge to continue operating the school. Declining enrollment, due to the integration of the public schools, and a shortage of nuns were contributing factors to the school's closure. However, the school had continued for over thirty years producing dozens of community leaders, including doctors, lawyers, educators, ministers, and nonprofit and corporate executives.

Alleghany County: An 1884 business directory lists the number of public schools for "colored" children at three and for white children at 26 (Bryan, 2009). The county schools were separate for the two races from 1884 until integration was accomplished in 1965. The schools were Gap Civil Elementary, Cherry Lane Elementary, and one that assembled at the Pleasant Hill Baptist Church in Laurel Springs. There was never a high school for black students in Alleghany County, but there was one for white students in Sparta. Bus transportation was provided for students who completed the eighth grade to attend Lincoln Heights High School in North Wilkesboro. At one time Clay Bryan served as the bus driver. Among the black teachers in Alleghany County were J.M. Hickerson, Ms. Paskal, Regina Brown Parham, Lucile Carson, and Byrdia Kilpatrick (D. Brewer, personal communication, November 19, 2009).

According to Bryan (2009), the new Cherry Lane Elementary School, built in 1950, had two rooms, two bathrooms, a basement, and a lunchroom. Two teachers divided the grades, with one teaching grades one through four and the other, grades five through eight. After the new building was completed, children from Gap Civil, Piney Creek, Laurel Springs, Ennice and Glade Valley attended school there. The school closed with the advent of integration.

Catawba County: While teachers were establishing schools in wide-ranging communities, education was still in need of help and of more committed teachers. Slavery had cast a dark shadow on learning that lasted for decades extending into the twentieth century.

Cherry Lane School in Alleghany County was built in 1950 and served black students until integration came in 1965. With no high school available in the county, students then traveled by bus to Lincoln Heights High School in Wilkes County. In 1940–41 Cherry Lane had a perfect average daily attendance record of 19 for its 19 students (courtesy Alleghany Historical-Genealogical Society).

In Hickory, John F. Smyre, the son of slaves, devoted his life and money to improving conditions for members of the black community. His parents had been denied an education. By the first decade in the 1900s, he was part of reversing the trend — entering the classroom as a teacher rather than being denied entrance as a student.

Juggling several jobs to accomplish his goal to help his neighbors, Smyre worked as a garbage collector, a janitor, and a yardman. In the early hours of the day, Smyre fired the furnace at Henkel Boarding House and made rounds waking other workers. In 1908, Smyre invested capital in a grocery store, which failed due to his overextending credit, but in 1912 he founded "Smyre's Charitable Institute," a school that stressed manners and character (Freeze, 2002). Limited to a $36 annual budget, Smyre trained black children during the summertime to master social skills as a means of coping with the challenges of living in a segregated society. Some of his white employers contributed small amounts to the institute.

The school continued into the 1940s. Beginning with only four students, the institute grew to an average attendance of between 50 and 75 students each session. The enthusiastic pupils met in churches and paid a dime a week in the beginning, then 15 cents a week during the New Deal with discounts allowed for families with more than one child attending. However, no child was ever turned away for lack of money. Working with his daughter Lottie Barbour, Smyre sought "to train children's heads, hearts, and hands for a life in progress." He and Barbour stressed the value of hard work and polite manners.

The curriculum, informal as it was, changed depending upon the age and abilities of the students. The students listened to Bible stories, learned the basics of sewing, drew pictures if paper were available, and developed basic reading skills by using books donated by white supporters. Always music was a part of the school day. More than 500 children attended the Institute, including future teachers such as Lottie Barbour, Carrie Johnson, Rose Agnes Gaston, and Taft Jordan. On Emancipation Day, which coincides with New Year's Day, Smyre modeled an appreciative spirit for freedom by providing celebratory music to any and all listeners on the streets of Bobtown (Freeze, 2002).

In Hickory itself, teachers faced other trials. Because Hickory was the largest town in Catawba County, the staff often had students from nearby counties: Alexander, Burke, and Caldwell. Black students from those counties lived with relatives or commuted to attend segregated schools. During times of economic crunch, black families found temporary living quarters so they could seek employment.

Blacks took advantage of local economic opportunities. At the turn of the century, gold mining was a successful industry in Catawba. The county was part of one of the largest gold producing areas in the entire country and provided jobs, though often arduous and backbreaking, for a lot of people. By 1904, Catawba was the site of 20 schools for black communities, eight of which were log, and all schools, for both white and black pupils, were equipped with desks built by hand from local materials. In 1910, with the graded school system established for county schools, 158 black students and 352 white students were enrolled. Soon schools in the prospering city of Hickory were overcrowded with 250 black students sharing four small rooms.

Despite its growth, Hickory was near the bottom of Western North Carolina towns in teacher salaries, and higher salaries often lured teachers to other places. During the 1920s, black schools received the benefit of new facilities, but their schools lacked centralization. After 1927, four schools received help from the Rosenwald Fund. By 1929, two black schools had buses or trucks. Though the white enrollment grew impressively, Bobtown student figures, increasing to 368 by 1925, were not notable. However, both white and black students ranked first in attendance in their respective categories in 1927 (Freeze, 2002).

Rutherford County: Thomas Kilgore, Jr., accomplished civil rights leader and minister who spent a large part of his boyhood in Brevard, North Carolina, began teaching in Rutherford County. In his memoir *A Servant's Journey* (1998), Kilgore shares the circumstances of his being hired as a teacher: A recent unemployed graduate of Morehouse College, Kilgore volunteered to drive his sister-in-law to Forest City where she had a job as a teacher. En route she asked to stop at the county school superintendent's office in Rutherfordton. At the office, Kilgore was approached by Mrs. Dennis, a Jeanes supervisor, who offered him a position as principal and teacher in the three-teacher school at Doggetts Grove. He accepted. His school was a three-room frame building on an unpaved road, but he was able to board with the family across from the school. Kilgore's salary was $58 monthly, and his room and board was $15 monthly.

The white superintendent advised Kilgore not to have school programs at night because the neighborhood was full of hoodlums and disorderly men. By the time he received this warning, Kilgore had already planned a Christmas program and had sent out invitations. Always innovative, he moved forward with the event. On the evening of the performance, parents and their children packed the two rooms that had been combined into an auditorium.

Before the program began, the courageous educator detected a fire burning near the school and found a group of men gambling at the edge of the school grounds. He invited them to the program, and all but two accepted the offer. In his three years as the school principal there were no problems with unruly outsiders.

Kilgore's wife-to-be, Jeannetta Miriam Scott, taught in the small village of Henrietta, about five miles from Doggetts Grove. As newlyweds in 1937, the Kilgores requested that she be transferred to Doggetts Grove and the superintendent granted their request.

During the 1938 summer, Kilgore accepted the position of principal in the public black school in Waynesville, a segregated three-teacher school. In addition to tending to administrative responsibilities, Kilgore also taught grades 7, 8, and 9. His wife had accepted a position to teach at Grahamtown High School in Forest City. Although their careers eventually led them far from North Carolina, the Kilgores contributed to the education of rural mountain children. Kilgore, educated at the Brevard Rosenwald School, was himself one of those children (Reed, 2004).

He exemplifies the student-turning-teacher trend as well as the socially responsive spirit. Teachers transformed, but first they were students whose minds were ignited by previous teachers, who came in all forms and served with loyalty and with distinction.

Lifted by Energetic Students

Regardless of race, families required mountain children to care for babies, look after younger siblings, pick apples, gather hay, stack fodder, feed animals, milk cows, and lend a hand in any way needed to contribute to family needs. Such tasks often conflicted with school attendance but served to reinforce the work ethic taught at home and in the classroom. However, conditions were primitive in fledgling schools for both white and black students. For example, toilet facilities in the early mountain schools were minimal. At times a certain stretch of woods or bushes was designated for boys to use and another stretch for girls.

Despite their difficulties, children always enjoyed a chance to play. Although early schools owned no playground equipment, children found ways to play: tag, leap frog, hop scotch, jump rope, marbles, kite flying, hide and seek, ball, ante-over, blind man's bluff, and playhouse. Their energy abounded and added resilience to their student lives.

Their stories still reverberate in the mountains of Western North Carolina. They also echo book learning and group yearning.

Libby Viola Payne: Payne's time at Edneyville School was sandwiched in between morning and evening chores at home. Sometimes students misbehaved — and that brought consequences. She remembered two punishments. Mischievous students were required to stand on one foot and to hold sentences in front of themselves.

"I wanted to learn, and it was hard," she recalled. "We got books that white students threw away. I believe children got better educated in segregated schools. The reason for integration was that no high school was furnished. We integrated to get a high school education." Recess provided an opportunity to play outside.

According to Payne, all her teachers were helpful, especially Sally Hill, who used her own car to transport her students — Libby, Frances Littlejohn, and Laurel Bell Payne — to town. On Fridays the teacher gave the students a party and served special treats, "little goodies," such as Jell-o and cookies. Pupils played games, sang songs and practiced reciting poetry. Once an Asheville church invited the school children to present a program for its congregation — a great opportunity for rural students. Every holiday there were school programs for the parents. Both parents and teachers made appropriate costumes for the young actors. After completing seven grades at Edneyville, students participated in a graduation ceremony with the girls dressed in white, if possible. Teachers borrowed sports jackets, white shirts, and ties for the boys. Each graduating student made a speech (personal communication, March 5, 2005).

Gladys Russell Freeman, a resident of Tampa, Florida, shared vivid memories of attending school in Edneyville. Her father, Calvin Russell, had served as a school committeeman in the 1920s with Cleo Waters and Richard Littlejohn. Russell's older siblings had Ruth Bell as their instructor, but when Gladys enrolled in the first grade in 1921, Belle Suddreth had replaced Ruth Bell and taught grades 1–6, and occasionally 7 and 8. Suddreth called each grade

Edneyville School in Henderson County received a caution regarding fire safety in 1942, but was abandoned for school purposes in 1947. John and Ruth Montgomery purchased the building, which, after renovation, became the living room of their home (pictured here), where they have lived for more than 50 years. Ruth's mother, Odie Mills Littlejohn, taught at the school (courtesy Henderson County Board of Public Education).

up front for its lessons. The front included a stage, a black board, and a teacher's desk and chair.

As at many black schools, a wood burning pot-bellied stove heated the facility. Freeman recalled what happened once when the stove overheated and the roof caught on fire. Local people rushed to extinguish the blaze, for there was no community fire station.

Freeman's memories of school life in the 1920s are remarkably vivid. She recalled names of teachers and students as well as the daily routine of school life. Living on the brink of the Great Depression did not prevent her family from buying their own school supplies. Her parents invested hard-earned money in books and in writing materials for their children. She detailed specifics about those provisions and about other physical features of the Edneyville School:

> Lunches—there was no free anything back then. We took our lunch. My parents bought our textbooks—pencils, everything—and it made my father mad because all the students whose parents couldn't afford them used our books. Our school was off St. Paul Road. At the school there were two toilets. Before they were built, people went behind the tree—that was what had to be done. One toilet was for the girls and one for the boys—but the one for the boys broke down. It rotted out so then there was only one [personal communication, February 15, 2007].

Freeman's comments also reveal facts about the lifestyles of the teachers as well as contrasts with the white community. According to Freeman, Emma Littlejohn allowed teachers to board in her large white house. Sally Hill may have boarded with Littlejohn. Also, the first male teacher at Edneyville was Henry Darity. Later a woman named Crawford began teaching, but during her second year she became pregnant and school board policy and community sentiment required that she resign, even though she was married (personal communication, February 15, 2007). It was deemed flirting with immorality to allow a pregnant woman in the classroom.

A low enrollment forced the closing of Edneyville Colored School, so for a time students traveled to East Flat Rock Colored School. Later consolidation opened the way for Edneyville's black students to attend Ninth Avenue School in Hendersonville. Freeman's father helped build the Edneyville School for white children, but its doors were closed to his own offspring. However, one of his descendants broke that barrier, for decades later, his granddaughter, Freeman's niece, graduated from Edneyville High School.

Both Payne and Freeman indicated that white Edneyville residents were their friends. Libby Payne and her new groom went to a corn shucking after their wedding that was a mixed black-and-white affair. One of their African-American friends lived and worked with a local white family. "We knew which whites to associate with and which not to," Payne said. "The Jones family would come to our house to borrow a cup of sugar or flour, and we would do the same. Others we avoided."

Freeman continued, "Some white children who rode the school bus would taunt the black children as they walked to their school. They would yell things like "Goody, goody, you're walkin' while we're ridin.'" Attacking children of another color of skin was so common that it was expected (personal communication, March 5, 2005).

Joe L. Mills: In his Brickton neighborhood near Fletcher, Joe L. Mills grew up where men labored in a brickyard to mine clay and to shape bricks that were hardened in kilns. Parents also aimed to build a better life a brick at a time. In this community, Mills attended Brickton School, erected in 1930, for five years. His teacher, Gustava Robinson, taught five grades in the two-room school, which had ample window space and a platform in one room that was used as a stage for special programs. Each grade consisted of only four students, 20 in all.

The normal procedure consisted of receiving the day's assignment, doing it, and being

Brickton School near Fletcher was designed by Erle G. Stillwell in July of 1928 and was constructed by blacks in 1930 but it ceased operating as a school in 1952 when Henderson County's black students began attending the consolidated Ninth Avenue School in Hendersonville. The Brickton building continued to be used by the community until its demolition at the close of the twentieth century. Among the teachers who taught Brickton students were Mary E. Hansberry, Adella L. Epps, and Emily M. Carson (courtesy Henderson County Board of Public Education).

quiet. Students had to do their lessons, know their lessons, or face being held back. There was no social promotion. Brickton students used a stage where plays were performed for the community's enjoyment.

Mills' hardships typify circumstances students had to overcome. After losing his father when he was nine years old, Joe Mills stayed out of school to help earn money to pay funeral expenses. Robinson told him he had completed enough of that year's work to be promoted, but there was another stipulation to move ahead to the next grade. Robinson required participation in an annual field trip to the Great Smoky Mountains as a condition of promotion and explained that if he failed to participate he would not pass. Since his work commitment precluded going the Great Smokies, Mills was not promoted, but he found happier school days when he attended elementary school in town. There he was a member of the school patrol, which was sponsored by the Veterans of Foreign Wars (VFW).

For Mills, as for others, special activities were uplifting. Once a year all patrol members from both white and black schools descended on the local VFW for an interracial event that included dinner and games. May Day activities provided another highlight with field day competition. Events included pitching horseshoes, a sack race, a ball toss, and 50- and 100-yard dashes. The day culminated with wrapping the May Pole. Someone found a pole in the woods, dug a hole, placed the pole there, and decorated it with beautiful crepe paper ribbons. According to Mills, the last one left standing won a prize (personal communication, March 12, 2007).

Clifford Lynch: Henderson County resident Clifford Lynch (personal communication, March 8, 2005) attended Ninth Avenue School, formerly Sixth Avenue, beginning in the first grade. Remembering teachers who made a difference, he described Mary Lou Cunningham and Annie Fowler as "good teachers." During his elementary years, Lynch's favorite pastimes were studying science and playing. He also believed music was an important part of school life. He clearly recalls other routines: Teachers opened school by calling the roll, reading a Bible passage, assigning one student to sharpen all the pencils, and collecting that day's lunch money. Being chosen as the class "pencil sharpener" was an honor.

Lynch vividly recounts the consequence of arriving at school without a completed homework assignment. For that infraction, he received a spanking with a thick paddle and a note to deliver to his parents. As was the custom in African American homes, a spanking at school meant a spanking at home. Lynch remembers the double dose of discipline, and he never forgot his homework again. However, he does admit to playing hooky. Passing up the school lunch, Lynch was allowed to eat at his cousin's house located near the school. On those days the temptation to cut afternoon classes was often too strong for a young fellow to resist.

In addition, he believes all personnel, whether teachers or the school staff, influenced the educational atmosphere. As proof, Lynch cited the school janitor, Earl Mitchum, as a positive influence on young pupils.

Elizabeth Haynes: The former student described Black Mountain's Carver School simply (personal communication, September 9, 2007). Students were typically confined to one classroom for most of the school day with lunchtime and recess allowing a change of pace. Carver's teachers emphasized basic subjects such as reading, writing, arithmetic, and English. Lunchtime brought appealing, nutritious foods. A special treat, according to Haynes, was the "fresh made-from-scratch baked bread."

Recess was joyful as the rambunctious youngsters played together. Parents were very much involved in the school and attended holiday activities, school plays, and competitive sports. A number of alumni from Carver have found success in education, in the ministry, and in civic organizations.

Clifton Roland: When he was 84, Roland shared his elementary school experiences (personal communication, November 16, 2007). During the late 1920s and the early 1930s, he attended Higgins School in Yancey County. He remembers a two-room school with two teachers and an outhouse and a pot bellied stove. He still recalls teachers' names: Mrs. Louis Kerns, Ruby Beard, Charity H. Griffins. However, his memories also reflect the poverty and the lack of adequate equipment. Teachers broke pencils in half so there would be enough to go around. Students carried sandwiches to school and drank water from a nearby spring.

Later Roland attended Weaverville and Hill Street, where boyish mischief led to a whipping. Roland learned to hate winter cold and summer heat in those classrooms. However, he believes teachers did all right "considering what they had to work with."

Students recall routine patterns and methods that they found annoying. However, they gave positive ratings to most of their school experiences because they knew they were learning. They recognized benefits that paid off in later life.

Patricia Roland (wife of Clifton): Like others, Patricia Roland recalls that her Hill Street instructor Beatrice Chambers disciplined her "quite a bit" (personal communication, May 23, 2007). Roland explained that her attention span was short, and Chambers found the little girl doing as she pleased rather than doing as she was told. Chambers' method of discipline was to bend the hand back and hit it with a ruler. Teachers, Roland said, were strict and focused on students learning their lessons.

After Hill Street, Roland attended Asheland Avenue School. Explaining that she walked to school, Roland related that school went on in all kinds of weather — rain, sleet, or sunshine. At Asheland, she found her teachers were also strict. Even as a child, she disapproved of the method used for reading instruction. "In reading we had to be able to recite what we read or stay after school or stay in," she said. "The teacher wanted word for word with no mistakes."

However, looking back, Roland believes she was taught well overall. She felt her schooling prepared her to assume the role of activist as a young married woman. Roland demonstrated in front of Winn-Dixie, a grocery where blacks could spend their money but could not be hired in any but menial positions. "I thought it was time for segregation to end so I picketed Winn-Dixie," Roland said. "I walked out front, and Lyndia [her young daughter] was with me. The manager wouldn't hire blacks."

Alma Lee Shippy: In Swannanoa, where there were two elementary schools, Upper and Lower Swannanoa, before consolidation, a student found a door to new opportunities. Shippy, the young man who was the first black student to enroll at Warren Wilson College in 1953, attended Swannanoa School, which remains on its original site but is now a private residence. In 1940, the principal was James T. Sapp, who also worked as a red cap at the railroad depot. Both he and his wife were well-trained teachers (Styles, personal communication, August 7, 2007). According to Shippy, Sapp was a dynamic teacher who knew how to work a classroom, to inspire learning, and to demand attention and respect.

The cloakroom, where coats, sweaters, caps and lunches were kept, also provided private space for corporal punishment, as at other schools. Sapp used his belt sparingly, but students realized they were faced with that possibility. At times a glance from Sapp was all it took to win a student back to his lesson. Shippy also recalled difficult circumstances during his elementary school experience. The school had drinking water piped inside the building, but outhouses provided toilet facilities. Students raised their hands to speak, but if they needed to request permission to use the outhouse, they raised only a finger.

The school opened on snow days, but early dismissal was a possibility. "We would stand by the pot-bellied stoves. There were two, one for each room," Shippy said. "One guy would be designated to come by and start a fire each morning. I think he got 25 or 50 cents, and then he would get to go to the store. We had to have permission to go during school, but Mr.

Buncombe County had an Upper and a Lower Swannanoa School for the black community and eventually combined the schools in this building. Swannanoa students received instruction in reading, music, art, chair caning, basket weaving, and making corn shuck mats, and displayed their crafts at the school and at the county fair. After this school closed in the early 1950s to consolidate with the school at Black Mountain, the building was converted to a private residence (courtesy William A. Reed).

Sapp loved Luden's or Smith Bros. cough drops. He just had to have them so sometimes I got to be the one to get his cough drops" (personal communications, January 31, 2006).

At lunch students retrieved their bags or buckets from the cloakroom, because there was no lunchroom at the school. Nearby a woman in her 70s or 80s would often plan a hot treat for the school children. She would carry goodies, baked apples, potatoes or roasted ears of corn in her apron and deliver the food to the school.

School programs, including plays, provided entertainment for the entire community. Programs were

The youthful James Thaddeus Sapp became the teacher and principal at Swannanoa School and later a teacher and the director of safety patrol at Carver Elementary School. Sapp taught 19 years in the Lower Swannanoa school and two years in Upper Swannanoa; when Swannanoa School, with an enrollment of 50, merged with the Black Mountain Elementary School for Negroes, with its enrollment of 101, Sapp continued his career in education at the new facility. He kept his teaching skills up to date by attending the Summer Institute for Teachers held at Hill Street School in conjunction with Winston-Salem State Teachers College (courtesy Swannanoa Valley Museum).

In 1952 Alma Shippy, former student at Swannanoa Elementary School and a graduate of Stephens-Lee High School, became the first black man to enroll in a private college located in the old Confederacy. A pioneer in the history of civil rights, Shippy hitched a ride in a friend's pick-up truck and rode to the other side of the tracks in Swannanoa to accept the invitation to enroll at then Warren Wilson Junior College — without fanfare, media coverage, or an armed bodyguard. This trailblazer in racial integration met with Rodney Lytle (right), and Billy Edd Wheeler (left) circa 2003 to plan Alma Shippy Day at Warren Wilson College. Wheeler, a white musician and songwriter, was Shippy's college roommate in the early 1950s. Rodney Lytle, a 1973 graduate of Warren Wilson College and now director of alumni affairs, said Shippy gained unprecedented support from the student body during the days of Jim Crow. When Shippy went to a movie, his white friends escorted him through the back door and sat with him in the theater balcony and when he was denied service in a restaurant his friends exited the building with him (courtesy Warren Wilson College Archives).

scheduled for the early evening so parents would be able to attend. Accordion doors would be pushed aside, and there was room for the entire neighborhood population to be seated. Families from Upper and Lower Swannanoa — Dillinghams, Smiths, Dorseys, Johnsons, Whittingtons — attended the plays and clapped enthusiastically for the young actors.

Shippy explained that the school also provided a venue for Saturday afternoon movies. "The floors would be oiled down, and adults could come for 25 cents and kids for 10 cents," he said. "Some folks sold roasted peanuts. A black guy from Asheville showed the movies, mostly old westerns. It was really a lot of fun" (personal communication, January 31, 2006).

For a time Sapp provided transportation to school in his own car. He started early and picked up students who lived too far away for easy walking. Later the state provided a small van, and finally the county arranged bus transportation. Mrs. Wilson, another teacher, drove "a little Ford" and picked up Shippy on her way from Asheville.

Later a third teacher, Mrs. Russell, rode the Trailways bus, got off on Highway 70 and walked to the school. Russell was a musician who played the piano and led in singing during the morning devotional period. After Bible reading and prayer, students sang the "Battle Hymn of the Republic" and pledged allegiance to the flag.

Shippy remembers that Sapp stressed lessons in arithmetic, spelling and English. Shippy participated in spelling bees, which created a competitive spirit even for poor spellers, who were caught up in the excitement of hoping their friend or favorite speller would win. Of course, the prize was only bragging rights, but parents and neighbors also kept up with who won that week's spelling bee.

Shippy recalled that a lot of stress was placed on the students' shoulders. Not only was each scholar expected to complete his assignment, but he also had to present it before the class, a difficult task for young children.

However, Shippy learned to speak to an audience and did that throughout his life. Before being accepted at Warren Wilson College in 1952, a young Shippy addressed a gathering of 300 individuals in the college chapel. In retrospect, Shippy appreciates the expectation on the part of both Sapp and Wilson that he would learn. Such teachers, described by Shippy as "firm" and "hard," often brought out the best in their students.

Sapp also allowed passers-by who wanted to attend class to come into the school. About 50 pupils attended regularly, but older students had Mr. Sapp's permission to sit in on classes when they could. A number of those young people hoped to learn to write their names, to read a few sentences, and to do a little arithmetic.

Shippy, who was raised by his grandmother, Ludie Lytle White, who could neither read nor write, became her teacher during his student days. "My grandmother raised me, and I had to show her respect," he said. "When I was in high school, I taught her how to read and write. She loved writing her name. When I went away, she could write me letters. Later I opened a class for adults who couldn't read or write. Writing their names was a really big thing" (personal communication, January 31, 2006).

As expected by the community, students completing the highest grade offered at their elementary school were honored at a graduation ceremony, a formal commencement exercise with dignified music. All graduates dressed for the occasion and spent time learning and practicing their recitations. The event filled the students and the onlookers with pride (Shippy, personal communication, January 31, 2006).

Having graduated from Swannanoa Elementary School, Shippy then traveled to Asheville to attend Asheland Avenue School. It was a larger school with six or seven teachers. However, the most "beautiful" time was recess when students were allowed to spend time outdoors. At times teachers would give out fruit—figs, raisins, or prunes—for students to snack on during recess.

Geraldine Coone Ray: In Weaverville, about 10 miles north of Asheville, another black school served several communities. The building itself remains in use as a community center. When the Reems Creek Road near Weaverville was being widened, the town of Weaverville rescued the school by purchasing it and moving it to a new site. Located at the bottom of a steep hill, the school was rolled on logs to its present location. Children gathered to watch men engaged in the arduous task of placing a two-room school on a makeshift pulley of logs so they could maneuver the building to the top of the hill. Later, Little Mt. Zion Baptist Church purchased the building.

One of today's Weaverville residents, Ray studied at the school and enthusiastically shared its history. According to her, Weaverville students who lived in outlying neighborhoods, such as Alexander, Reems Creek, Dola Springs, and Barnardsville, traveled to Weaverville where eight grades of study were available.

Ray explained that transportation to the school was at times a hardship. "I had to walk a half mile to catch the bus. We didn't have a good bus. There was lots of pushing and walking when the bus broke down. The buses were hard to heat. We finally did get a panel-like bus when I was in eighth grade," Ray said.

Ray described her teachers: Amanda Horn, "a fine lady who lived near the school," and Monnie Jones. Horn taught the primary grades, and Jones taught the upper grades. "Both were very strict," Ray said. "Monnie was my cousin, but she was serious about her teaching. I had to tow the line." During the time that Ray's parents, Howard and Odessa Coone, attended Weaverville Colored School, Ethel Mills (née Kennedy) taught there. "She taught there when it was just a one-room school."

When students arrived on cold mornings to begin the school day, Weaverville Colored School was already warm. "We had a pot bellied stove. We stored coal underneath the school. There was a cellar with a square door and steps.... Boys would go down and carry the coal up.... Boys picked up branches and sticks to get the fire started," Ray explained. "We burned coal, and the cinders were spread out on the wet playground.... Two rooms made up the school's study space. Inside there was a kind of cloakroom with nails to hang coats on ... like a wall that was a room divider. We could slide two doors [for special programs]. There was a table for us to set our lunches on until time to eat."

At lunchtime, students were allowed to sit at their desks or outside on the porch. "We had baloney sandwiches and beans. Some days my future husband's mother, Elizabeth Ray, brought vegetable soup and bread. On that day we each carried a bowl to school." Older students were often allowed to walk to Weaverville. "There they could visit the drugstore, and at times teachers sent them into town to run errands," she said.

Ray described other details about the school routine: Mornings at school began with music and devotions. Lessons at Weaverville Colored School included Bible classes each Wednesday. For years the Reverend Dendy conducted the classes. Later Dorothy Russell replaced him. Ray recalls the excitement of Russell's flannel graph stories. The Bible classes were part of the school curriculum because students were tested and graded on the material.

While Bible knowledge was emphasized once a week, every day there was spelling. "We'd line up around the blackboard from the smartest to the slowest," she said. "We'd write the words on the board or spell it out loud." Ray emphasized that reading, arithmetic, and penmanship were also stressed. Once a year the school handed out academic awards, such as plaques and certificates. Also, promotions were not guaranteed. Failing students had to repeat their grade.

According to Ray, the students and the community took pride in keeping the building well maintained. She recalled the activities in remarkable detail. It was the scene of community activities after school hours. There were games, suppers, and meetings about parent concerns. PTA meetings were held so public awareness of the building's condition contributed to its being well kept. Janitors, such as John Ray, Robert and Daniel Cowan, and Nathaniel Brooks conscientiously cared for the school.

The example they set was emulated by the students of yesterday and by Weaverville citizens today. For such an old structure, "our school," as the community center is frequently called, is amazingly well preserved.

The joy of recess reigned at the Weaverville School, but boundaries were set. "Girls and boys were not allowed to play together at recess. Girls played on one side and boys on the other," Ray said. "We girls played ball, hopscotch, ring around the rosy. It was fun! On Fridays, if it didn't rain, we would play up on the hill, play ball, and some Fridays we would walk down to the creek and back—a long hike. On Friday all of us had ball games.... We had no equipment ... had to make do. We used outside toilets."

Ray also recalled that her ideal school sometimes experienced conflict. Weaverville teachers were challenged by student misbehavior. In Ray's recollections, "cutting up" and "fighting" were two common causes for punishment. If spankings were necessary, teachers marched the offenders to the cloakroom to suffer their humiliation in semi-privacy.

Students were trained to take part in special school events, such as plays and oral recitations. Ray remembered the tradition of drawing names for Christmas gifts and planning a Christmas program. Ray had the lead role in "L'il Red Riding Hood." For that performance she was costumed in a red suit. For musical programs, Monnie Jones played the piano. Also, May Day activities featured special field day competitions. At the eighth-grade graduation ceremony, each student received a diploma and best wishes.

Substitute teachers were rare at Weaverville Colored School. However, teachers sometimes attended classes to renew or advance their certificates and missed work. For example, Monnie Jones studied in Rogersville, Tennessee, and Rosa LaPearl Jones filled in during her absence. Horn was seriously injured in a train wreck on a trip to Philadelphia. During her absence, Margarite Dixon McArath took over. McArath is reported to have been the granddaughter of the renowned Isaac Dickson.

White people expressed interest in the school. R.A. Tomberlin, principal at the Weaverville White School, routinely visited the school and made efforts to get what the teachers needed. A dentist also periodically checked students' teeth. According to Ray, Weaverville was an integrated community with a lot of interaction between the races. Children of both races resorted to name-calling, but the Golden Rule was generally put into practice. However, blacks had to use back doors and take back seats. At restaurants in Weaverville, blacks placed their orders at the rear entrance.

Although Ray enjoyed her elementary school experiences, she sometimes wishes there had been a lunchroom and an indoor toilet. Like many black children whose parents had been forced to leave Western North Carolina to earn a better wage, Ray was raised by grandparents Chedester and Estella Coone. Her grandfather farmed and made extra money by cutting wood and logging. He also owned a blacksmith shop. After graduating from Stephens-Lee, Ray opted not to continue her education so she could care for her grandmother, whose rheumatoid arthritis had confined her to a wheelchair. Ray, however, was able to study art by correspondence.

All students have to take their first steps on the road to educational accomplishments. Otherwise, learning never happens. However, once it begins, even students who explore distractions on sidetracks eventually return to the main path, which always goes upward. They soon learn to ask, "What's next?" Happy school experiences, as evident in student memories decades afterward, increase the chances that learning may "take." For African Americans in Appalachian North Carolina, that "next" became help from an outside source and the possibility of completing high school — turning a dream into a reality (personal communication, November 28, 2007).

Oddie Cox: "Professor" Cox, the grandson of slaves and a teacher-principal at Bristol School for Negroes in Ashe County, studied during the summers at the Agricultural and Technical (A&T) College in Greensboro. Beginning at age 46, Cox commenced with basic classes in spelling, writing, and arithmetic because his elementary school had failed to prepare him well. Then he continued with courses such as botany, biology, chemistry, geography, and child psychology for 23 summers. What motivated him in course selection was not what was required to earn a degree, but what would benefit his students as he worked with them in the classroom. He explored course offerings to determine which would most interest and benefit his students.

The summer before Cox's death, Lewis C. Dowdy, A&T's acting president, in conjunction with his associates at the college decided Oddie Cox should receive a degree based on his accomplishments, which could be presented either then or at the college commencement.

Given a preference, Cox chose to wait until the graduation date to accept his degree so he could receive it formally with pomp and circumstance dressed in cap and gown with friends looking on from the audience. Sadly, a fire at his home took Cox's life before that graduation event occurred, but his success as a teacher lives on. His degree was awarded posthumously.

Cox exemplifies the ideal student-teacher. He both taught and learned. Also, he led and inspired. The school where Cox performed the role of student-teacher still stands, but more importantly his model still lives. He did not have a desk in an elementary school, but he was a man memorializing the value of an energizing education and of assisting youth to make the most of school experiences and to yearn for higher-level learning experiences that were yet to come for African Americans.

Victimized by Segregation

One drop of "colored" blood confined an individual to the label "black." Members of school boards became embroiled in demands that a child was ineligible to attend a white school. The 1916 Buncombe County school board minutes document a sad episode. In Fairview township, hostile white parents objected to admitting the children of O.G. Cox into the white school because Cox's father was supposedly a "colored man."

Numerous witnesses testified that Cox was considered a member of the white race. His mother, a woman of advanced years, provided an affidavit stating that Isaac Lyda, a white man, had fathered her son. Those challenging the right of his two school-age children to enroll in the white school were required to produce evidence that Cox was indeed colored. In subsequent sessions, Cox identified the mother of his children as his wife, a white woman, and offered an explanation for his father's identity being shrouded in secrecy. Cox said his own mother was unwilling to identify Isaac Lyda as her child's father because Lyda was married to another woman at the time of his conception and birth. Such a revelation would have unnerved the Lyda household and the community. His mother, refusing to stir flames of notoriety that would have hurt her lover's family, chose to raise her child alone.

Cox asserted that he himself had not been denied the right to attend white schools in Henderson County. His neighbor, J.J. Taylor, testified that Cox's people were of a dark complexion and that Isaac Lyda was also dark complexioned. Other witnesses swore under oath that Bill Owens, a colored man, was Cox's father. Attorneys presented affidavits building the case for both sides. No evidence in the days before DNA testing could be objectively analyzed. However, the challenge undoubtedly created stress and unhappiness in the Cox family. The time-consuming conflict indicated how rampant racial charges were throughout Western North Carolina (Buncombe County Board of Education minutes, 1916).

In the early 1900s, Watauga County's Board of Education ordered the superintendent to give notice to one father that his children were ineligible to attend the white school because their blood was not pure. Two months later, the parent received official notice that he should withdraw his children from the white school—"it being shown to the satisfaction of the board that they have some strain of Negro blood" (Corbitt, p. 45).

Buncombe County schools implemented another extreme that included an unconventional segregated institution for members of the Anderson family and others. Students assigned to the Anderson School near Barnardsville were predominantly white with the racial characteristics of Caucasians. Forcing the extended Anderson family, regarded as a mixed race, to attend a school specified for neither whites nor blacks resulted in heartache and bitterness. It is sometimes difficult to distinguish between fact and fiction concerning the Barnardsville citizens.

Geraldine Coone Ray explained that, according to family stories, her aunt had moved to Maney Branch in North Buncombe County and there had married an Anderson man with roots in Darlington, South Carolina, a union that crossed racial lines. The Anderson family shared a burial ground with Ray's relatives (personal communication, November 28, 2007).

By 1904, the county school system references a dilemma about providing for offspring of a mixed race or of interracial marriages. On March 12, the board ordered that contracts be awarded to provide a school building for children of a mixed race in the Ivy Township so school could commence that spring. The order did not designate that an actual school building would serve such children, but that space be found in which to conduct classes.

A long list of apportionments made from the general school fund, 1917-1918, to black schools at the April 3, 1917, county school board meeting included the amount of $75 for Anderson School in Ivy Township, District 10. Other schools receiving these allotments are labeled colored, but the Anderson School is designated "mixed." On April 1, 1918, after ordering an appropriation of $30 for the Colored Summer School, the board again allotted District 10, Mixed, of the Ivy Township the sum of $100 and provided the same amount to District 11, Colored. In 1918, the two schools received identical amounts: $135.

According to the December 11, 1926 minutes, board members gave permission for Ruby Hicks' child to enroll at the Paint Fork School. A few weeks later, February 7, 1927, the board ruled definitively that Paul and Lillie Hicks were not colored children. According to S.G. Bernard, a member of the Buncombe County Board of Education, the Hicks children were not more than one sixteenth Negro. Classified as "not colored," they were eligible to attend a school for whites. Addressing the racial heritage of students proved to be a frequent task for school boards throughout the region.

On May 6, 1927, the board decided it would be best for the Anderson children to have their own school. That decision may have been the board's way of protecting children of a mixed race from being persecuted at an all-white school. However, the decision also raises a serious charge about the brutality of segregation.

Evidence indicates that, though isolated from potential white and black classmates, the Anderson clan received routine administrative services, such as the appointment of citizens to oversee the material needs of Anderson School. However, the board bypassed questions about self-esteem and psychological effects. In 1930, the school board appointed the following school committeemen: Burch Anderson, Meade Anderson, and Bob Anderson. In 1931, the makeup of the committee changed to Lloyd Anderson, Meade Anderson, and Ruby Hicks. The inclusion of Hicks indicates her children, labeled as 1/16 black, were attending the Anderson School. Had they left the white school to escape harassment?

Additional concern about providing a high school education for students at the Anderson School surfaced at the July 7, 1947, board meeting. Appearing with a delegation of interested citizens, Anna B. Metz, a former missionary, requested a high school program be provided for the Anderson Cove children. After explaining the manner used to allot North Carolina teachers and the impossibility of acquiring an additional instructor, the board directed its secretary to contact the State Board of Education regarding the Anderson dilemma "at his convenience."

The record also includes a letter from Nancy Brigman of Barnardsville requesting that her daughter be permitted to continue her schooling beyond what was offered at the Anderson School, a high school education. In 2009, Henderson County School Superintendent Steve Page, who was a former associate superintendent of Buncombe County Schools, explained that tuition had been paid for Anderson students to attend Rabun Gap School in Georgia (personal communication, April 24, 2009).

The next day Superintendent T.C. Roberson drafted a letter to Paul A. Reid of North Carolina's State Board of Education, stating,

> At the meeting ... on July 7, 1947, a delegation from ... Anderson Cove was present with a group of citizens from the City of Asheville requesting the Board of Education to provide high school instruction for the Anderson Cove children.... This is a section where a mixed race is found and the patrons of Barnardsville District will not permit the children to attend school with the white children. Therefore, the children are provided an elementary school with one teacher, the average [daily attendance] being approximately 15....
>
> The Board of Education ... is willing to build an additional room to the present building if this is the solution. We realize that an additional teacher would be a greater expense than we would be able to provide [Letter filed with Board of Education minutes, July 7, 1947].

In a response, dated July 14, 1947, Paul A. Reid, comptroller for the State Board of Education, requested additional information regarding the problem of providing high school instruction at the Anderson School on behalf of the State Board of Education; among the information needed were the number of prospective high school students, the possibility of their attending a nearby high school, and the ability of the Buncombe County School Board to provide tuition of $10 per month per child for the children to attend elsewhere. Evidence of any follow-up to this letter or to the problem at Anderson Cove does not appear in the record.

The Anderson School was inspected two years later by the appointed delegation from Raleigh. In reference to the Anderson School, the committee stated:

> It is difficult to say what should be done with the Anderson School. It is a matter of court record that at least some of the children ... have a very small mixture of Negro blood. [However,] it was difficult for the Committee to detect any in the children.... Undoubtedly community sentiment will not permit these children to be enrolled at Barnardsville [Elementary School], and certainly they would not attend a school specifically designed for Negro children.
>
> Your Committee, therefore, recommends that a permanent building of brick structure be erected for the benefit of these children and that this school be supplied with the best teacher available.... furnished an adequate elementary school program, but they should not be denied the opportunity for a high school education. Every effort should be made to find a high school to which they can be admitted, and the county should bear whatever extra expense is necessary for their attendance in this school [Report of State School Survey Panel, 1949, p. 6].

In 1950, the board awarded the contract for a new Anderson School at its August 25 meeting to architect Henry Gaines; designated Guy Ensley, Don Riddle, Lee Hensley, Woodrow Dillingham, and Mrs. W.C. Embler as the school building committee; developed building contracts on September 18; tabulated bids on October 6; and provided for drilling a well at the Anderson School on June 6, 1951. School officials addressed the needs of at least a dozen children prohibited from attending white or black schools.

Though the Anderson children were not allowed to attend Barnardsville Elementary School, their photographs appeared in the white school's yearbook, according to Barnardsville resident Frankie T. Littrell (personal communication, March 30, 2009). Also, Houston Henderson, a teacher at the Anderson School, and the Barnardsville Elementary School principal transported pans of food from the white school cafeteria to Anderson students.

One former female student, now a senior citizen, spoke emotionally about treatment of Anderson students. "We were treated like trash," she asserted, scowling and pointing her finger for emphasis. "Even Barnardsville churches shut us out. Only the Church of God would allow us to enter their doors. Later on, a missionary church welcomed us, but we started our own church — and that was good."

The former student's husband, not an Anderson School student, expressed the conviction that the name T.C. Roberson should be torn off the high school named in honor of the former school superintendent because, in the gentleman's opinion, Roberson did not improve conditions for students at Anderson School. A Baptist Association group from outside Barnardsville took an interest in providing religious instruction for the Andersons. Another group from Asheville annually brought gifts to students (personal communication, Mary Alice Maney and Frankie T. Littrell, March 30, 2009).

The community mentioned Anderson teachers: Hargrove Carter, Houston Henderson, Flossie Emory, and Louisa Burleson Brigman. Anderson teachers conducted classes for grades 1–7 in a single room. Emory, who had a reputation as an outstanding teacher, taught only at Anderson School prior to integration. Following integration, she taught at Barnardsville Elementary School (Mary Alice Maney, personal communication, May 4, 2009). Alumna Louisa Brigman said Emory was a "hard teacher, very strict, a devil"— a no-nonsense teacher focused on students' learning their lessons and postponing play.

After completing the eighth grade, Anderson students were forced to seek additional education in private schools. Some attended Crossnore School in Avery County. Others went to Rabun Gap in Georgia. A few attended Berea College in Kentucky. Both white and black public schools in Western North Carolina shut them out.

Pearl Hicks, whose mother had also attended the school, was allowed to attend Barnardsville schools, where she excelled. "I wrote her a letter of recommendation to be accepted at Berea College in Kentucky. She went there, became a nurse, and got even more education," said Mary Alice Maney, former Barnardsville postmistress. "We were all proud of her. Others from the school did well. Today the Anderson family excels in business in a big way." (personal communication, March 30, 2009). Though the Anderson family's business acumen has won them success in the twenty-first century, discrimination suffered by earlier generations has left enduring scars.

Stories about elementary schools corroborate the huge leaps required to guarantee eight years of education. However, what nineteenth century North Carolinians did not know is that help was on the way for the next climb upward. Yes, blacks were helping one another to progress higher on the educational trail, but they needed more and better buildings and access to secondary schools. Special help would come with the creation of the Rosenwald Fund, soon to add a major boost from the outside.

Conceptual Path to Schools

It took both an outsider and an insider to stimulate cohesive community effort to nurture educational progress for blacks. Sears Roebuck executive and philanthropist Julius Rosenwald contributed to aiding black rural schools by first forming an interracial partnership with a transplanted Appalachian African American, educator and political leader Booker T. Washington. The partnership added a major impetus to expand and enrich black education in a joint venture with the white community throughout Appalachia and other parts of the South.

The two leaders worked to produce an intense desire in the heart of a community—the key to accomplishing a project dependent upon unity and vision among its players. The goal of the Rosenwald program was to bring about interracial teamwork, not simply to construct newer and better school buildings (Embree and Waxman, 1949). To realize the goal of the Rosenwald-Washington partnership, white and black communities needed to work shoulder to shoulder. By cooperating to provide the means to improve an existing school or to erect a new building, individuals stimulated a strengthening of educational values in rural homes, homes in which parents seldom had more than the most rudimentary formal learning experiences. Parents eking out a living in remote rural communities in Western North Carolina caught the vision of schools that would inspire their sons and daughters to seek learning as an escape from the endless chain of poverty experienced by most rural black families in Appalachia.

The exterior force, especially that initiated by Washington and Rosenwald, can be historically documented, but development also required an interior force to create a community entity, a solidarity that went beyond simply a working side by side to construct a building. In Western North Carolina, the interior force required building interpersonal relationships to stimulate an environment that valued education. The buildings provided the place for the education to happen. The values provided the motivation to accelerate education.

An examination of how the exterior-interior forces interacted confronts essential questions: How could this kind of interactive community happen? With what reciprocal outcomes? What would this kind of community do to help black students learn and to enhance a cooperative spirit between learners and citizens?

Southern states, including North Carolina, inadequately supported black education, especially in school construction. Black educators, many who had little education themselves, were often forced to conduct classes in churches, in private homes, in lodge halls, in corncribs, in abandoned structures, and in other makeshift locations. Learning did take place in such environments, but the subtle message that education for black students was not a priority promoted the "propaganda" that those who learned in such unattractive quarters were themselves inferior.

Fortunately, the two prominent outsiders, Washington and Rosenwald, challenged the assumption that substandard classrooms were adequate. In contrast, they supported building well-planned schools to provide a more inviting environment that fostered respect for both teachers and learners. The collaboration and commitment of Washington and Rosenwald resulted In 4,977 such institutions in 15 southern states as citizens constructed buildings to create an acceptable environment for learning. Those buildings became a center of pride in communities (Embree and Waxman, 1949). The effort was so noteworthy that its success influenced the highest level of leadership. Responding to the program, President Franklin Delano Roosevelt asked for a schoolhouse to be constructed in Warm Springs, Georgia, well after the 1932 termination of the Rosenwald school program. His wish was honored, and the president dedicated the school on March 18, 1937 (Embree and Waxman, 1949).

In addition to helping finance schools, the Rosenwald organization funded 217 teachers' homes and 163 shops in which to train young men how to use basic tools needed for carpentry and rudimentary repair of machinery (Embree and Waxman, 1949). Beginning with the first Rosenwald school built in Alabama in 1912, the program aroused enthusiastic interest and support among black citizens throughout the South but especially in North Carolina, where Rosenwald schools became the headquarters for primary, intermediate, and advanced students seeking to fulfill their parents' dreams. Teachers conducted classes in such schools until integration closed their doors.

Today what were once the most architecturally sound rural schools in the South have been destroyed or converted for other uses. Some are private homes or community centers. Some have become tobacco barns or storage facilities, and others are museums spotlighting the local history of the African American community or the site for showcasing the arts of canning and drying food or other dying domestic arts so prevalent in homes during the first half of the twentieth century. Once the site of academic challenge and boisterous play, those Rosenwald schools that have survived the challenges of age and changing times are now only landmarks whose original purpose, until recently, has been forgotten or ignored by the public.

In 2002, the National Trust for Historic Preservation placed Rosenwald Schools near the top of the country's most "endangered places." The decision kindled a national campaign to save existing buildings, which are historic schools dating from 1912 to 1932. The history of those structures deserves special consideration, for the Rosenwald program symbolized educational empowerment for small rural communities of blacks. Confronted by overwhelming odds barring an adequate education for their sons and daughters, the intervention of the Rosenwald program challenged a society favoring and partial to white achievement. During the era of segregation, chronic failure by white legislators and school board members to provide adequate funding for black education in the South forced such neighborhoods to conduct elementary classes in substandard buildings. Conditions often included the absence of windows, so interior lighting was dim. In addition, electricity was not available; roofs leaked; small stoves—the picturesque cherry-red pot-bellied heaters—provided tremendous warmth with little opportunity to regulate blistering or chilling temperatures. Depending on the location of the stove, a student might be burning hot on the side nearer the heater and freezing on the other side. Students farthest from the stove might be chilled to the bone. Occasionally the teacher built a fire on the school grounds and allowed pupils to take turns warming themselves outside the classroom (Embree and Waxman, 1949).

Furniture was typically makeshift, with wooden desks or benches. The size of the student often did not match the size of the furniture, but such discomfort was accepted. Embree and Waxman described typical school benches as having no back support and so high that small pupils were elevated with their legs dangling uncomfortably far above the floor. Room ventilation was another problem. Extremes of temperature resulting from poorly ventilated space created discomfort so intense that frigid, sweltering, or stifling conditions often interfered with learning. The improvements that occurred after philanthropist Julius Rosenwald provided incentive funds for school construction were enormous.

The philanthropist determined to improve the life of the Negro after reading two works of nonfiction. Rosenwald read Booker T. Washington's autobiography *Up from Slavery*, which, along with *An American Citizen*, the biography of William Henry Baldwin, Jr., he referenced as two books that changed his life. The philanthropist resolved to meet the extraordinary educator. That opportunity came in 1911 when Washington visited Chicago to raise funds for the Tuskegee Institute. Soon the two, after their initial meeting, developed a friendship. Rosenwald became a member of the board for the Tuskegee Institute and directed some of his philanthropic largesse toward that school (Embree and Waxman, 1949). Rosenwald agreed wholeheartedly with Washington's philosophy of self-help and his emphasis on "industrial" education as the road to economic success for black southerners (Hanchett, 1988).

During Rosenwald's visits to Tuskegee, the black educator and the Sears Roebuck executive frequently engaged in private conversations about ways to improve and to expand the mission of the institute. The Rosenwald program of school construction was the outcome of one such dialogue, during which Booker T. Washington asserted that the educational need surpassing all others in southern black communities was the provision of well-constructed elementary school buildings. Washington suggested that Rosenwald's money would be best invested, not in erecting other Tuskegees, but in providing rural elementary schoolhouses in which the most basic education would be available to black children. The opportunity to pursue that idea occurred when, as a way of celebrating his fiftieth birthday, Rosenwald donated money to a number of worthwhile causes, including a $25,000 grant to Tuskegee Institute to assist in providing matching gifts to teacher training institutions. Finding that $2,800 was left over, Washington sought permission to use that amount to build rural elementary schools in Alabama — and thus Washington's dream of improving elementary schools for black children resulted in almost 5,000 school buildings being constructed in the South, most of which were not built until after his death (Hoffschwelle, 2003).

On this one matter advocated by Washington, his academic adversary W.E.B. Du Bois agreed. Du Bois asserted that the cause of widespread illiteracy among blacks was the result of too little emphasis being placed on elementary schools. The scholar spared no one in his furious condemnation of poorly trained teachers, untalented principals, and parents indifferent to the quality of their children's education. He condemned existing elementary schools, describing them as "quarters ill-suited physically and morally" to provide an appropriate setting in which young black students could master the basic skills of reading, writing and ciphering. He further stormed that no college professor could damage a student who had mastered the basics of learning (Du Bois, 1973). Du Bois placed himself squarely on the side of Washington and Rosenwald in their alliance to construct rural elementary schools.

Rosenwald partnered with Washington by establishing an office at Tuskegee Institute to filter and to finance requests for school buildings. At first schools were built only in Alabama with financing directed from the Tuskegee campus. The staff at Tuskegee simply could not efficiently handle the multitude of requests pouring into their office as word spread about schools being built. Consequently, in 1917, Rosenwald established the Julius Rosenwald Fund, at first housed in Chicago but later re-located to Nashville, Tennessee. The fund was incorporated in Illinois stating as its purpose "the well-being of mankind" (Embree and Waxman, 1949, p. 28).

From the beginning, the Rosenwald school building program placed significant value on architectural design. An early booklet of school designs for the black population was published in 1915 by Tuskegee Normal and Industrial Institute of Alabama. Funded by both the John F. Slater and the Ash Fund and titled *The Negro Rural School and Its Relation to the Community*, the booklet included designs for three different types of buildings: the one-teacher school, the central school, and the county training schools. The focus at that time was the one-teacher rural school, for such buildings provided the formal learning environment for the majority of rural Negro students in Alabama and throughout the South. One-room schools were also the norm in isolated Appalachian settlements.

A central school for all grades was not considered a realistic possibility (Dresslar, 1915). As a result, the Tuskegee committee recommended designing such buildings to attract students from a radius of several miles for only four years of schoolwork, which would be primarily vocational. Since Mitchell County in Western North Carolina had too few black students in any one district to merit building a schoolhouse, its officials chose to use state funds allotted for the education of its Negro population by building one central Negro school (Van Noppen and Van Noppen, 1973). Such a central school caused hardships for students living at a distance, particularly during inclement weather.

Education focused on basic academic skills. On the other hand, county training schools were expected to provide a few advanced courses in home economics for female students and in agriculture and trades for males. Such schools were also designed to house teacher-training classes for students aspiring to become educators in rural communities. The design for each type of school reflected its purpose. An architect specializing in school design provided the blueprints. The designer of rural schools and their grounds, as depicted in the booklet previously referenced and published by Tuskegee, was Fletcher B. Dresslar. Bulletin 585, containing numerous drafts of buildings and landscape designs for school plots, was available from the United States Bureau of Education and advertised for a cost of 50 cents. Southern school boards could afford such a price to obtain standard blueprints for school construction. Dresslar's designs also provided a source of architectural material for Samuel L. Smith as he dealt with the demands of an ever-expanding building program (1915).

The move away from Tuskegee and eventually to Nashville resulted in standardizing the kinds of buildings erected and allowed incorporation of the latest architectural concerns into drafting designs for schools. Popular during the period of Progressive Education, the concept of sound architecture resulted in a building effectively designed to improve the learning experience of students in those schools, as indicated in "Progressive School Architecture," included in *An African American One-Room School—Reading 2*, which cites articles such as James Oscar Betelle's "New School Buildings, State of Delaware" (*American Architect* 117 [June 1920]: 751–788) and "Architectural Styles as Applied to School Buildings" (*The American School Board Journal* 58 [April 1919]: 75–76); and other architectural sources (retrieved from http://www.nps.gov/history/nr/twhp/wwwlps/lessons/58iron/58facts2.htm).

As evidence of the importance of the concept, the conviction that architecture influences the educational process has impacted additional eras of education as well. The learning environment was accepted as a standard way to stimulate student learning, and the construction of a well-designed building conveyed a subtle message that education was valued. Today's modern educators view the learning environment as a viable tool of instruction.

The Rosenwald team had access to a model of architectural prioritizing that existed in one state to the north. The structural design of the small rural school had been a major focus in the Pierre S. du Pont school initiative in the border state of Delaware, a state that did not require Rosenwald funding. Du Pont hired a famous school architect to draft floor plans for his program in Delaware. Recognized for his effective school blueprints, James Oscar Betelle preached a doctrine of design that contributed to the health and safety of school children. He practiced equality in creating schools for both white and black students. Because Delaware's black population was small, its children required smaller schools than their white counterparts, but Betelle asserted that schools, large or small, should be equal in design and in construction.

He considered maintenance cost a priority and emphasized the need for using natural light effectively and the benefits of moveable desks as well as the existence of cloakrooms and space for preparing hot meals (Department of Public Instruction, Division of Negro Education, Special Subjects File, Box 11). His convictions, shared by Fletcher Dresslar and by Dresslar's student, Samuel L. Smith, impacted the more than 5,000 Rosenwald buildings erected in the southern states.

Building on the architectural advancement of Betelle and Dresslar, schools constructed with assistance from the Rosenwald Fund used sound principles of school design. Samuel L. Smith supervised the development of plans for Rosenwald schools that were up-to-date architectural models for schools of that period. For example, few rural schools could tap into electricity, and Smith directed his Rosenwald planners to draft blueprints with the idea of maximizing natural light as a means of protecting students from eyestrain, which could result in near-sightedness. Details about placement of banks of windows, the location of student desks, and positioning the teacher's desk and the blackboard were carefully outlined. The plans recommended placing student desks so right-handed students—the majority—would not be hampered by shadows cast across their work. Smith's incorporation of banks of windows was due to the influence of Dresslar, who declared that east-west exposure of light was more beneficial to student comfort than north-south exposure (Hanchett, 1988).

Smith's plans included two versions to ensure that Rosenwald schools could be constructed on any site and be allowed to draw on the availability of east-west sunlight. Lighter shades of paint were recommended to make the most of interior light. As much as possible, the goal was to eliminate interior corridors that tend to minimize light. As a way of incorporating the latest in educational reform for blacks, each school also included an industrial room designed as a place to teach girls to cook and to sew, and to provide boys an opportunity to work with simple tools. The inclusion of an industrial room echoed the conviction of Washington that economic tools were vital for the black student if he or she were to find gainful employment and reflected the view of the white masses that a black student should be taught to work with his or her hands.

Rosenwald schools were also designed with annual service to the total community in mind. The school provided for a few months of instruction in classrooms, but Smith expanded the purpose of the building beyond the school term, encompassing twelve months' use. Plans provided for moveable partitions that could be retracted to provide a room for community meetings yearlong (Hanchett, 1988). Ideally, each school could serve the total community for 12 months of the year, according to his bulletin published in 1924. In Transylvania County, the Parent-Teacher Association and other community groups pushed the folding partition to the side to convert their school into an auditorium. The typical black school provided space for other public programs. Musical programs such as barbershop quartets, magic shows, and movies were popular events (Reed, 2004). Because of rigid Jim Crow dictates of segregation, few other venues were available.

So frequent was the demand for full sets of community school plans that the Rosenwald Fund issued its *1924 Community School Plans, Bulletin No. 3*, which detailed specifications for all school plans used for the building program up to that time. Samuel L. Smith had combined all his school plans into a single format. His priorities included the total school campus, its buildings, its play area, its garden and landscaping, and its sanitary outhouse. Not only did the Rosenwald plan establish new buildings or improve existing ones, but it also designated that the school campus be large enough to accommodate a useful play area and to provide an area for raising vegetables. Detailed suggestions for landscaping each campus were included. The plans also provided designs for sanitary privies and their placement on school property. At least one privy seat should be made low enough to accommodate small children, and Smith recommended that one seat be constructed for every 15 to 20 children. Precautions to prevent water contamination were outlined in detail. All the required amenities were addressed.

In the bulletin's foreword, Smith pointed out that his plans exceeded the standards set by the National Education Association's Committee on Schoolhouse Planning and Construction. For example, the NEA Committee recommended that 50 percent of the total floor area of a school be used for instruction. Smith proudly stated that in his plans up to 75 percent was used for that purpose. He also indicated how effectively his design incorporated natural illumination: "The Footlight Meter has been used ... to demonstrate clearly that they have ample light at all times of the year provided the windows are constructed according to plans, the interior painted in keeping with directions, and the high skylight not shut out by dark green ... shades ... or by trees or other obstructions" (Smith, 1924, Community School Plans, Bulletin No. 3 in DPI, DNE, Special Subjects, Box 8).

However, frustration at the state level developed when local superintendents and boards revised or ignored the approved Rosenwald plans, a frequent occurrence at the beginning of the regional project. Not willing to relinquish local concerns to their partners on the state level, county officials felt they could save money by modifying the plans or using others, and the manpower in the state department was not adequate to inspect every building during construction; after-completion evaluations allowed little opportunity to correct defects (Westin, 1966). Smith and Newbold's team developed strategies to deal with such alterations, but even limited success required constant vigilance and no one wanted to dampen enthusiasm for the building program. Any adequate construction was deemed an improvement in the black school system.

Newbold included a directive to Superintendent W.R. Hill in Rutherfordton in a letter dated May 3, 1916:

> I am today recommending an appropriation of $350 to aid in building your colored school ... for which you asked aid some time ago. I hope you will be able to go right to work on this building. Please let me know when you want the money. Also, I shall be glad if you will send me a detailed outline of the plan of your building, as the appropriation is made by Mr. Rosenwald on condition that all buildings are built in accordance with plans approved by the State Department [DPI, DNE, GCD, Box 11].

Thus Newbold gave emphasis to the need to build according to approved blueprints.

However, Hill's response bypassed any agreement to use recommended plans or even to build a school at New Hope. Nature had altered local priorities. In July of 1916 the Rutherfordton superintendent asked if a postponement would mean the loss of the funds designated for the New Hope Colored School. He explained, "You see the flood has damaged the crops of all the farmers and almost ruined the crops.... It will cost $100,000 to repair roads and bridges. We want to reduce our school expenses as much as we can not to impair efficiency too much. To do this we have decided to cut down our buildup program ... we will not build a single house this year ... unless it [will cancel any possibility] of getting an appropriation from you." He ended by saying, "If we must build this year, it will be necessary to begin soon" (DPI, DNE, GCD, Box 11). Newbold's August 3 response indicated that he was unable to guarantee the $350 would be available for New Hope in the coming year but he felt certain help would be available, leaving the decision to build or not build up to Hill. Hill was torn between the decision to relinquish the needed money for school construction and the great need to improve mountain roads.

Problems began before the establishment of the Division of Negro Education. In 1915, Superintendent James Y. Joyner approved the employment of Charles H. Moore as an agent to promote Negro education under Newbold's direction (Westin, 1966). From September 1915 to June 1916 Moore traveled 12,050 miles in 35 counties. His first annual report identified a major problem: a lack of qualified black teachers, some never having completed elementary school. When a qualified instructor was not available, superintendents hired incompetent applicants simply because a warm body was needed to run the school. Moore also discovered a reluctance on the part of many white superintendents to endorse or provide funding to improve their black schools, with money often diverted to white schools. Moore even railed against black communities that could not agree about school matters. For example, in 1919 he reported that in one community in Wilkes County the construction of the Rosenwald school was being delayed by a "factional fight" (p. 348). He felt it would be best to withhold approval from such communities until the Negroes were able to resolve their differences. Obviously, the Rosenwald initiative did not provide an instant solution to every problem.

Although the Rosenwald Fund provided both seed money and school plans, communities had to apply for grants and to meet the requirements set up by Rosenwald. Initiative to submit an application and to follow through with fundraisers and campaigns to elicit community support fell into white and black camps, which further increased the need for constant monitoring to bring the project to fruition. Nevertheless, North Carolina benefited from dynamic leadership at the state level and from relentless efforts by Negro leaders in local communities. As a result, the state succeeded in erecting considerably more schools than did any other in the South. Of the nearly 5,000 Rosenwald schools built in the Southeast, North Carolina was home to more than 800. Such success can be attributed to the state's leaders, who helped local educators and students in Western North Carolina. Shortly after the Department of Instruction organized of the Division of Negro Education in 1921 with N.C. Newbold as its director, Newbold appointed William F. Credle, a white educator, and George E. Davis, a black professor, as his assistants at the State Department of Public Instruction in Raleigh. The director and his team traveled throughout the state to check on the educational needs of black communities and to stimulate interest at the grassroots level in the prospect of building new elementary schools. Their commitment to the task energized the program statewide. As a result of much hard work, applications flooded their office. Newbold wisely placed additional blacks on his team.

Soon after assuming his role as Supervisor of the Rosenwald Fund, Credle attended Peabody University to take graduate classes in schoolhouse planning. The World War I veteran and former school superintendent provided service to both white and black communities by conducting surveys statewide to assess educational needs. An outstanding member of Newbold's team, he divided his time between preparing budgets, working with the Nashville office, and doing necessary field work overseeing the construction of Rosenwald schools. When Credle expressed an interest in 1929 in joining the staff at the Nashville office, Rosenwald is reported to have jokingly replied, "Go ahead and employ him. He is building so many schools in North Carolina we will save money by bringing him into our office" (Smith, 1950, cited by Hanchett, 1988).

George E. Davis, a native of Wilmington, North Carolina, had served as Biddle University's first black professor and later as the dean of its faculty (Hanchett, 1988). Davis tirelessly campaigned for grassroots support for Rosenwald schools. A diligent worker who had been blessed with a uniquely privileged upbringing, Davis introduced the possibility of new school construction to black leaders and to the white public school officials in each county he visited. Davis was often the featured speaker in school rallies that gave opportunity to raise money for new schools. Fundraisers, conducted in local black churches, triggered the investment of private dollars in new construction and elevated an intense interest in improving black education in elementary schools.

Applications poured into Raleigh from throughout the state as the fever for new schools spread. Fewer Rosenwald buildings were constructed in the western part of the state because of its sparse black population, but in the 27 or so counties at that time comprising Western North Carolina, various legislative budgets ranging from those for 1918-19 to 1929-30 included funds for the construction of 44 Rosenwald buildings. However, recalcitrant local school officials and warring Negro communities delayed the construction of better schools at times. Another delay resulted from the need to postpone a building program in areas with slim black populations. However, the state department designated at least 20 of the Western counties as sites for Rosenwald schools and for one teachers' home in Jackson County. In a report dated June 1925, Dr. George E. Davis, whose official title was supervisor of Rosenwald buildings, had this to say regarding Sylva and Jackson County:

> This beautiful little town is nestled snugly in between lofty mountain ranges on a level valley in which meanders the Pigeon River on its way to the Gulf of Mexico ... a veritable "Happy Valley." ... All these "lost Provinces" of Western North Carolina are feeling the wholesome effects of ... modern schools. There are only 600 Negroes in the county.... Those who do not live in ... Sylva are brought there ... in trucks provided by the county.... The school at Sylva was completed in October. We went to inspect the teachers' home just completed at a cost of $1,857.91, of which amount the colored people, few in number and poor, gave $626.99. This shows only about $300 was paid by the county. The building is very well constructed and is occupied by the principal and his family of eight fine children [DPI, DNE, Special Collections, Box 8].

In his June 1925 report, Dr. Davis also records his impression of the school constructed in Haywood County: "The town of Waynesville has built at a cost of about $12,000 a very good four-teacher building. It is a brick construction and steam heated. The location, though accessible, is not all that we could wish, but is perhaps the best that could be obtained in this rapidly growing summer resort" (Box 8).

Directives for a sense of ownership by the black community resulted from the requirement that only a designated portion of the funds necessary for school construction would come from the Rosenwald Fund. Local citizens had to raise money, donate labor, land or materials, or provide in some other way a direct contribution to the expense of the construction. Although some individuals gave out of their meager life savings, others sponsored entertainment events with the proceeds earmarked for the new school (Embree and Waxman, 1949).

Community social events included box suppers and musical programs designed to bring in a trickle of coins to be used for the new structure. While individuals donated a portion of their crops to raise money, others felled trees and sawed lumber. Occasionally white landowners donated a few acres to be used as the site of the black school, and records indicate some white men contributed money from their bank accounts to support the school building program.

However, the problem of uncooperative white officials continued to be a constant threat to the program's success. In 1927 G.E. Davis reported that in Surry County the school board was withholding approval of a $2,400 loan to build a Negro school, but the same men were willing to borrow $20,000 for white schools. Even more frustrating to Davis was the fact that the board had demanded $900 from its poor black community and, after $500 was raised, had announced that no school would be built. Indignant about the entire episode, Davis stated, "I could get the four hundred from the colored people, poor as they are, tomorrow if they were assured that this would buy justice" (Westin, 1966, p. 363). Negroes were encouraged to pressure local officials in a courteous way to take advantage of the Rosenwald Fund to improve their schools.

A letter, dated 1922, from J.H. Michael of Asheville to Newbold solicits aid in dealing with white board members (Westin, 1966). Michael found that although his recommendations were well received, no action was taken. The plans perished in committee. Michael called on

Newbold to write letters to win approval for improved facilities. However, it was not until 1927 that a Rosenwald school was built in Buncombe County.

Such examples demonstrate an extreme irony when compared to the original goal of black-white teamwork. The Rosenwald program was designed to stimulate a spirit of cooperation between the majority and minority communities—and in some sections that proved to be the case. Members of the white community played a role in fundraising, and public funds from the state and county also contributed toward accruing enough money to provide the final cost of each new building. The school-building program enabled a rural black community to boast of its ownership in the new structure, and that sense of accomplishment boosted community pride. However, the program was not designed to last endlessly. Rosenwald's conviction that philanthropic funds should not continue in perpetuity and his directive that all the money be spent for present needs spelled an early climax to the program. Rosenwald firmly believed that "the generation which contributed to the making of wealth should be the one to profit by it.... He wanted dollars to be spent for clear needs today rather than left to accumulate until they had multiplied even a hundredfold for possible uses in the remote future" (Embree and Waxman, 1949, p. 37). When the trail-blazing philanthropist died in 1932, the schoolhouse building initiative soon ended.

7

Pragmatic Path to Schools

The Rosenwald plan for elementary schools was obviously important, but as with any plan, achieving total success was difficult. The challenge was enormous because both structural and educational upgrades always depend on the visionary viewpoint of community leaders. The architectural framework and the lessons taught within that framework provided a foundation for learning, but the essence of education — the learning process itself — emerged within the structure, whether influenced by buildings or by curriculum.

Architects design frameworks for school buildings. Builders construct schools using available material — logs, finished lumber, river rock, granite, and brick. Historians evaluate how the frameworks shaped the society, for architecture is itself a historical document and reveals elements of what a society valued. Historians also examine local Appalachian city and county boards of education that determined when, where and how to build.

The Appalachian influence affected the entire 125-mile east-west width and the 75-mile north-south sweep of Western North Carolina. However, even within the area, opportunities varied widely. Poverty and population were two contributing factors. Less money did not eliminate a budget for black education, but the minimal amounts clearly resulted in fewer opportunities. In addition, a smaller black population made it easier to overlook the needs of those students, just as a larger white population made it easier to justify expenditures for their better-equipped buildings and for their better-trained teachers. In all areas, though, the historical results refute the simplistic claim of "separate but equal." That slogan may sound appealing, but it simply never happened. The goal was worthwhile, but the climb was too steep and covered with a myriad of obstacles.

Rosenwald scholar Thomas Hanchett (1988) documented Western North Carolina's Rosenwald structures. Those buildings replaced dilapidated shanties that housed black elementary schools in remote communities. From Ashe County, bordering Virginia and Tennessee, to Cherokee County, bordering Georgia and Tennessee, new buildings dotted the landscape.

Whenever a new elementary school was erected or a new addition was attached to a school, blacks experienced a sense of achievement. The new construction was a source of delight, for it resulted from community effort. However, having the space was only a part of that achievement. Triumph resulted from the learning that occurred within those rooms. A close look at representative schools in Western North Carolina reveals the value placed on learning for students in the schools and the power engendered by those educational experiences.

As senior citizens reminisce about their experiences in segregated schools, several themes are prevalent: teacher appreciation, daily routines, special projects, community interest in each child, and celebratory programs. Those who taught at the schools generally focus on memories quite similar to those of the students, but they sometimes refer to racial bias as it affected their classrooms, to white interest in their schools, to class routine ranging from discipline to special projects, and to their interaction with the black communities they served. Many teachers boarded at homes in their school's community and returned to their residences on some weekends or during holidays. The minutes of the local school boards include sparse information about their black schools, but there are records of citizen activism as parents made demands for their children's education. In addition, the white attitude of smug superiority often appears as decisions are made for the black schools.

History speaks. Individuals remember. Obscure records come to light. Out of the past comes reality, no matter how remote the geographical area or how long ago events happened. Eventually citizens discover how actions and decisions shaped lives in the past as well as how those actions and decisions have led to present limitations or to opportunities of the future.

From school board minutes, from county and state reports, and from communication within the state come hundreds of documents filed every year. Fortunately, no matter how leaders feel about decisions or where they file away documents, eventually the public learns what has happened in the past — sometimes with pride and occasionally with shame. Even though almost a century has passed since the Rosenwald project attempted to change the educational landscape for blacks, those affected by segregation and those energized by new hope still recall the pain and the pleasure of their past.

The records reveal that 12 Western counties had one Rosenwald School; four counties, three Rosenwald Schools; and five counties; four or more Rosenwald Schools. While the funding and the construction methods were similar, the details of the historical records vary. However, an intensive and exhaustive search for existing information reveals patterns in the process and in the classrooms were similar. The names and places change, but the goal of educating black students remains the highlight.

Prototype in Transylvania County

Located at the western edge of Brevard — a town that now houses the respected liberal arts Brevard College and a nationally renowned summer music program — the Brevard Rosenwald School clearly illustrates the transformation of the Rosenwald movement in Western North Carolina. The tight-knit black community in that town responded enthusiastically to the concept of a cooperative effort to construct a building on what is now the site of the central office for Brevard Schools.

The three-teacher Rosenwald school construction — renovation — in Transylvania County cost $4,850. Of that amount, blacks contributed $1,195; the Rosenwald Fund, $900; and public funds, $2,755 (Reed, 2004).

In every way, the effort illustrates the power of combining an outer force, the munificent philanthropist, with the inner force, the conscientious parents of black children. The school, built in 1920–21, exemplifies all the goals, challenges, curriculum, and involvement that happened elsewhere, as detailed in *The Brevard Rosenwald School: Black Education and Community Building in a Southern Appalachian Town, 1920–1960,* the forerunner of this more extensive study (Reed, 2004). There were games, spelling bees, work projects, and celebrations as well as the expected emphasis on the three Rs: reading, writing and arithmetic. However, there were also struggles, challenges, disappointments, parental contributions, heart-warming achievements, and a determined principal, Ethel Kennedy Mills, who carried on the educational tradition as she hoisted the educational torch passed on from her father, the legendary Rev. James T. Kennedy.

Out of darkness came light even after a fire that destroyed the original school — an accident that appears all too frequently in the historical record of these schools. But the light led to learning, promotions, and graduations. And those patterns emerge again and again during the century of the black journey to integrated education in Western North Carolina. The roadblocks were many; the persistent eventually succeeded. While one story illustrates the effort, the many stories document the tenacity and the perseverance of black highlanders.

Decisions in Buncombe County

A much different story emerges in a community in South Asheville. In 1895 when George Vanderbilt purchased property for his Buncombe County, North Carolina, estate, he made provisions for black residents to move to the Shiloh area, a short distance away. As a result, Vanderbilt established housing opportunities for those whose former property occupied an area on his newly acquired land. One resident refused to part with his treasured piece of real estate. An aging black property owner lived in the heart of the newly established Biltmore Estate, according to Lenwood G. Davis (1984). When Vanderbilt offered to purchase the man's nine acres for $10,000, the black man turned down the offer. Tradition affirms that the "old darky," as he was called, explained that it did not bother him to have a rich man for a neighbor. After his death, however, his heirs sold the property, but they settled for a smaller sum. According to Ella Mae Harper (personal communication, August 11, 2004) and Anita White-Carter (personal communication, March 5, 2007), the tycoon also relocated the black cemetery and the community church from his estate to the Shiloh community.

Prior to the decision to build the Shiloh School, the only Rosenwald school in Buncombe County, the board dealt with the business of educating Shiloh students. The May 1905 minutes of the Buncombe County Board of Education documents the decision to sell a one-quarter acre school lot in the Shiloh community, located near what is currently known as Biltmore Village, and to purchase one acre for a school from George Vanderbilt. A few months after the August appointment of A.C. Reynolds as a new superintendent of schools, the matter of selling a lot at Shiloh and purchasing another was again an item of business. The next year, in February 1906, the board ordered Superintendent Reynolds to buy a schoolhouse site near Shiloh Church from the Vanderbilts and to sell the lot owned by the county for $30. Subsequently, on May 23, 1906, the board ordered the removal of an old schoolhouse near Biltmore to the lot at Shiloh to be set up for the colored community. The transaction may be regarded as another example of passing on used, worn, and unwanted school items to the black community in what the whites regarded as acts of kindness.

The board, according to its July 5, 1909, minutes, voted to serve the Shiloh school by appointing the following committeemen: G.W. Payne, Jack Foster, and W.E. Logan. In 1917, Payne and Logan were still serving as committeemen. All school committees were informed that if attendance fell below 50 percent, the teacher and the school committee would be required to appear before the school board and explain why school should not be discontinued at that site and to provide for interested students to attend other schools.

However, a drop in school attendance did not disrupt education in the Shiloh community. In 1916, G.W. Payne appeared before the board to request repairs to the Shiloh school building. The board agreed to match any funds raised in the district to meet that need. The board apportioned $400 in April 1916 for use at the Shiloh School. In 1918, the board considered adding an extra teacher to the staff at Shiloh. Funds needed for a four-month term at Shiloh amounted to $465. In 1919, the board discussed the need to provide a new building for the colored students. Apparently no action was taken, for on May 3, 1920, J.W. Foster, a colored man acting on behalf of Shiloh's black citizens, attended the board meeting. Pointing out that, due to overcrowding, there was an urgent need for a new school building, Foster called the old one inadequate. The board assigned secretary Katherine Lipe and Superintendent Reynolds to look into the matter. Reynolds and Lipe were also instructed to check with state officials to see whether additional help might be available (Buncombe County Board of Education minutes, 1916–1920).

At the May 16, 1927, meeting of the Buncombe County Board of Education, Mrs. G. Latta Clement offered to sell a piece of property to be used for the site of the Shiloh colored school. Her price was $1,250 per acre for up to eight acres. James Roberts and A.C. Reynolds were asked to investigate the offer and to report their findings to the board. On June 27, 1927, the board agreed to provide $25,000 of the state loan to the Shiloh district. In addition, the board decided to provide four teachers for the South Asheville colored school and designated that $1,500 be included in the budget for the construction of an additional room. The following September the board made the following appointments as Shiloh district committeemen: J.T. Bradshaw, W.T. Payne, and L.W. Williams (Buncombe County Board of Education minutes).

On October 17, 1927, the board, according to its minutes, awarded the contract to build a schoolhouse in the Shiloh District to Lucius Williams. It made these stipulations: Williams was instructed to use the specifications of the Julius Rosenwald Plan No. 6A and to provide "three stools for boys and three for girls" in the basement. The basement became the designated site for student restrooms. Board members instructed Williams to install two hot air furnaces under each end of the auditorium, to use adequate wiring for light, and to provide sufficient plumbing.

Shiloh School was constructed by using Rosenwald funds and by using Rosenwald plans for a Type 8 school under the 1927-1928 state budget (Rosenwald Fund Card File Database, retrieved from http://rosenwald.fisk.edu). However, board minutes specify a Type 6 school. No explanation exists for the discrepancy. The school, located on a four-acre site, cost a total of $32,200. Of that amount, the Rosenwald Fund contributed $1,700 and public funds amounted to $30,500. The Shiloh record on file at Fisk University does not designate a specific amount provided by the black community.

School board minutes reveal numerous facts about the Shiloh School. In 1960, additional land was acquired to increase the total school property to seven acres. In 1928, the basement area was 3,203 square feet, and the first floor consisted of 6,690 square feet. By 1950, the gross floor area amounted to 21,121 square feet. In 1965, the Shiloh school had an enrollment of 245 students.

Like other black communities, the Shiloh neighborhood was close-knit with families frequently interacting with one another and watching out for one another's children. Adults, sitting on their front porches in the evening, rested after a hard day at work and talked about community events. Sometimes a family started singing, and the melody was picked up from porch to porch as neighbors relaxed and joined in the evening concert. Some of the Shiloh residents participated in gospel groups that performed at churches and in other venues. There were also stores in the community where neighbors congregated to chat and to catch up on current happenings (Lyndia Roland Chiles, personal communication, April 26, 2007). Ella Mae Harper's father operated a café in the basement of their home. There was music, probably a jukebox, and couples danced. Ella Mae met her future husband there when he dropped by after a basketball game. She waited patiently for him while he served in World War II. During their 56-year marriage, the couple became involved in school events as a result of having their seven children enrolled at Shiloh School (personal communication, August 11, 2004).

In the Shiloh community, which prized its school, over the years students learned from a dedicated faculty. Delores Carnegie, who taught first grade, and Franklyn Owens, who taught in the upper grades, remembered special events, which included creating and producing an original operetta. Owens incorporated songs the children had learned about animals into a story and built an operetta around those melodies. Included were "Old McDonald Had a Farm" and songs about "Peter Rabbit." Carnegie described costumes made from crepe paper and reinforced with coat hangers designed by Mary Jackson. Some children portrayed chickens, and one little "rooster" was provided with a string attached to his "tail" so he could make his tail feathers wiggle by pulling on the string. The children wore a variety of costumes to depict different animals. Children delighted the audience as they danced while they sang. Carnegie and Owens explained that such performances were often used as fundraisers. Owens regretted that Shiloh School was eventually phased out, with some students going to such schools as Biltmore, Oakley, and Estes. Teachers were also sent to other schools. For example, Carnegie was assigned to a school in Black Mountain (personal communication, January 16, 2004).

Linwood Crump, who attended Shiloh School, was known as the unofficial mayor of the Shiloh community. He claims he became the mayor "by raising sand with the City Council." Among the teachers he remembers most vividly is Guy Bass, a strict teacher who taught eighth grade and "really knew how to use a paddle." Monnie Jones—he called her "Money" Jones—was his fifth grade teacher. He felt Ms. Jones was an effective teacher, especially in math. "Mayor" Crump also vividly remembers being punished by her. "I thought: Now I'm finished, and POW! There came the strap." He identified Ms. Carnegie as the grade 1 teacher, Ms. Anderson, grade 2; Ms. Cowan, grade 3; Ms. Owens, grade 4; Ms. Jones, grade 5, and Mr. Bass, grade 8. There were some combination classes during his tenure at the school (personal communication, February 11, 2004).

Typically, the normal day at Shiloh began with an early morning Bible class. Crump explained that songs were a part of every day's routine. "Mrs. Cowan taught music and dance, square dancing ... and we had really good workers at the school," he said. The janitor and cooks, Agnes Jones and Pauline Seabrook, were an important part of life at Shiloh. "They served good food, especially potato salad, pinto beans, greens, meatloaf—lots of good stuff" (personal communication, February 11, 2004). Anita White-Carter described the aroma of delicious rolls prepared in a kitchen in the basement of the school. With delight, Crump recalled the excellent meals made by Mrs. Thompson and the other workers (personal communication, March 5, 2004). As at other rural black schools, former students often sing praises for lunchroom workers. They remember food as an important part of institutional life.

With less enthusiasm, students such as Linwood Crump have little difficulty remembering the kinds of punishments routinely meted out. According to Crump and others, Shiloh teachers would hit an offending student's hand with a ruler. "That hurt, but it wouldn't kill you," Crump said. "Nor did whippings. And we didn't get put in jail." Crump believes such disciplinary measures were effective and paved the way for responsible citizenship during adult life. Crump described Shiloh Principal J.C. Daniels: "He was a hard man. Nice to you, but when he said to bend over, he would just wear you out. He used a strap with holes in it."

Principal Daniels received praise from the faculty, students, and community. He was touted as a fine man who ran a tight ship. Franklyn Owens described Daniels as "a good man to work for." Both Harper and White-Carter, former Shiloh students, spoke of Daniels with admiration. His first wife, Lillian, taught at the school and invited the "little ones" from the community to drop by her home to learn their ABCs. After Lillian Daniels' death, Principal Daniels remarried. His second wife was also an educator and was described as "a good teacher who thought a lot of all children" (Ella Mae Harper, personal communication, August 11, 2004).

Anita White-Carter highlighted experiences from her student days at Shiloh, where she attended from 1951 to 1959 (personal communication, March 5, 2007). White-Carter treasures her Shiloh educational experience. She described classes, conducted by Mrs. Cowan and Mrs.

Payne, that emphasized black culture. "We read Negro poetry and grew to love it — poems by Langston Hughes, James W. Johnson, and Paul Lawrence Dunbar. Negro culture and history were a direct focus of the curriculum," she said. "That is something that is lost for our kids now, and that is sad." Others also expressed regret that the historical achievements of blacks have not received the recognition merited by their achievements in modern schools. Black history month typically is celebrated by a bulletin board display in the school library. Individuals such as Anita White-Carter believe black history and literature should be a part of the mainstream curriculum.

Students enjoyed recreation during recess, and in the evenings they returned to the school to continue playing. Sometimes girls played hopscotch. Ella Mae Harper (personal communication, August 11, 2004) described a 10 o'clock recess when all students marched out of the school and organized ball games on the playground. There was softball and basketball. At times the girls played on the school steps. Games included "I spy," hopscotch, and hide-and-seek. On rainy days students played inside.

White-Carter recalled that girls received instruction in sex education, quite a progressive move at a small school in the 1950s. "Mrs. Cowan conducted a girls' seminar. She named it: 'You Are Becoming a Woman.' It was about sex," White-Carter said. Education at Shiloh also included character education and provided incentives for focusing on academics by presenting annual academic awards and a much-coveted citizenship award. During White-Carter's tenure at Shiloh School, teachers sent report cards home every six weeks with a letter grade for each subject and one for citizenship. The school held a graduation for eighth graders and recognized both a valedictorian and a salutatorian. Girls wore white dresses, and the boys wore suits for the occasion. Music was a special part of commencement with Mrs. Franklyn Owens playing "Pomp and Circumstance" and other pieces. The eighth-grade valedictorian and salutatorian spoke. During Harper's student days, students presented an annual musical program with a chorus or glee club. Girls wore white tops and back skirts, and the boys dressed in white shirts and dark pants. Although education at Shiloh was effective in White-Carter's view, her chief disappointment was the scarcity of library books. "I worked in the library. There just were not enough books" (personal communication, August 11, 2004). Today White-Carter is the research services coordinator at D. Hyden Ramsey Library at the University of North Carolina at Asheville.

Other celebrations at Shiloh followed traditional patterns that were common in most of the black schools in Western North Carolina. Harper recalled that the school celebrated May Day, which occurred near the end of the school year, by wrapping colors around the flagpole. Also, near the closing of the school year, all black schools were invited to the McCormick Baseball Field, home of the Asheville Tourists, to participate in sports events, to have races, and to share in a time of relaxation with refreshments and entertainment.

Music was a part of the daily routine at Shiloh, but special programs were also built around music. According to White-Carter, students sang the Negro National Anthem each morning as the school day opened with devotions and prayer. Students presented Easter and Christmas plays with appropriate music added to the script. In addition, there were seasonal plays, and teachers involved their students in orations and speaking contests. "I always participated in those. We also read poems aloud and often recited poetry," she said. "There were operettas which involved the total student population at one time or another" (personal communication, March 5, 2007).

Parents were actively involved in school events and in school fundraisers, often in connection with the Parent-Teacher Association. Harper, who served a term as the PTA president, remembers that mothers frequently made costumes, rehearsed with students, and raised money to fill the school coffers. Parents organized an annual October festival with a bazaar to increase school revenue. "Dishes were cooked. There were booths and tables, and at one table you could play games. You could toss a ring around a bottle for a prize or bid on a cake. There was also a cake walk" (White-Carter, personal communication, March 5, 2007). Black citizens were active in solving community problems, so sponsoring such events to garner financial support for their schools was a widespread part of black culture. Like past parents, twenty-first century citizens, whether poor, middle class, or affluent, have learned to regard such economic assistance as a normal school activity.

Examining research compiled by the faculty provides a unique view of the internal workings of Shiloh School. In March 1963, J.C. Daniels, a life-member of the National Educational Association, presented a self-study report of Shiloh Elementary School as part of the accreditation process for the Southern Association of Colleges and Schools. According to the report, available at the Buncombe County superintendent's office, the original Shiloh Elementary School had been constructed as a two-room building, which was later destroyed by fire.

A Rosenwald building, which replaced the original Shiloh structure, grew to a 10-classroom and a 10-teacher school. The majority of the students' parents worked in domestic and custodial positions, with 80 percent having only an elementary school education. The school facilities were also used by clubs and by churches. Also, Boy Scouts met there.

In addition to Daniels, the professional staff was composed of the following teachers: Dolores Carnegie, first grade; Ratherline Simpson, second grade; Myrtle Brittian and Maxine Teamer, third grade; Franklyn Owens, fourth grade; Agnes Anderson, fifth grade; Jacqueline Scott, sixth grade; Wylma James, seventh grade; Mrs. R. Beatty Payne, sixth and seventh grade; and Guy Bass, eighth grade. At the time of the study there were 295 students—33 students were enrolled in first grade, 30 in second; 61 in third; 31 in fourth; 34 in fifth, and 23 in sixth plus those sixth graders in the Payne combination class. James and Payne were teaching 53 sixth and seventh graders, and Bass had a pupil load of 30 eighth graders.

Supervisory staff included Lucy S. Herring (colored), Ann Sherward (white), and Helen Wells (white). Carrie Wood was the lunchroom supervisor. Dr. Irma Henderson, Dr. D.W. Dudley, and Mrs. L.F. Woodfin served as director of health services, school dentist, and school nurse, respectively. The custodian, Charles Williams, had student assistance in mopping and sweeping. T.C. Lewis, Leonard Collington, James Weston, and John Gilliam were the bus drivers. One section of the school's philosophy, Daniels declared, was creating an appreciation for the interdependence of mankind, a conviction that all work is honorable, and the principle that each individual has a unique purpose in life. In a sense, Daniels indicated that custodians, cooks, and teachers all had an important, even vital, function in the grand scheme of school life. He proposed that the role of each member of the staff, professional or nonprofessional, was a means of enriching the total educational experience for students.

Daniels also pointed out that there should be mastery of the basic skills of reading, writing, spelling, speaking, and doing arithmetic. However, his staff also valued independent thinking, appreciation of diversity, and an understanding of the important principles of human relationships. Daniels encouraged his staff to preserve each pupil's individuality while emphasizing honesty and critical thinking as well as encouraging them to assume responsibility for their actions and the needs of their community. Daniels provided practical experiences in accomplishing these goals within the school. Students were assigned tasks such as making announcements, doing housekeeping chores, answering the telephone, and cooperating in ongoing class projects to promote their skill in functioning within the community. Although the self-study involved only one school year, it provided a valuable overview of how the school was organized and how it functioned.

Integration closed Shiloh Elementary School, with its students being bused to T.C. Roberson and to Biltmore. Leaving their neighborhood school led students to new experiences that were often unpleasant. "At T.C. Roberson the Shiloh kids were called names, the N-word and told, 'Gypsies, go home.' The school board decided there were too many blacks at T.C. Roberson so half of them were reassigned to the Oakley District and to A.C. Reynolds. By then, there was no trouble" (Ella Mae Harper, personal communication, August 11, 2004).

The irony is that the solution, integration, also caused problems for black students as they adjusted to new scholastic environments. Once again, it was the underserved students who had to deal with the challenges of school board decisions and pressures from white citizens.

Expectations in Henderson County

In nearby Henderson County, East Flat Rock's black community had a long history of placing a high value on education. Linda Culpepper, in her unpublished history of the Mud Creek Missionary Baptist Church in East Flat Rock (2002), credits New Era Institutes with strengthening education among rural black communities, such as the one at East Flat Rock. Culpepper specifies that development of the institutes was the outgrowth of teamwork by the North Carolina Baptist State Educational and Missionary Convention in collaboration with Shaw University in Raleigh. Rural families believed their success depended on living according to Christian values and on obtaining an education. In response to that premise, ministers and scholars traveled throughout the state to present lectures focused on being loyal Baptists and on obtaining an education. From 1897 to 1901, they presented lectures in Asheville, Waynesville, Brevard, East Flat Rock, and Flat Rock. Though different from the Washington-Rosenwald approach, the lectures are further evidence of how outsiders stimulated building a community that nurtured educational progress for blacks.

In 1912, a lecture was sponsored in Hendersonville and attended by county residents. Rural citizens were advised of the importance of self-help and of learning. Shaw University, located in Raleigh and founded in 1890 for blacks, used such lectures to advertise its program of studies to interested young people and to their parents (Culpepper, 2002). In the East Flat Rock community, black parents sought opportunities to instill in their children a willingness to learn and to provide schools where learning could take place.

As early as November 25, 1905, George Potts and Robert Alston, trustees of the Mud Creek Missionary Church, had deeded one-half acre of land to Henderson County. They cited the "more or less" one-half acre as bounded on the north by A.R. Guerrard, on the east by Rhett's Mill Creek, and on the south by the church property. The provision of a building site demonstrated interest in meeting local educational needs. The land in East Flat Rock was designated as a site for a school building (Culpepper, 2002).

Henderson County also became the location of a Rosenwald school on a four-acre campus on Mine Gap Road. During the early 1920s, the community campaigned successfully for a new school. Known as the East Flat Rock Colored School, the building implemented a three-teacher type plan for which funds were included in the legislative budget for 1922-23. Construction costs amounted to $4,781. Of that amount, the Rosenwald Fund provided $900; blacks, $1,423; and public funds, $2,458 (Rosenwald Database).

In his June 1923 report, W.F. Credle, North Carolina's supervisor of the Rosenwald Fund, included this information: At East Flat Rock in Henderson County, "we have erected a most excellent three-teacher school, using our Community School Plan #3. This is the first Rosenwald School [also the only one] to be erected in this county. Superintendent [R.G.] Anders is pleased with the building and with the appropriation which we have made" (Department of Public Instruction, Division of Negro Education, Special Subjects, Box 8).

William Darity, who had been an outstanding student at the school, testified to the emphasis placed on learning in the typical black home in East Flat Rock. Following the traditional view of education as a means of improving life, Darity's parents, Aden Randall and Elizabeth Smith Darity, urged him to attend college. "All we ever heard from Mother and Father was—you are going to college. My father said, 'I can't spell college, but you are going.' Of course, he could spell college" (personal communication, November 6, 2004). It was the normal pattern for East Flat Rock residents to attempt to instill high expectations in their children.

Teachers at any school influence their pupils in ways beyond classroom instruction. John Potts, who served as teacher and principal at East Flat Rock, was such a man. Potts dressed professionally and impressed young William Darity with his wardrobe. Darity determined to own a three-piece suit, like the one Potts modeled. Darity expressed his admiration in this fashion: "I emulated John Potts. I wanted to be just like him. He dressed in a three-piece gray suit.... He was tall—about 6' 3"—and he wore that suit. He was an imposing figure and a terrific role model. I wanted to be like him. I saved my money—$16.95—and I bought my first suit. I worked all summer to save that money" (personal communication). In the vernacular of that day, the principal's manner of dressing was "swell." Potts maintained contact with Darity throughout his former student's career. Although he was a conscientious disciplinarian, Potts furnished guidance and a feeling of security for his students. He expected students to make something of themselves.

Both Audrey Davis, who attended the East Flat Rock Colored School, and Hortense Potts, retired educator, regarded the principal as the model of a successful educator. After his leadership at the East Flat Rock school, Principal Potts served for many years as president of Voorhees College in Denmark, South Carolina. Other East Flat Rock teachers were Marie Thompson, Mary Jones, Mary Hansberry, Gustava Robinson, and Mrs. Jackson from Tryon. John Simmons, a former East Flat Rock student who later became a dentist with a practice in California, also taught at the school (Hortense Potts and Audrey Davis, personal communication, March 26, 2004). Teachers expected learning to take place and established a challenging atmosphere in the classroom.

Although Davis and Hortense Potts recall that instruction focused on the three R's, Marie Thompson provided experience in crafts for the students. Thompson acquired bottles and instructed the students to paint them, often with flowers, a frequent artistic theme. She also gave pupils blocks of wood to smooth and shellac. Pupils then glued a calendar to the surface. Students gathered sprigs of thorns and pinned gumdrops on them to create bouquets. Thompson also taught the students to weave baskets out of grass. Because of her method of enriching the curriculum, Thompson was popular with her students. "I was sick with whooping cough when I found out Mrs. Thompson was going to leave," Potts said. "I cried and cried and cried."

Another event that impacted Potts in a positive way was winning an oratorical contest in closing activities at the school. Hortense Potts, Lydia White, and Pauline White made a speech, and Potts received a medal for her achievement, a medal that she cherished (personal communication, March 26, 2004). Hands-on activities provided relief from being bound to academic learning acquired from books, often mastered by rote learning, and relieved the pressure of work at student desks. Musical activities and oral recitations also enriched the educational experiences of elementary students.

Assigning special responsibilities to students was routine. For example, Guy Payne had the task of ringing the school bell for recess. He kept a schedule on his desk. When the time came, the young boy walked to the hall and rang the bell. A short recess provided an opportunity to go to the bathroom and to get a drink of water. There was a longer recess for outdoor games. During that break, Payne placed the black-handled brass bell on the windowsill. He chuckled as he remembered the peer pressure when he walked over to end their playtime. "The kids would say, 'Can't you wait? Walk slow then'" (personal communication).

Betty Payne, Guy's sister and a retired educator, takes pride in one special accomplishment of hers at the East Flat Rock school. There was no library, but some books, which had been donated, were stored in a closet. Motivated by her passion for reading, Payne begged permission to organize the books and succeeded in establishing a school library, located in that small room, which benefited both teachers and students (personal communication, March 7, 2007).

Audrey Davis remains convinced that segregated schools had great merit because teachers provided individual attention and a sense of security for their students. Anecdotal evidence abounds that teachers were interested in pupils as individuals both in and out of the classroom. Mary Jones invited students to spend a night or a weekend at her home. Guy Payne spent one night there and received a toy airplane as a gift. That was a highlight in the young child's school experience. His sister Betty also accepted Jones' invitation and has a letter written to her mother by Miss Jones, in which the teacher's generosity is documented. Jones gave Betty a winter coat. Such individual attention was common in many black schools.

Davis recalled with pleasure a program, planned by the PTA, in which other schools in the county were invited to participate. For the county program, the East Flat Rock pupils prepared a play about marriage. "I was the bride, and teacher was the groom," Audrey said. "We made little speeches, interrupted with lots of cheering and clapping. We enjoyed it. I was happy to be in that play" (personal communication, March 23, 2004). Davis also found physical education enjoyable, but Potts preferred other recess activities. Later Betty Payne appreciated going to Mrs. Cook's house, located within walking distance of the school, to pull candy made from molasses. Cook's mother led the students in this fun at her home (personal communication, March 7, 2007). Of course, the highlight of the excursion was being allowed to take the candy home.

Payne also shared her memory of an important field trip during which all the older boys and girls were bused into Hendersonville for a performance by the North Carolina Symphony Orchestra under the direction of Dr. Benjamin F. Swalin. In preparation for attending the concert, students learned about various musical instruments. There was also an annual spring event, held at the Baptist assembly grounds near the school, to provide students with field day activities, which included softball games (personal communication, March 7, 2007). Involving students in hands-on projects and extracurricular activities made learning experiences more vital and school far more appealing for most students.

The school was heated by a pot-bellied stove, which became crimson with heat during the winters. Often, Israel Simmons, Jr., and Charles Darity made fires before the school buses arrived. The school would be warm and welcoming. Children responded enthusiastically to the toasty warmth as a reprieve from the walk to school or the long bus ride from other communities. Live coals were banked during the night to allow ease in igniting the morning fire. Teachers stored coal in a small building near the school (Audrey Davis, personal communication, March 26, 2004).

Black students were bused from Bat Cave, Brickton, Clear Creek, Etowah, Edneyville, and Horse Shoe to create a consolidated black school in East Flat Rock (Guy Payne, personal communication, November 13, 2006). According to Betty Payne, the long ride was not a pleasant experience. Waiting for the school bus adjacent to the Etowah Elementary School for white children, the black students became uncomfortably cold. Guy Payne said they gathered corn stalks and pine cones, put them in a bucket, and built a fire by the roadside to keep warm. Occasionally the school bus would not run, and students joyfully embraced an unexpected holiday (personal communication, November 13, 2006). The children took up their vigil near a facility that, had state law not mandated segregation, would have allowed them to study within their community of residence and avoided an uncomfortable wait and an extended bus ride.

Community life was also enriched by inter-family support. Blacks in most Western North Carolina communities looked after other families confronted with unexpected hardships and invented novel ways to ensure the availability of cash. For example, the father of Dr. John Simmons formed the Society of Necessity. The society raised money to help poor families with medical bills and winter heating costs. Teachers needed only to indicate that a student or his or her family was in need to spark a move to help in difficult situations.

Of course, having the money required raising funds, and that was accomplished in a variety of ways. To ensure there would be a community chest of funds to purchase coal, to assist in paying doctor bills or to buy needed winter clothing, a summer rally was held at the Baptist assembly grounds with a lot of competitive activities as well as special music and great speakers. Edward W. Pearson was involved, and the Rev. E.W. Dixon, pastor of an Asheville church and moderator of the assembly, supervised the construction of a grandstand so busloads arriving at the picnic could view the entertainment in style. Records mention two popular speakers: Stanley McDowell and Mae McCorkle. Each was an impressive speaker, but McDowell was described as a "great orator." There was a merry-go-round and a Ferris wheel, provided by Pearson. Local families donated baked and canned goods and set up tables or booths to sell their wares for the Society's benefit. White people were asked for donations. Local white farmer Seldon Hill, known for wearing bib overalls, supported the black community's fund-raising activities by buying food and other products. The event was great entertainment for the colored people from miles around, and it was one avenue to sell goods for funds for the Society of Necessity, but there were other means of getting money as well (Potts, personal communication, March 26, 2004).

Hortense Potts has special memories of the assembly event held near the Fourth of July or on Labor Day. Her father served as deputy to maintain order. As his daughter, she did not have to pay the $1 fee to attend, and she could ride without paying (personal communication, March 24, 2004). Her father, Fred Potts, was a leader in the East Flat Rock community. Not only did he serve as a school committeeman, but he also became president of the local NAACP. Fred Potts earned his living by doing landscaping, yard work and occasionally as a chauffeur. However, he performed other services for the community. For example, if a child died, he routinely constructed a coffin and gave it to the family to use for their loved one's burial. He also helped as an officer with the Society of Necessity (personal communication, April 6, 2004).

One student who came to East Flat Rock by bus from the Etowah community was Hannah Logan Edwards. During recess she and her classmates collected kindling and pine burrs from the nearby woods. During her student days, teachers used those materials to kindle fires. Recess was also a time for Edwards and her classmates to play games and to pretend. One popular activity was "Little Sally Walker Sitting in a Saucer." Female students played "house" and made furniture with pine needles. Students were especially fond of playing softball. At times Ed Potts, who lived in the nearby woody area, showed up at school during recess to play ball with the children. The boys and girls were impressed with his ability to knock the ball out of sight (Hannah Logan Edwards, personal communication, November 16, 2004).

Edwards worked in the school lunchroom in exchange for her meals. Early in the school's history, parents had provided food, especially during the winter months, to allow students to partake of a nourishing midday meal. Soup and peanut butter sandwiches were common fare. By the time Edwards attended the school, a small staff prepared hot lunches with Corabelle Walker serving as the cook (personal communication, November 16, 2004).

At times boys were excused from the East Flat Rock school for a haircut. Ed Potts was one barber, and there was a second community barber, Artie Lynch, who also cut the pupils' hair. In this way school officials encouraged careful personal grooming. Lessons other than those derived from books prepared the students for adult living. Occasionally students were allowed to walk to Charles Hill's General Merchandise Store or to Stepp and Walker Store in the business section of East Flat Rock. A lucky student might have a dime to spend. Hortense Potts occasionally accompanied her playmate Daisy Downs to the Stepp and Walker Store to purchase a veal chop for Daisy's grandmother (personal communication, November 16, 2004). Visiting either store exposed students to the local white population. While black and white children played together at East Flat Rock, they did not visit one another in their homes. Tradition designated one side of the streets for blacks and the other for whites.

More information about the colored school at East Flat Rock appears in the board of education minutes for August 4, 1924, with J.A. Hudgens, J.W. Morgan, and H.E. Erwin in attendance. The board agreed to wire the East Flat Rock colored school. An $80 bid submitted by J.H. Bangs was accepted, but the board decided that wiring could not take place until the community had installed lead wires into the building. Citizens in the neighborhood were required to contribute toward the solution of the school's problem. Eventually the arrival of electricity at the school was an exciting event, especially for the educators and their students. In the minutes for March 1, 1926, East Flat Rock resident Henry Simmons asked the board to sell one lot off the colored school site in his community to be used for the construction of a church. The board did not approve, so Simmons had to pursue other options.

Another issue related to the colored school at East Flat Rock is recorded in the June 6, 1927, school board minutes. Beatrice Dill, whose son had damaged the school building, offered to pay for repairs. The board agreed to withdraw the warrant for her son's arrest upon restoration of the property. Dill had stepped forward not only to protect her son but also to assume responsibility for the damage incurred by his youthful prank. A second item of business affected the East Flat Rock School. The board announced the appointments of Fred Potts and Willie Williams as additional committeemen for the school.

Ledgers containing information from the 1920s can be found at the Henderson County central education offices. One entry indicates that at East Flat Rock in the Hendersonville Township, a total of $836.10 had been debited to the cost of the school site, $4,195.22 to the cost of the building, and $300 to the cost of equipment.

Beginning in the late 1930s, business matters related to insuring schools and their contents, as well as a concern for safety, gradually became routine items of business. An engineer generally surveyed the schools and provided concise reports as to their conditions, their value, and the value of their contents in addition to suggesting needed improvements and estimating the insurable value. In July 1947, engineer Stewart B. Foulke submitted his findings about the condition of the school, describing the East Flat Rock Colored School as a one-and-a-half story frame building with an ordinary wood joisted roof covered with metal. Brick piers supported the entire building. Its interior finish was of double wood joist floor with pine wearing surfaces. The sidewalls, partition walls and ceiling were wood sheathed. It was lighted by electricity and heated by stoves. The cafeteria was equipped with a coal range. All units were vented to brick chimneys built from the ground. Foulke indicated the building contained two classrooms and one combination classroom as well as an auditorium and cafeteria. Because one of the stoves had a cracked bowl at the time of the inspection, he recommended its repair and suggested that one of the metal mats under a stove should be replaced by a larger one that should extend at least 12 inches from the outside edge of the stove on all four sides. The insurance appraiser valued the building and its contents at approximately $4,000 (Foulke Survey, July 1947).

The East Flat Rock Rosenwald School received funding in the 1922-23 legislative budget and was constructed for $4781. In 1947 its insurable value was $6,200 but county-city consolidation of black schools closed its doors in 1951. Today all that remains is a chimney, two cement steps and an old pump. John Foster Potts, who served as president of Voorhees College from 1954 to 1970, was its principal in the 1930s (courtesy Henderson County Board of Public Education).

Having a more modern structure in which to conduct classes was important and highly motivational, but the interaction of educators with their pupils and parents made the difference in maximizing the elementary school experience. Annie Fowler taught at the Edneyville and at the East Flat Rock schools. Speaking through her caregiver, Charlotte Harper, in 2009, Fowler lamented the deplorable conditions that existed in the schools for colored children. She also expressed regret that teaching so many little children created hardships. For example, if a young child needed to use the bathroom, he or she often required assistance. The teacher had to leave a crowded room to tend to a single child in the outhouse. Some young students had a fear of falling into the privy pit. "The kids were fine," she said, "but the conditions were horrible." The school frequently required warmth from a heated stove that had a pot of boiling water on top of it. That was necessary, but it could be a danger.

If lunches were brought from home, Fowler required that they be kept out of sight during student lessons. During school lunch period, she seized on the opportunity to instill manners and encouraged sharing if appropriate. There was more to teaching and learning than the ABCs. Fowler taught without proper equipment and strived to incorporate art and music into her students' classroom experience. Much improvisation was necessary, and often she, like her colleagues, invested personal time and money to improve learning opportunities. During end-of-term closing exercises teachers gave each child an opportunity to display his or her knowledge and skill (personal communication, April 9, 2009).

Eventually the board consolidated the students residing in the county with the city students. Students were then transported to Sixth Avenue and Ninth Avenue Schools in Hendersonville. The buildings, including the one funded by Rosenwald, were vacated. Abandoned schools are mentioned in the February 8, 1954, minutes. The board of education, comprised of B.B. Massagee, chairman, and W.O. Waters and L.C. Youngblood, decided to advertise abandoned schools for sale at a public auction. P.G. Cornelius offered the highest bid, $2,000, for the East Flat Rock colored school property. It was determined that the money acquired from the sale of abandoned schools should be used to construct new buildings.

Attitudes in Madison County

Another district, named for the fourth President of the United States, shared similar hardships of rural life in a depressed community. Located deep in the Appalachian region on the Tennessee border, Madison County was home to at least five schools for black children in the late 1890s. According to the state school superintendent's *Biennial Report of 1904*, the school term for Madison County's black students lasted 15 weeks; the term for the white students lasted 17 weeks. For that year the county's black male teachers received $22 and black females received $23.66. Their white counterparts were paid $28.42 and $25.25 respectively (Van Noppen and Van Noppen, 1973). During the early 1900s, illiteracy was widespread among both white and black populations in Madison County. Survival was a more pressing need than education. However, small community schools, generally one room, were symbols of the possibilities open to those who became educated.

North Carolina's 1928-29 legislative budget provided funds for constructing a Rosenwald school in Madison County. Built on two acres of land, the Long Ridge School cost $2,093. According to documentation at Fisk University, the black community provided $200; the Rosenwald Fund, $750, which included an additional $250 because Madison was designated a "backward county;" and public funds, $1,143 (Rosenwald Database).

Long Ridge School, called Mars Hill School in Rosenwald Fund Records, included grades 1–6 in the beginning, but most years seven grades were taught there. Occasionally the school included eighth grade. There were two teachers and two classrooms. Pot-bellied stoves heated each classroom, and the school campus included two outside toilets, one for boys and one for girls.

A unique piece of research documents enrichment activities at Long Ridge School. Professor Edwin B. Cheek of Mars Hill College interviewed at least three former Long Ridge students as a part of an oral history project in 1983. His interview was published in *The Hilltop Online* of Mars Hill College (retrieved from http://hilltop.mhc.edu/). The students had attended the one-room school that served as the forerunner of the Rosenwald structure.

Professor Cheek interviewed Augusta Ray, who attended Long Ridge in the 1920s and 1930s, on June 15, 1983. Her teacher, Ruby Fortune, taught the children how to use red clay to make pottery. Fortune showed them how to make mats, dolls, and other things from corn shucks. Ray's family maintained lifelong contact with another Longview teacher, Sallie Ledbetter Davidson.

Seventy-year-old Shirley Sewell recalled making pottery under the guidance of teacher Ruby Fortune. After gathering the clay, wetting it, working and shaping it, students then placed their work on racks, using bricks to hold the heat, and fired it. The firing took place outside in the schoolyard. Fortune also taught students to make belts, whiskbrooms, picture frames, and corn shuck rugs. The children used pictures from magazines to fold into sections to create a belt. Parents were invited to drop by to view students' work on display in the classroom. Though Sewell finished her schooling in 1927, she recalls that her last teachers, Miss Luck and Miss Davis, took time to provide individual attention for each student. Luck and Davis encouraged pupils to look to the future and to build productive lives for themselves.

Both Sewell and Ray recalled a visit to their school and community by John D. Rockefeller, the nationally known creator of the General Education Board, which was founded in 1902,

Known originally as Mars Hill Colored School, Long Ridge was renamed in its final days as a functioning school the Joe Anderson School. Long Ridge School was built with funds included in the legislative budget for 1928-29. This is the only Rosenwald school remaining in the mountain counties and renovation is underway in 2010 to restore the building and use it as a community center (North Carolina Office of Archives and History, Raleigh).

an organization especially active in supporting black schools in the South. A lot of preparation went into setting up an exhibition for the wealthy philanthropist's benefit. Pottery and other crafts were placed among floral arrangements for his inspection. Wearing a hat, Rockefeller arrived at the school in a Model T Ford. The Standard Oil billionaire expressed admiration for the students' wares and purchased some of their crafts. He also made a donation to the school.

Manuel Briscoe, who enrolled at the Long Ridge School in the late 1920s, shared his experiences with Professor Cheek on June 18, 1983. His teacher Charity Hazard of Abingdon, Virginia, taught pottery as a special craft project. Hazard sent students to a nearby stream to fill buckets with soft clay. The pupils then formed vases, bowls, and pitchers from the clay. After their pottery was dry, the boys and girls painted them. Then during the fair organized by E.W. Pearson for Western North Carolina's black citizens on a vacant lot at McDowell and Southside, those wares and others were placed on exhibit. Pearson, who was responsible for promoting agricultural fairs for blacks throughout Western North Carolina, provided prizes for crafts (Ready, 1986). Briscoe won a blue ribbon one year, and another Long Ridge student won a shotgun.

Briscoe recalled the names of his other Long Ridge teachers: Ms. Mackie, Ms. Roseberry, Ms. Phillips, Ms. Davis, and Ms. Conley. Also, he shared another memorable experience: "Our teacher trusted me and another boy to take her check, about $50 a month, to the bank." Other students have similar memories of being allowed to run errands for teachers because the students were considered responsible. In their advanced years, school alumni express pride in having achieved their teachers' trust.

Charity Ray, curriculum coordinator at Mars Hill College (personal communication, April 17, 2008), shared her memories of attending classes in Long Ridge School, which had two rooms divided by a sliding door. One teacher taught grades 1–4, and a second teacher instructed grades 5–8. During Ray's school days there was neither a lunchroom nor an inside bathroom. Students carried lunches to school. They came from as far away as Marshall and Hot Springs. The travel distances influenced the school board's decision to end the school day at 2 P.M. to allow time to transport commuting students safely back to their homes on what in those days were especially treacherous, winding mountain roads.

The interviews also show that school provided multiple occasions for celebration, some for holidays and many for daily experiences. Recess at Long Ridge was a time for laughter and fun on the playground. Students enjoyed swinging on grape vines in the woods near the schoolhouse. Charity Ray also recalled the exhilaration of playing softball and "snap the whip" as well as preparing Scottish folk dances to perform for special audiences. Student dancers were outfitted with costumes made of bright blue and yellow crepe paper with hats created from plates, and shoes festooned with paper ruffles. The dance team visited other schools, such as the white Marshall Elementary School, to perform. There were other special programs and events, such as commencement and May Day celebrations. Those generally took place outdoors. Members of the community built a stage and put up a May Pole. Parents were special guests on those occasions (personal communication, April 17, 2008).

Mary Jane Wilson (personal communication, April 4, 2008), reminiscing about her teaching experience at Long Ridge School, affirmed that many of her students had made her proud. She used music to promote her goal of making school more enjoyable for students by celebrating "everything." Her young students sang songs such as "Oh, be careful, little hands/What you do/Father up above/Looking down on you." Wilson's glee club often performed for the community, sometimes on Sunday afternoons so most parents could attend.

Wilson also encouraged her students to beautify the school and its grounds. Under their teacher's supervision, they planted flowers in the yard and prepared exhibits inside the school. She worked tirelessly to instill her students with pride in their school. Wilson made herself a part of the community by living there during the school week and returning home to Asheville on weekends. That way she became acquainted with the people who lived in Mars Hill and acquired a more intimate view of the families of her pupils. Wilson boarded with Thelma Young and taught Young's two sons.

The Mars Hill community bought into the widespread practice that every child was a treasure of the total community. According to Charity Ray (April 17, 2008), Mars Hill was a neighborhood where "everyone raised everyone else's children." Madison County's black parents received support in child rearing from church leaders, from senior citizens, and from other adults. The community claimed to have a loving regard of Madison County's children — a concern that extended inside the school walls as citizens fostered institutional caring. According to former students and leaders, every single student mattered.

As was customary in other Western North Carolina elementary schools, Wilson's opening exercises included singing followed by morning devotions. She required that every child recite a Bible verse as part of her plan to use the first minutes of the school day to focus on a spiritual lesson and on character education to settle the students down for serious instruction. Learning focused on the basics of reading, spelling, and arithmetic. There was also an emphasis on penmanship. To keep up with the modern trends in education, Wilson attended summer school courses in Asheville or in Winston-Salem, where Winston-Salem Teachers' College offered classes. Courses offered to practicing teachers ranged from mental hygiene to reading improvement (J.H. Michael, Summer School Instructor's Report, July 15, 1938, Winston-Salem Teachers' College).

Like peers in other counties, Wilson punished her students when they broke the rules. "I would have them stand in the corner or take minutes off their recess. Sometimes they would write sentences," she said. Wilson also recalled that her pupils enthusiastically participated in weekly spelling bees and the year's May Day activities and graduation. Men from the community built the May Pole, and students danced around it as they wrapped it in many colors of crepe paper streamers. Music came from the piano inside the school, and graduation, in Wilson's words, was "hard to describe." Workmen constructed a platform outdoors, and she considered the community turnout "impressive." School days for most of the Mars Hill students ended with their graduation from seventh or eighth grade.

Other teachers at Long Ridge were Ida Sigmon, Grace Owens, and Addie Best. Those women taught the lower grades. Charity Ray identified Best as a teacher during her school days.

Although Madison County's citizens did not offer unconditional backing for minority students, Mary Wilson praised the support she received from the white community. The superintendent visited the school and occasionally stayed to observe classroom procedure. He was generally pleased with what he saw. There was also a cooperative relationship with Mars Hill College. "If I needed anything, I'd tell Mrs. Vann [Cornelia Vann], and she would supply us with whatever it was," Wilson said. "She was a lovely person ... very artistic."

Students, under Wilson, carried buckets to a nearby spring to get water. Most of the students drank from a paper cup or their own individual cup. Charity Ray explained the water sometimes became contaminated so, as a result, students were ill. Boys and girls continued to use the two outdoor toilets. As in other black schools, Wilson used coal for heat. A man from the community came early in the morning to build a fire so the school would be warm by the time the boys and girls arrived. Wilson would add coal during the day to keep the fire going.

Madison County's Board of Education minutes reveal that the name of Long Ridge School was changed. A short time before Madison County Schools were integrated, school board member Zeno Ponder recommended that the Long Ridge School, which in 1965 had only 12 pupils enrolled, be renamed. He suggested that the name should be one that would associate dignity with the building. Although Ponder's recommendation is recorded in the minutes, the actual baptism of Long Ridge School as the Joe Anderson School did not happen. Floor plans housed at Madison County's administrative offices designate the building as Joe Anderson School. However, perhaps due to the immediacy of integration following the new designation, community tradition persists in calling the school Long Ridge. The building still stands but has fallen into disrepair. In 2009, the Madison County School Board appointed a committee to investigate the possibilities of preserving the old building.

The African American grandfather of some of the Long Ridge students, Joe Anderson, a slave belonging to the Reverend J.W. Anderson, was, by default, one of the original trustees of Mars Hill College, the oldest college in Western North Carolina. The 25 original trustees of that institution contracted to have a building erected. When the time came to retire their debt, the trustees were $1,875 short. To ensure prompt payment, the contractors seized Joe Anderson and jailed him as collateral for the debt. Once the men were paid, the jailer released Anderson (D. Glanton, May 22, 1977. "A Former Slave's Granddaughter Retires at Mars Hill." *Asheville Citizen*). His story brings a degree of notoriety to the history of the Baptist college. Being held as security for payment of a debt incurred by white men signifies disrespect for Joe Anderson's humanity.

In contrast, now the college community has displayed its high regard for Anderson's contributions. In modern times Joe Anderson has been lauded for his brick-making skills, for his winning personality, and for the achievements of his descendants. In 1932, the college arranged to move Anderson's remains to a permanent site on campus. In 1999, Mars Hill College honored Anderson by formally distinguishing him as an original founder of the school. On a slab of granite near the college president's residence, the man once imprisoned as surety for the school's debt is memorialized in these words: "In memory of Joe Anderson, slave, who was taken by contractors of the first building on this college as a pledge for the debt owed them." His granddaughter, Mrs. Doskey Anderson McDowell, was honored 125 years later for her 36 years of service as a cook in the college cafeteria (Glanton, May 22, 1977). Anderson's great-granddaughter, Oralene Graves Simmons, became the first African American to attend Mars Hill College. While Joe Anderson and his descendants have been an important part of Madison County history, the change in their status reflects how Mars Hill College leaders dramatically illustrate a turnabout in attitudes.

Changes in Macon County

In Franklin, North Carolina, there existed a strong black presence even though the population was not large in Macon County. Early schools existed in various communities. Following the "separate but equal" ruling, schools were established for black children. One report in the 1870-71 North Carolina Legislative Session Book indicated delay in providing a building for the students in the Mill Shoal community and the intention to remedy that need as soon as possible. Another black school, located at Cowee, employed a single teacher, Mrs. S.C. Anderson, a white lady. Having a white teacher for black students may seem unusual, but in Macon County white teachers taught in the black schools until qualified black teachers became available. According to an article in *The Franklin Press* on May 2, 1957, the Cowee School originally occupied a log cabin that was later replaced. Subsequently the school merged with the Chapel School inside Franklin's city limits. The community of Alarka, which at that time remained a part of Macon County, claimed only one school age child, a female, for whom private instruction was being provided (Barbara McRae, 1987).

Prior to the establishment of a Rosenwald school, the black community received a boost to educational provisions for its children with the 1887 arrival, from his native Charleston, South Carolina, of the Reverend James Thomas Kennedy, the father of educator Ethel Kennedy Mills. He

Ethel Kennedy Mills taught at Arden Colored School, Weaverville School, Everett Farm School, and the Brevard Rosenwald School. Her formal career commenced in 1916 at the Arden school when she was fifteen years old and continued until 1966 when she resigned from Transylvania County Schools. However, she continued to work in varied capacities following retirement, including Head Start and organizing library materials at the public schools' central office (courtesy Ethel K. Mills).

The two teacher Chapel School in Franklin in Macon County received appropriations earmarked in the legislative budget for 1922-23 and was constructed for a total cost of $3,000. During the 1940-41 school term 21 high school students and 122 elementary students were enrolled with an average daily attendance of 16 and 110 respectively. In 1935-36 there were 113 elementary students and four teachers. Principal R.B. Watts worked with D.B. Barber, Emma S. England, and Beulah Martin during that school term. Located two miles from Franklin, once the site of slave auctions, Chapel was the only colored school in Macon County in the 1940s (North Carolina Office of Archives and History, Raleigh).

established a decided emphasis on black education in Franklin and influenced his students throughout their lives—and through them, their children. As an educator, he influenced the future.

According to Ethel Mills (personal communication, June 9, 1999), her father built both a church and a school easily viewed from her childhood home. The Reverend Kennedy was a young bachelor when he responded to an advertisement in the Connecticut based publication *The Church Record* (1886), according to Hall (1998). The ad appealed for a church worker in Macon County, North Carolina. The Reverend John A. Deal, the Episcopal priest responsible for mission work in southwestern North Carolina, requested that young Kennedy make himself available in Franklin on January 1, 1887. There the 22-year-old commenced his work with only two students, age 8 and 30. However, that number grew to 85 by the end of the year with students ranging in age from 6 to 60. Gradually he established a Sunday school with approximately 100 members, adults as well as children.

The Reverend Kennedy included manual training as a part of the curriculum, an addition for which he was remarkably qualified. Kennedy was a skilled craftsman. Daughter Ethel Mills proudly displayed, in her home, pieces of furniture constructed by her father. She explained that the wood (lumber) was rescued from the streets of Chicago when prohibition closed the doors of saloons. Her uncle had saved the wood from being burned at Chicago's city dumps by loading it up and giving it to his brother in North Carolina (personal communication, June 9, 1999). Working with the Reverend Deal, Kennedy helped build St. Cyprian's Church and Mission School. In the church he created an altar rail, a lectern, a service desk and a cross made from curly maple. Philadelphia resident W.W. Frazier provided money and tools for the new classes. Kennedy added cooking and sewing to a curriculum that included arithmetic and writing. He served in Macon County before accepting an appointment to St. Matthias in Asheville, where he was ordained to the priesthood (Hall, 1998).

Two former Kennedy students shared their memories of their teacher in *The Heritage of Macon County* (1998). Kennedy served as a role model, much like John Potts at East Flat Rock and Mr. Jordan at Texana School in Cherokee County. He left an indelible imprint on the lives of students Blanche Ray Means and Carrie Stewart. Means described Kennedy as man who dressed meticulously and influenced his students to do so. She recalled his wearing a blue serge suit, a white shirt with starched collar and cuffs, and a felt hat. Based on her memory from childhood, Stewart described Kennedy as a very tall man, who insisted that students be responsible for sewing on buttons, carefully combing their hair, and using proper speech. He fostered a belief that a true education is more than "book learning."

Means remembered that neatness of appearance and work was a standard emphasized in the classroom and that nonstandard speech such as the use of "ain't" was not acceptable. She recalled no whipping or use of corporal punishment, but she has a vivid memory that any student showing up with uncombed hair would be taken to a small room and have his or her hair combed with something resembling a wool carder. Kennedy reinforced habits of acceptable grooming, correct use of language, and courteous behavior in all his interactions with his pupils.

Stewart, as recorded in her *Foxfire 5* interview (1979), described her "wonderful teacher" at St. Cyprian's Mission School in this way:

> You didn't pass anything half way with him. You had to know it [the lesson]. I remember we wore out the page in the book learning the multiplication tables. That was the hardest thing to learn. He made us stay right there till we learned those tables. In the 5s and 10s, we could just rattle on, but we couldn't keep up with the others. He made us stay right with it till we learned all of them. We had to learn and ... I'm proud of it, too. If he had let us go on, I'd never have known my arithmetic" [Wigginton, 1979, p. 88].

Kennedy apparently adhered to the principle that idle hands were bad. When Stewart married, Kennedy advised her to keep her children busy, if nothing more than giving her daughters a needle and thread with a few pieces of cloth. He recommended that they sew on that cloth until they could get the stitches straight, no matter how many times the stitches had to be pulled out to make a fresh start (Hall, et. al., 1998). She also indicated that the Reverend John A. Deal, with the assistance of Sally Stalkup, held regular classes in sewing on Thursdays. By practicing sewing squares together to improve her stitches, Stewart learned the basics for future success in quilting (Wigginton and Bennett, *Foxfire 8*, 1984).

Stewart knew Kennedy in a more personal way than did the other students because he had boarded with her family upon arriving in Franklin. Even around the family dining table, Kennedy persisted in educating the young. He insisted that children use proper table manners, such as avoiding placing arms on the table, keeping knives at the back of the plate, using the fork to eat with, and not allowing crumbs to fall on the floor. That same teacher insisted that students keep their hair combed. "He taught from the bottom up. He didn't spare nothing," Stewart said (Hall, 1998, p. 57). Her teacher discouraged asking other students for help when one could not grasp a concept. Stewart's friend was slow in learning addition and subtraction. When Kennedy overheard her asking for help from a fellow classmate, he demoted the friend to the beginning section for that lesson. Stewart believed Kennedy's strictness encouraged learning (Wigginton and Bennett, 1984).

During a second interview for *Foxfire 8* (1984), Stewart revisited her school days. Although she did not name her instructor, she cited habits reminiscent of her description of the Reverend Kennedy in *Foxfire 5*. If a girl showed up for class with a missing button on her blouse, which Stewart called a waist, the teacher instructed her to ask her mother to sew on a button before wearing it again. Finally, in 1865, at the age of 90, the oldest active black Episcopal priest in the United States was asked what he viewed as important about his life. His answer: "I just did what had to be done. I accepted life ... and liked it. I think the greatest of my accomplishments was teaching people to read and write. The results of that work reach down to the present day (pp. 87–88)."

Foxfire 5 includes a further account of Macon resident Carrie Stewart's early education. Initially Stewart attended a three-month school at New Hope under the tutelage of William Bessman Hopper, known as "Bess" and as a black teacher throughout Macon County. Stewart and the other children at New Hope sat on slabs of lumber suspended on pegs. It was an uncomfortable arrangement, but Carrie's father solved the problem by making benches for her and her siblings to use. Carrie explained that only five years of study were offered in rural schools such as New Hope. To acquire more schooling, two hurdles had to be crossed. School officials in Franklin required that county students enrolling in the city school pass an examination. In addition, the student's family had either to provide transportation or to allow the young child to board in town. Unless those hurdles could be overcome, the pupil's education came to a halt at the fifth grade level.

Viola Lenoir, whose mother had been a classmate of Carrie Stewart, had a unique education in Macon County. A woman named Elizabeth Kelly took her into her home and taught her there. Lenoir's family had fallen on hard times and had little food to eat. Kelly supported the family and made a place for Lenoir to thrive. Providing lessons in the privacy of the child's bedroom, Kelly instructed her through the seventh grade. Despite seeing and hearing about the mistreatment of Negroes, like those beaten in Cherokee County and those lynched in Canton, North Carolina, Lenoir found it impossible to hate white people because the white Miss Kelly and her friends had saved her life and those of her family (Wigginton and Bennett, 1984).

So before the Rosenwald Fund offered stimulus money to erect schools in the Appalachian area of North Carolina, the Reverend Kennedy, William Bessman Hopper, and others had already provided an opportunity to learn in Franklin and Macon County. St. Cyprian's School was not supported with public funds, but its school term for black pupils was three times as long as that sponsored by the public domain. The term at St. Cyprian's was nine months, and the public school term lasted only three months. Although secondary education was not a part of that tradition, an interest in educating children was firmly entrenched in the mindset of the black community. Nonetheless, the big push by local school officials was to enhance educational opportunities for local white Appalachian students.

However, as recorded in the Fisk University Rosenwald Database, in the second decade of the twentieth century, black education received a boost with provision in the 1922-23 state budget for one Rosenwald school to be built in Macon County. Known as the Chapel School, the building was a two-teacher school constructed on a two-acre campus for a total cost of $3,000. The Rosenwald Fund contributed $700; the black community, $750; and public funds, $1,550. In his June 1923 report, W.F. Credle documented a visit to Macon County (Department of Public Instruction, Division of Negro Education, Special Collections, Box 8). Credle indicated that the building at Chapel was complete and noted that both material and workmanship were "good." He also commented that Superintendent Billings "is justly proud of what the county has done for the colored people at this place."

Resistance in Clay County

Another western county, named for Henry Clay of Kentucky, blended the efforts of white and black citizens to fund a school for the black population. As provided for in the North

Carolina legislative budget for 1922-1923, Clay County built a one-teacher school that cost $1,500. Of that amount, blacks provided $495; the Rosenwald Fund and public funds, $500 each. The record also shows that $5 was contributed by the white population (Rosenwald Database at http://rosenwald.fisk.edu). That single contribution may have been an effort directed toward rounding out the total amount to $1,500.

According to records in the State Archives and at Fisk University, the community called the school Hayesville Colored School number 1. In the Clay County Board of Education minutes for August 22, 1922, the secretary recorded an order for $150 to be appropriated from the Building and Incidental Fund to assist the Rosenwald Fund in building a Negro schoolhouse. Then, in the February 23, 1923, minutes, the board designated that T.M. McClure be paid $15 for extra work on the Negro school. On July 2 of that year, the board agreed to pay $75 for painting both Chigger Hill School and "the Negro school."

Three years after the school repairs, a delegation of "colored citizens" confronted the white school board to request the provision of a one-teacher school in Hayesville. However, the board, citing the sparse number of black students, denied the request. School records for March 1, 1926, state, "There being a request from the Col[ored] citizens before the board asking for a school in Hayesville on the basis of one teacher, it was ordered by the board that such request be not allowed on account of insufficient number of pupils to justify a school." Such a demand may have resulted either from the lack of funds or from the lack of an available teacher for that school term. No clear explanation is discernable.

By the next year, though, the board appointed Charles Mauldin and Harley Worley to serve as committeemen for the Hayesville Colored School. On October 3, 1927, the Board designated an amount not to exceed $100 for the purpose of digging a well at the "colored school."

During the remainder of the 1920s and during the 1930s, black men such as W.M. Herbert, C.H. Mauldin, H.B. Worley, Moody Nicely, and Charley Lloyd served as committeemen at various times, as documented in the school board minutes. In the late 1930s and into the 1940s, the board annually approved Elma R. Dennis, a native of Texas, as the teacher at the Hayesville Colored School.

Despite the recognition of scholastic education for blacks, the process was not smooth. The school board deemed it necessary to interrupt normal school terms and to shut down the schools from time to time. At various times epidemics of measles, infantile paralysis, whooping cough, and other illnesses led to closing both the white and black Clay County Schools. A measles epidemic occurred in November of 1939 and again in December of 1940. An epidemic of infantile paralysis occurred in August of 1944, and schools closed for two weeks in September of 1954. However, beginning in 1929, the board asserted that school would no longer stop for pulling fodder, a common practice in mountain communities. School terms began during the summer months and stopped during harvest season, thus creating a split term. Schools traditionally shut down for a few weeks each year to allow students to help their parents harvest crops, dry fruit, and can meats and vegetables.

The decision to end that tradition incurred objections from farm families, both black and white. Clay County's board, however, was only one of several to place school business before community custom in this regard, probably due to pressure from Raleigh. The calendar dispute, affected by economic concerns, seems less outdated when compared to the 2004 North Carolina law, supported by the business influence of the state's tourism industry and requiring all schools, including those in mountain counties, to delay the start of the academic year till late August. Though social convenience now influences the calendar, in the past family survival determined the calendar.

A major school decision in Clay County occurred during the war days of the early 1940s.

The local board affirmed its commitment to comply with the compulsory attendance law beginning in the fall of 1943. In late 1949, the board initiated a school construction program, but records provide few details other than the board's choice of Ronald Green as architect. On February 20, 1950, the board ordered that the two-acre property of Hayesville Colored School, the building recorded in Rosenwald Fund records, revert to its original owners because the building was no longer in use as a school and the board of education possessed no title of record for the property.

That decision is equally puzzling because one of the Rosenwald mandates asserted that school property be transferred to the public school system to house a building subsidized by Rosenwald funds. However, historians surmise that no building was constructed for Clay County's black population during the 1950s. New buildings listed in the minutes for November 6, 1951, are Hayesville High and Shooting Creek Elementary with additions at Ogden and with repairs at Elf School. There is no reference to a black school. In 1953, kitchen improvements at Elf School cost $6,354.70. In 1955, the board purchased an automobile to be used for driver education classes. Such records of school expenditures imply an ongoing indifference to the black community. Oral tradition indicates that, due to the small number of Negro students in Clay County, its few black students were routinely bused to a school in Murphy, North Carolina. Mark Leek (2003) documents the use of a pickup truck in which Clay County pupils rode and later the purchase of a small bus to carry students from Hayesville to Murphy to attend Texana School.

The practice of transporting students to Cherokee County may offer a partial explanation as to why Clay County school records are silent about black education for several years. That silence was broken on August 16, 1955. Board Chairman Paul Caler indicated to members R.L. Long and R.L. McGlamery a need to plan for 1955-56 pupil assignments. The board then appointed a committee—H.S. Beal, Ora K. McGlamery, B.M. Nicely, M.H. Payne, and Neal Rogers—to study the "problems created by the Supreme Court decision" requiring integrated schools. Though the board noted that the school at Murphy was not accredited, it ordered that the administration of Murphy City Schools be asked to allow Clay County students to attend its Negro school and that a request be made to the State Board of Education for an allotment of funds to assist Negro students to attend accredited schools outside the county. Another business decision, which probably indicates a concern about the need to comply with civil rights legislation, pertained to hiring attorney T.C. Gray as its legal representative by giving him a retainer of $100 (Clay County Board of Education minutes, August 16,1955).

Both white and black students were impacted by a change in Clay County's administration of public schools. On April 16, 1956, long-serving Superintendent Allen J. Bell died. Hugh Scott Beal, principal of Hayesville High School, replaced him. The community expressed appreciation for Bell's service to public education and sadness at his death.

Charles F. Carroll, a former principal of Hayesville High School, served as state superintendent of education from 1952 to 1969. As a result, Clay County enjoyed close ties with the Raleigh office during the increasing fervor of the civil rights movement. During those years, the Clay County Board of Education continued the practice of segregation. On July 7, 1956, it assigned white pupils to attend schools located in their residential districts, but it requested permission from the Murphy City Schools administration to transfer Clay County's Negro children to its Negro school and again requested assistance from the state to fund educating black students at accredited Negro high schools outside the county. The elementary students were expected to attend classes in Murphy, North Carolina. The same procedure was adopted on March 9, 1957, for the coming school term. On June 1, 1957, the board approved spending up to $300 to improve the Negro school building in nearby Murphy (Clay County Board of Education minutes).

School board minutes indicate that the board welcomed the opportunity to approve a class trip to the nation's capital for its white students in 1958 and confirmed its willingness to join Cherokee and Graham Counties along with the cities of Murphy and Andrews to form a partnership to secure a district vocational school in the region. The board made these progressive decisions but continued its backward policy of segregation. On May 24, 1958, school officials affirmed the local policy of sending black students to Texana School in Murphy and to the black Stephens-Lee High School in Asheville. Transfer information for black students was duly and impersonally noted on end-of-the-year report cards.

A hostile response came from the black community on July 19, 1958, according to the records of the Clay County school board. African American parents were displeased and angry about the second-rate provisions for their children's education. A delegation of 12 Negroes met with the board. The group indicated it had no desire to send its children to Clay County's white schools—that integrated schools were not their choice. Instead, they requested that either a satisfactory school be provided in Clay County or that the facilities and the building at Murphy's Texana School be improved. Complaints about Texana School included its lack of running water, its use of pit toilets, its inadequate heating system, its lack of provision for a lunchroom, the existence of only a single door to the outside, the need for new floors and other repairs. Such problems were absent from neighboring white schools in 1958.

The group demanded that an accredited high school be built in Murphy to serve Clay as well as Cherokee County. Board members assured the group that they were in complete sympathy with their requests and that they would do everything within their power to improve conditions at the Texana School. However, the board's statement made no reference to providing a school in the black group's home county. The board then instructed Superintendent Beal to confer with Murphy City Schools officials about the community's concerns and to provide $500 for the school's improvement. With this decision, officials continued to avoid compliance with the national law of the land.

Because instruction at the Texana School was offered only through the tenth grade, students could not earn a high school diploma. If an African American student in Clay County wished to attend and graduate from high school, he or she traveled to Asheville to enroll at Stephens-Lee (Clay County School Board of Education minutes, 1921–2003). Students boarded within the Asheville City district and returned to their homes in Clay County on holidays and between school terms (B. Dorsey, personal communication with Mark Leek, June 18, 2003).

Five years after the *Brown v. Board of Education* ruling, a sharp contrast in treatment of students, on the basis of race, characterized decisions made by the Clay County Board of Education. As recorded in the minutes for April 4, 1959, members approved a trip for its white students not only to Washington, D.C., but also to New York City. In the same meeting, the school officials affirmed their policy of segregation by assigning Negro students to Texana School and to accredited Negro schools "anywhere." Poor mountain students who were white had the new opportunity to visit major metropolitan areas, but poor mountain students who were black shared no such prospect.

Subsequently, on August 21, the board granted approval for three black high school students to attend West High School in Morristown, Tennessee, during the 1959-60 school year. The board agreed to pay $25 per month per child and to use an additional $25 from state funds for each student's expenses. In addition, it assumed the responsibility of paying transportation costs for students Allen Nicely, Jerry Lloyd, and James Corn to and from Tennessee. As the 1960s arrived, black students in Clay County coped with powerful barriers to a continuation of their education following grade school.

In 1961, segregation continued for student assignments during the coming year. The board assigned elementary students to Texana School and high school students to West High School in Morristown, Tennessee. In June 1962, the board received notice that B.M. Nicely had submitted a request to the governor of North Carolina that black students be allowed to attend school in Clay County. Nicely was notified that such a request first had to be submitted to the local school board. The board adopted a "wait-and-see" policy. Until a request came from black parents, no action would be taken. In the meantime, the policy of segregation continued. Following the previous pattern, all Negroes were forced to attend school outside Clay County. Negro high school students were assigned to attend Stephens-Lee High School in Asheville, West High School in Morristown, Tennessee, or Butler School in Gainesville, Georgia. Change came only after implementation of the Civil Rights Act of 1964 (Leek, 2003).

Silence in Cherokee County

The history of Cherokee County's schools for blacks is similar to that of Clay County. However, Cherokee County's schools for white children were sharply criticized by W.F. Credle in his 1939 educational survey, which was inserted in the county board of education minutes. Referring to the county's white schools, Credle described them as "almost indescribably poor ... they are wretched, and in their present condition are wholly unfit for school purposes." Credle labeled the majority of the county's white schools as "insanitary, unhygienic and unfit for use." Such schools, he declared, were likely to create an aversion to education (1940).

Although Credle referenced the existence of 60 Native Americans and more than 300 blacks in the county's total population of 16,151, this representative from Raleigh made no specific references to the quality of education for minorities. Credle was working for the white board of education when conducting this survey, but the omission is perhaps puzzling, since he was a vital member of the staff that guarded the black students' learning environments. It was obvious that poverty and rural conditions, such as remote residences and poor roads, created severe handicaps for all students and teachers. Every citizen in Cherokee County — white, black, and Native American — faced obstacles to achieving a higher quality of life regardless of race.

Credle documents the lack of professional training for Cherokee County's teachers and acknowledges that its "white children" were long overdue for a fair and equitable opportunity to receive a decent education. The county's buildings, deemed inferior, were often fire hazards. Credle urged that the Tennessee Valley Authority be approached about allowing their soon-to-be-vacated buildings to be converted for school purposes— white schools— after the completion of the Hiwassee Dam project. Such a transfer allowed Cherokee County to consolidate its many small rural schools, but Credle did not document any concern about schools for the county's black children — another chilling example of racially charged silence.

Ignoring black students obviously was the normal practice in Cherokee County, as indicated by the nonexistence of standardized testing for those students. Credle cited statistics from the scores on the 1938 Metropolitan Achievement Tests and the Iowa Silent Reading Test. On the entire battery, Cherokee County's white students scored consistently lower than the state average. The report, however, contained no statistics regarding the achievement of minority students. Also, there is no indication recorded of administering the advanced battery of tests to black students. The normal practice of recording test results would have differentiated between scores for white and for black students. The omission raises this question: Did the expense of providing the test to the majority student population hinder extending the program to include the black population?

However, the county's black population actively sought better conditions in schools for its children. Black parents were risk takers when it came to making demands to improve education conditions. Cherokee County parents succeeded in persuading the local school board to approach Raleigh for assistance. Cherokee County requested that a Rosenwald school be constructed for its black residents. North Carolina's legislative budget for 1925-1926 provided funding to build a two-teacher type school near the county seat. The community constructed the school on a two-acre site in the Texana Community, located a short distance from downtown Murphy. The total cost of the school amounted to $2,880. Blacks provided $650; the Rosenwald Fund, $700; and public funds, $1,530 (Rosenwald Database, retrieved from http://www.rosenwald.fisk.edu).

The Texana School and its community were named for Texana McClelland, a black woman whose parents, Isaac and Lucy McClelland, moved to the Appalachian region of North Carolina from Texas in the mid-nineteenth century. After Texana's marriage to Henry McAdams, the couple settled on a mountain site outside Murphy, and the neighborhood developed into the Texana community. The locale received national attention when in the best selling *A Walk Across America* (1979) Peter Jenkins wrote about his stay with the families who lived there ("The North Carolina Language and Life Project," retrieved from http://www.ncsu.edu/linguistics/nclip/sites/Texana/php).

The creation of a Rosenwald school elevated Cherokee County's black education to a higher status. Before its construction, because of the prevailing practice of segregation, public school sites had been reserved exclusively for white pupils. As was often the practice in early twentieth century communities of Western North Carolina, Cherokee County's black students attended classes during a three-month school term in the local church, a building made of logs, which tradition indicates were hewn by the women of the community. Later a small school provided a separate space for the children and their teacher, Mr. Hooper of Asheville (Satterwhite, 1995).

The Rosenwald building replaced a small one-room schoolhouse. The new two-room building provided space for grades 1–7. No high school courses were available. During the 1930s, Lori Jones and George Henry were the teachers (Satterwhite, 1995). Pat and Gwyn Kincaid, 2009 residents of Cherokee County's Texana community, live near the site of the Texana School, which they attended during their childhood years (personal communication, June 22, 2009). Pat Kincaid recalled that Elma Dennis had a teaching degree from Texas and taught the upper grades. During Kincaid's early student days, Ella B. Ragsdale taught grades 1–5. Ragsdale, who died in 2009, was a 1945 graduate of Winston-Salem Teachers' College. In 1958, she earned a master's degree in education from A&T State University. Better qualified than most of the white teachers, Ragsdale taught in the Murphy City School system for 20 years. Gwyn Kincaid, who is younger than her brother Pat, identified Texana teacher Helen Smith Miller as a "sweet person." Other teachers praised by the Kincaids were James Austin, Mr. Jordan, Mr. Franks, and Henry and Gertrude Pierceson, a husband and wife team.

Jordan organized a basketball team, which included Johnny T. Summerous, Charles Sutton, Don Colbert, and Neal Cowart, for the Texana students. According to Summerous, the team donned their uniforms to play Sylva, Bryson City, and Murphy High Schools (Johnny T. Summerous, personal communication, August 12, 2009).

Often teachers in the mountain communities boarded with families in the communities and returned to their homes on weekends or during holidays. Ms. Dennis and Ms. Ragsdale lived with Agnes Carter, the Kincaids' grandmother. "Our grandmother was the best cook in the county, and she always kept us laughing," Pat Kincaid affirmed enthusiastically. Teachers who lived with her received home-cooked food and benefited from an environment accented by daily humor. Later on, Ragsdale moved into the home of Lucy Siler, and Helen Smith Miller lived with the John Summerous family. The living pattern of teachers working away from their home communities brought them into intimate family circles. A number of other teachers lived with the Summerous family (Grace Mauldin, personal communication, August 12, 2009). Local residents generally regarded it a privilege to have a teacher share their homes.

Professor George Henry, a gentleman who became an integral member of the Texana school family, worked at the school as a janitor and as a substitute teacher. An older man with a reputation for being "very strict," Henry was also active as the community's scoutmaster.

Pat Kincaid had also worked as the janitor at Texana School. He oiled the floor and cleaned the ashes from the potbellied stoves used to heat each classroom. Kincaid recalled that during his time as a student, the school had outdoor wooden toilets, which were later replaced by a cement block building that had water. "We could wash our hands," he recalled. Perhaps as late as 1963 the men dug a well and installed two huge water tanks, one for the school and the other for the community (personal communication, June 23, 2009).

Class work and extracurricular activities enriched the lives of Texana students. Pat Kincaid readily admits that he had little enthusiasm for schoolwork, but Gwyn Kincaid enjoyed all classroom work except math, which she "totally hated." She recalled the pleasure of participating in school plays for Christmas, Easter, and the closing of the school term. Students performed musicals directed by Mr. Jordan. Said Gwyn: "You better not miss even one word or sing off key." Pat added, "And there better not be an incorrect verb when you speak. [Jordan] would lose it, and that would scare you to death" (personal communication, June 23, 2009). Students at Texana learned that standards existed both for music and for speaking if Professor Jordan had anything to say about it.

Clay County continued to transport its black students to Texana. On September 4, 1948, the Cherokee County Board of Education ordered payment to the "colored bus driver from Clay County" each month to assist in the cost of transporting students to Texana School. According to the Kincaids, Moody Nicely drove the bus from Clay County and spent the day at their home until time for the return trip. "There was no carrying on on that bus," Pat said. He affirmed that rules for safety were in play on the school bus and were enforced by the driver.

In 2009, Texana was home to about 153 residents who live on the same hillside where Texana McClelland first set up housekeeping. Although Texanans live in the Great Smoky Mountains of Appalachia — an area that is primarily populated by whites and Native Americans — they celebrate their heritage annually. Each year at homecoming, community members gather to recount anecdotes of the early history of their community. Often their stories chronicle events at Texana School.

Breakthroughs in Alexander, Ashe, Avery, Jackson, Stokes, Surry, and Yadkin Counties

Rosenwald elementary schools spread to other counties, but the records sometimes have become difficult to track down. Ashe County was the site for the construction of a two-room building, Crumpler Elementary School, for which the North Carolina legislature allotted funds in its budget for 1919-1920. Nearby Avery County was home to Elk Consolidated School, another type two-room school that was included in the state budget for 1921-1922. The Elk Consolidated School, constructed on a two-acre campus, cost $2,400. Of that amount, Negroes raised $600 while whites provided only $200. The $800 taken from public funds matched the amount provided by the Rosenwald Fund (Rosenwald Database).

Surry County erected four Rosenwald schools: Combstown, Mount Ararat, Sandy Level, and Woodville. Both Combstown and Sandy Level had two teachers at the time of construction, while both Mount Ararat and Woodville had four teachers. The Mount Ararat School cost $5,385, and Woodville cost $5,174. The Mount Ararat School cost $5,385, and Woodville cost $5,174 (Rosenwald Database, retrieved from http://rosenwald.fisk.edu). Thompson (personal communication, July 29, 2010) documents a school known locally as Ararat Colored School. Apparently the community never used Mount Ararat to identify the school, simply Ararat. The two-room school housed grades 1–6. In 1916 the Rev. Albert Jenkins and his wife, Ada, taught there. By 1926 with help from the Rosenwald Fund, a new three-room building replaced the earlier one. As often happened in those times, the school burned in 1938. The Mount Airy Colored School replaced the Rosenwald structure and housed elementary grades through high school.

The first two Rosenwald buildings in Western North Carolina housed students in Surry County and in Swain County. The Surry County structure was Sandy Level, a two-teacher school (Hanchett, 1988). A third room was added to the Sandy Level building, which was heated with a coal burning heater, and students carried drinking water from a spring. Teachers allowed students to walk home for lunch or carry their lunch to school (Thompson, 2005).

Citizens in Alexander County erected Moser School on a two-acre tract of land at a cost of $1,631 (Rosenwald Database). The Rosenwald Fund provided $400, and the remainder, $1,231, came from public funds. The project was included in the 1926-27 legislative budget, and the Moser School was insured for $1,000. Other Rosenwald schools in Alexander County included Happy Hollow (Plains) and Third Creek.

Sylva Consolidated School, included in the 1924-25 legislative budget and located in Jackson County, cost $7,850. Whites provided $900; Rosenwald, $1,300; Negroes, $1,500; and public funds, $4,150. In addition, $120 was donated to fund for the school's elementary library.

The 1918-19 budget provided for a Stokes County building, the Walnut Cove School, which accommodated four teachers. The same legislative budget provided for Yadkinville School, a two-teacher type school, in Yadkin County. In the same county was the Huntsville School, a one-room structure allotted for in the 1921-22 budget (Hanchett, 1988).

Innovation in Swain County

In Bryson City, two school districts for the colored race existed from 1889 until about 1909, when four such districts are documented (Thomasson, 1965).

In its budget for 1918-1919, the state legislature allotted funds for the Bryson City Rosenwald School, one of the first two Rosenwald buildings. By the early 1920s, the facility was in use with a small group of students. The one-teacher school, which was said to be a poorly maintained structure, provided instruction for grades 1–7. Mountain roads, coupled with distance, proved to be an obstacle to attendance. Enrollment at the school was quite low. During one year students were able to pursue high school classes, but that claim is misleading. According to a compilation titled "Annual Statistical Reports" by the superintendent of Swain County Schools, cited by Thomason (1965) in Table III on pages 91–92, five students were involved in high school work at the colored school in 1939. That work was on an eighth-grade level. At that time elementary subjects were designated only through the seventh grade. Eighth grade was then allocated as a secondary school grade.

One factor limiting opportunities at the school was enrollment. From 1937 until 1964, the student population numbered fewer than 20. During 1953 and 1956, the black pupil population did not exceed 15 for all seven grades (Thomasson, 1965). Of course, in those early years, any black student desiring a high school education met with the frustrating decision of resigning himself or herself to having none or, if conditions could be met, of leaving home

The renovated Walnut Cove Colored School in Stokes County is currently the site of the Walnut Cove Senior Center with Vicky East as its director. Closed as a school in 1952 due to the construction of London School, which included a high school with John Neal Hairston as principal and made it unnecessary for students to travel to Forsyth or Rockingham to attend secondary schools, it is now a gathering place for former Walnut Cove students to reminisce about their school days. The old Walnut Cove school operated from 1910 until 1952 with educators such as Troy Lee Williams (principal), Sally Joyce, Catherine Goolsby, Ethel Lewis, and Cora Hairston; the new five-room building opened in 1921 (photograph by Laura A. W. Phillips; courtesy of the North Carolina Office of Archives and History, Raleigh).

to attend school. Having a school partially financed by the Rosenwald Fund was an advantage to the black students, but the practice of segregation cheated black students from acquiring an education that kept pace with that of white students.

In June 1945, the Swain County Board of Education recommended to the N.C. Board of Education that black students eligible for high school work be bused to Jackson County to attend Sylva High School for Negroes. By September, the state had approved that plan as the means of providing secondary education to Swain County's minority black students, and the practice continued until school integration occurred (Thomasson, 1965).

In addition to the school in Bryson City, there was also a school for blacks located in Swain County's Birdtown, with one teacher. However, a sparse pupil population resulted in change. In 1932, W.F. Credle, C.S. Noble, Jr., and Superintendent C.F. Carroll, Jr., who later served as the state superintendent of public instruction, surveyed school conditions in Swain County. The school census and enrollment in Bryson City was 37 and in Birdtown, 21. Bryson City achieved a daily attendance average of 36. The enrollment of 16 in Birdtown School had an average daily attendance of 13. The survey committee recommended that there be only one elementary school for the colored students (Thomasson, 1965). However, no efforts to provide high school work were mentioned; even with the school merger, the pupil population failed to merit offering secondary classes. However, combining the two schools did provide a more efficient use of Swain County resources designated for its black population.

Funding for Swain County's Rosenwald school — the first in Western North Carolina — was appropriated in North Carolina's 1918-19 legislative budget. In 1935-36 Lois Chambers taught grades 1–7. The school's 1940-41 enrollment was 32 with an average daily attendance of 30 (courtesy the North Carolina Office of Archives and History, Raleigh).

Expansion in McDowell County

From 1920 to 1926, McDowell County received money for six schools: Old Fort Number 1, Old Fort Number 2, Bridgewater, Marion Graded (a term that came into being to show an upgrade over one-room schools), Old Fort Number 3, and Marion Number 2 (Hanchett, 1985). The Rosenwald Fund Card File Database at Fisk University provides additional information about some of those institutions. In 1921-22, the Bridgewater School was constructed at a total cost of $2,000. The black population invested $250; the Rosenwald Fund, $500; and public funds, $1,250. Bridgewater was a one-teacher school built on two acres of land. In the same year, the Marion Graded School, a six-teacher school, was built on a two-acre site for $12,000. Negroes contributed, $1,250; the Rosenwald Fund, $1,600; the public, $9,150 (retrieved from http://rosenwald.fisk.edu).

In the *Marion Progress* for August 4, 1921, an article reported the business of the McDowell County Board of Education as it considered bids to erect a "school house for the colored race." The contract was awarded to John F. Pead, an experienced black contractor who was required to secure a bond prior to beginning the actual construction. Pead was hired to construct a building with six classrooms, an auditorium and other rooms, which the news article reported was to supply all the "educational needs of the colored race" living in the area around Marion. In addition, the building was designed to provide high school classes for black students. The new schoolhouse was built near the black church known as Addie's Chapel and was to replace the Corner School, which would no longer be needed. The article contained words of praise for the black community's enthusiasm for the new school and for their efforts to raise money to assist in funding the new structure.

However, only four years after its construction, the Marion Graded School fell victim to a destructive fire. Attached to the card file database website at Fisk University is this note:

"The building burned on the night of 2/20/1925; Insurance $6,000." There is also a paragraph from the McDowell County Schools superintendent with this explanation: "The colored people were having a school program and in some way yet undetermined the building caught fire and in a few minutes burned to the ground. It was impossible to save the building or contents" (from http://rosenwald.fisk.edu).

An article, "Colored School Building Burned," in the February 25, 1925, edition of the *Marion Progress* indicates that a public entertainment was going on when the fire alarm sounded, but all escaped without a single injury. The source of the fire, according to the article, was an accumulation of rubbish and trash papers in one of the classrooms. A student went to that room to retrieve stage equipment for the program and struck a match. The lighted match apparently sparked the flame, and a blaze quickly engulfed the room. Fortunately, an alarm was sounded immediately so the crowd was able to exit the building and to escape harm. Editors of the *Marion Progress* credited the building's modern design, which included fire escapes, as the probable reason that no one suffered injury or loss of life. The auditorium was emptied within a matter of minutes. The school principal worked with the school board to arrange facilities for the completion of the school term.

In its August 9, 1928, edition, *The McDowell News* included an article written by Mary Poteat, which was headlined "Schools for Colored Race Show Progress." According to Poteat, during the previous decade the attitude of the black community had undergone tremendous change, moving from a state of apathy to motivation to improve their schools. Poteat described the change resulting from catching the vision of better schools from their white neighbors. The result was prominent in modern school construction in Marion, Old Fort, Bridgewater and Dysartsville. Citing the black community's pride and care of its schoolhouses and the regularity of school attendance as evidence of their eagerness to become educated, Poteat praises the way blacks were taking advantage of opportunities open to them. She documented attendance in the colored schools as being near 100 percent. One school with 17 students had achieved a perfect attendance record for a six-month term, according to Poteat.

Citing the careful maintenance of the black schools, Poteat said nine schools for "colored children" existed in McDowell County in 1928. The Marion School provided some high school level classes. A truck transported students to Marion from the Glenwood community, and efforts were underway to establish a standard high school in Marion for all black students in McDowell County. Two new schools served the needs of the black community at Old Fort. Prior to the construction of those buildings, classes were held in the upstairs lodge rooms at Old Fort, with one teacher at each site. In 1928, a three-teacher school existed in District 1 and a four-teacher school in District 2. Other schools had only one room and one teacher.

The Rosenwald incentive provided tremendous advancement for black education in McDowell County. Once again an outsider moved a community to nurture educational opportunities for blacks. Investing in functional structures advanced a positive attitude toward learning.

Progress in Polk County

Polk County offered an additional venue of black education during "Jim Crow" days. However, minutes of board of education meetings are no longer available at the county schools' administrative offices, but some records exist on microfilm at the State Archives. According to Hanchett (1988), Polk County hosted five Rosenwald schools: Coxes, Pea Ridge, Rosenwald, Tryon, and Union Grove. All but the Tryon School were two-teacher facilities. The state budget for 1920-21 included Pea Ridge School, but the Rosenwald Fund Card File Database at Fisk University provides no information about that building. However, the Rosenwald School, built in 1921–22, had a 2.5-acre campus and cost a total of $3,400. Of that amount, the Rosenwald Fund contributed $800 and public funds, $2,600.

Coxes School, constructed in 1923–24 on a two-acre site, cost $2,000. Of that amount, Negroes contributed $250; the Rosenwald Fund, $700; and public funds, $1,050. Union Grove School was constructed on a four-acre campus at a total cost of $2,670. The Negro contribution was $550; the Rosenwald Fund, $700; and public funds, $1,420. The largest building, the Tryon School, was a five-teacher facility built on a 3.5-acre site for $7,500. Of that amount, Negroes contributed $450; the Rosenwald Fund, $1,300; and public funds, $5,750. W.F. Credle, supervisor of the Rosenwald Fund for North Carolina, made this note: "The five-room building with auditorium at Tryon is one of the nicest small town buildings for the colored people to be found anywhere in the state. Our Community School Plan Number 5 is used and the results are very pleasing."

In Polk County, two boards of education existed. Tryon schools were administered through its city board of education. Other schools, including those in Saluda, fell under the jurisdiction of the Polk County Board of Education. For many years, Lola M. Jackson taught the children of the small black population in Saluda and served as principal at Saluda Elementary. Jackson, who held a Grammar A teaching certificate, spent six hours teaching her pupils, according to an annual principal's report she filed with the state Department of Public Instruction for the 1943-44 school year (Department of Public Instruction, Division of Negro Education, Elementary School Principal's Annual Report, Box 29). That year she taught 11 students in grades 1, 3, 4, and 7. Jackson retained one of two first graders and all three seventh graders.

One responsibility Jackson completed was a pre-school clinic and a beginner's day program. Only one pre-school child participated. Jackson issued report cards monthly and completed records for the state's assigned cumulative record folders. Students either brought lunches to school or went home for lunch. Jackson devoted Friday afternoons to involving her pupils in both speaking and singing activities. She also promoted crafting by teaching the pupils to create stools, bookends, baskets, and other objects. She enriched the curriculum by teaching simple sewing and art.

Coxes School in Polk County may have derived its name from the Franklin Coxe family who owned the Green River Plantation. It was built as a two-teacher school in 1923-24, but, along with Stony Knoll, and Pea Ridge, was consolidated at Union Grove in 1950. At times high school students received instruction at the school, such as the 17 secondary students in 1935-36. In 1945 the school's advisory committee was made up of Roy E. Simpson, Thomas Gray, and Monroe Twitty. Mary B. King was the teacher (North Carolina Office of Archives and History, Raleigh).

Jackson's one-room school boasted no indoor toilets, but soap and paper towels were available along with a pail of water and a basin for washing hands. A stove provided heat, and, according to Jackson, lighting and ventilation were adequate. However, she questioned the adequacy of fire protection. Her classroom contained only one blackboard and had no shelves, window shades, or bulletin boards. She and her students beautified the grounds, wrote Jackson, as much as possible. Her school program targeted improvement of effective reading skills, mastery of writing fundamentals, development of strong bodies, appreciation of music, and knowledge of safety principles, among others. Jackson modeled oral participation for her pupils by telling stories and by expecting them to recite orally by regaling their classmates with stories of their own.

Some historical data has been gleaned from the black community, especially by the efforts of the Polk County Historical Association. According to Anna Pack Conner (2008), after the turn of the twentieth century blacks first attended school in a log cabin located on Melrose Avenue in Tryon. Later Edmund Embury donated land for a second school for black children on Tryon's Markham Road. That school was known as Tryon Industrial Mission School.

During the 1920s the community erected the Tryon Colored School. Its name was subsequently changed to Embury School. In 1940, fire destroyed that schoolhouse and rebuilding occurred in 1942-43. During the interim, educators conducted classes at the Church of the Good Shepherd and above the Furnan Miller Store. Classes then continued in the new Embury School until integration occurred in 1967. About 30 years later fire again played a role in the destruction of the former school for black students. In 1994, flames engulfed the building and destroyed it.

Future scholars praised educators in those historic Appalachian schools for being committed to providing a sound education for their students. They did this despite being inadequately funded, often being forced to use their own money for needed materials. W.H. Greene and J.A. Tillman served as principal of Embury School at different times, and one Embury teacher, highly regarded by students, was Orline Wiggins.

Teachers were respected by parents and students. Among those educators serving at Tryon Colored School in the elementary grades during the 1943-44 school term, with Jacob Ayers Tillman as principal, were V.R. Candler, first grade; E.B. Robinson, second and third grades; G.E. McKissick, fourth grade; H.H. Hannon, fifth and sixth grades; and Wiggins taught seventh and eighth grades. Tillman noted the inadequacy of library materials and indicated the purchase of *Friends Here and Away, Jolly Number Tales* and *Friends Around the World*. Though it had an enrollment of 157 pupils on the elementary level, the union school owned only 10 pupil dictionaries.

Tillman authorized the purchase of a hectograph duplicating machine, a volleyball, ping pong balls and other athletic equipment. He noted that music was the latest addition to the curriculum. Tillman's school had four outdoor lavatories furnished with soap and paper towels and two drinking fountains, in working order, along with a swing, basketball and volleyball courts and a ping pong table. However, Tillman officially declared the outdoor toilets were in poor condition and had not been approved by the North Carolina Board of Health. Although bulletin board space, blackboards, heating, and lighting were adequate, in Tillman's opinion, Tryon Colored School needed shelves, better lighting, window shades, and increased fire protection.

In Tillman's annual elementary school report for 1943-44, he also said the school sponsored a glee club, a newspaper, and a baseball team. The school had its own lunchroom and an active Parent-Teacher Association. Of the school's 157 students, 53 were retained at the close of that school year. In Tillman's report for 1944-45, the student enrollment had increased to 161, and 31 pupils were not promoted to the next grade level. That term Tillman purchased a radio, recreational games, and two American flags. The school boasted a new cafeteria, and Tillman reported that his staff had created a stronger curriculum. Such records indicate the professionalism and concerns of black administrators during the extended period of segregation (Department of Public Instruction, Division of Negro Education, Elementary School Principal's Annual Report, Box 29).

On March 4, 1986, Leona Loy made a presentation entitled "One Room Schools in Polk County" to the Polk County Historical Association, which is on file at the county library. She identified the following schools for blacks: St. Paul, Union Grove, Rosenwald, Melvin Hill, Collinsville, Stony Knoll, and Pea Ridge. Schools were the centers of community life, and within the school organization was the key to learning. Parents supported the efforts of teachers and encouraged the students. One reason for the success of these small schools was the help older students provided for the younger ones. Successful teachers planned well-structured lessons with reinforcement from mature students who coached younger pupils and listened to them read. The process, which required review, enhanced the learning of both older and younger students.

Cathy Calure interviewed former career teacher Della Jackson on August 24, 1988. That conversation, recorded by the Polk County Historical Association, is on file at the county library. Because Polk County offered no high school for its black students, Della Jackson had completed a teacher-training program at the Allen Home School in Asheville, North Carolina. She earned a Class A Elementary Certificate for Teaching. She earned a bachelor's degree and completed course work for her master's degree by attending extension classes and summer school sessions. This piecemeal approach to earning a college education and a state teacher's certificate was the only way many future educators in Appalachian regions, white and black, could achieve their ambition to become qualified educators (Della Jackson interview by Cathy Calure, August 24, 1988, Polk County Public Library, Columbus, NC).

Jackson began her career as an educator in 1927 in Stony Knoll, her home community. She taught seven grades and at one time had 68 students in a single room. It helped, she said, that many of them were older, more responsible students. In the 1930s, Jackson relocated to the Embury School in Tryon. Embury was a union school with grades 1–11. However, Jackson missed being at Stony Knoll, so she returned there after the first term. She also taught at Pea Ridge School, a Rosenwald-sponsored schoolhouse. Jackson had two classrooms at her disposal and a smaller industrial room, which she converted into a school lunchroom, the first lunchroom established in any of the Polk County black schools. One of the older students was enlisted as the school cook, and Jackson felt the plan worked out well, especially because all students were able to eat lunch at the same time. Jackson then taught at another Rosenwald school, Union Grove, which also had begun to serve school lunches.

However, in the mid–1930s Jackson returned to Tryon to teach at Tryon Colored School, later called Embury School, for a monthly salary of $90. In 1950, three rural black schools— Coxes, Pea Ridge, and Stony Knoll — were consolidated at Union Grove. Della Jackson became the first principal of the consolidated school. Jackson described Union Grove as a "beautiful school." Then, in 1951, according to Della Jackson, all the schools for black students combined to form Cobb Elementary School, which was located in the Green Creek Community. The new school building provided for eight grades with seven teachers and a principal. Jackson (presentation, May 5, 1987) also identified two private schools for black students, the Love Joy Institute in Mill Spring and the Good Shepherd School in Tryon, that offered eight years of education (interview with Calure, August 24, 1988).

Advancement in Wilkes, Burke, and Catawba Counties

Other Rosenwald structures were sprinkled across the mountains of Western North Carolina, each with its own rich heritage, but in some ways similar to the ones previously discussed. The Wilkes County black population profited from the construction of six buildings. One was a nine-teacher county training school, which allowed a unique opportunity for older black students to benefit from advanced studies in agriculture and in home economics as well as for training to become teachers. From 1923 until 1927, the state legislature budgeted funds to construct five Burke County schools: Morganton, McElrathe Chapel, Willow Tree, Rock Hill, and Rosenwald schools.

Hanchett (1988) cataloged the existence of Rosenwald schools in Catawba County, which at various times provided educational opportunities for blacks commuting from nearby Caldwell County. Although Catawba is in the Piedmont, a portion of its mountainous territory extends into Western North Carolina. Catawba School was a two-teacher building included in the legislative budget for 1927-28, but the addition of third room included in the 1929-30 budget increased its total cost from $2,680 to $3,530, as indicated in the Rosenwald Database at Fisk University. Maiden, a three-teacher school, was constructed on a large four-acre campus for $4,560, to which whites contributed $200; Negroes, $300; Rosenwald, $850; and public funds, $8,210. The Maiden School also housed an elementary library that received a donation of $120 from the Rosenwald Fund. Newton Consolidated School was a large five-teacher facility built on a two-acre site, the minimum amount of land acceptable to Rosenwald standards, and a teacher's home was also located on that campus (Rosenwald Database).

Gary Freeze documented the educational history of Catawba's black community, where during the 1890s, leaders exerted effort to create more adequate schools. Generally white schools were frame, resulting from the availability of steam sawmills, but half of black schools remained log, an indication of the racial attitudes of that time. In Hickory, black residents made their homes on one side of the railroad tracks in the south end of town. From its early days, the black community was known as Bobtown. The white community named it after Bob Simonton, a freedman who, according to E.L. Shuford, became the first black man to establish a home there. Simonton, known in the language of the day as "a good darkey" to his white neighbors, exhibited a strong work ethic as he completed his duties as a woodchopper for the depot (Freeze, 2002). Later the community changed its name to Ridgeview, but, according to Hartsoe (2001), it was also called Colored Town or Southside, and residents frequently referred to that neighborhood as "the hill." J.W. Clinard (1962), in his collection of vignettes about the Hickory community, confirms the account of both Freeze and Hartsoe.

Catawba County residents had shown an interest in education in the late 1800s. In 1902, Catawba College invited Governor Charles B. Aycock to deliver its commencement address. The governor emphasized his efforts to improve education statewide, and the gospel of public education inspired prominent county leaders. Catawba was the first county to inaugurate a complete system of redistricting the schools. By 1905, Newton had erected its first school, described by Dr. Gary Freeze (2002) as the result of "the contagion for graded schools" spreading throughout Catawba County. St. James and Claremont built schools for white pupils during the summer of 1905, and school representatives selected a site in Snow Hill for the construction of a colored school. A contrast exists between a two-story 10-room white school designed to accommodate 763 white children and the frame building that would serve approximately 100 black students.

Obviously the difference in the number of students to be served was a factor, but the dual educational system again increased the cost of providing schools for the two races. Combining the white and black student population into one school would have been a more efficient use of funds and buildings. G. W. Setzer oversaw the construction of both schools. Contractors began erecting the black school on December 4, 1905, and construction commenced on the white school on February 6, 1906. Ninety percent of white girls attended schools at the turn of the century, and 60 percent of white boys, but black students maintained a slightly higher attendance percentage (Freeze, 2002). By the late 1920s, when Rosenwald seed money was allotted for black schools in Catawba County, parents and interested community leaders had built a foundation for the education of its black students.

The Rosenwald Investment

Rosenwald's philanthropy was an extension of his Jewish faith's emphasis on practicing charity, and North Carolina's black population benefited from his generosity. The success of the Rosenwald school building program is obvious because 5,357 elementary schools, teachers' homes, and shops resulted from the enterprise, but the vision of building an alliance between the whites and blacks with a public-private partnership proved futile. Total triumph was lacking because the carefully planned measures of building a cooperative spirit between the black and the white communities never materialized.

According to Hanchett (1988), that aspect of the Rosenwald-Washington plan failed. Although the Fund brought about cooperation between the white boards of education and the black community leaders that led to improving the education of the minority population, the credo of Jim Crow prevailed. Despite dramatic improvements in school resources for black students, the public-private partnership never took root. Whites persisted in viewing their black neighbors as less than equal and continued to squelch efforts to elevate the blacks' opportunities and civil rights to a level equal with their own. That victory would come from the federal courts. However, in the short run, new and improved facilities enhanced the learning arena for the blacks of Western North Carolina.

Rosenwald's plan to involve both white and black citizens in improving schoolhouses for black pupils was a wise one. According to Embree and Waxman (1949), conditions had to be met by each community receiving support from the fund. State and county officials had to cooperate with local citizens of both races to win approval for a grant. The overriding conviction that white leaders must be involved on the local level to ensure the success of the program for southern blacks meant that some money had to find its way from white wallets into the treasury reserved for each school's construction. Records show a lack of disbursement in some communities, but public funds derived from both white and black taxpayers represented the largest donation for every construction record available. In addition, blacks emptied their pocket change into the enterprise, a contribution comparable to the widow's mite praised in the Bible, for during that period in history the typical black had minimal material goods and even fewer dollars.

Although Washington demanded an emphasis on industrial education and Rosenwald plans included accommodations for that aspect of the curriculum, over time the schools stressed academic courses as well, such as the Rosenwald School in Brevard, North Carolina, whose faculty bought into the educational principles of Du Bois as well as those of Washington (Reed, 2004). Rosenwald classrooms were scenes of learning mathematics, poetry, history, and foreign language and served as venues of oral declamation and drama. The curriculum included opportunities to learn sewing, cooking, using tools for carpentry, and brick making as well as other practical skills. By the conclusion of the elementary grades, students had received a well-rounded education.

Though the schools aspired to academic success, a major transformation failed. The dream of both Washington and Rosenwald to elevate the education of black student to an equal playing field with that of the white student was accomplished only by demanding civil rights through courtroom and legislative action. Those changes happened in the 1950s and in the 1960s, but the process took decades to affect all counties.

The focus on elementary schools provided the firm foundation advocated by both Du

Bois and Washington. However, efforts to enhance secondary education were missing because counties in the western part of the state typically failed to provide opportunities for black students to earn a high school education. However, resourceful black families willingly sacrificed to enable their sons and daughters to relocate so their children could advance their learning beyond the basic skills emphasized in their elementary school experience. Separation from family was not easy, but necessary, if additional education were to be acquired. The struggle was great, but a determined group of learners plunged forward to achieve their dreams and the dreams of their parents.

Leaders in Secondary Education

Blacks utilized education as a means of creating community. Black neighbors did not necessarily agree with one another on political and educational matters. Like all human beings, their inclination was to draw their own conclusions based on how issues affected their personal lives, but school needs were a common ground with the potential of building unity and like-mindedness. Despite that commonality, there were occasional rifts centered on the school. When problems needed to be addressed, the neighborhood meeting place was frequently a classroom or a school auditorium. Because community centers had not become the established norm in black neighborhoods, schools and churches functioned as such during the first half of the 1900s.

As a result of underfunding, black citizens in Western North Carolina banded together locally to publicize school needs and to broadcast desirable additions as they congregated within their own school buildings. The necessity to provide for student needs unified them as they explored solutions. In the late 1930s and early 1940s, communities banded together to address a major problem: the lack of standard high schools in the region. Union schools—which spanned grades 1–10 with grades 8–10 operating typically as secondary classes—possessed limited space designated for high school rooms. Secondary student enrollment in union schools was normally small, with few students completing the requirements for graduation. However, even with the limitations characterizing those schools, community members garnered satisfaction in knowing that at least a few high school training classes were available. Black citizens believed that some opportunity surpassed no opportunity. Even with the limited offerings available, parents continually encouraged their children to learn as much as circumstances permitted.

A powerful stimulus to community esteem was derived from student success in academics and in extracurricular activities. Because of the pride triggered by athletic and academic teams, community building was a natural outcome of the development of high schools. As pride in young athletes ballooned, parents and fans combined forces to raise money for sports uniforms and equipment and to provide for bands and cheerleaders. The poorest fan pocketed coins to buy tickets to attend local games to achieve personal enjoyment and to support aspiring athletes. Other extracurricular activities won parental approval, as adults learned their offspring were talented in public speaking, in sewing, in masonry, in spelling, in reading, or in memorizing historical facts or famous speeches.

The Local High School Treasure

According to a 1962 report by G.H. Ferguson, North Carolina's director of the Division of Negro Education, the majority of North Carolina's blacks had by 1921 chosen either to enroll in the secondary department of a state college or to attend private boarding schools. Summarizing the 1921 situation, the superintendent of public instruction reported to the governor that 85 of the state's 100 counties lacked an accredited high school for its rural student population, including both white and black. In fact, the superintendent confirmed that 35 North Carolina counties lacked a standard/accredited high school for any child, either urban or rural (DPI, DNE, 1898–1961. General Correspondence of the Director [GCD], Box 1). Ferguson praised W.A. Robinson, who shouldered the responsibility for secondary schools in the Division of Negro Education and who had spent a decade assisting urban educators to improve their schools and to encourage rural communities to develop high schools.

Due to the reluctance of local school boards to allow such institutions to be designated as high schools, the schools were known as "county training schools." Their instructional staff offered secondary subjects as well as classes in teacher training. The George F. Slater Fund and the General Education Board provided money for the purchase of instructional equipment and emphasized that the schools develop programs in industrial training. Criteria for receiving funds included expanding the school term and providing money appropriated by local school boards for teacher salaries (Anderson, 1988).

The decade of 1930–40, in addition to improving both instruction and organization in elementary schools, saw a movement to increase the number of high schools available for black communities and to improve existing ones. From 1940 to 1950, the emphasis shifted to preparing high schools for accreditation. The 1950–60 bond issues created funds to expand elementary and secondary school facilities. The investment led to a movement to consolidate schools and to provide improved student transportation (Ferguson, 1962).

During the 39-year history of the Division of Negro Education, high school enrollment rose from 16,817 in 1921 to 68,255 in 1960. The number of accredited black high schools in the state increased from seven in 1920 to 208 in 1960. In 1960, there were 10,837 high school graduates, quite a contrast to the 59 in 1921 (DPI, DNE, GCD, Box 1). A hard-working staff in the Division of Negro Education, along with the support of local communities, brought about such improvements.

Bringing the dream of a high school education within reach propelled the black community forward. The process involved adding high school classes to the elementary curriculum and developing local independent high schools, both public and private. The histories of six established schools, as revealed in school board minutes, in newspaper accounts, and in archival materials such as letters, printed programs, and documented reports, illustrate the deterrents encountered and the persistence required. Interviews, oral tradition, and online sources add firsthand verification about the schools. Families who valued learning played an important role. Also, black educators, as showcased in success stories, worked relentlessly to increase opportunities for their students

Each course and each service made available in pre-secondary schools and continued as a part of the secondary program were building blocks enabling pupils from the black community to achieve a creditable secondary education. Music, which was a daily part of elementary programs that enriched the culture of communities, became a typical addition, often extracurricular, to high school studies. The emphasis led to the formation of glee clubs and choral groups, to the production of musical programs and to the establishment of school bands. Eventually high schools in Appalachian North Carolina enrolled musical groups in annual competitive concerts, which strengthened those programs and enhanced individual contributions.

Opportunities to learn a second language, such as French, Latin, and Spanish, enriched the educational experience. Classes in home economics, industrial arts, and physical education led to a number of extracurricular opportunities and strengthened learning that had a daily practical application. The addition of guidance programs allowed exposure to college and to job-training opportunities. Annual reports, which the state required high school principals to file, document the changing emphases in black high schools. The reports are filled with pertinent accounts that detail enrollment, average daily attendance, daily schedules, the qualifications of professional staff, the number of graduates, and other statistics.

There were instances in which white opponents denounced providing public high schools for black students. But that attitude had existed for decades in the South. Nancy C. Curtis (1996), in her *Black Heritage Sites: An African American Odyssey and Finder's Guide,* quotes from a 1933 pamphlet printed in Alabama by G. Woodford Mabry and entitled "A Reply to Southern Slanderers: In Re to the Nigger Question." "The taxing of poor white people to furnish 'HIGHER EDUCATION' for Negro wenches and sassy bucks, is an OUTRAGE upon the WHITES and an injury to the negroes," the pamphlet states. "The schools ... are turning loose on the country thousands of Negro men and women who have been taught the smattering of the higher branches ... who ... consider it beneath their dignity to work with their hands. There is absolutely no place in this land for the arrogant, aggressive school-spoilt Afro-American, who wants to live without manual labor" (p. 15).

In 1933, southerners, in general, believed opening up avenues to a high school education for African Americans to be of dubious value. Most whites frowned on advancing black education because it would encourage learners to develop an unrealistic level of aspiration and arm black students with non-marketable skills. Formal learning for blacks, as preached by Booker T. Washington and supported by whites, should be directed toward developing skills that would enhance the black worker's ability to find employment in jobs involving manual labor. Such skills ensured economic survival. Even some leading educational leaders frowned on an expansion of educational options for black students.

As late as 1938, one public school superintendent in Western North Carolina offered the opinion that a curriculum made up of job-related skills on the elementary level was probably more appropriate for black students than one offering a basic secondary course of study. In a January 17, 1938, letter to N.C. Newbold, director of North Carolina's Division of Negro Education, A.J. Hutchens, superintendent of the Canton Public Schools in Haywood County, wrote:

> As I said in my letter to you the other day, I doubt very seriously whether the matter of a standard high school is of nearly so much importance to these colored children as the matter of specific training for some specific job. I do not profess to know the answer. I am entirely willing to learn it.... My thinking for the colored children runs very much on the same line that it does for white ones. The main purpose is to make happy, useful, good citizens. The question is, "Which form of training will do most toward this desirable end?" [DPI, DNE, Special Subjects, Box 11].

Hutchens revealed an open mind as to the truth of his musings, but the late 19th century conviction that an academic curriculum was inappropriate for the black student resonates in his mid 20th century message. From the late 1800s into the 1970s, blacks zealously banged on closed doors barring advanced learning as they sought the establishment of schools, secondary as well as elementary, in Western North Carolina.

The state legislature established public high schools in 1907, but that law abided by North Carolina's constitutional approval of separate schools, barring black students from the benefit of secondary education. Though high school training was offered in 66 rural black schools, the Public Laws of North Carolina, 1907, which claimed to offer all of North Carolina's children equal opportunity for educational advancement, was in actual practice only for white students (Moses, 1989). Secondary schools as the educational norm for rural black communities would come later.

With the 1913 establishment of the Division of Negro Education and the appointment of

N.C. Newbold as director, there was increased effort to establish county training schools to prepare black teachers for their roles in the classroom. Newbold strongly supported the training school movement, and those institutions laid the foundation for North Carolina's first black high schools. Victory in the educational arena for honoring community requests for black high schools came unhurriedly as white leaders dragged their heels, but the battle lines had been drawn. Newbold's leadership and that of his staff succeeded in advancing the movement toward secondary education for blacks.

In Western North Carolina, Negro communities were small. In 1920, Graham County in the extreme west had only five black citizens. In 1928-29 and later, it reported no enrollment of black students (Cooke, 1930). Because the black population of the western counties included few school age children, opportunities for students residing in rural communities to pursue a high school diploma were virtually non-existent unless the student relocated either to Asheville, to Hendersonville, to private schools in other North Carolina towns, to public schools in Tennessee and in Georgia, or to more distant venues.

To attend a secondary school, black students in Transylvania County opted either to board at the private Allen Home School in Asheville, to ride a bus to Ninth Avenue School in Hendersonville, to live with relatives near Lincoln Academy in Kings Mountain, to board in Concord at the Barber-Scotia school, or to relocate to faraway Illinois or to Washington, D.C. (Reed, 2004). Attending the high school available in their county of residence was a privilege denied to them. Until the 1960s, Brevard High School opened its doors only to white students.

Help came from an unlikely source: Viola Barnett. For her persistence in seeking opportunities for the children of her community to advance beyond a seventh grade education, Barnett, a laundress at Mars Hill College in Madison County, has been hailed as a pioneer in black education (*Madison County Heritage*, Vol. 1, 1994). As a mother of nine children, Barnett realized that with no black high school in Mars Hill, her children would have no opportunity to earn a diploma. Once a student completed seventh grade at Long Ridge School, if he or she wished to continue learning in a formal setting and lacked transportation to attend the high school in Asheville, the student could choose one of two options: drop out of school or keep on repeating seventh grade over and over again. Such a practice made no sense whatever to Barnett.

With the encouragement and financial assistance of the men and women for whom she worked, Barnett was able to send her first born, David, to St. Augustine's in Raleigh and others to the private Lincoln Academy in Kings Mountain (Wilson, 1983). When the time came for her youngest, Herbert, to attend high school, she became pro-active. She wrote North Carolina's superintendent of public instruction, probably Clyde A. Erwin, who served in that office from 1934 to 1952, to ask if bus transportation could be provided for students from Madison County to Stephens-Lee High School in Asheville.

The reply took months, but eventually the answer came. Barnett received a letter announcing that buses had been secured. As a result, the way was open for all black students in Madison County to pursue a secondary education. One part of the superintendent's letter praised Barnett for her initiative on behalf of youth. The letter assured her that students from other communities, as well as from Mars Hill, would benefit from her action (Wilson, 1983). A simple effort had a dramatic effect: One woman's self-imposed mission to convince state authorities that transportation was a must to enable Mars Hill students to attend high school impacted all deprived students of Western North Carolina in a positive way.

The crusade to extend educational opportunities for black communities had been waged for decades before Barnett became a front-line soldier in the melee. In the early part of the twentieth century, educators struggled with the need to provide secondary schools for black students. A paper entitled "Negro Education in North Carolina" and dated February 1933 (Department of Public Instruction, Division of Negro Education, Special Subjects, Box 4) provides statistics for black high school enrollment.

The enrollment in the state's Negro public high schools, as recorded in that paper, for the 1924-25 term was 4,715, a figure representing 1.9 percent of the total Negro enrollment for all grades. In 1930-31, that figure had climbed to 16,817, representing 6.5 percent of the total enrollment. During the spring of 1932, public and private high schools graduated a total of 16,125 students. A larger number — 11,283 — completed secondary training in public schools while 4,842 completed courses in private institutions. The Department of Negro Education called for the establishment of high schools in every county having a black population large enough to ensure a successful secondary program. The need in Western North Carolina was acute due to its sparse black population and to the indifference of local school boards, which made minimal efforts to provide secondary education for black students.

A hastily scribbled note labeled "For Asheville" and probably penned by N.C. Newbold outlines information to be presented to educators at a Western North Carolina district meeting. In its margin, the note contains these words: "Attach to last letter from J.H. Michael" (DPI, DNE, Special Subjects, Box 11). Michael served as principal of a school in Asheville and as director of a western summer school program for teachers. He had previously worked as a Jeanes supervisor, a position supported by money from philanthropist Anna Jeanes. Her foundation provided a portion of Jeanes supervisors' salaries and enabled them to assist teachers in developing programs of industrial education (Anderson, 1988). Michael's leadership role in black education was far-reaching in Western North Carolina, and his communication with the N.C. Department of Public Instruction was frequent. Newbold depended upon Michael to keep him abreast of educational needs in the western counties.

In this note, the writer, presumed to be Newbold, listed pertinent topics to be hashed over with educators in the region around Asheville, such as facts about school transportation, about the role of leadership, about high schools in 32 counties in Western North Carolina, about how the people could assist in getting high school facilities, and about the intent to appoint a district committee to assess the problem. The note indicates that the committee could include from five to 20 members. The group was expected to engage in a methodical study of the 32 counties, and select two or three leaders in each county to form a large district committee that would then create a plan of consolidation for the entire district with maps and supporting data to present to local school boards.

The final entry in the memo states: "If this can be done in a statesmanlike manner by March 1, 1937 [we] may be able to do something about it." Though not clearly defined, "it" seems to be a reference to providing additional high schools in the western part of the state. The value of the note is that it clearly indicates serious consideration was being given to strengthening secondary education options for black communities. However, information about any follow-through by 1937 is missing.

Director N.C. Newbold initiated a campaign to expand high school opportunities by making them more accessible in the 1930s. Recommendations stored at North Carolina's State Archives in Raleigh include data for 24 counties in Western North Carolina in a list labeled "Suggestions for High School Facilities for Negro Children 1935–1936" (DPI, DNE, Special Subjects, Box 11). In this list, proposals imply the inadequacy of school boards in Western North Carolina to meet the needs of its secondary school population among blacks and point to indisputable concern at the state level to make it possible for black students to attend high school. State officials seriously pondered data for the mountain schools. The number of individuals in each county's black school population, the number of school units, and the availability of high school work guided the decision of state officials as they interpreted facts and figures from the far western counties. Those recommendations included the following observations.

Alexander County, with its one school unit and a pupil population of 364, had adopted a plan to develop a four-year accredited black school and was in the process of doing so. The list contains no additional advice for Alexander County. State officials suggested that Alleghany County, with its four school units and a student population of 88, send its high school students to an outside facility. For Ashe County's high school population, officials recommended that two years of secondary instruction be offered at Crumpler School and that both juniors and seniors be assigned to an outside school. For Avery County, the state proposed a similar plan: that two years of secondary study be offered at Elk Park and that "upperclassmen" attend an outside school.

A plan to send black high school students away to school — outside their communities of residence — was proffered for Cherokee, Clay, Madison, Mitchell, Swain, Watauga, and Yancey Counties. The school population and number of school units for that group ranged from 10 students with one school in Mitchell County to 125 students with two schools in Cherokee County. Clay claimed 24 students in one school; Madison, 67 and two schools; Swain, 40 students in two schools; Watauga, 62 students in two schools, and Yancey County, 56 students in two schools.

Solutions for the other counties were similar to those for both Alleghany and Ashe Counties. After completing their freshmen and sophomore years locally, juniors and seniors in Haywood, Macon, and Yadkin were to be sent away to complete high school. There was a notation that two years of secondary classes were available in Transylvania County with its school population of 252, but the committee urged that all Transylvania high school students be sent to nearby Hendersonville. Yadkin County, credited with a pupil population of 312 served by nine school units, had a second alternative suggested — that all secondary students would benefit by attending Houstonville in nearby Iredell County. In a few counties, the standard recommendation was consolidation. Those included Buncombe with 5,406 students; Burke, with 1,141; Caldwell, with 1,095; Henderson, with 622; McDowell, with 700; Polk, 684; and Wilkes, 855.

Buncombe and Burke were to concentrate on the high schools in Asheville and Morganton, respectively. In Asheville, two high schools existed: Stephens-Lee and Allen. In Morganton, there was Olive Hill. Caldwell County had an accredited school at Lenoir, and it was recommended that all students from Harpertown, Dulatown, and Warrior be transported there. In addition, the committee suggested that high school students from five school communities in the northeastern section of the county and three in the southwestern be transported to Lenoir.

The committee strongly urged that Henderson County schools combine with the Hendersonville city school system. Henderson County was home to five rural schools at that time. Brickton, eight miles from the black school in Hendersonville, had a student population of 68; Clear Creek, with 26 students, was only four miles from town; Horseshoe, with 36 students, was five miles away, as was East Flat Rock with 37 students. Edneyville's 45 students would have to travel 12 miles to reach the city school. Consolidation would enable 417 elementary students and 155 high school students to attend the same school. Although transportation problems required thoughtful solutions, the larger number of students would increase the efficiency of the educational provisions for black students and would provide benefits for black teachers. The increased student population for the high school would enlarge the number of courses available and increase extracurricular opportunities.

In addition, a chart entitled "Number of Negro School Units by Size, 1935–36" (DPI, DNE, Special Subjects File, Box 11) indicates there were no colored schools, elementary or high school, in Graham County, but seven small high schools occupying from one to two classrooms existed in Alexander, Avery, Haywood, McDowell, Polk, Rutherford, and Transylvania Counties. Burke, Caldwell, Henderson, Rutherford, and Wilkes had high schools with three to five rooms. Buncombe County alone had a building with six or more rooms. An analysis of the total number of black schools—13 offering secondary education; 134, elementary education — evokes a conviction that the black community had been cheated of normal educational growth for its children. The chart, which reveals that only the one high school in Buncombe County had adequate classroom space, documents the problem of unfair treatment.

The enrollment in high schools in Western North Carolina ranged from 13 in Transylvania County to 620 in Buncombe County, according to a chart entitled "Enrollment ... in Negro Schools 1935-36 (Department of Public Instruction, Division of Negro Education, Special Subjects File, Box 11). The three largest high schools following Buncombe County, according to this table, were Rutherford with 170 students, Wilkes with 150, and Burke with 102. The total high school enrollment for that year was 1,386. However, in the 25 counties considered, the elementary school enrollment totaled 9,753. The total suggests that quite a large number of students completing the seventh grade did not continue their education.

Director N.C. Newbold initiated a follow-up of possible solutions to the high school problem in the western counties. He appointed another committee to secure information in an attempt to pinpoint strategic locations for high schools in the mountain region. In Box 11 (DPI, DNE, Special Subjects File, Box 11), there is a folder labeled WNC Negro Education, 1936–1942, which records the membership of a committee recruited to study public school facilities for Negro children in 27 Western North Carolina counties. Members from Asheville College were William H. Morgan, John Miller, and Elah Cowart; from Western Carolina Teachers College, John S. Seymour, William A. Ashbrook, and Cordelia Camp; and from Appalachian State Teachers College, Wiley Smith, J. Harold Wolfe, and Amos Abrams. Newbold assigned the task of identifying local school needs to professional educators working in the western counties.

The 27 counties were divided among the teams based upon geographical proximity to their institutions. To successfully complete their assignment, committee members used a prescribed strategy: forge liaisons with local leaders to formalize a total picture of the elementary schools and the prospects of offering high schools in those counties or in adjacent counties. The committee recognized that assistance from prominent members of black Appalachian communities was essential to overcome a reluctance to assume ownership of plans to enlarge educational prospects in targeted counties.

Newbold carefully planned the survey with the intent to limit its cost. Noting that a considerable amount of information had already been assembled and that Negro members employed at the state level would be able to travel to gather the needed information and to aid in interpreting the data because the project would fall within their area of service, Newbold also indicated that a member of the faculties at Duke University and at the University of North Carolina would willingly assist. He endorsed the involvement of L.R. Reynolds of the Commission on Interracial Cooperation and allowed members of the commission to prepare and present the final report. By involving these leaders with those on the local level, Newbold believed a plan of consolidation with high schools serving more than one county might be accomplished more effectively.

The study included consideration of both day-school services and boarding schools. One key would be the ability to transport students from homes in remote communities to a day school. If that were not feasible, then acquiring contractual services with private boarding schools was another option. Still another possibility was to persuade local boards to provide partial payment for costs, other than instructional, for boarding students. Newbold outlined the need to determine per capita cost for instruction in each county and the average per capita cost for all the counties involved, on the basis of total school population and not by race alone. The plan would include data about the cost of transportation, the cost of instruction, and the cost of boarding. By bringing enough students to schools in a central area, the potential of developing high schools became more likely.

The prospect of creating joint-county schools was deemed desirable if two or more counties were willing to commit to providing money to supplement state funding. Newbold directed the committee to compile information about school buildings, equipment, and school grounds, including area, drainage, elevation, and beautification. Facts about heat and ventilation, as well as the value of each building, equipment, and site, would be necessary. Finally, Newbold requested that a Kodak picture be made of each school building.

In addition, the committee was instructed to obtain information about each teacher's training and certification as well as the enrollment and average daily attendance of students. If a school contained more than one room, Newbold wanted a record indicating how many pupils were assigned to each room. Teacher qualifications, school attendance, and environmental issues, such as overcrowding, were deemed important matters for maximizing improvements in the educational sites.

In conclusion, Newbold asked that numbers be compiled of potential high school students by age — not only the number of pupils who had recently completed seventh grade but also those who had finished seventh grade in the previous three to five years and had been unable to acquire a high school education. By expanding the search for secondary students to a variety of ages, Newbold was fighting for an enrollment large enough to justify the support of rural high schools.

An impressive compilation of statistics resulted from the committee's investigations. To plan school bus routes, local citizens marked the location of students' homes on county maps. Team members, with the aid of local school officials, compiled data that included student enrollment, average daily attendance, and number of teachers in each school. The committee focused its attention on the need for more centrally located high schools in western counties. The committee submitted noteworthy data to Director Newbold. The charts and tables indicated the number of students who had completed seventh grade (DPI, DNE, Special Collections, Box 11). In 1940, there were no high school facilities in eight counties, but there were potential secondary students: Alleghany, with four black students; Ashe, with 19; Avery, with four; Cherokee, with 10; Macon, with 24; Madison, with eight; Watauga, with eight; and Yadkin, with 23. "Non-standard" or "inadequate" was the label used for five high schools: Sixth Avenue in Hendersonville with an enrollment of 79 black students; County Training School in Sylva, with 30; Hudgins High School in Marion, with 54; Walnut Cove in Stokes County, with 30; and Brevard High School in Transylvania County, with 27. Perhaps most significant is the fact that eight counties had no high school facilities, forcing the young people whose families lived there to forfeit further training after seventh grade or to move away from home to continue their education.

Enrollment in Negro Schools 1935–36

County	Elementary Grades 1–7 incl.	High School	Total	Seventh Grade Only
Alexander	315	49	364	28
Alleghany	84		84	3
Ashe	154		154	
Avery	52		52	3

(continued on page 168)

Enrollment in Negro Schools 1935–36 (continued)

County	Elementary Grades 1–7 incl.	High School	Total	Seventh Grade Only
Buncombe	2,887	620	3,507	437
Burke	771	102	873	53
Caldwell	609	84	693	66
Cherokee	99		99	4
Clay	23		23	1
Graham	None			
Haywood	172	22	194	26
Henderson	416	68	484	35
Jackson	187		187	9
Macon	136		136	8
Madison	54		54	12
McDowell	439	62	501	30
Mitchell	10		10	
Polk	413	46	459	42
Rutherford	1,636	170	1,806	160
Swain	40		40	2
Transylvania	174	13	187	26
Watauga	62		62	
Wilkes	691	150	841	67
Yadkin	277		277	47
Yancey	51		51	5
	9,752	1,386	11,138	1,064

Courtesy of the North Carolina Office of Archives and History, Raleigh.

School Population and Average Daily Attendance 1935–36

County	School Population Ages 6–21	Average Daily Attendance		
		Elementary	High School	Total
Alexander	364	295	38	333
Alleghany	88	69		69
Ashe	156	116		116
Avery	78	49	10	59
Buncombe	5406	2549	483	3032
Burke	1141	677	95	772
Caldwell	1095	519	67	586
Cherokee	125	74		74
Clay	24	15		15
Graham	None			0
Haywood	258	149	21	170
Henderson	622	377	61	438
Jackson	227	150		150
Macon	214	115		115
Madison	67	47		47
McDowell	700	386	55	441
Mitchell	10	9		9
Polk	684	307	43	350
Rutherford	1915	1349	147	1496
Swain	40	37		37
Transylvania	252	135	11	146
Watauga	62	57		57
Wilkes	855	594	133	727
Yadkin	312	242		242
Yancey	56	43		43
	14,751	8,360	1,164	9,524

Courtesy of the North Carolina Office of Archives and History, Raleigh, North Carolina.

Schools, Number Negro Teachers, Enrollment, and Average Daily Attendance of 27 Counties in Western North Carolina

County and City Units	Name of School	1941–42 No. Teachers and Principals		1940–41 Enrollment		1940–41 Average Daily Attendance	
		H.S.	Elem.	H.S.	Elem.	H.S.	Elem.
ALLEGHANY	Cherry Lane		1		19		19
	Gap Civil		1		31		31
	Glade Creek		1		22		22
	Prathers Creek		1		19		19
ALEXANDER	Happy Plains	3	9	94	358	94	358
ASHE	Bristol		1		21		17
	Creston		1		24		22
	Crumpler Institute		1		47		46
	Pine Swamp		1		13		11
AVERY	Elk Park		2	7	43	7	42
BUNCOMBE	Black Mountain		3		108		103
	Leicester		1		16		14
	Shiloh		6		203		194
	South Asheville		5		157		156
	Swannanoa		2		51		49
	Weaverville		2		53		52
ASHEVILLE	Ashland Avenue				369		336
	Burton Street				120		109
	Hill Street				432		385
	Livingston St.	47	20		434		420
	Mountain St.				451		425
	Stephens-Lee			759		660	
BURKE	Corpening		2		46		45
	Connelly Springs		1		14		8
	Drexel		2		53		47
	Maple Grove		1		14		13
	Mission		3		21		21
	Willow Tree				73		63
GLEN ALPINE	McAlpine		4		137		133
	Rock Hill		1		22		21
	Rosenwald		1		31		25
	Shiloh		1		50		49
	Morganton	5	8	159	271	149	256
CALDWELL	Adako		1		25		21
	Franklin		1		13		9
	Bush Town		1		27		21
	Dula Town		1		37		33
	Granite Falls		1		12		12
	Harper Town		2		55		47
	Kings Creek		2		61		57

(continued on page 170)

Schools, Number Negro Teachers, Enrollment, and Average Daily Attendance of 27 Counties in Western North Carolina (continued)

County and City Units	Name of School	1941–42 No. Teachers and Principals		1940–41 Enrollment		1940–41 Average Daily Attendance	
		H.S.	Elem.	H.S.	Elem.	H.S.	Elem.
	Mars Hill		1		19		19
	Freedman	4	5	135	186	117	175
	West End		3		95		85
CHEROKEE	Andrews		1		37		26
	Texana		2		70		65
CLAY	Hayesville		1		11		8
GRAHAM	(None)						
HAYWOOD	Waynesville	1	2	19	59	17	52
	Reynolds		2		69		64
HENDERSON	Brickton		1		45		39
	Edneyville		1		29		18
	East Flat Rock		2		79		63
	Hendersonville Hi.	3	6	79	252	67	218
JACKSON	Colored Consolidated	1	5	30	129	29	123
MACON	Chapel	1	4	21	122	16	110
MADISON	Hot Springs		1		8		8
	Mars Hill		1		42		40
McDOWELL	Bridgewater*		2		54		49
	Dysartville*						
	Old Fort		4		118		113
	Vein Mountain		1		15		14
	Hudgins	3	5	54	201		192
	Glade Elem.		1		18		18
MITCHELL	(None)						
POLK	Coxes		1		35		31
	Melvin Hill		1		56		39
	Pea Ridge		1		34		29
	Rosenwald		2		75		52
	Stoney Knoll		1		22		19
	Union Grove		1		28		16
	Saluda		1		12		9
	Tryon	2	4	48	153	46	145
RUTHERFORD	St. Johns**		4		108		92
	Antioch**						
	Uree**						
	Bostic		1		27		27
	Broad River		1		27		22

Schools, Number Negro Teachers, Enrollment, and Average Daily Attendance of 27 Counties in Western North Carolina *(continued)*

County and City Units	Name of School	1941–42 No. Teachers and Principals		1940–41 Enrollment		1940–41 Average Daily Attendance	
		H.S.	Elem.	H.S.	Elem.	H.S.	Elem.
	Bryants		1		24		20
	Buck Shoals		1		28		15
	Caroleen		2		54		46
	Chapel Hill		1		24		15
	Cliffside		2		69		54
	Doggetts Grove		3		107		94
	Duncan Creek		1		27		24
	Grahamtown	4	6	122	254	111	224
	Henrietta		2		59		48
	New Hope	6	7	185	268	166	248
	Spindale		4		161		139
	Union Mills		4		122		113
	Webbs		1		30		25
STOKES	Walnut Grove	1	4	30	235	280	210
	Danbury		1		15		10
	Dry Hollow		2		67		56
	Brown Mountain		1		21		18
	Francisco		1		18		14
	Brim's Grove		1		36		30
	Locust Grove		1		24		23
	Prestonville		2		50		45
	Pine Hall		2		75		63
	Pinnacle		1		46		39
SURRY	Combstown		2		53		52
	Elkin		2		72		66
	Little Richmond		1		31		30
	Pilot Mountain		1		26		26
	Pisgah		1		24		20
	Red Brush		1		26		24
	Ridge		2		60		45
	Sandy Level		2		73		65
	Westfield		2		64		56
	Ararat	4	5	120	185	109	171
	Virginia St.		2		69		62
SWAIN	Bryson City		1		32		30
TRANSYLVANIA	Glade Creek		1		45		31
	Rosenwald	1	4	27	113	22	94
WATAUGA	Boone		2	2	58	2	48
WILKES	Darby		1		6		5
	Lincoln Heights	6	9	170	291	154	282
	Parks Grove		1		15		14
	Rock Creek		1		15		14

(continued on page 172)

Schools, Number Negro Teachers, Enrollment, and Average Daily Attendance of 27 Counties in Western North Carolina (continued)

County and City Units	Name of School	1941–42 No. Teachers and Principals		1940–41 Enrollment		1940–41 Average Daily Attendance	
		H.S.	Elem.	H.S.	Elem.	H.S.	Elem.
	Ronda		1		20		16
	Thankful		2		66		53
	Traphill		1		33		25
	N. Wilkesboro		5		146		142
YADKIN	Barney Hill		1		25		23
	Boonville	2	3	38	57	31	56
	Enon		1		15		14
	Huntersville		1		16		16
	Jonesville		2		80		83
	Kingknob		1		18		17
	Yadkinville		2		47		44
YANCEY	Burnsville		1		42		40

Courtesy of the North Carolina Office of Archives and History, Raleigh, North Carolina.
*Bridgewater and Dysartville use combined numbers for both schools.
**St. Johns, Antioch, and Uree use combined numbers for all three schools.

By 1940, Western North Carolina counties with standard high schools for blacks—standard meaning those with state accreditation—included Buncombe with the private Allen School and Stephens-Lee High School, Burke with Olive Hill School in Morganton, Caldwell with Freedman High in Lenoir, Rutherford with New Hope High in Rutherfordton and Colored High in Grahamtown of Forest City, Surry with Ararat Colored High in Mount Airy, and Wilkes County with Lincoln Heights in Wilkesboro. Of the 27 counties surveyed by the WNC committee, only one other was home to a standard high school: Alexander County with the Happy Plains School of Taylorsville. Three other secondary schools—in Hickory, Catawba and Newton—were in Catawba County, located mostly in North Carolina's Piedmont with only a portion in the mountain region. Within the 27 or 32 counties considered by the Department of Public Instruction to be western, there were 13 secondary black schools.

As they became aware of the sudden spotlight on their educational needs, Appalachian black communities no doubt rejoiced that Raleigh seemed on the threshold of meeting their desire for more advanced schools. White community members may have also noted that state officials were exploring regions far from the capital. The committee's response to their assignment resulted in gathering extensive information. Additional data includes correspondence from Superintendent of Public Education Clyde A. Erwin and correspondence between members of the committee, white superintendents, and Newbold, as well as between principals of black schools and Newbold, and plans for acquiring the targeted information.

Letters from the principal of Lincoln Academy in Kings Mountain, North Carolina, illustrate the need to provide additional opportunities for secondary education in the western counties. In an August 6, 1941, letter, Henry C. McDowell indicates Lincoln Academy had accepted more than 20 applications for its boarding program from youth residing in homes scattered throughout several western counties, despite their parents' inability to provide much more than clothing and travel. He requests that Newbold support his request of N.C. Larabee, state director of the Division of Student Work for the National Youth Administration in North

Carolina. As a part of the New Deal Program, students, both boys and girls, could earn from $6 to $40 a month for completing work-study projects at their schools. McDowell asked Larabee to grant work scholarships to those students residing in counties in which high school programs were not available. Newbold complied with that request in an August 8 letter that heartily endorsed McDowell's request (Department of Public Instruction, Division of Negro Education, Special Subjects, Box 11).

Officials in the state Department of Public Instruction were concerned about the legal aspects of designating public schools to serve more than a single county. North Carolina's attorney general determined that no laws would be broken if central high schools were established to accommodate multiple counties. In an October 20, 1937, letter addressed to state Superintendent Clyde A. Erwin, Attorney General A.A.F. Seawell summarized his findings regarding school law related to joint schools and the powers of the board. He interpreted the original statute, C.S. 5482, as allowing those schools serving more than one county to be legal, as not having been repealed by any of the School Machinery Acts, and therefore, in his judgment, still in force.

Seawell concluded that school boards could establish high schools to serve contiguous counties. The legal decision encouraged school boards to seek alternative locations in which to provide high school training for their black students. Seawell also attached an article from the School Law of West Virginia — Chapter 18, Article 5, Section 16 — stating, "In districts in which no high school is maintained for Negro pupils and no provision for high school training ... such board shall transfer said pupils to the high school department of one of the state-supported ... institutions ... in which said pupils may be trained. In which case said board of education shall pay to such institution ... the sum of $10 per month to be applied to the general expenses of said pupil at such institution...." (DPI, DNE, Special Subjects File, Box 11).

In addition, a reference to another law follows Seawell's letter in the file. The 1939 legislature, in response to a request from Yadkin County, enacted a law requiring that the Yadkin County Board of Education pay a reasonable portion of the cost of a student forced to attend high school in another county until such time as Yadkin County provided a high school for its black students. Soon thereafter Yadkin County built a high school and began offering training on the secondary level (report attached to Seawell letter, DPI, DNE, Special Subjects File, Box 11).

The prospect of hosting a secondary school for two counties appealed to educators in Macon and Jackson Counties, thus giving rise to a fierce competition between educators there to win state approval for the establishment of a local consolidated high school. Such remote counties had too few students to create a standard secondary school. Even with their combined populations, problems still persisted.

A search of the annual secondary principals' reports at the North Carolina State Archives (Boxes 6–18) reveals noteworthy statistics about specific secondary schools in Western North Carolina. Such reports document, among other details, curriculum, physical education offerings, number of graduates, annual improvements, annual enrollment declarations and average daily attendance as well as faculty members and their qualifications, lunchroom management, the price of lunch, average number served daily, and extracurricular activities, including sports and clubs.

The reports are authentic historical documents, although errors are occasionally glaringly evident. From time to time, the Department of Public Instruction added requests for additional information, and notes indicate what practices the state viewed as desirable. For example, state officials showed interest in enrollment in home economics classes, such as the number of male students taking those classes, additional duties of the teacher of home economics, the existence of lessons exchanged with other departments, whether adult classes were offered, and other details. Official forms also contained detailed questions about counseling services as well as about science departments and their offerings and equipment.

Innovation at Stephens-Lee High School

Stephens-Lee High School, located in Asheville, became the most prominent black secondary school in Western North Carolina. The school, known for its rich history of educating the youth of the black community by enlisting the services of outstanding educators, was erected near the site of Catholic Hill School. Actually, the phoenix-like Stephens-Lee building rose from the ashes of Catholic Hill, at the eastern edge of downtown Asheville. Designed by architect Ronald Greene in the Gothic academic style so popular with universities of that time, the community it served dubbed it the "Castle on the Hill." The new building, which faced west on Valley Street, was brick with a white trim. The central part of the school was three stories high with multiple windows encircled with granite. A four-story brick tower with two-story oriel bay windows accented the north end. An arched entrance surrounded by granite enhanced the ground floor. A two-story auditorium with a gable roof was behind the tower to the north, and at the south end there was a three-story square entrance tower. The main portion had a flat roof (Swain, 1981).

After being forced to attend classes in makeshift accommodations, black high school students were elated to begin attending the newly constructed school in January 1923. Because of segregation, counties with no high school facilities for their black students transported

From 1923 until 1965 the premier high school in the western counties for black students was Stephens-Lee High School — The Castle on the Hill — photographed in 1951. Its first graduation occurred in May of 1924, and through the years notable graduates included Albert E. Manley, former president of Spelman College; Floyd McKissick, first black graduate of UNC's School of Law; and Harlow Fullwood, 1990 inductee into the Central Intercollegiate Athletic Association Hall of Fame and president of Fullwood Foods. All the high school building except the gymnasium was torn down in 1975. In 1940-41 there were 759 students enrolled with an average daily attendance of 660 (North Carolina Office of Archives and History, Raleigh).

them to Stephens-Lee. Eventually the school served young people from Henderson, Madison, Yancey, and Transylvania as well as from Buncombe County. School officials honored two educators by naming the school for them: Hester Lee, the deceased wife of Principal Walter S. Lee, and a much loved teacher, and Edward Stephens, a native of the West Indies who had been the principal of Catholic Hill School. Stephens, who had been educated at Cambridge University in England, had studied at other European universities. He is acknowledged as the visionary who conceived of an institute for the young men of Asheville and who, with the support of businessman George Vanderbilt, known for his Biltmore Estate landmark in south Asheville, succeeded in establishing the Young Men's Institute, still located near Eagle Street (Ready, 1986).

Principal Lee had been educated at Livingstone College near Salisbury and at Columbia University in New York City. He enthusiastically embraced and practiced the curriculum espoused by Booker T. Washington, but he also added Shakespeare, music, and drama. Lee championed the dignity of manual labor and of self-help. At Stephens-Lee, an industrial education, enhanced by classical studies, prevailed (T. Andonaras, August 15, 1995, "The Castle on the Hill," *Asheville Citizen-Times*). In some ways, Lee merged the educational philosophies of Booker T. Washington and W.E.B. Du Bois, but he favored that of Washington. Courses at the high school included carpentry, radio repair, welding, home economics, cosmetology, music, drama, and English literature in addition to more traditional subjects. According to Ready, Stephens-Lee "enhanced the spirit as well as the intellect of black mountaineers" (1986, p. 54).

Stephens-Lee was more than fortunate in its capable school administrators. Later principals included Albert Manley, Joseph E. Belton, and Frank Toliver. Manley earned his doctorate at Stanford University. No doubt his being a role model for the school's students inspired them to seek success in adult life by making their own contributions in their respective communities. Throughout its existence, Stephens-Lee's principals demonstrated strong leadership and exhibited exceptional professional qualifications.

The school's first graduation took place in 1924. Among that year's graduates were Mrs. Ruth C. Carolina, who later returned to her alma mater as a teacher, and Mrs. Willie Knuckles Robinson, who later joined the faculty of the Mountain Street Elementary School. Another graduate who returned to teach at Stephens-Lee was Lucille Pearson Burton, who earned a bachelor of arts degree at Spelman College and a graduate degree from Columbia University in New York City. She served more than 40 years in the Asheville City Schools as a teacher, as vice principal, and as principal.

In 1925, Principal Lee completed an annual report showing a nine-member faculty and 26 graduates and a student enrollment of 234. Lee's 1925-1926 principal's report listed a faculty of 10 with annual salaries ranging from $725 to $1,025. Most salaries that year were in the $900 range. He listed the names of 17 graduates. Frank A. Toliver's 1947-1948 report cited a total enrollment of 545 students, 21 faculty members, and a graduating class of 109, of which 11 were identified as members of the Accelerated Veterans' Classes. The Toliver 1948-49 report indicates a student enrollment of 511, 19 faculty members, and 85 graduates. In the 1949-50 report, the number of students totaled 514, with 22 faculty members and 104 graduates. Stephens-Lee was frequently used as the site of conferences for principals, supervisors, and teachers covering a range of topics. For example, on October 15, 1957, the conference theme was "Cooperative Planning for Curriculum Improvement." In 1958, principals pondered the pros and cons of using television in schools (Department of Public Instruction, Division of Negro Education, State Supervisor of Elementary Education, Conferences 1957 and 1958, Box 3).

Stephens-Lee's music program, a source of tremendous school pride, and its drama productions enlivened community life. In the 1930s, music enhanced the school's status with the formation of its first marching band, a musical group that enriched the events of both white and black communities with stirring performances. In 2007, residents of the area, both black and white, spoke in glowing terms about the exciting routines by the Stephens-Lee band. For decades the band built a reputation for performing with rhythm and energy that thrilled onlookers.

In an article published in the *Asheville Citizens-Times* on February 13, 1994, alumnus Henry Robinson wrote, "Under the direction of Madison 'Doc' Lennon, the Stephens-Lee marching band, used to thrill WNC residents with its jazzy music and high-stepping drum major supported by a corps of pretty majorettes." Both white and black spectators were delighted to watch the Stephens-Lee band perform.

Stephens-Lee created a rich history of competitive sports, which eventually became an integral part of school life. Oliver W. McCorkle and Clarence L. Moore (Ready, 1986) were among the coaches lauded as professionals who had used the athletic program to benefit all students, not only gifted athletes. In 2004, the North Carolina High School Athletic Association inducted Moore, whose career spanned 1928–68, posthumously into its Hall of Fame. The association named Moore as a top North Carolina coach and cited his two successful stints at Stephens-Lee, where he coached football, basketball, and baseball from 1934 to 1940 and from 1948 to 1968. From 1941 to 1947, Moore was owner of the well-known Asheville Blues Baseball team, which is featured in the Baseball Hall of Fame. In 1957, his Stephens-Lee team became the undefeated state football champion. In 1958, the baseball team won awards. In 1962, the basketball team won the Negro 4-A championship by defeating Atkins High of Winston-Salem with a score of 66 to 59. The association also identified Moore as the high school coach of the legendary Henry Logan, the All-American black player at Western Carolina University (*NCHSAA Bulletin*, Vol. 56, No. 2, Winter 2004). Eventually competitive sports became an integral part of school life.

In addition to coaches, Henry Logan, who played professional basketball, and Bennie Lake, who later played for the Harlem Globetrotters, were popular athletes. Logan and Willie Maples were the Bears' two All-State players. Logan broke the color barrier when he accepted an invitation to play in Buncombe County's Blue-White All-Star Games. No other black athlete had been invited to participate. Officials named Logan, by then well known in the region for his remarkable talent, the Most Valuable Player. The next year his friend and fellow athlete Johnny Bailey played in the Blue-White All-Star Games.

Moore is not remembered solely as a coach. Harlow Fullwood praised his performance in the classroom as a chemistry teacher. At the Stephens-Lee Bicentennial Celebration Luncheon, Fullwood said, "Clarence L. Moore taught me the true significance of education. Although I was drafted by both the Colts and the Bills of the NFL, I chose to pursue college, service, and loyalty to my community. Thanks to Mr. Moore and the other teachers at Stephens-Lee I grew up understanding that no one rises alone" (Editorial, Stephens-Lee Bicentennial Celebration Luncheon, from *Asheville Citizen-Times*, n.d., in files at Asheville City School Offices, Asheville, NC).

Lake and Johnny Bailey, both part of the legend of the Stephens-Lee Bears, compiled a sports history of their school, *The Greatest Sports Heroes of the Stephens-Lee Bears* (2001), which has also been made into a documentary film. Stephens-Lee was also the alma mater of Fred Worley of football and baseball fame and Wayne Coleman, who was drafted by the Baltimore Orioles (Henry Robinson, "Stephens-Lee School Opened in 1923," *Asheville Citizen-Times*, February 13, 1994).

An *Asheville Citizen-Times* editorial (August 19, 1995) described the majestic school on Catholic Hill as Western North Carolina's largest school for black students and as a "major cultural center" as well as a "symbol of excellence and achievement" for the African American population of Asheville. A member of the graduating class of 1950 and a veteran of the Korean Conflict, Clarence Chavis praised the Stephens-Lee building as wonderful in design for a high school and as having been improved with the 1941 addition of a gymnasium (personal communication, April 14, 2009).

The parents, students, and professional staff were surprised that a distinguished committee appointed by the N.C. Department of Public Instruction examined the Stephens-Lee facility in 1949 and found the site limiting as a school location. Their State School Survey Report (1949) states:

> When one visits the Stephens-Lee High School, one wonders why this plot was ever selected for a school site. It seems necessary to continue the high school ... since it is too good a building to be abandoned. Early consideration, however, should be given to the selection of a larger and more adequate site with the intention of eventually constructing a new building to house the high school and of converting the present building into a junior high.... Immediate consideration should be given to ... acquiring additional land ... and developing ... more suitable play space at this site [p. 9].

Because its location severely hampered enlarging and modernizing the Stephens-Lee facility, eventually Asheville erected another high school for its black students. The school was vacated in 1965 as black students began to attend the new South French Broad High School.

While Stephens-Lee High School was a public high school valued by black Asheville residents, there was also a private black school that helped provide a solution for black families who wanted their children to graduate with a high school diploma. Allen School, which became a four-year high school in 1924, appealed to families who could afford to send their children to a boarding school.

Playing a prominent role in the history of secondary education in Western North Carolina, Allen School, sometimes referred to as Allen Home School, drew students from many states and from foreign countries. The Allen School Women's Home Missionary Society of the Methodist Church founded the school in 1887 in an attempt to fill part of the void in educational opportunities for young black children and for uneducated adults. Allen High School was accredited by the state of North Carolina in 1924 and received accreditation by the Southern Association of Colleges and Secondary Schools in 1940. From 1941, Allen Home operated under the wing of the Woman's Division of Christian Service (Julia Titus, "History of Allen School," 1962, retrieved from http://toto.lib.unca.edu/).

The L.M. Peases of New York City donated a tract of land near Buncombe County's Beaucatcher Mountain to be used as a school site. Marriage Allen, a resident of London, England, contributed money to construct a dormitory, which was built in 1897. The school assumed Allen's name and became a boarding school. Its beginnings were primitive, with the first classes being held in an abandoned livery stable, but a rigorous curriculum combining vocational and classical studies developed (Ready, 1986). When turning the school over to the Women's Home Missionary Society, the Peases stipulated that it sustain a graded, industrial school for black people. And sustain it they did, by providing a remarkable education. The society re-opened the school on October 30, 1887, with two students, but a few weeks later 70 had enrolled. By the end of its first year more than 200 students were studying at Allen, often using books from home, such as Bibles, worn from use, and Blue Back Spellers (Reinhardt, June 14, 1995).

An excerpt from the school's 1965-66 student handbook outlines its distinctive mission: "Through small classes, religious services, discussions, cultural programs, social events and recreational activities, the school seeks to help each girl understand herself, develop her abilities and accept her limitations. The school is concerned that each girl show continuous growth in the acceptance of responsibility for her own actions, a concern for others, an understanding and appreciation for her Christian faith and heritage, and an attitude toward life that will enable her to communicate and work effectively with others" (p. 3).

Students were warned in advance that those whose behavior contradicted these ideals and standards would be sent home. The school's unwavering mission also included meeting the school's scholastic standards. Failure to do so resulted in the student's withdrawal. In addition, there was a third standard, a spiritual one, that each student was expected to demonstrate. Bible was taught, and Bible reading was encouraged. The school also offered studies in the history of the early church in its Religious Education Department (*Allen School Student Handbook*, Collection 278. Allen High School Collection of Papers, W.L. Eury Appalachian Collection, Appalachian State University, Boone, North Carolina).

Not only was there a rich and varied curriculum, but also the Allen campus had a number of organizations available: National Association for the Advancement of Colored People, Y-Teens, Girl Scouts, Student Council, Dramatic Club, and Crown and Scepter Club. The latter was a state honor society. Graduating from Allen School provided status as a black student who had earned a desirable degree and as one who had been exposed to a high level of culture.

Respected principals were responsible for upholding the lofty Allen traditions. Alsie B. Dole, who served as principal and superintendent at the school for more than 30 years from 1887 until 1920, added an industrial department for girls and women. Eventually adults attended classes in the evening and children during the day. In 1948, Allen Home School joined the Southern Association of Colleges and Secondary Schools, one of only two Western North Carolina schools to earn such accreditation. By 1947, the school's enrollment had climbed to 135, including both boarding and day students. Its campus contained three buildings and employed 16 college-trained staff. By the 1960s, Allen sent more than 50 percent of its graduates to college ("Historical Note," Collection 278, Allen High School Collection of Papers, W.L. Eury Appalachian Collection, Appalachian State University, Boone, North Carolina).

Veda Stryker, who served as the principal from 1924 to 1930, reported a 1929-30 enrollment of 58 with an average daily attendance of 56. The school employed 11 teachers, of whom four taught in the high school full time; four were part-time high school teachers; and three were elementary teachers. In her 1935-36 report, Principal Carmen Lowry listed nine instructors, each with a college degree and three master's degrees (DPI, DNE, High School Principal's Annual Reports, Box 7). In her 1938-39 report, Principal Julia Titus indicated advanced math courses that included geometry and algebra, foreign language study in both Latin and French, and science classes that included biology and chemistry. There were also classes in typing, handcrafts, piano, and vocal training.

Textbooks for most high schools were those recommended by the state, but at Allen the approved texts were different. As expected a number were used for religious instruction in Bible: *From Desert to Temple*, *Hebrew Life and Times*, and *Jesus' Ideals of Living*. Students participated in a Boost-Your-School Club, a Moentita Club (a name based on the first two letters of money, energy, time, and talent) Student Council, Art Club, and Home Economics Club, and 98 students were involved in the Queen Esther Society. There was an activity for any interest. As the school developed its physical education program, the staff rented the gymnasium at the YWCA.

In her 1956-57 annual report, Principal Titus provided the following information: The school had settled into a new building containing an auditorium with a seating capacity of 288, two music studios and six practice rooms. There was also ample space for the home economics classes. The science department had two classrooms plus a storage room and a darkroom. In the two-story brick building there were an additional six classrooms, offices, and a faculty lounge. The French instructor was using a tape recorder to improve pronunciation and accent. In the ninth grade, general math classes were organized into ability groups of four or five students with assignments to be completed at a speed comfortable for the group. Negro history was a part of the curriculum. By the next year the school had paved an outside recreational area and marked it for tennis, volleyball, and basketball. Students were allowed to engage in outdoor activities, including roller skating. Typing and shorthand were offered (Box 27). Adhering to professional standards, the faculty added to and improved opportunities for their students.

Most of the instructors at Allen School were single white women, but when Charity Ray attended in the early 1950s there were both black and white teachers (personal communication, April 17, 2008). Dolores Lassiter found a strict and loving environment at her alma mater. There she learned to believe in herself and to stretch to accomplish her dreams. One of her teachers, Frieda Morris, explained the goal of the Allen staff for their students: "We tried our best to prepare them to ... earn a good living, to be a part of the mainstream. Most of the girls came from communities where there were no high schools for black people." Morris found her students were eager to learn even though their school environment tolerated no nonsense (Reinhardt, June 15, 1995).

Though it has been more than 40 years since Allen closed its doors after integration opened up more doors for black high school students, the Allen status still stands as a superior learning opportunity. The limitation, of course, is that its private- and boarding-school status limited enrollment to females whose families were able to afford the board and tuition.

Transformation at Hendersonville School

About 25 miles away was another secondary school serving black students. Henderson County became home to Ninth Avenue High School, which developed from a union school called Sixth Avenue School. Both schools fell under the administrative offices of the Hendersonville Board of Education. In Hendersonville, individuals, whether committed leaders or aspiring students, worked continually to introduce improvements and expansions of programs. However, the official records, especially financial details, show how difficult it was to achieve progress, whether in construction or in equipment. For sure, though, everyone kept working and targeted success as an institution and success as students engaged in developing academic and industrial skills.

In the beginning, Sixth Avenue was located in a two-story school building at Sixth Avenue and Valley Street. Although Sixth Avenue School was primarily for elementary grades, high school work was offered intermittently. By 1936, a nine-month term had been established and high school grades added, for which two secondary teachers were employed. In the two-story frame structure, which housed the Sixth Avenue School and provided a community center for more than three decades, classrooms were on the ground floor. The upper floor was the site of an auditorium that could be converted into classrooms. When overcrowding occurred, curtains divided the auditorium into classrooms. Until 1936 only elementary classes were taught at the school (Greene, 1996).

In 1936, however, education for Hendersonville's black students received a boost as a result of a Work Projects Administration project initiated to provide employment for the jobless of the depression era as part of the New Deal. A brand new stone gymnasium was constructed at the all-white Hendersonville High School. As a result, the old gymnasium was dismantled and assembled to serve as an annex at Sixth Avenue School (Greene, 1996). Dubbed simply the "Annex" or the "gym," the structure provided space for high school classes, eventually becoming Ninth Avenue School. At last Henderson County's African American students had the opportunity to pursue a high school diploma without being exiled from home and family. The black community's dream of local access to secondary education had become a reality. Accepting students from other counties allowed a larger teaching staff and an expansion of courses to be studied and a larger number of extracurricular activities. Although Hendersonville students had secondary education available in their front yards, students traveling from Transylvania and Polk County experienced dislocation and sometimes felt like outsiders who did not truly belong.

The "Annex" was a big plus for Sixth Avenue students. Nevertheless, what the white community regarded as a grand gesture toward their black neighbors served to reinforce the black consciousness of educational inequality. The Annex was another example of passing on "white hand-me-downs" to the black community. Similar to the bitterness that resulted from the transfer of textbooks from schools for white children, who found excitement when their names were written in newly issued texts, black students would have been less than human not to have compared the new gymnasium at the white school with a reassembled structure on their school grounds.

The gymnasium transaction, a new one for a white school and a used one for a black school, provided a permanent image that publicized how educational decisions shortchanged financial investments for black schools year after year. The budget decisions documented in school board minutes and other records are convincing because the dollar shortcomings occur repeatedly. In contrast to those financial figures stands the integrity of industrious figures—principals, teachers and students—who rose above the circumstances because they recognized the value of a high school education and the satisfactory results students could experience.

Sixth Avenue Principal W.R. Robinson was a compassionate educator. Greene (1996) elaborated on the multiple phases of Robinson's dual role as principal and teacher. Robinson provided numerous janitorial services by gathering wood, stoking fires, and cleaning rooms. Also, he actively solicited assistance for needy families. Citing a taped 1986 interview, Greene affirmed that Alberta Jowers helped Principal Robinson provide for individuals enduring difficult circumstances. The multi-talented Jowers was a nurse, a newspaper publisher, an owner of a beauty shop, a sponsor of a local black baseball team, and a leader in Girl Scout Troop No. 7. Any one of those positions would have made her a valuable contact for Robinson. Jowers had a wide network of sources able to assist needy blacks. Because she owned and drove a car, Jowers was able to provide additional help for Robinson's referrals. The two remarkably competent individuals united their efforts to alleviate suffering in the black communities (Greene, 1996).

Robinson was not only compassionate, but also he was skillful in handling school business. Professionalism was his trademark as a school administrator. In 1925, Robinson filed an annual principal's report for Sixth Avenue School. Of the 321 students, 19 were enrolled in the high school program, which included eighth and ninth grades. Eleven units were required for graduation, and those included classes such as English, literature, algebra, history, Latin, and home economics. Robinson described Sixth Avenue School, built in 1918 for $4,500, as a two-story frame building with six classrooms, an auditorium, and an office. He stated that heating and ventilation were satisfactory, as was the equipment for home economics. At that time the school owned 250 books.

There were nine graduates in 1925 (DPI, DNE, HSPAR, Box 1). For the 1931-32 term, 47 students enrolled in high school classes covering grades 8–10 with an average daily attendance of 42. Beyond the graduation statistics, puzzles abound. Robinson, documenting the work of a home economics teacher, writes, "The equipment for home economics is satisfactory. This department is supervised by a splendid teacher." However, no home economics classes are listed in the high school curriculum, but Robinson verifies that a home economics teacher manages the lunchroom.

In his 1931-32 report, Robinson writes, "Equipment for home economics is modern.... We hope to make other improvements when conditions will permit. A [great] deal of interest is shown by those taking this course. We get splendid cooperation from patrons. Funds are raised from time to time ... to ... purchase sewing materials and food for demonstration lessons." In Section IV, Robinson indicates that cooking and sewing are offered to grades 5–9. The assumption is that those subjects were presented to combination classes so the arrangement may explain why no home economics classes are listed in the report of the high school course offerings.

Robinson lists Mary J. Mills as a high school teacher in the 1933-34 report, but there is no class listed for her in the high school daily schedule (DPI, DNE, HSPAR, Box 5). According to later reports, it appears that Mills began her career in home economics at Sixth Avenue in 1927, but she may have been assigned to the elementary section. Another puzzling piece of information is the title *Francois, the* text used for the Latin classes (DPI, DNE, HSPAR, Box 4). The same text was used several years for Latin. Later French became the second language offered to Sixth Avenue students.

In the mid–1930s, Robinson filed another annual high school report, but the name of the school is cited as Hendersonville Colored School, which suggests that it was prepared in the superintendent's office without involving the school's principal. This 1934-35 report is unsigned. Often white staff referred to a black school in their system simply as "the colored school." The report cited an enrollment of 76 students for grades 8–10, with an average attendance of 65, which represented an increase of approximately 50 percent after a decade. A note added, "We will have the eleventh grade next year for the first time" (DPI, DNE, HSPAR, Box 6). Only one page contains any information, another indication that the central office staff failed to confer with Robinson.

However, the 1935-36 report is complete and is signed by W.M. Robinson. He documented a total enrollment of 68 with an average of 10 students absent each day. That term the home economics teacher supervised the school lunchroom. Robinson, who had studied at Benedict College, assumed responsibility for teaching English, mathematics, sociology, economics, and Latin. Helen G. Prince, an alumna of Clafflin University in Orangeburg, South Carolina, taught mathematics, science, history, and civics. Mary J. Mills, a graduate of Teachers College in Winston-Salem, taught home economics and English. Mills used three texts for home economics classes: *The Girl and Her Home, Everyday Foods,* and *Fabrics and Dress.* Each teacher supervised a daily 40-minute noon recess, which included the lunch period (DPI, DNE, HSPAR, Box 7).

In Robinson's annual report for 1936-37, he specified that the high school students continued to average 10 absences daily. Robinson also indicated that the school library contained 750 volumes and noted that white friends regularly donated a large number of magazines. For home economics classes, Mills had acquired a new text: *The Home Economics Omnibus.* Attached to the report is a copy of a letter from Harold L. Trigg, high school inspector for the Department of Public Instruction. He requested that Robinson report annual salaries for the high school personnel. That year Robinson earned $787.20; Prince, $604; and Mary J. Miller [*sic*], $660 (DPI, DNE, HSPAR, Box 8). Robinson recorded the home economics teacher's name as Mills, but communication from Raleigh identifies her as Miller. Finally, Robinson's report in 1937-38 referred to the ongoing attendance problem and the library's acquisition of an additional 25 volumes.

Sixth Avenue, even with no physical education teacher, had organized both a baseball and a basketball team. An earlier football squad involved 15 players. There was also a glee club and a literary club, which sponsored a literary digest. The Dramatic Club had 25 members, almost one-third of the students. Extracurricular activities brought additional challenges for the staff but enriched the education of secondary students (DPI, DNE, HSPAR, Box 9). The number of graduates at Sixth Avenue ranged from eight in 1936, which marked the addition of the eleventh grade, to 16 in 1937. Evans K. Mims, a native of East Flat Rock and a 1937 alumnus, was an outstanding student who returned after completing college to serve as principal of the elementary grades. Four members of the Class of 1937 entered college, and three enrolled in normal school. Almost one half of that graduating class pursued additional education.

Spencer E. Durante and John Marable, later principals, contributed to the expansion of educational options at Ninth Avenue School. Durante arrived in 1939. During the 1939-40 term, Durante taught biology, geography, general science, mathematics, physics, and algebra. Other teachers included Mabel Gunn, social studies; John Simmons, two sections of English and three of mathematics; and Mary J. Mills, English in addition to home economics. Both Mills and Durante invested one hour daily in the school's guidance program (DPI, DNE, HSPAR, Box 11). Durante's 1940-41 report recorded no home economics classes but indicated that a home economics club, with a membership of 20, had been organized. Durante noted that new science equipment had been added and that 90 minutes was allowed for science labs. There were also physical education classes (Box 12).

William A. Darity, who graduated in 1941, described the Sixth Avenue School that he remembered:

> There was Sixth Avenue School, which eventually had a four-room Annex, in Hendersonville.... The Sixth Avenue School was an old building that looked like it was about to fall down. All the high school was in one room with each teacher holding class in one corner of the room. Durante became the principal [after Robinson].... Later there were four rooms in the annex and a gymtorium for sports and meetings. There were four teachers: Durante taught all the sciences and math; Marable taught English and French. Mrs. Joyce Mills taught home economics; Mrs. Helen Prince taught social studies, government, and civics. There was homeroom for the four classes: 8, 9, 10, and 11. We were constantly moving. There were six or seven classes, one at a time.
>
> Homeroom was at the back of the class, and there was study hall. There was a little room that was supposed to be Mr. Durante's office, but books were donated, and he turned his office into a library. I used to run the library. When I look back, I feel cheated, but they were good teachers who made us feel we could achieve. We were motivated [personal communication, November 6, 2004].

Darity, calling himself a leftist, railed against such injustices in his 1941 valedictory address. On November 6, 2004, at the Siena Hotel in Chapel Hill, he had this to say:

> I went to Sixth Avenue School where four teachers taught in one room. We eventually had a four-room Annex in Hendersonville. This was ... later called the Ninth Avenue High School. There were no laboratory facilities, but we learned theoretical physics, chemistry, and biology. We caught frogs to dissect. Not having good equipment helped me realize how horrible segregation was. Down the street at the white high school, there was fine equipment, microscopes, slides, etc. I was a leftist even then. Sure, I felt resentment. I talked about it in my valedictory address. Instead of fostering intellectual capacity, segregation impaired it. Made me feel I'm not as good, but made me determined to succeed. Another thing [that strengthened my outlook] — I had teachers who were not afraid to say "you're black" or "you're a Negro," but you are just as good as anyone else [personal communication].

Minutes of the school board meeting on August 22, 1944, confirm Darity's viewpoint. Discrepancies of monumental proportion existed between the educational equipment and classes available for the two races. For example, architect Erle Stillwell provided the following valuation in 1944 on school buildings and their contents to J.C. Morrow for insurance purposes:

High school (White)—Building $240,000, Contents $30,000
Elementary (White)—Building $35,000, Contents $3,000
Gymnasium (White)—Building $50,000, Contents $5,000
6th Avenue (Colored)—Building $6,000, Contents $1,000
9th Avenue (Colored)—Building $15,000, Contents $1,500

Considering that in 1951 and 1954 respectively the enrollment at Hendersonville High School was 351 and 388—and speculatively 344 and 381 in 1944—and less than 85 at Ninth Avenue, a rough figure is that the board designated expenditures of $213 for each black student and of $1,170 for each white student. Accounting for a definite margin of error, the investment in a white teenager's education was almost five times as much as the investment in a black teenager's education.

The board agreed to provide insurance based on the above valuations for a period of five years at a total cost of $2,691.16 and designated Chairman O.A. Meyer to complete the contract. The white school population was larger than the black school population, but considerably less money was invested in the schools for black students. The amount seems smaller when the role of black parents as taxpayers is factored into the equation. Such records highlight the need for integrating schools to provide equality in educational opportunities (Hendersonville City Board of Education minutes, August 22, 1944).

Although the board approved adding another grade, it was not prepared to act immediately. Instead, the seventh grade was to be placed in the high school—a decision that would serve as a delaying tactic until funds became available for the additional twelfth grade. The August 20, 1940, meeting also addressed the problem of adding the twelfth grade. Each board member shared the opinion that such a change was desirable, but postponement was again deemed a necessity. The board directed the superintendent to include seventh grade in the high school system in readiness for a future change to the 12-grade system. The addition of the twelfth grade came with the 1944-45 term.

The following spring, after debating the propriety of extending an invitation to Rabbi Robert P. Jacobs to deliver the baccalaureate sermon—a debate that ended with the decision to confer with the local ministerial association—and after discussing the effectiveness of defense classes, which provided training in metal work, welding, and auto mechanics for individuals over the acceptable school age, the board again reviewed the installation of the heating plant in "the colored school." Although the heating plant was functioning, the funds allotted for that project proved insufficient to provide for the purchase of a new boiler, which was much needed. The board concluded that installation of heating in the gym would not prove a costly proposition for the next year and added that intent to its list of projects for the 1941-42 school year (Hendersonville City Board of Education minutes, March 25, 1941).

In Hendersonville's school board minutes for November 21, 1944, Superintendent F.M. Waters requested, on behalf of the Colored Parent-Teacher Association, that a new elementary school be constructed. The board passed a resolution to the effect that they would strive to provide better facilities for the colored community as soon as possible. Following that business item, J.H. Flanagan asked that the Bond Committee in the black community be allowed the use of both the Hendersonville High School auditorium and gymnasium for a rally on December 7. The board firmly denied permission for the colored community to use white school property, although it had granted such permission in the past. Flanagan was instructed to report this decision to the black community's Bond Committee.

On January 10, 1945, following a lengthy discussion of the county board of education's debt of $20,255.32, owed for both black- and white-school expenses, with the surprising decision to accept $2,500 and forgive the remainder. Flanagan brought up the problem of outside groups using school properties at a time when there was a severe shortage of coal. Board members unanimously supported the motion to limit property rental to agencies directly involved with the war effort. Because the business matter seems directly related to white requests, the decision suggests that limitations were being placed on whites as well as on black groups.

On June 25, improvements to school properties were itemized. Sixth Avenue Colored School had been painted on the interior, and new doors and windowpanes had been installed. The colored gymnasium, the "annex," had been painted on the outside, and its door had been repaired. On August 15, repairs at the colored school were enumerated, but additional work was needed. Also, a monthly salary schedule for janitors allotted $80 for Walter Allman and for Lewis Clay and $60 for William Owen at the "Colored School."

There being no quorum on September 18, 1945, the two members present, Bruce Drysdale and H.B. Crowder, held an informal meeting with a delegation of colored citizens. The highly respected Sam Mills led the delegation in outlining its case for needed improvements of the city's black schools. The chief request was that a new building be constructed near the colored gym because the Sixth Avenue School was no longer adequate to meet the needs of both elementary and high school students.

The board concurred with the group's delineation of shortcomings at the school site and affirmed that they would direct their efforts toward modernizing the facilities as soon as possible. In addition, the board chairman O.A. Meyer asked Superintendent F.M. Waters to inform the state board of education about the problems, to investigate state plans for Negro education in Western North Carolina, and to explore the prospect of securing financial aid.

On October 9, 1945, the full board approved the business of the informal meeting held in September and discussed the building project for the Negro community. The school superintendent had contacted Newbold of the North Carolina Division of Negro Education and had been assured that there would be state support for the building project. The local board invited county commissioners to assist with an inspection of the "colored school" to develop informal plans for a new building. A follow-up discussion during the November 23 meeting revealed unanimous support for completing a new building as soon as possible, so the superintendent was instructed to communicate the desire to the county commissioners. By the January 16, 1946, board meeting, the commissioners had sent a letter to the board of education to intensify their determination to expedite the construction of the new building for the colored citizens.

Though Superintendent Waters resigned at the March 8, 1946, school board meeting to accept the position as Gastonia city school superintendent, the Hendersonville board honored its efforts to improve the colored school while searching for Waters' replacement. An attachment to the records of the school board on March 15, 1946, itemizes future improvements to the colored school building: $75,000 for expansion to include 10 rooms, a library, a cafeteria with a seating capacity of 250 and an area of 3,000 square feet; and repairs: $800 for a heating system installed in the gymnasium; $500 for roof repairs on the east side; $250 for improvements in the school shop; $500 for expansion of the home economics department; and $1,000 for two coats of paint. Total repairs would require $2,250, and total output, including the building, would amount to $77,250. Numerous changes and repairs would also be made to the white schools (Hendersonville Board of Education minutes, March 8, 1946).

Showing a concern for the buying power of its educators' dollars, the board of education explored the impact of reduced wages and discussed providing a bonus to faculty members on August 16, 1946. The bonus idea was necessary because the commissioners had cut the board's proposed budget, which included a 10 percent supplement for teachers. The board decided that each teacher with less than an annual salary of $2,000 would be given $100 to assist with the increase in the cost of living. The number of white and black teachers eligible for this allotment was not itemized. In another item of business, board members accepted the bid presented by Pace Heating and Plumbing Company for heating improvements in the colored gymnasium.

On September 20, 1946, the school board focused on the building program. The board instructed Superintendent A.D. Kornegay to solicit help from the state department to plan a new school for Negro students as well as an auditorium for Rosa Edwards School and a new shop and activities building for Hendersonville High School. Whenever a project was adopted for the black community, board members capitalized on the opportunity to win public support for improving white school facilities.

Again, as part of a full agenda on December 20, 1946, the board reviewed planned improvements at the Ninth Avenue High School. The gym floor needed to be sanded and refinished. The school would make an effort to provide payment of one half of the cost of materials, amounting to $170, according to Superintendent Kornegay. Two of the system's janitors, supervised by Paul Newton, one of the shop instructors, would do the work to keep expenses at a minimum. The board agreed to underwrite the balance.

One item in a report by treasurer J.H. Flanagan to the school board was the receipt of $55 for rental of the colored school gymnasium. In a penned notation, Flanagan is identified as "former treasurer." Kornegay presented a report on the state of the budget on January 17, 1947. Items in his 1946-47 budget designated $600 for Negro elementary teachers' salaries and $4,670.09 for white elementary teachers. The amount set aside for Negro high school teachers was $200 as contrasted with $5,305 for white high school teachers. An equal amount for white and Negro home economics teachers was stipulated: $2,370 plus $100 for their travel. Wages for the Negro janitor were $350 and for the white janitor, $700.

Other items were not separated for white and black professionals. However, the salaries for both elementary and high school principals are not classified racially—a factual detail that may suggest that those who provided administrative duties at the black school were categorized simply as teachers. It was rare to eliminate the use of "Colored" or "Negro" in such records, but the dual role of black administrators appears to have been a matter of convenience for their employer. Total capital outlay in the budget amounted to $5,450. On July 1947, board chairman Bruce Drysdale wrote a letter to the county commissioners to request support of the school budget. He specifically asked that the commissioners levy the full 25 cent tax rate required to support the budget.

Support for the Ninth Avenue Negro High School is evident in a paragraph in the May 21, 1947, school board minutes. Adding a lunchroom under the "back end of the gymnasium" was approved. The board felt the benefits to students outweighed the minimal cost for doing so. The board also appointed a committee, which included Sam Mills, James Pilgrim, and Neal Woodson, to oversee programs presented in the Negro gymnasium. The board felt such a committee would "insure decency and also protect the building" (p. 29). The committee was authorized to terminate offensive programs and to take appropriate action against any groups abusing the privilege.

Another item of interest in the board of education's May 21 meeting pertained to a state law requiring all students to attend the school in their residential districts. If students were allowed to enroll in a school outside their home communities, their home schools would not receive credit for attendance and state and county funds for their training would be withheld. No mention was made of the impossibility of black students' attending school in their residential areas. The omission suggests that possibly a waiver existed for black students.

Sixth Avenue School with its Ninth Avenue Annex continued serving the educational needs of elementary and high school students until 1951. That year the new school building was dedicated, and Sixth Avenue School was sold and renovated to become an apartment building. By 1982, the building had become so deteriorated that, at the request of its owner, the Hendersonville Fire Department razed the structure.

However, its historical influence continued in the segregated education available at the new Ninth Avenue School. In 1950, Frank Wilson, who became a Henderson County educator as an adult, enrolled in first grade, taught by Odell Rouse. After completing first grade, Wilson attended the new Ninth Avenue School for grades 2 through 12. During his high school days, Wilson enjoyed learning science in Lorraine Jackson's classes. He described her as an "outstanding educator" who "did not play around, demanded you be prepared" and who advocated "no fooling around ... build on what you have ... and do your homework" (personal communication, March 10, 2009).

Ninth Avenue School was dedicated on October 28, 1951. It was an occasion for much jubilation. State Superintendent Cyde A. Erwin traveled from Raleigh to deliver the keynote address. The school was intended to serve students not only from Henderson County but also from Polk and Transylvania Counties as well. The two county schools for blacks, Brickton and East Flat Rock, closed their doors as they consolidated with Ninth Avenue, a union school.

William Darity, who brought acclaim to his alma mater, considered dropping out after his first year at Raleigh's Shaw University. With a twinkle in his eye, Darity explained that spending time with the girls during a summer of working in Atlantic City hindered him from saving money for his second year. With no money saved, continuing with his education seemed impossible. His parents, however, insisted that he return to Shaw. "My parents bought me a train ticket, put me on the segregated train, and sent me to Raleigh with orders to talk to the finance officer at Shaw, which I did" (personal communication, November 6, 2004).

Darity graduated from Shaw University with a degree in biology and chemistry and earned a master's degree in public health at North Carolina Central University in Durham. Employed by the World Health Organization for 10 years in the Middle East, he cites that experience as beneficial in preparing him to attend a university with few black students. *The Fountain* (Spring 2001), a University of North Carolina publication, quoted him as saying, "The whole social situation was not as difficult as people might think it was because I had worked for the World Health Organization overseas. Coming back into the situation where there were few blacks—well, I'd worked in various countries in the world where there were no black Americans." Being in the minority at the university did not fill him with a sense of inferiority. He was strongly motivated by his experiences at Ninth Avenue.

When Darity earned his Ph.D. from the University of North Carolina at Chapel Hill in 1964, he was the first African American to do so. At a time when the nation was embroiled with civil rights issues that sparked violence, marches, and innumerable demonstrations, Darity received his doctorate in public health ("Carolina's First Black Ph.D. Graduate," retrieved from http://www.gradschool.unc.edu/fountain/spr_01/darity.html).

However, he does not share the attitude that it was an honor to become the first black to earn a Ph.D. from UNC–Chapel Hill. Darity describes his monumental achievement as underscoring the shameful discrimination of that time. "I think it's disgraceful. That's why I don't talk about it. My parents paid taxes for people to have good schools to go to, and we had to take whatever they threw at us." However, he praised the black teachers who struggled in poor, ill-equipped schools, on behalf of their students: "Black teachers then were probably some of the best teachers. I think that they realized what you needed to make a success in life so they gave you the best they could ... without things like laboratory equipment" (personal communication, November 6, 2004).

Darity evaluated his achievement with discretion and with appreciation for his parents' encouragement:

I don't really feel I have accomplished that much, but I am probably most proud of making my parents proud of me. They saw me get married, knew my children, and were living when I received my Ph.D. from the University of North Carolina–Chapel Hill.... My mother — that woman was perceptive! A short period before she died, she told me, "You did pretty well. You didn't have any money that one summer because you spent it all on girls, but I am proud of you." Both my parents died with ... satisfaction [personal communication, November 6, 2004].

Prior to Darity's senior year at Ninth Avenue School, the board of education began developing plans for improving the black school. State public school officials believed Ninth Avenue High School should direct its efforts toward accreditation. Budget matters dominated the city board of education's meeting on July 23, 1940. A discussion of capital outlay led to approving a motion to authorize the installation of a heating plant in "the colored school." Attention was also focused on meeting the requirements of the Southern Association in regard to the recommended number of library books. The decision to add the twelfth grade affected the schools of both races. A handwritten note at the top of Durante's 1940-41 report indicated "possible accreditment." Sixth Avenue School achieved accreditation in 1942 (DPI, DNE, Special Subjects, Box 1).

The 1944-45 report refers to Ninth Avenue as Hendersonville Colored High School and seems to have been completed by someone other than Durante. His signature, which appears on a form attached to the report, indicates that no high school students were involved in "Pre-induction Training for the War Effort." The report affirms that the 53 students enrolled in high school classes had access to a gymnasium with showers available for both boys and girls. The report also states that a fourth year of high school, the twelfth grade, had been added (DPI, DNE, HSPAR, Box 16). However, the next report, also revealing that the name of the school is Hendersonville Colored High School, divulged that no students were enrolled in the twelfth grade.

Though no senior class existed, in 1946 there was one graduate, Tony Cunningham (DPI, DNE, HSPAR, Box 17). He probably completed his classes as independent studies within the framework of other classes or in the library. Durante could hardly have scheduled classes for a single student.

By 1951, Ninth Avenue High School had enrolled 141 students, but the average daily attendance was 116, approximately a 275 percent increase compared to the 1925 record. Six instructors established the program for high school students, and counseling services were available. Money had been invested in science equipment, and audio-visual equipment was available. The home economics program had expanded to include adult classes serving 18 students. In addition, 61 students were doing home practice, and lessons were being exchanged with the science and economics departments (DPI, DNE, HSPAR, Box 11). In her 1946-47 vocational education report, Mills indicated she had taught units on topics such as courtesy, personal grooming, food preservation, and personality development. Mills had sponsored a fall festival, a PTA benefit, adult study groups, and a Christmas gift exhibit. She had supervised the renovation of the home economics department and had traveled 2,680 miles during the year to complete job-related projects (DPI, Division of Vocational Education, Home Economics Section, Annual Reports, 1935–1952, Box 9). Although Mills won praise for her professional expertise, unfortunately she lost the support of the community when a personal conflict occurred in 1946.

John Marable, an instructor in French and English, had replaced Durante as principal at Sixth Avenue in 1946. Prior to the opening of the new Ninth Avenue School, Marable achieved one of his chief contributions when he organized a football team and served as coach. Marable stipulated that the players would have to raise enough money to purchase their uniforms. Enthusiasm and community support was so high that only six weeks later the newly formed Tigers proudly manned the field in uniforms (Greene, 1996).

Turnout at Ninth Avenue's first game was a response to the enthusiastic publicity. In its October 14, 1947, edition, the Hendersonville *Times-News* introduced the story with this headline: "Colored High School Teams Play Friday." The Tigers, coached by Marable and Oliver Summey, Jr., opened their first season of organized football against Carver High School of Spartanburg, South Carolina. The Tigers, with an average weight of 160 pounds, had been practicing for only three weeks and operated from both the single wing and T formations. The team relied on offensive play against a much heavier team.

The Ninth Avenue Tigers, in their historical debut in organized football, ended with an 18–6 defeat, but the game initiated the football culture that became prominent for the remainder of the school's existence. The October 17, 1947, headline proclaimed: "S.C. Eleven Nips Colored Team Here." The article succinctly summarized the competition: "The Tigers grabbed an early lead. Taking the opening kickoff, they drove for a touchdown with fullback Clyde Davis making the score. Carver came back to tie the score, and the half ended 6 to 6.... The visitors scored again near the end of the third period and sewed the game up by returning an intercepted pass for a touchdown in the fourth period.... Coach John Marable said he was well pleased with the play of his team."

Of the 35 male students in the high school, 25 had gone out for football, and these first-time players were praised as outstanding in the line: John Cash, Alonzo Payne, and Carnell Brooks. Equally acclaimed for their success in the backfield were Alexander Greene, Clyde Davis, Jr., and George Mitchum. A crowd of more than 1,000 spectators braved a rainy night to watch the game. An important phase of Ninth Avenue history had begun. Soon the prowess of the athletes captured strong support from white citizens with an interest in sports.

Ninth Avenue's team used the football field at the white Hendersonville High School when it was available. Sports historian Patrick Gallegher pointed out that a football player's academic work could be impacted negatively due to the rigor of having games scheduled during the school week (personal communication, January 15, 2008, data and news reports of Ninth Avenue's Sports Program in Gallegher's personal files). However, in response to the stimulation of football, young men pursued eligibility by remaining involved in schoolwork.

Frank Wilson enjoyed the challenge of football, basketball, and track at Ninth Avenue. He explained that the expectation that boys would participate in sports was a given. Wilson recalled with pride that, during his last two years of high school, Ninth Avenue School had a winning football conference (personal communication, March 10, 2009).

Other extracurricular activities were appealing. There was a glee club and a chapter of Future Teachers of America as well as a National Honor Society and a Student Council. "I am proud that I was voted into the National Honor Society," Wilson said. "I also enjoyed running for president of the student body, but I lost to another guy. Later I was asked to replace him ... so indirectly I became student body president" (personal communication, March 10,2009).

Marable's annual report for 1953-54 documents the services of Eddie Young, who taught brick masonry (DPI, DNE, HSPAR, Box 11). According to Eddie Young's son Morris, the elder Young was a motivator who spurred young men to acquire skills that would "put food on the table." The craftsman had no patience with laziness and pushed his students hard to be prepared. Ninth Avenue students earned three units of credit for masonry. Though some students were interested only in earning those three units, Young taught them to take pride in their work as well as to create walls that were neat, straight, and in order. If a student were told to make an 8 by 10 wall with a diamond pattern, there were consequences if he did not do the job correctly. If it was not done the way Young directed or if it was not finished in a certain amount of time, the teacher said, "Tear it down." He encouraged students to guarantee their future employment by building a reputation for doing their jobs with care and with attention to detail. "My father was a disciplinarian," Morris Young said. "He was teaching more than bricklaying. He was teaching about life from the lessons he had learned" (personal communication, October 31, 2006).

Praise for Young's classes came from outside the school community. The Hendersonville City Board of Education minutes for November 20, 1953, records the following: "Praise was given to the new masonry class program at the Ninth Avenue High School and the group told of a letter ... from General Manager H.B. Foster of the Brick and Tile Service, Inc., who stated, 'I just wanted you to know that among all the classes we have had at the Institute we believe this one appears to have gotten off to the best flying start.'"

Eddie Young oversees his masonry class at Ninth Avenue School in Hendersonville. Men trained by Young, who served on the faculty from 1957 to 1960 and from 1963 to 1965, were equipped to earn a living by applying their skills and putting his lessons into practice (courtesy Morris Young).

Subsequent entries in board minutes for January 15, 1954, and February 12, 1954, continue documenting the success of Young's program. His class poured a concrete walk from the school lunchroom to the street. One entry states: "The fine work being done by the Ninth Avenue High School masonry class and the lunchroom storeroom that they had worked on were described. Also reported was ... that a new counter had been constructed in the ... lunchroom, giving it a ... good chance for an 'A' sanitary rating ... at next inspection." Joe Mills attributed the success of his brother, who took second place in a brick mason contest, to Young's insistence on doing the job right. "Walter came in second because he wouldn't rush. He wanted the job done right, just like Mr. Young taught us" (personal communication, October 31, 2006). Young's former students such as David Ballard have earned a living by applying the skills and principles with which he endowed them. Examples of his students' masonry abound in Henderson County.

Graduation at any school is a time of celebration. Graduates of Ninth Avenue school were awarded a special memento in honor of their milestone accomplishment. James Pilgrim, an astute businessman and outstanding civic leader, provided silver dollars, one for each graduating senior, to be awarded along with the much sought-after high school diploma (J. Mills, March 12, 2007). Receiving a silver dollar for a job well-done provided yet another reason to celebrate.

The Ninth Avenue High School band was another source of pride for Hendersonville. Earl H. Martin, a white music teacher and conductor, organized a small band at Ninth Avenue in the late 1950s. Martin found the students able and interested. He also acknowledged that the band parents were supportive and that help was available from white citizens and from the school officials. "At first cooperation from the school system was minimal, allowing a teacher one hour a day and a room in the gymnasium but little, if any, funds for instruments and equipment," Martin said. "The principal and faculty at Ninth Avenue were very much in favor of a band but unable to help with needed funds. We simply scrounged around, parents buying or renting some instruments, using one or two school-owned instruments from the Hendersonville High School band and maybe a donation here or there" (personal communication, December 9, 2009).

Martin began with a small class of beginners, but the young musicians worked their way up to a concert band. Six or seven students enrolled in the first class, and, although never very large, the number grew to include 18 to 20 students. Once Martin established the band, he then offered two classes. One was an advanced "performing group and the other a beginning band-feeder group." In the beginning, the band played in the stands but eventually performed on the football field. It also performed in school programs and played at civic festivities (personal communication, November 23, 2008).

"The Ninth Avenue School band program was started ... during a time when there was a growing unrest about the inequities between the white and black schools," Martin writes. "These so-called 'separate but equal' schools were beginning to be seen in their true light. The differences were real and profound in terms of most criteria that would define equality of educational opportunity" (personal communication, December 9, 2009).

Martin supported the organization of a band boosters club. The club's efforts helped, though he recognized the support was a sensitive issue. "Several students," he said, "became good musicians, including Zenobia Crosby, who made First Chair in the All-State Band the first year that our schools were integrated. Technically, this young lady was ... a wizard and could play as fast and read as well as any student I ever taught. A marvelous young man, William Green, our first drum major, was also a stalwart during those years" (personal communication, December 9, 2009).

Martin became acutely aware of the inequities and the handicaps faced by black people in every aspect of daily living. "When we first began making trips to other towns for football games, I noticed the kids came to the bus with their lunches, which would have been highly irregular with our [white] band at Hendersonville High School," Martin wrote. "They explained later that they could not buy food any place so it would be their only access to food while away. On down the road on this first trip, some of the students wanted to stop for a 'toilet break.' I said, 'Why don't we stop at a filling station?'... which we did in just a few minutes."

At the service station, Martin experienced another reality his black students had to deal with. "The operator would not allow my students to use his restroom so we stopped on the road. Students got out of the bus and went in all directions among the trees to find some privacy, did their thing, and returned to the bus" (personal communication, December 9, 2009). Two of life's most basic needs—food and restroom facilities—were routinely denied to African Americans traveling in Western North Carolina and throughout the southern states.

Another racial issue, one that becomes transparent only with persistent research, emerged when the school board, on November 20, 1953, determined to use the gymnasium at the Ninth Avenue School for the children of migrant workers. Later the workers erected Quonset huts. Teachers designed classes for children who lived in the county until the agricultural jobs ended. When the growing season was over, their parents took them elsewhere as they followed work opportunities. In 1963, the migrant school moved to the Blue Ridge Assembly Grounds near the site of East Flat Rock School for black children.

That small example is another illustration of segregation, this time for children of migrant laborers, most of whom had a brown skin color. The participation of students, though, reinforces the conviction that humans, no matter what ethnicity, desire to learn with whatever assistance possible. The objective is always to advance despite the suppression that happens too frequently. Progress, though, requires countering turmoil before achieving reconciliation on the forward journey.

9

Turmoil in Secondary Education

Patterns in schools located in larger towns, such as Asheville and Hendersonville, prevailed in other counties too. But so did turmoil, which became apparent in places such as Mitchell and McDowell. However, progress and reconciliation happened more smoothly in many counties, such as Rutherford, Wilkes and Yadkin. The two stories—turmoil and reconciliation—accentuate the obstacles and the accomplishments in the educational journey for blacks in Western North Carolina.

Cleansing in Mitchell County

In Mitchell County white citizens found the most economical way—and at the same time the most offensive way—to solve the problem of providing schools for blacks: simply transport the county's blacks elsewhere. Denise Byrd Russo, a middle-aged white woman, was subjected to tales of her grandfather's part in Spruce Pine's racial cleansing and exposed to the shame he felt for having safeguarded his existence at the expense of his black neighbors. Freeman spent his life recalling the unfair treatment of Spruce Pine's blacks and his sense of regret at having personally participated in making the purge happen (personal communication, August 17, 2010).

According to Russo, a Spruce Pine native, her reluctant grandfather helped oust the blacks from Mitchell County. Following the alleged rape of a white woman, black residents of Spruce Pine were rounded up at gunpoint. "According to Grandmother Ora Mae Freeman, blacks were loaded in cattle cars and sent to Shelby, North Carolina. The story was that one black man had been caught looking at a white woman" (personal communication, August 17, 2010). However, investigation of the alleged rape resulted in the arrest, trial, and electrocution of John Goss, an illiterate black man. Elliot Jaspin, the author of *Buried in the Bitter Waters* (2007) reveals testimony by family members of the victim, Mrs. Mack Thomas, that she may have been more fearful of a black man than actually having been the victim of a crime.

Russo's family history has eliminated the actual crime because members have focused on the grandfather being forced to participate in a racist event that he did not endorse. Freeman participated because, as Russo puts it, "To refuse would have resulted in his being forced on board the cattle car and sent away."

However, Russo's story includes one positive outcome: George Jackson, a black man respected by the white community, was allowed to remain with his family. Jackson was the custodian of the police station, the school and other public offices. He continued to live near Spruce Pine, and his children attended school there.

According to Russo, there were no schools for black children in Mitchell County, but Jackson's family eventually attended integrated schools and one of his grandchildren dated white girls without provoking reprisals other than gossip. Russo also laughed about Jackson's response to affluent whites wanting to buy his property at Swiss Pine Lake. In essence, Jackson told the prospective buyers to forget it.

Russo's grandmother told the story of a black man and a white woman who were interested in one another. "A group of rednecks imprisoned him in a pig pen and fed him like a pig. Grandmother had no idea how long that went on," Russo said (personal communication, August 17, 2010).

Documents confirm the validity of the Freeman family's shared memory about hostility in Mitchell County. The governor sent General Van Metts to Spruce Pine to investigate and to report back to him. Citizens were filled with fear because a rare crime, rape, had been reported in Mitchell County. In 1923, those who lived in the small mountain hamlet were confused about how to deal with the situation. When Metts arrived, he discovered a situation so tense that he ordered National Guard units to report to Spruce Pine to maintain order. The small town instantly became a heavily fortified base.

More than 100 men set up camp near the Toe River with machine guns trained on downtown Spruce Pine. Feelings were running high, so additional troops were ordered to report for duty. Upon their arrival, 240 troops were available at "Camp Mitchell." Governor Cameron Morrison telegrammed Metts to protect the prison camp near the town and to cooperate with the sheriff to protect black workers and to uphold the law and to fight mob rule at any cost (John Silver, "Silver Threads," February, 2007, retrieved from http://homepages.rootsweb.com/~silver/south/).

In the meantime strong business interests represented by R. Fred Bower, general manager of the Clinchfield Products Corporation, indicated in a September 28, 1923, letter that the company had imported black laborers, accompanied by families, to fill the void in hiring qualified workers. Bower maintained that his employees were law-abiding citizens and that it was a crime to drive them from their home because someone else had supposedly committed a crime.

The chairman of the North Carolina Highway Commission received a letter, dated September 27, 1923, informing him that workers in Avery County were accosted by 150 men, armed with shotguns and pistols, who ordered all the black workers to march the five and one half miles to Spruce Pine. Despite the pleas of P.H. O'Brien, author of the letter and owner of the construction company that had brought its own black laborers from Alabama, that his labor force be respected and allowed to stay on the job since not one of them had been out of camp and knew nothing about the rape of an older white woman in Mitchell County, the mob insisted that his laborers be out of state by the next day.

"Fifteen of the Negroes ran away when they saw the mob coming, and we only have between 25 and 30 in the camp tonight as best as I can check them over," O'Brien wrote. "We will not have a man to bridle a mule tomorrow at noon, and both of our steam shovels are shut down tonight. They loaded at Spruce Pine ... two box car loads of Negroes and have run them out of here and three more carloads of them went out ... today on the passenger train" (John Silver, "Silver Threads," February, 2007, retrieved from http://homepages.rootsweb.com/~silver/south/).

The white population quieted down in the charged atmosphere once they sent blacks in the county away, as indicated in a telegram sent to the governor by Metts. However, the event pushed newspaper editors and reporters into a frenzy. Front pages focused on Spruce Pine activities daily. Once the accused, John Goss, was apprehended, the family of the victim indicated that they would let law enforcement deal with bringing him to trial. They did, however, hope to see him get the electric chair. James Thomas Rusher (2003) describes the trial and sentencing of John Goss, "colored." The judge ordered that a charge of electricity was to pass through his body until he was dead. Rusher points out that "colored" is used so extensively in news and court accounts of John Goss that it could be interpreted as a part of his name. Ruther also said it was reported that Goss confessed to assaulting Mrs. Thomas (*Until He Is Dead: Capital Punishment in the Western North Carolina History*, retrieved from http://books.google.com/books).

The cleansing went far beyond Mitchell County. Van R. Newkirk (2009) documents deaths by lynching throughout North Carolina, from the coast to the mountains. In 1903 and in 1904, there were two attempted lynchings near Hickory in Catawba County. Also, police arrested a young black man for winking at a white girl. In *Catawbans,* Freeze (2002) says that blacks throughout Western North Carolina, and indeed the South, seldom appeared in the papers—only when accused of crimes or other negative actions. The bias was so widespread and the hostility so common that it obviously restricted blacks from acquiring an adequate education by prolonging segregated education.

The strain was severe in Mitchell, but other western counties were sites of less pervasive attempts to keep the black population in its place. One such event occurred in Henderson County, as related by Gladys Russell Freeman (personal communication, March 19, 2007). Accompanied by her children, Freeman was visiting her family in the Edneyville community. She learned that her husband had died. In the grip of grief, she decided his body should be sent to Henderson County for burial and that she would relocate and enroll her children in school. On the day of the funeral, several friends hugged her saying, "Don't worry." Only when the funeral cortege arrived at the cemetery did she understand the motivation behind their words. A group of men in a pick-up truck blocked the way to the open grave. The men shouldered shotguns and rifles. "Mr. Pilgrim went ahead and spoke with them. Then he came back and told me, if I were willing, we would wait another day to bury my husband, but if I wanted it to happen that day, it would.... Mr. Pilgrim could usually handle any situation. We buried my husband the next day ... one row over from the first spot. Those men claimed his grave was in the white section of the cemetery." Such events were common throughout Western North Carolina.

Episodes prompted by fear permeated the experience of black and white mountaineers, and such events provide a backdrop against which children attended school, an institution that usually provided a safe haven for the two races. Tension in the community negatively affected learning and made reconciliation even more desirable.

Stalling in McDowell County

In McDowell County the black community succeeded in gaining a high school for students completing the seventh grade. The Marion City Board of Education minutes (Vol. 2, 1933–50) documents the existence of Hudgins School for black students. In his 1931-32 report, Principal A.P. Conley explained that Hudgins provided two years of high school work and seven of elementary classes (Department of Public Instruction, Division of Negro Education, High School Principal's Annual Report, Box 4, North Carolina State Archives, Raleigh). There was only one high school teacher with nine students enrolled. The two-story school building, erected in 1925 and valued at $14,500, was heated with a coal stove and located on two acres, part of which had been landscaped. The school site had a value of $6,000. One of the school's six classrooms was available for high school classes. A separate room was maintained for the library, which contained 115 volumes. According to Conley, there were 10 reference books, five history and biography, five works of poetry, 15 of standard literature, and 65 labeled miscellaneous. The school subscribed to one magazine and to one daily newspaper.

Well-educated, A.P. Conley had earned a bachelor's degree at Johnson C. Smith University and had done graduate work at Columbia University. A veteran educator of 20 years, Conley taught all classes for the eighth and ninth grades and indicated that he held a high school "C" certificate. His annual salary amounted to $633. Eight units were required for graduation, and there were eight graduates: Essie Brown, Mildred Jackson, Hubert Logan, Bishop Martin, Andrew Roberts, William Sisk, Mary Smith, and Lynell Withrow.

Although not required to do so, Conley's report listed the names, grades and salaries of the school's elementary teachers: Franklyn Brown, first grade, $522; Louise Springs, second grade, $452; Alma Ross, third grade, $540; Margaret Greenlee, fourth and fifth grades, $558; Lorna Jenkins, sixth and seventh grades, $576 (DPI, DNE; HSPAR, Box 4,).

According to other annual principal reports, in the 1930s, F.M. Beaver, who had earned his bachelor's degree from Johnson C. Smith University in Charlotte, North Carolina, became the school's principal and had the certification for the position. For an extended period the school's history moved forward under his administration, but eventually blacks charged him with inadequate leadership in a series of events that stamped a negative image on the Marion school.

After Beaver became the principal, faculty members were always college graduates. During its June 1934 meeting, the board elected the following faculty members: Bessie Newsome, Annie Louise Jones, Greenlee Corpening, Margaret Greenlee, Alma Ross, Franklyn P. Brown, and Sarah Bynum. On June 25, 1935, the board added Charles Graham as a science teacher and boys' adviser. Because Hudgins was a union school, both elementary and secondary teachers served on the staff. Teacher salaries during that time frame ranged from $518.40 to $600 (DPI, DNE, HSPAR, Boxes 7 and 8).

Despite its small faculty, extracurricular activities were regularly available at Hudgins High School. In his 1936-37 report, Beaver verified the existence of a math and a science club in addition to dramatics, baseball and basketball (DPI, DNE, HSPAR, Boxes 7 and 8).

In 1939, the Marion public schools achieved a record that would foster pride in any school system when the North Carolina School Commission released statistics for the 1937-38 school term. The Marion school system ranked third in the 111 city school units in attendance with a rate of 98.3 percent. Also, Marion's black school tied with a school in Lexington for first place in the state with an attendance rate of 97.1 percent (Marion School Board minutes, November 9, 1939).

Marion school girls dressed in white, perhaps for a graduation ceremony, a celebration, or for performing in a musical production. The city's first Rosenwald sponsored school, which was destroyed by fire, was replaced by another in 1925-26 at a cost of $13,500. The school's combined elementary and secondary enrollment in 1940-41 was 255 with a combined average daily attendance of 244 (North Carolina Office of Archives and History, Raleigh).

The black community developed a strong interest in erecting a gymnasium on school property. Faculty members were eager to solicit funds from the school board to make that a reality. However, on November 19, 1945, the principal of Hudgins School reported to the school board that he had advised his faculty to withdraw their request for funds to construct a gymnasium at the black school.

Instead, Beaver asked the board to approve funds up to $500 to improve the school grounds. However, because no money had been allotted in the budget for that project, the board postponed any action on the matter. The campaign to add a gymnasium gained momentum over the next several years. The Marion City Board of Education had regularly done routine maintenance work at the school, such as painting both the interior and the exterior, but no action was taken on the community's desire for a gymnasium.

On June 28, 1945, local patrons of the Negro school asked for permission to use the white athletic field for a July 4 celebration, but the Marion Central PTA had a recreational program that required the use of the field. In October 1946, Principal Beaver asked the board if the Hudgins students could use the white gymnasium, Once again, no action was taken. The board tabled the matter to be considered later. In April 1948, the board explained that there were insufficient funds to erect a metal building to be used as a gymnasium for the "colored students." In May, the school board asked the board of commissioners for funds to build a gym, but no decision was made.

On August 18, another complication arose with the request for a new colored high school. The school board debated whether to continue looking into funding for a gym. However, on August 24 the board again discussed the gym. The following December board minutes indicate that little progress had been made in providing a gym because there was not enough money available. Beaver appeared at the December 9, 1948, meeting to ask that Hudgins School be allowed to play its home games in the white Central High School gym. The board declined "inasmuch as a gym project is under consideration for the Hudgins School." The instance implies that the board was taking action, but their denial of the request did not solve the problem for the black community.

Instead of improvement, years of inaction continued. On April 22, 1949, the board extensively discussed building a Negro gym and decided to investigate buying land adjacent to the school owned by W.H. Hawkins. He was willing to sell the plot for $12,000. By August 11, the board decided to buy a parcel of land from Hawkins for $7,000. On November 29, board attorney Paul J. Story reported that he would sign the certificate of title for the property "with reservations" based on legal technicalities, but the board refused to finalize the arrangement until there were no reservations by their attorney. After the attorney obtained a quitclaim deed from B. Greenlee Corpening and Norman Calicutt and explained that he considered the lack of such a document from a colored man named Moore to be harmless, the board still refused to take action, according to board minutes for March 30, 1950.

On January 24, 1950, Principal D.A. Horne requested the use of the white high school gym for basketball games. Town Manager Reece Snyder pointed out to both Horne and the board that the Negroes had use, regular use, of a community building for athletic and social events, and therefore no action was taken. Snyder recommended that the city board of trustees and alderman meet to discuss the matter, which happened. At that meeting the Negro delegation submitted requests to the Marion City Board of Trustees, but the record failed to itemize those.

On July 1, 1950, Hugh Beam announced that state Superintendent Clyde A. Erwin advised that the board proceed with its plan to construct a new city-county consolidated school in Marion. On July 20, 1950, the Marion Board of Education met with the McDowell County Board of Commissioners and decided to expedite the work on the Hudgins athletic field and to remodel the school. In the same joint meeting, the Marion Board of Education agreed to provide for all the colored students in the county, thus paving the way for a county-city school consolidation.

A new decade arrived, but the same request surfaced annually from black citizens. On November 9, 1950, the black community urgently requested the board to provide a gymnasium before the basketball season commenced. A basketball court was badly needed, but again it was the same theme: no action was taken. Unfortunately, basketball fans in the white community suffered a tremendous setback when fire destroyed much of the white gymnasium. At the November 28 meeting, the school board learned that the entire west end of the building had been destroyed on the morning of November 27. For classes to continue, the white school's band and both the physical education and the home economics departments required temporary housing. A further setback occurred on December 11, 1950, when the board determined that there could be no further use of the white gymnasium until the insurance claims were settled (Marion City Board of Education minutes, Book 4, 1950–1959). Perhaps the problems confronting the physical education instructors at the white school created sympathy for the black school's dilemma. However, the matter of a gymnasium for black students was not solved until after the construction of the new Hudgins School. The continuing gymnasium conundrum probably cast a dark shadow over the school leadership.

Beaver himself became the object of criticism in the black community. In a November 25, 1940, report (DPI, DNE; General Correspondence of the Director [GCD], Box 14), Assistant Director G.H. Ferguson commented on his visit to Hudgins School in Marion. "Unfortunately, the principal is too concerned about holding his job for another nine years ... for him to ... to give the attention he should to the proper organization of his school," he stated. "Unless he can change his point of view, the Negro patrons of this community will never have a good school while he is principal. He is ... conscious of some of the shortages but unfortunately spends his time making excuses rather than explaining his plans for amending conditions. I had a conference with Superintendent Beam.... He is not conscious of all the ways he might be able to assist the principal, and I doubt he will render much help professionally." There is no doubt that the language sounds as strong now as it must have 70 years ago.

Ferguson was convinced that Beaver had an interest in the Negro school, but his report indicates that a new principal was needed for the school to be effective. As opposition grew, the African American community rejected any efforts by Beaver to convince them that he was able to create an effective educational environment for their children. How that turmoil affected the educational process cannot be fully determined, but obviously as the principal became the center of a major controversy, both teachers and students were distracted in their pursuits of teaching and of learning respectively.

Influential members of the community asked that Beaver be replaced as principal. At first the objection to his administration was that it showed a lack of significant forward steps to improve Hudgins School. A delegation of eight black citizens, led by Richard Erwin, met with Marion's school board on October 16, 1947, and expressed their wish that Beaver be asked to resign. The superintendent agreed to personally review progress at the school since 1932, but the board refused to relieve Beaver of his position. Turmoil increased. The delegation responded by vowing to prefer charges against Beaver.

The board responded by determining to confer with other black citizens as soon as possible. The obvious question is whether Beaver's decision to deny support for the need to finance a gymnasium may have contributed to his unpopularity, which was evident for more than a decade.

His black opponents took drastic action by lodging charges of immorality against Beaver, as recorded in the board of education's minutes for January 9, 1948. School board members planned the hearing carefully. They decided the public inquiry would take place in a courtroom on January 15 at 10 A.M. The total investigation would be oral with a stenographer keeping a record of the proceedings. First, though, the principals involved were notified. Attorney Paul J. Story represented Beaver, and attorney Roy W. Davis represented the patrons bringing the charges. The date appears to have been changed to January 20 when two teachers, Helen Janet Moye and Catherine Cowan Fisher, were questioned and excused. The conclusion was unanimous that there was insufficient proof of immorality by Professor Beaver and that he should not be dismissed from his position. A short time later at its March 23 meeting, the board again analyzed the transcript of the hearing and then agreed to turn it over to attorney Paul J. Story.

However, the delegation, led by Richard Erwin and Will Crisp, Jr., again approached the school board, according to the May 25, 1948, board minutes, and reaffirmed their objections to allowing Beaver to stay on as principal of Hudgins School. According to spokesmen for the group, they were unhappy with Beaver's management of school affairs and with his uncooperative spirit. The matter was left open for board action. On June 2, Professor Beaver appeared before the board to respond to objections about renewing his contract.

Once again the board chose to endorse Beaver to serve as Hudgins' principal. However, during the initial vote, one board member responded negatively to Beaver's contract, but the dissenting member then reconsidered and made the decision unanimous. Having a unified front gave the board's decision more power in the public domain.

Beaver's opponents were unyielding. Details about the Marion conflict reached Raleigh. A group of eight men traveled to the state capital and apprised Director N.C. Newbold of their unhappiness with the Marion school board's denial of their request that Principal Beaver be replaced. Newbold visited Marion to investigate the problem and was assured that Beaver had been exonerated of all accusations and that he was suitable to continue as principal. Later a petition opposing Beaver's appointment was delivered to the board at its August 18 meeting, but the board took no action. No doubt, the superintendent and members of the board realized the depth of community disapproval with their school's principal.

As the 1948-49 school term drew to a close, on May 24 the board again retained F.M. Beaver as principal of Hudgins School. Then, on June 3, the superintendent recommended that a Negro advisory committee be appointed for the Hudgins School. The board authorized the committee and specified that the superintendent and board chair select its members (Marion City Board of Education [BOE] minutes, Book 3, June 30, 1949).

Opposition to Beaver escalated. By September 6, members of the board feared that trouble would develop, according to the board entry on that date. Consequently, they ordered the superintendent to request Beaver's resignation, though they stipulated that "said resignation was not a demand." Trouble did develop. According to a caption with a photo of picketers at Hudgins School, parents and patrons of the elementary and high school assembled each weekday morning at the campus and displayed posters that proclaimed: "We Want a New Principal" and "Give Us a Principal." Leaders of the group emphasized that the picketing would continue until the school board replaced Beaver ("Negro School Is Picketed," *The McDowell News,* Marion, NC, n.d. in "African American Scrapbook," Vertical File, McDowell County Public Library, Marion, NC).

At a called meeting of the Marion City Board of Education, the superintendent reported that Beaver had declined to resign. No action was taken, by then a well-known response, and the board agreed to await further developments. Two weeks later, September 23, 1949, the board called another meeting at which the Rev. M.O. Owens, minister of the First Baptist Church of Marion, offered to facilitate a compromise between the two opposing factions. The outcome of that plan is not part of the record, but by October 25, 1949, Beaver had submitted his resignation (Marion City BOE minutes, Book 3). He stipulated that he would continue until a replacement was hired.

At the same meeting the board unanimously chose D.A. Horne to replace Beaver, hired Paul Dusenbury to teach at the school, and appointed a committee of black citizens to work with the black Hudgins School. During the entire period while the board continually frustrated the black community, both the board and the school superintendent had failed to take action. Theirs was a difficult role, but perhaps if they had chosen to act, the impact on the educational process would have been less severe. Had Beaver chosen to resign, the matter would have been quickly laid to rest, but he may have wrestled with the fear that such a move would destroy his career.

At the board's next meeting, November 29, 1949, teacher B. Greenlee Corpening submitted a bill itemizing damages to his home that had occurred "when unknown hoodlums threw rocks into his windows and shot through his doors during the Negro school strike." Denying any legal responsibility for those damages, the board refused to disburse any funds. Corpening, a member of Hudgins' faculty, was assumed to be a supporter of Beaver. The attack on his home demonstrates further the barriers to learning that resulted from the split in community support for school personnel. The reference to a "school strike" defines the depth of disagreement about this matter. Although no details are included in the official record, the suspicion was that students and other members of the community wreaked havoc as a result of the strong feelings surrounding demands for the principal's resignation. Marion was a community in turmoil.

Confronting Personnel Disputes

In McDowell County, Horne was employed as Hudgens' principal for only one year, 1949-50. Beaver's replacement faced wavering support. He filed his High School Principal's Report (DPI, DNE, HSPAR, Box 24) on June 13, 1950, and noted that Hudgins had seven graduates that spring. According to Horne's report, Madge Logan had provided counseling services for students. In response to the question: "What ... are the chief handicapping factors preventing an effective counseling service in your school?" Principal Horne stated, "Lack of community and school cooperation." That comment suggests a continuing split in support of Hudgins School.

The monitoring committee — which included Lee Cooper, Rodney Wilkerson, Clyde Forney, Melzo Rutherford, Charles Martin, Curtis Henry, and Marvin Swepson — objected to Horne's continuation as principal. That recommendation, along with the committee's submission of their choice for his replacement, occurred at the March 30, 1950, board meeting, but no action was taken. The committee again appeared before the board at its May 30 meeting and asked that Principal D.A. Horne and B. Greenlee Corpening not be rehired and that qualified teachers replace them. The superintendent and board chairman assured the committee their suggestions would be given careful consideration. Later minutes indicate those leaders felt the person the committee recommended as the new principal was too inexperienced and agreed to look elsewhere.

Marion City Schools was not alone in facing tough calls about school personnel. A conflict in Hendersonville City Schools occurred about the continued employment of Joyce Mills as home economics teacher at Ninth Avenue School. In Madison County community residents demanded a replacement for the respected Gladys Wilson, an elementary school teacher at Long Ridge School. Both incidents illustrate that internal pressures, in addition to white pressures from outside the school, can interfere with the educational process. Ironically, that is one way both black schools and white schools were "separate but equal," as white teachers also became the objects of dissension and petitions were circulated in white communities asking for the dismissal of principals.

Personal conflict interrupted the educational process at Ninth Avenue as community members took sides in a personal vendetta. Joyce Mills, wife of Sam Mills, a respected community leader, taught home economics, but her job fell into jeopardy after she allegedly attacked another teacher in school. The confrontation occurred during the absence of Principal Marable, who had been called away due to the death of his mother. Reportedly Mills and Alma Forest, a substitute teacher, "exchanged heated words, spat on each other, and struck blows," according to board minutes for October 18, 1946. The physical confrontation resulted in Forest's glasses being broken, which led Forest to take out a warrant for Mills' arrest. However, that issue was settled out of court.

After months, with patrons pressing for her removal and school officials noting that Mills' classroom performance was good, even outstanding, the board decided that she would not be rehired. The board's solution included hiring a male teacher who could provide needed assistance for Principal Marble. By its August meeting, the board had secured the services of Mary Louise Valentine to replace Mills as home economics teacher and had hired Evans K. Mims as assistant principal of the "Sixth Avenue Negro School" (Hendersonville Board of Education minutes, August 27, 1948).

In Madison County, residents criticized Wilson for her classroom practices. According to the minutes of the Madison County Board of Education, school patrons objected to Gladys Wilson's sense of ownership of Long Ridge School and demanded that she be replaced. At first the board refused but eventually determined to honor the community's wishes by hiring another instructor. The matter reached a critical point when, on January 4, 1954, a delegation from the community again asked that a new teacher be hired. The group presented a list of five reasons that, from their perspective, justified Wilson's dismissal.

Those reasons are paraphrased in the following assertions: (1) Wilson had been there too long and acted as if she owned the school; (2) Her students were not adequately prepared to do high school work; (3) She displayed a critical spirit, criticizing parents to their children and criticizing individual students in front of the class; (4) Often she did not ask for homework assignments in a timely manner and punished students who were unable to present their work when she asked for it at a late date; and (5) Wilson "carried on" with men and boys in the community. The delegation also asked that M. Grace Owens be replaced (Madison County BOE minutes, January 4, 1954).

Nevertheless, Wilson retained only positive memories of her career at Long Ridge School and took pleasure in the success of her former students (personal communication, April 4, 2008). Despite the negative actions, the community in future days spoke of Wilson with respect. However, the board approved Lillie A. Love as the new Long Ridge teacher at its meeting on May 20, 1954, and rejected Wilson and Owens.

At the June 1, 1960, board meeting, after the board elected Dora B. Bass, a substitute teacher at Long Ridge, as the teacher at Mars Hill Colored School, Zeno Ponder, a burly political activist, formally recommended that future appointments at the school be left up to the school's committeemen and that the board adopt a policy of approving the recommendations of those committee members. As a result, the school was under parental control as far as the hiring of professional staff.

Disputing School Locations Within the County

In McDowell County, another area of dissension arose regarding consolidation of county and city schools. On February 7, 1950, a joint meeting was held with Marion Board of Aldermen and the Marion City administrative unit to discuss the "Negro situation as it exists in Marion." The leaders decided to contact the McDowell Board of Education and to explore the building needs for both black and white students in the city and in the county. On March 30, Superintendents Hugh Beam and N.F. Steppe agreed to invite Dr. Clyde A. Erwin, state superintendent of education, to send a survey team to determine their long-term needs.

The team visited the county in April and sent a report recommending that one central school be erected at Marion for all the black pupils in the county. School officials agreed to ask the county commissioners to place $40,000 in the city's school budget for 1950-51 for a school for the black children of the entire county and to provide an additional $40,000 to supplement a bond levy for 1950-51. The board made a resolution to erect and equip an additional building at Hudgins (Marion City Board of Education minutes, Book 4, July 25, 1950; August 5, 1950).

However, on August 29, 1950, board members learned that residents of Old Fort in McDowell County opposed the attempt to consolidate black schools. The board acknowledged the opposition but took no action. J.E. Hunter of the Division of Teacher Allotment in Raleigh had sent a telegram requesting that the City of Marion accept seven or eight students from Mitchell County to attend Hudgins School. Adding students was favorable for the Marion school because there had been an insufficient enrollment to support a high school, and that was an obstacle in earning accreditation. In September, the black community at Old Fort again refused to send their children to Hudgins School. S.E. Duncan, state inspector of Negro high schools, recommended a compromise, but no action was taken. In October the N.C. Department of Public Instruction recommended postponing consolidation for twelve months. Both the county and the city agreed to the postponement, and Superintendent Hugh Beam transferred two teachers to the county system so that the plan could go into effect immediately.

Catawba View Grammar School at Old Fort was abandoned in the early 1950s due to consolidation of McDowell County Schools with the Hudgins School in Marion. Just as consolidation brought resistance in Watauga County, Old Fort citizens boycotted the move and fought in the courts to retain their school. Citizens such as Bob Keaton, Watt Twitty, and Col. D.W. Adams begged school authorities to leave the building intact to serve as a community center, but, despite their pleas, the building was razed (North Carolina Office of Archives and History, Raleigh).

With that delay in consolidation the board focused on plans for building specifications. Working together, the city and county boards of education determined that 12 classrooms would be needed, as would a combination gymnasium and cafeteria that would seat 250, a library, a teachers' restroom, a clinic–first aid room, and offices for the principal and other personnel. Marion City — with its black school fund of $73,000, a fire settlement estimated at $55,000, and a state allotment for city and county of $421,000 — had a total of $549,000 for expenses. That amount was to be supplemented by a $1 million bond issue. The amount of $260,000 was earmarked for the construction of the consolidated black school and the remainder was to be divided between the city and the county. The city board formally resolved to build a consolidated school for black students living within McDowell County. Lindsey Gudger's architectural firm was to provide a new building at the school site as rapidly as possible (Marion City BOE minutes, Book 4, 1950–59).

On September 13, 1951, an architect's depiction of the soon-to-be constructed Marion

Jackson County Consolidated School in Sylva also served students from Swain, Macon, and Haywood Counties. In the early 1940s, 30 secondary students and 129 elementary students were enrolled with an average daily attendance of 29 and 123 respectively. This was the only high school for Negro students west of Canton. In the late 1940s and early 1950s during the scurry to provide "equal" facilities for black students, Jackson County build a modern brick school with indoor plumbing and a central heating system in 1956; however, in 1954 the county appraised the old frame building with six classrooms, a combination auditorium and gymnasium, and a library, and deemed the school to be in fair condition, although there were no indoor toilets and the building was in dire need of renovation (North Carolina Office of Archives and History, Raleigh).

Consolidated Negro School, considered "both modern and attractive," appeared in the local paper. The November 15, 1951, edition of *The McDowell News* announced, "Work Started Tuesday At Hudgins School; To Erect New Negro Consolidated School." Marion City Superintendent Beam, according to the article, had arranged temporary sites for classes to continue while the construction progressed. Grades 1–4 would meet in the basement of Addie's Chapel. Classes for grades 4–7 would meet in the basement of Mt. Moriah Baptist Church, and high school students would attend classes at A.M.E. Zion Methodist Church. Makeshift arrangements, scheduled for the entire school year, would allow students to continue their education. School officials affirmed that "unless the National Emergency becomes more acute and shortages develop in critical material that ... the Building should be ready ... at the beginning of the next school year."

Black residents in Old Fort continued to object to being forced to attend a consolidated school in Marion, at least 15 miles away. By the end of October 1952 only a few had enrolled in the new school. Board minutes for October 28 indicated that the dissenters had established a private school in Old Fort. County Superintendent N.F. Steppe had conferred with D. Hyden Ramsey of the state board of education. Ramsey advised that school officials exercise patience because he believed the private school would fail and force Old Fort students to attend school in Marion.

However, by November 25, 1952, Ramsey, who had changed his mind, stated that Old Fort citizens "were in open defiance of the law." He deemed that legal action was required and recommended that the local board take the matter to court. School board minutes for both McDowell County and the city of Marion confirmed ongoing disputes into the late 1950s from citizens who wanted their children to attend school in Old Fort. On July 21, 1955, *The*

McDowell News headline read, "McDowell Board of Education Answers Petition of Negroes: No Class Space, Modern Negro School Comprise Reply to Negro Requests."

E.P. Damerson, county board of education chairman, had received a formal petition from Old Fort parents requesting that their children be allowed to attend school in Old Fort, their home territory, for the 1955-56 school term. The board instructed its attorney, Roy Davis, to answer them. The parents, in turn, had enlisted the services of Raleigh attorneys Samuel A. Mitchell and Herman Taylor to handle the matter. Davis, speaking on behalf of the board of education, cited the construction in Marion of an up-to-date, modern, and well-equipped school that had cost approximately $300,000 and the lack of classroom space at Old Fort as the basis for denying the request. However, the matter did not go away. The August 5 and 24, 1957, county board minutes recorded another request that their children be allowed to attend school in Old Fort. Citing crowded conditions there, the October 14, 1957, minutes indicate a denial of individual requests for reassignment to Old Fort.

Disputing School Locations Between Counties

In addition to concerns about the geographical location of schools within a county, such as McDowell, there were also disputes about where a black school should be located when it was supposed to serve two or more counties, which made the distances farther. While daily traffic can consume hours on today's better roads, it is easy to imagine how distance could affect travel time and student motivation on less developed highway systems in mountain regions with many curves and elevations. In addition, location of schools had strategic economic benefits, especially as school activities expanded.

A conflict developed between Jackson and Macon Counties regarding the location of a standard high school. Educators in each county coveted the prospect of having a high school with enough students to ensure success for a program of secondary education. Neither county had a large black population, but by combining their pupil populations with those of other counties, a successful school could pave the way for more students to earn a high school diploma, to find better job opportunities, or to gain acceptance into black colleges.

Because elementary schools with small enrollments were allowed to include high school classes for grades 8 and 9, both Macon and Jackson had fledgling high schools. One such institution was Franklin's Chapel School, which attempted to provide advanced training. In a letter to N.C. Newbold, Chapel Principal R. B. Watts suggested that to benefit those students in nearby western counties, a full high school with dormitory facilities should be established in Franklin.

The Watts Plan, as this recommendation became known, espoused a standard high school with boarding facilities that would allow students to spend more time in classes and in study activities by avoiding long daily bus rides. However, Principal John H. Davis of Sylva in Jackson County campaigned for a central high school, to be located in Sylva, with daily bus service. The competing proposals initiated a lively disagreement between advocates of the Davis Plan and of the Watts Plan (DPI, DNE, Special Subjects, Box 11). A flood of correspondence commenced between Watts and Newbold as well as between Davis and Newbold because each county coveted being the site of a consolidated high school.

In his February 19, 1938, letter, to Newbold, Watts supported his plan by stating that the town of Franklin was the more central location for the counties involved, that it was a growing town with amicable relations between the races, and that it housed a two-acre school site with additional acreage leased for recreational purposes. He maintained that the Franklin colored community was experiencing growth, and, to top it off, he affirmed that Franklin site was far

Grahamtown School in Forest City had an enrollment of 122 high school students and 254 elementary students in 1940-41 with an average daily attendance of 111 in the high school and 224 in the elementary grades. The original building was constructed in 1926-27 for $4,900, of which the Rosenwald Fund contributed $1,100. Following the opening of Carver High School in Spindale, the school's name was changed to Dunbar Elementary School (North Carolina Office of Archives and History, Raleigh).

more scenic and attractive than that of Sylva. In conclusion, he documented the distance to Franklin from Canton was 52 miles and from Murphy was 62 miles. Watts built a strong case for building a dormitory in Franklin to save hours of daily travel for students.

In his July 15, 1937, letter to Newbold, Principal John H. Davis, who managed the education of Jackson County's black children from 1919 until 1942, had requested an additional teacher to consolidate Haywood, Swain, Macon, and Jackson Counties. A census indicated that, even with the combined students of those four counties, there would not be a sufficient number of students to establish a standard high school. He also asked that the Department of Public Instruction consider reducing the minimum number of students required for an additional instructor to 20. In his opinion, such an action would reduce the costliness of consolidation and make it more effective because two teachers would be designated for full-time high school instruction (DPI, DNE; Special Subjects, Box 11). Despite Watts' persuasive arguments, the Davis Plan won state approval.

Jackson County Consolidated School, located in Sylva, educated its own students and others from nearby western counties. As a union school, one with elementary and high school grades occupying a single building, it had received stimulus money from the Rosenwald Fund in the 1924-25 legislative budget for a Type 5 school referenced as Sylva Consolidated School (Hanchett, 1988).

In the 1930s, according to annual reports filed by the school's principal with the North Carolina Department of Public Instruction, the school's enrollment ranged from 19, with an average daily attendance of 10, in 1935, to 21, with an average daily attendance of 16, in 1939.

In his annual report Davis wrote, "This high school work has been classified as supplementary because of the limited number of high school pupils and [has been] encouraged by the various superintendents. Pupils have taken the two years [of] courses and have entered senior high schools very creditably."

The name used for the school varied on state reports. At times it was Negro Consolidated, Colored Consolidated, or Central Consolidated. By 1942, the school boasted an enrollment of 41 students with an average daily attendance of 34. During Davis' tenure, additional extracurricular activities became available, and the school library grew substantially.

In 1935-36, the school employed a part-time coach to supervise 18 students playing baseball and 20 playing basketball. It was quite a coup for a school the size of Sylva's Consolidated Negro School to purchase the services of a physical education instructor. Another improvement, academic in nature, was the purchase of a globe plus additional political and physical maps. The principal's involvement in teaching geography and United States history no doubt underscored the need for such learning materials.

John Wade became principal of the Colored Consolidated School when John H. Davis retired. In an attempt to elevate the professional standards of his staff, Wade hired only teachers who had standard college degrees, not degrees from normal schools (Murray, 2002). Employing a new teacher in 1944 merited a feature story in the *Sylva Herald*. The black community expressed thanks to Senator Gertrude McKee and Superintendent A.C. Moses for their help in locating a qualified teacher, which allowed the addition of high school classes. Four years later the school was able to expand to a complete high school program and to hire additional teachers. Neighboring Macon and Swain Counties transported their students to the Consolidated High School.

In the early 1940s, W.F. Credle, supervisor of the Rosenwald Fund and of construction, surveyed Jackson County Schools at the request of the board of education. Despite rising costs of construction related to war conditions, the board began tentatively developing long-range plans to improve all its schools. Because the high school for black students served two counties in addition to Jackson, money for building a new school for the black community would also come from Macon County and Swain County. The Jackson County edifice was the sole secondary black school west of Canton in southwestern North Carolina.

Turmoil was widespread and surfaced in numerous ways. Adults contrived ways to achieve racial cleansing, made excuses to delay essential improvements, addressed complex personnel disputes and problems, and argued about school locations. Despite the obstacles, Western North Carolina educational and civil rights leaders kept working to achieve reconciliation and the end result: integrated schools.

10

Reconciliation in Secondary Education

Decade after decade tension spread throughout North Carolina's Appalachian communities as leaders coveted an accessible neighborhood school, adequately equipped and staffed by well-trained teachers. Black citizens reconciled themselves to the obvious fact: their schools would never equate with white schools, but advancing degrees of improvement lessened their frustration. They recognized that schools were moving forward step by step. Also, black citizens were endowed with hope and with a spirit of reconciliation, especially after the 1921 establishment of the North Carolina Division of Negro Education and its efforts to advance the cause of black education.

Secondary schools create unique challenges for teachers and administrators. As the secondary school program developed for Appalachian black schools, the process involved planning new curricula, developing behavior and discipline policies, providing career and academic counseling programs, expanding vocational offerings and adding new opportunities. In the past, student improvement in basic skills was an overriding objective. In the twenty-first century, concern about training North Carolina's students to become globally competitive has impacted the objectives of classroom activities. However, though global concerns prevail today, basic skills still provide the foundation for today's more sophisticated goals. In the mid-twentieth century, parents and educators recognized the need to achieve a major goal: allow students whose dreams included more than elementary education to have an accessible route to fulfill their aspirations.

Earlier, county training schools and normal schools, as well as private schools, provided an option to continue learning beyond seventh grade. By the late nineteenth century private high schools, such as Lincoln Academy in Gaston County, offered secondary education for blacks. With ongoing twentieth century development, public elementary schools added classes designated for high school study. The state's public school system is largely a product of the twentieth century, and the development of secondary schools for blacks was especially tardy. As late as 1924, only two public high schools for blacks existed in Western North Carolina (Van Noppen and Van Noppen, 1973), and the one located in Hendersonville was a union school with four corners of a large room designated for high school classes. By 1933-34, a decade later, ten secondary schools existed in 24 western counties (Hawkins, 2001).

Leading by Commitment

Jacob A. Tillman was principal of Burke County's Olive Hill School in the late 1940s. His numerous responsibilities, as indicated in his annual high school reports, included providing weekly counseling services, which included administering standard tests in mental ability, achievement, aptitude, and interest (DPI, DNE, HSPAR, Box 19). Tillman blocked off two hours each week to interact with individual students about their future plans. In addition, he assigned himself the responsibility of teaching two 55-minute classes: dramatics and mathematics, which required striking differences in content and lesson preparation. Tillman had completed enough classes himself to earn a principal's certificate on the master's level.

Tillman's annual reports indicate he led a staff of six teachers at Olive Hill. J.A. Arnold assumed responsibilities for health, science, and physical education. John H. Carson taught both English and French; Mrs. E.B. Worrell, home economics and eighth grade; Mrs. I.R. Fleming, history and eighth grade English; and Miss M.G. Clark, mathematics and science. Olive Hill, located in Morganton, followed a standard secondary curriculum with each of its instructors handling at least two separate courses. Their contribution to school effectiveness depended upon the success of their classroom procedure, the level of response of each student to the challenge of learning and the rapport established within the classroom. If their principal supported and encouraged their efforts while challenging them to improve their knowledge and techniques, he led them to raise the standards and the performance of their students. How that role of leadership can be measured by analyzing past performance defies any system of evaluation. However, as a leader willing to shoulder the workload, to be in regular contact with students on a one-to-one basis, and to invest effort in personal advancement, Tillman provided a role model for faculty as well as for students. His efforts showed black parents and students that it was possible to progress up the educational ladder.

Principals of black secondary schools normally had little time to fulfill the duties implied by their titles. Those men and women taught most of their working day. Administrators, by partnering with other staff members to instruct students, bolstered the spirits of their teachers. Ralph H. Davis, principal of Reynolds High School in Haywood County, taught three sections of English as well as health and physical education, according to his 1951-52 annual report (DPI, DNE, HSPAR, Box 6). At Lenoir's Freedman High School, Principal Julian J. Spearman, according to his 1947-48 report, taught one math class, three sections of English, supervised two study halls, and assigned himself to spend one hour doing office work (DPI, DNE, HSPAR, Box 20). During the 1948-49 school term, J.R. Edelin, principal of Lincoln Heights High School in North Wilkesboro, taught sociology and economics in addition to carrying out his duties as principal.

In Watauga County, Principal Bertha M. Neal, in her 1947-48 report, indicated that she taught classes during the entire school day to allow four students to earn credit for two years of high school work (DPI, DNE, HSPAR, Box 27). Her additional duties as principal were accomplished before and after school. In Surry County, Principal L.H. Jones counseled seniors two hours weekly and provided a placement service. He also taught mathematics and manual training (DPI, DNE, HSPAR, Box 26). James O. Gibbs, in his 1947-48 report for Grahamtown High School, listed his duties as including classes in mathematics and science and providing counseling services as well as being principal (Box 26). V.C. Ramseur, Jr., principal at New Hope School, taught biology, chemistry, physical education and first aid during the 1947-48 school year (DPI, DNE, HSPAR, Box 26). To provide for the academic needs of students, principals contributed to the variety of courses offered to their secondary students.

In the 1940s, Pigeon Street School, an embryonic secondary school with O.W.H. McCorkle serving as principal, was located in Waynesville. In 1941-42, while the eighth grade was still designated as a high school class, the school offered two years of secondary classes, eighth and ninth. The High school Principal's Annual Report for that year indicates that 15 students were promoted. The length of the school term was eight months or 160 days. The lone male instructor was responsible for all high school classes. Two female teachers taught the elementary students. Pigeon Street School contained an auditorium, a lunchroom, and a single classroom that was used for the high school.

The Pigeon Street lunchroom was controlled by the W.P.A. and the P.T.A., according to McCorkle's report. There was neither a library nor a gymnasium. No physical education classes existed. Two levels of English, eighth and ninth, were taught; students had a study period during the time paralleling the other grade's instruction. Citizenship, mathematics, history, and science were the same for both grades. Welton Reynolds provided instruction for the high school students and was the acting principal for both the elementary and high school classes (DPI, DNE, HSPAR, Box 13). In his annual 1946-47 report, Principal McCorkle, who was completing his fourteenth year as an educator, indicated that a ninth grade had been formed with seven students and that was the only secondary class at Pigeon Street School.

McCorkle, a college graduate, taught five subjects: English, mathematics, general science, citizenship, reading (as indicated by the entry "Good Companions") and spelling. Except for reading and spelling, all classes lasted 45 minutes; the time slot for reading and spelling was 30 minutes each (DPI, DNE, HSPAR, Box 18).

In Catawba County, Phairlever Pearson, who saw Newton's black high school for the first time when he became its principal in 1945, took a personal interest in encouraging students to advance their education. He arranged for them to visit black college campuses. His school had eleven grades in a single building and from day one on his job, Pearson took steps to advance the cause of black education. Soon after taking charge, he invited the patronizing white school board to inspect a building in great need of repair. One school official called Pearson "a smart little fellow." After the war the school received a new cafeteria, a gymnasium and a shop (from "The Civil Right Movement Comes to North Carolina," retrieved from http://www.mystatehistory.com). Monte Mitchell, writing "Community Remembers Educator, Leader" for the *Observer News Enterprise* on March 23, 1999, called Pearson an ambassador, a bus driver, a cook, a counselor, a custodian, a motivator, a teacher, a principal.

The black principal's workload was extensive — all part of the requirement to have a functioning high school.

Fulfilling Dreams of Progress

In the 1930s Yadkin County was home to scattered, remote communities with nine elementary schools. When Director of Negro Education N.C Newbold and Asheville educator John H. Michael were collecting data to learn how many students completing seventh grade wished to go on to high school (DPI, DNE, Special Subjects, Box 11), a Yadkin County leader approached Raleigh in 1938.

Newbold received a letter, dated June 15, 1938, with a map designating the location of the elementary schools and the county roads in and near Yadkin County from E.L. "Emmett Leroy" Cundiff. The county resident wrote:

> We colored citizens are deprived of any high school ... in the two counties Surry and Yadkin, in the interest of the students ... I have made a survey and find that ... over 100... [who have] finished the seventh grade in the last few years ... are anxious to have high school training, but their parents are not able to send them away to a boarding school. Then, too, we don't have a boarding high school.
> Through our board of education I learn that the state is trying to work out a program where two ... counties might combine and build a high school.... The colored students might be brought together by bus ... Boonville ... as you ... see from the map is more central located.
> From the farthest point it's only about 14 miles, I am wandering [*sic*] whether we could get ... at least a junior high school this year with ... two buses. We have a nice two story building well

lighted black-boards, electric lights, and good heating.... This building is a community center [DPI, DNE, GCD, Box 13].

Cundiff invited Newbold to send a representative to inspect the building offered for a school. In his June 24, 1938, reply, Newbold expressed a willingness to investigate the possibilities and, after having done that, to offer his recommendations to the county officials who, he indicated, would have the final word. On July 12, in still another letter, Newbold advised Cundiff that H.L. Trigg, high school supervisor for the state department, was studying the matter seriously and would welcome additional suggestions from community leaders. The Division of Negro Education worked with local school personnel to win approval for improving or constructing black school facilities. Again Newbold asked the Yadkin County committee to notify local school officials of their interest in the project. The Division of Negro Education made it their policy to operate in conjunction with local white school boards. Newbold indicated that ideally a high school could be built at both Yadkinville and at Mount Airy, the Yadkin and Surry seats, but he pointed out that having a high school is far more important than its location (Box 13).

Cundiff is an outstanding example of an effective community activist. A 1917 graduate of North Carolina Agricultural and Technical College (A&T) in Greensboro, Cundiff taught school in Stokes, Surry, and Yadkin counties (Thompson, 2005). In the 1920s, his salary was $75 per month. By organizing locally and by enlisting help from Raleigh, Cundiff worked diligently to provide secondary education for black students. His efforts and determination resulted in making Yadkin County's vision a reality.

Successful principals displayed an interest in and a concern for students as well as for the staff. In McDowell County, V.E. Carson, principal of Mountain View School during the late 1950s and early 1960s, acquired a reputation as a caring principal and as one whose progressive outlook included issues such as teen marriage and pregnancy. According to former students, he addressed such matters in a forthright manner. While Carson encouraged students to invest in their education, he warned them not to take on the role of parents until they were old enough to assume those responsibilities in an adult manner. Addressing issues straight on was one technique by which Carson invested personal wisdom in the lives of his students. Reba Jackson, a 1958 graduate, said, "He was more or less ahead of his time. He was always looking out for our welfare." Jackson, who attended Hudgins School in the 1950s as an elementary student, recalled the family-like spirit in her classes, where the principal and teachers were role models. (M. Conley, "Before Integration, Black Students Attended Hudgins, Mountain View," *The McDowell News*, February 21, 1996, p. 1).

White superintendents and board members created opportunities to improve educational conditions for black students residing in their counties. Wilkes County Superintendent C.B. Eller hired Miss A.R. Wilson as a Jeanes supervisor in 1952 (Ingram, 1954). The entire community benefited from having a Jeanes supervisor, who provided instruction and support for classroom teachers but frequently taught adult education classes and organized special events to display student accomplishments. In Rutherford County, according to school board minutes for August 17, 1961, the superintendent hired Mattie Carpenter to be the Negro school supervisor. Providing professional support for black educators provided another avenue to reconciliation.

White school superintendents also assumed leadership responsibilities in persuading Raleigh to address needs in black schools. Caldwell County Superintendent C.S. Warren applied to the Board of Equalization in Raleigh and explained the urgent need for a black high school in Lenoir. Pressured by congestion at Morganton's Olive Hill High School and at Hickory's Ridgeview, Lenoir school officials addressed the needs of local high school students

(Hawkins, 2001). Previously students had attended high schools in adjoining counties. However, other students traveled to Asheville and to North Wilkesboro as well as to schools in Tennessee. Citizens knew that establishing a high school in Lenoir would save hours of travel time and allow families to pocket money saved.

Upgrading School Facilities

Once the state gave its nod to add high school instruction to Lenoir's black school system, the local board did so for the first time. The plan began with an initial enrollment of 43 pupils in grades eight to ten. The board hired Oliver W. Flemming of Morganton to assist Principal J.J. Spearman. Both Spearman and Flemming had earned degrees at Johnson C. Smith University, and their colleague Edna Rogers had graduated from Winston-Salem State Teachers College with a degree in home economics (Hawkins, 2001). The white school board provided space for secondary classes and a staff to make education possible — actions that brought a degree of reconciliation.

Throughout the western part of the state during the 1930s, '40s, and '50s, high school facilities were either constructed, renovated, or updated, especially in the late 1940s and early 1950s. For example, an attractive modern building replaced the old Hudgins High School in McDowell County. Perhaps in the spring of 1953 or at the dedication service for the new school, its name was changed to Mountain View School. By 1956, board minutes refer to Mountain View, not to Hudgins. Oral tradition specifies that the original name — Hudgins — honored Carter Hudgins, a white man who contributed funds for the school's original construction. Upon completion, the new Mountain View Elementary and High School in Marion contained a 600-seat auditorium, which could be converted into a gymnasium (an addition greatly desired by the black community), and featured departments of music, home economics, and visual education. The school had a full-time librarian and boasted both a health room and a darkroom (M. Conley, February 21, 1996, "Before Integration Black Students Attended Hudgins, Mountain View," *The McDowell News*, p. 1).

In 1938, the county and the city superintendents in Haywood County and Canton combined their efforts to secure state approval to construct a union school for the black community, many of whom lived in Gibson Town. By including high school classes in the new school, officials aimed to free students from being forced to attend schools outside the county. However, World War II blocked immediate achievement of new-school construction. It was not until 1948 that the county erected an eight-room brick building on a nine-acre tract in Gibson Town. The building included a library, a workshop for vocational classes, a lunchroom and a gymnasium-auditorium (J. Messer, T. Tucker, M. Forney, W. Eggleston, and R. Mitchell, "The Story of Reynolds High," *Asheville Citizen-Times*, n.d. from copy in files of Wilbur Eggleston). In 1955-56, in another effort to defuse tension, the school installed student lockers and renovated the home economics department, which included the purchase of a new stove and refrigerator. Also, Principal Ralph H. Davis purchased audio-visual aids and other equipment (DPI, DNE, HSPAR, Box 38).

During the late nineteenth and early twentieth centuries, the Freedman School fell under the oversight of Lenoir Graded School Trustees (Hawkins, 2001). Freedman School began as an elementary school in 1904 but evolved into a high school by 1932. Each improvement was a welcome milestone. In 1907, Lenoir school officials began using the Odd Fellows' Lodge for Freedman classrooms and continued until 1912, when the school officials began renting the Finley high school building for its black students. After fire destroyed that building on September 11, 1917, students attended classes in two separate buildings. In 1926, the brilliant scholar and dedicated schoolman Theophilus Lacy Phillips, a man of Irish and African descent with a facility in several languages, succeeded in having the Freedman School relocated to a building with four rooms, which accommodated seven grades and housed a chapel (Pearson, 1991, and Hawkins, 2001).

Following the 1926 election, school officials launched a school building program. Two new black schools replaced the old ones occupied by West End School and Freedman School. Six years later, on October 3, 1932, the *Lenoir News-Topic* reported: "Following approval last week by the State Board of Equalization, the Lenoir Board of Trustees today established the first colored high school ever formed here. There were 43 students on hand for the courses, which include work from the eighth to the tenth grades inclusive" (cited by Hawkins, 2001, p. 68).

A clipping on file at the Caldwell Heritage Museum in Lenoir contains a picture of Freedman High School with the following caption: "A new four-room building was built in 1927. Heated by coal stoves, the structure had a small auditorium and two small extra rooms that served as needed for an office and a library. Thanks to a WPA project during FDR's administration in 1936, an addition doubled the classroom space, added sanitary facilities, a modern heating system, an impressive home economics department, and the installation of water to one class room to allow ... demonstrations in science." ("Freedman High School," April 27, 1939, *Lenoir News-Topic)*. Continuous improvements marked the history of Freedman High School.

Prior to extending classes to include high school work, Caldwell County students routinely traveled to Burke, Catawba, Wilkes, and Buncombe counties as well as to schools in Tennessee (Hawkins, 2001). A new building with ten classrooms, a library, home economics and science departments and a band building became home to Freedman High School in 1957-58 ("History of Freedman High School," *Freedman High School Student Handbook*, n.d., on file at Caldwell Heritage Museum, Lenoir, NC).

Examples of other upgrades include investing money in establishing a well-equipped marching band in North Wilkesboro at Lincoln Heights High School, a band that annually scored well in regional competition and won awards in music festivals. In 1956, the Watauga County Board of Education established a planning and advisory board, which included Bertha M. Neal, principal of the black school (Board of Education minutes, May 7, 1956). Also, the board, in a clearly needed move, employed Marjorie Grimes to provide janitorial services at the black school (Watauga County BOE minutes, May 18, 1956).

Historically, numerous work opportunities were available to blacks in Rutherford County. There business opportunities existed in both agricultural and industrial companies as well as in gold mining. Prior to the 1849 California gold rush, the center of the nation's gold mining industry was in Rutherford County. Two residents, Christopher and Augustus Bechler, had received a license to mint gold coins and had enjoyed the profits from that enterprise from 1831 to 1842. A century later the chief industries were agriculture and textiles, with agriculture netting $5 million annually and textiles, $12 million. Resorts at Chimney Rock and Lake Lure brought in tourist dollars that increased the region's prosperity and provided employment for many black citizens (Truesdell, 1954).

The large black population permitted the establishment of two high schools: New Hope and Grahamtown. Grahamtown High School was located in Forest City. In the late 1930s, Jeanetta Scott Kilgore taught there (Kilgore, 1998). Jeanetta Kilgore and her husband, Thomas Kilgore, became active in the civil rights movement on the national level. Grahamtown alumna Leatrice Roberts Pearson evaluated her alma mater:

> This segregated facility ... was far inferior to the brick structure provided for the white students of Rutherford County. To reach Grahamtown High, black students were bused from the Chesnee,

South Carolina, line through Cliffside, Avondale, Henrietta, Caroleen, Ellenboro, and Forest City. The weekly journey began at dawn and ended at dusk. My father, especially in winter, drove me to the bus stop in the mornings and waited for me to get off the bus in the evenings.... Young people, who wanted to learn, excelled in spite of all the obstacles placed in their way [personal communication, November 16, 2009].

New Hope School had an enrollment of 145 with an average daily attendance of 121 and a graduating class of 23 students, according to V.C. Ramseur's 1947-48 report. New Hope used six of its classrooms for the high school. Fifteen of the girls who were enrolled in the two levels of home economics participated in home practice (DPI, DNE, HSPAR, Box 26). Students from Polk County, with the school board's permission, attended New Hope High School. In the minutes for June 4, 1946, the board agreed to comply with Superintendent N.A. Melton's request by allowing a few students who had completed the eighth grade to enroll in high school classes in Rutherfordton (Rutherford County Board of Education minutes, June 4, 1946). Gaining new students could have a positive effect on a school's teacher allotment. Also, having an additional teacher often led to improving the quality of a high school's program of studies.

However, in the 1940s an urgency to erect a new high school developed. In the entry for February 5, 1946, the board instructed the superintendent to compile a detailed list of needs in the Negro schools by the next meeting. The June 3, 1947 entry, which documented a report to the board of commissioners, describes the inadequacy of the county's Negro schools, especially its high schools. Such deficiencies as the lack of an auditorium and low enrollments at New Hope and in Grahamtown suggested that a consolidated school would be more efficient.

A large amount of money went into providing a high school at Spindale. Rutherford County's school board developed a plan to have Carver High School erected by 1948-49 for an estimated cost of $75,000. Although the board's minutes provide no documentation for the delay, a building was not constructed by the deadline. On May 12, 1949, Charles Dalton, Lloyd Williamson and four black men from Spindale called on the board to erect a building as soon as possible. The board agreed, and the plan moved forward with the employment of architect V.W. Breese to submit blueprints, not only for the high school but also for an elementary school in Forest City. The board completed plans to consolidate the county's black schools into two elementary schools and one high school.

At its December 8, 1949, meeting, the board learned the county commissioners had earmarked $7,000 toward the cost of land needed for the black schools. The board began interviewing potential faculty members in January and, at a specially called meeting on April 10, 1951 (Polk County BOE minutes), elected Joseph C. Duncan to be principal of the new school, which apparently opened for the 1951-52 school year. On December 4, 1951, the board granted permission to the black school to hold a May Day celebration in the spring of 1952. In January 1952, S.E. Duncan, the high school supervisor for the Division of Negro Education, visited the new Carver High School and consulted with Principal Joseph C. Duncan (DPI, DNE, GCD, Box 19). Dwight Long, who attended Carver High School from 1963 to 1967, was an enthusiastic student of industrial arts. He especially admired instructor E.D. Roberts. "His class prepared me for the world of work. I learned to read blueprints, to use tools for measuring, and to build things, " Long said (personal communication, June 23, 2010).

On June 3, 1952, the board changed the name of Grahamtown School to Dunbar Elementary School. The minutes indicate that the reason stemmed from the discovery that Graham was a person of bad character. The community honored Paul Lawrence Dunbar, a renowned African American poet, by renaming their school for him. In October, the board approved blueprints for two plaques, one to be mounted at Carver High School and one at

Dunbar Elementary School. In December, the board agreed to purchase land for an athletic field at Carver.

The next mention of black schools occurred on May 14, 1953, when the principals were elected for another year. On January 19, 1954, the board endorsed a cultural opportunity for both white and black students: a concert by the North Carolina Little Symphony Orchestra — one concert for whites; one, for blacks. On June 22, 1954, the board agreed to hire a vocational agricultural teacher for Carver if the state agreed to pay a portion of his salary. That decision was approved at the July 6, 1955, meeting, and J.J. Spearman was elected principal at the New Hope Elementary School. At its June 7, 1955, meeting the board received a delegation from Spindale that included Max Padgett, P.D. Nanney, Charles Deveny, and John Jones asking for a suitable athletic field at Carver. The board agreed to enter into a 50–50 arrangement to upgrade the field but indicated a cap of $600 on their contribution.

Appreciating Community Help

In Polk County, the early history of black education became enmeshed with the history of the Good Shepherd Episcopal Church (http://www.goodshepherdtryon.org/aboutus.html). In the 1890s, Mabel Plaisted founded a school for black children living in Tryon. Milnor Jones erected a log cabin with classrooms for school children and a sanctuary for families to worship. By 1905, the building needed to be replaced, so it was sold. Through a substantial gift by Edmund Embury, the community erected a new school and chapel. In 1908, the Episcopal Missionary District of Asheville, Diocese of Western North Carolina, officially acknowledged the institution as a missionary chapel and named it the Good Shepherd Mission School.

By the 1920s, the school began accepting boarding students. The mission and its grounds housed the principal's home, a student dormitory, classrooms, an industrial room, a science room and a chapel. Focused on the conviction that students needed to learn marketable skills (industrial education), the staff provided classes in bricklaying, agriculture, carpentry, sewing, and cooking. In 1936, because the Tryon and Polk County school systems offered more options in the public schools, the mission school closed its doors. However, in 1940 the church and school reunited due to a misfortune. Arsonists destroyed the public Tryon Colored School in 1939, and the Good Shepherd Church provided accommodations until other facilities became available (Millwood, Joey, "God and Education," accessed at http://tryon1971.blogspot.com/2008_09_01_archive.html). In 1941, a new building for the black children in Tryon was under construction.

According to the August 30, 1941, issue of Hendersonville's *Times-News*, school would commence for Negro children on September 1 and would continue at the Good Shepherd Church until completion of the new building. Upgrading in Tryon occurred frequently throughout its history of black education, but discrimination also continued. The 1949-50 annual report summarized changes. The school was listed in the identification blank not as Tryon Colored School but as Edmund Embury School with an enrollment of 37 and an impressive average daily attendance of 36. Of the school's seven classrooms, two were used for high school classes. The school had purchased a radio and claimed the distinction of publishing a newspaper. Fourteen boys had enrolled in home economics classes. Principal W.H. Green listed eight graduates: F. Pickens Browne, Ulysses Counts, Josephine Browne, Luvenia Glenn, Rachel Hannon, Ruth Hannon, Mentha King, and Rena Twitty (DPI, DNE, HSPAR, Box 25).

In 1924, Wilkes County celebrated the replacement of an older frame school with a brick building. With money from the Rosenwald Fund, community officials hired Creven and Kendall to erect a new building using a recommended Rosenwald plan. According to Ingram

(1954), the new school contained 12 classrooms, a home economics room that permitted a focus on industrial education, a principal's office and a small auditorium. Originally, according to Hanchett (1988), the county training school built in Wilkes County was based on a Rosenwald Type 9 plan, which suggests a nine-room edifice. Possibly additional rooms were added to convert the building into 12 rooms, as the state legislature allotted additional money for the same school in its budget for 1926-27. Ingram documented later improvements, which included the addition of central heating, four more classrooms and a building for physical education and other activities. The latter was a frame building erected by members of the community with assistance from the county. Such local initiatives were characteristic of black communities striving to maintain and to improve educational opportunities for their young people.

Central High School in Newton was an eyesore when newly hired principal Phairlever Pearson first visited it. The building, which housed eleven grades, had broken windows, bare light bulbs suspended from the ceiling, and only one pot-bellied stove. After World War II, the county built a cafeteria, a gymnasium, and a shop, a major update long overdue ("The Civil Rights Movement Comes to North Carolina," retrieved from http://www.mystatehistory.com). In 1953, there were a number of improvements at the Catawba Rosenwald School, which added secondary classes in 1937. Both the cafeteria and vocational departments were renovated, a steam heating plant was built, and the athletic field was improved.

A major piece of upgrading occurred at J.J. Jones High School in Surry County. It was established in 1939 as Mount Airy Colored School as a consolidated black school, but the community renamed the facility to honor former principal J.J. Jones, whose son Leonidas H. Jones also became its principal. The white school board and the black community joined hands to erect a much-needed gymnasium in 1947. According to Thompson (2005), the community raised $2,000 while the board of education gave $4,000. Educator E.T. Sellars supervised the construction. Workers salvaged lumber while Sellars purchased additional lumber from sawmills. A local automobile dealer provided rock and Sellars' students broke up stones and put their knowledge of the "trowel trade" to good use to raise the walls of the gymnasium. Students, under Sellars' direction, also made cement blocks and laid brick, contributing thousands of dollars in the cost of labor.

Upon completion, the value of the new gymnasium was an estimated $30,000, but its value in showing what can be accomplished when citizens are motivated is much greater. As evident in other counties, the Surry County cooperation illustrates how reconciliation endorsed the dream of high school education for black students.

Expanding Curriculum and Opportunities

The program of studies offered in a high school is of particular importance. In the early 1900s, the emphasis on industrial education carried over from the previous century. A prevalent belief among educators was that black students needed to learn how to make a living and that an emphasis on academic subjects was wasted. In his 1932 study "Public Secondary Education for Negroes in North Carolina," Hollis M. Long recommends the most desirable education for black students would result in their acquiring employable skills and that an injustice would be done if their education resulted in their being economically disabled. Long was apparently convinced that the state course of studies was suitable for white students but education required a more practical emphasis to benefit black students.

A drawback, noted by Long, was the lack of instructional supervision in black high schools. He based his conclusion on the need for principals to teach most of the school day and the infrequency of any oversight from the county or city office of education. Such a deficiency, in his opinion, handicapped teachers because they were left alone to cope with overcrowded classes, meager equipment, discipline needs, and lack of adequate texts. Education in such circumstances, according to Long, was stigmatized by a hit-and-miss fashion. He also lamented the unrealistic level of aspiration of most black students, which called for wise counsel. In the course of his research about North Carolina's black secondary schools, Long discovered only one high school in the entire state offering a formal guidance program. In his opinion, that lack represented an injustice to black students. Reports about numerous schools support Long's concerns, but they also show faculty efforts to offer comprehensive secondary education.

In its high school division during the early 1950s, Reynolds School near Canton offered social studies, including North Carolina history, French, English, shop, home economics, chemistry and art, in addition to physical education and health. In typical fashion, the Reynolds faculty taught more than one subject. One year Margaret Kemmer taught four levels of home economics and two of social studies, but another found her teaching geography, health, and citizenship in addition to supervising a study hall. Joyce Mills, who originally taught home economics at Ninth Avenue School in Hendersonville, replaced Kemmer in 1953, but Mills taught only one section of home economics. Mills' other classes included civics, United States history, geography and North Carolina history. Football coach Wilbur Eggleston, a legend in Southwestern North Carolina, taught physics, industrial arts, mathematics, and art.

As implied by the class assignments, teaching in a small school required frequently switching areas of academic discipline. Despite the inconvenience, there was an important reason: a major responsibility of the administration was to ensure that seniors would have an opportunity to earn the necessary units of study required for graduation (DPI, DNE, HSPAR, Box 38).

Also, in the late 1950s, Reynolds students had the opportunity to participate in a wide variety of extracurricular activities (DPI, DNE, HSPAR, Box 6). Davis' 1959-60 annual report mentions clubs organized around subjects such as drama, music, science and home economics. Students could also engage in physical activities ranging from pitching horseshoes to calisthenics to involvement in team sports, such as volleyball, softball, football and basketball (Box 38).

The Caldwell Heritage Museum in Lenoir has a student handbook for Freedman High School on file, undated but probably issued to students in the early 1960s. It contains a numerical listing of events in the school's development that highlights curriculum development and the expansion of extracurricular opportunities.

In 1934, when Julian J. Spearman was principal, seven students made up the school's first graduating class. In 1945, Freedman added the twelfth grade and extended the curriculum to include chemistry and physics, taught by C.F. Erwin. During the 1949-50 school year, J.T. Mitchell organized the school's first band and served as its director. In 1952, the school's home economics department launched a chapter of the New Homemakers of America. In 1953, Mrs. I.C. Jones created a vocational home economics department. M.L. DeVane became Freedman's principal in 1954. That year the school offered classes in typing and founded a chapter of the Crown and Scepter Club, an honor society. In 1955, the school's student council became affiliated with the state association. With the construction of a new building in 1957, the principal added a business education department offering courses in shorthand and typing. What may have been, from a student perspective, the most exciting curriculum change came in 1957-58 with the addition of driver education (Freedman High School Student Handbook).

The *Freedman High Student Handbook* indicates indirectly the faculty emphasized character education by its inclusion of a code of conduct. Students were expected to be considerate and respectful, to refrain from discrediting others by careless statements, and to care for the building, grounds, and equipment. The handbook also includes a wide variety of extracurricular activities: Student Council, Crown and Scepter Club, New Homemakers of America, Future Business Leaders of America, Glee Club, Science Club, Library Club, newspaper staff, dramatics, boys' and girls' athletics and cheering squad. The *Freedman High School Herald*'s stated aim was to promote school spirit and to keep the school and community informed about activities as well as to provide hands-on training in journalism.

In Wilkes County, Lincoln Heights High School functioned as a union school in 1927 with an enrollment of 920 pupils and 27 teachers. Its elementary school population was 775, and its high school provided four years of secondary study for 69 students ("Rosenwald Fund," Special Collections, Box 341, Fisk University, Nashville, TN). Two notes attached to the chart, which lists public high schools for Negroes in North Carolina, state that Lincoln Heights is a "county training school" and that enrollment figures contained in the chart are not accurate but represent the best available information.

North Wilkesboro's Woodlawn Elementary School Principal Milton J. Ingram, Sr., in "A History of Negro Education in Wilkes County, North Carolina" (1954), reports that Lincoln Heights High School offered extracurricular activities that included a school band and a meaningful vocational education curriculum, the latter being especially important for students residing in a predominantly agricultural community. By the late 1940s, according to J.R. Edelin's annual high school report (DPI, DNE, HSPAR, Box 27), the Lincoln Heights students published a newspaper. The school included a daily activity period for club meetings, assemblies, and homeroom activities. The curriculum included advanced courses in agriculture and home economics with high promotion rates in both subjects. Agriculture teacher George C. Corbett taught one class for military veterans in addition to his regular courses. The curriculum included standard course offerings in English, social studies, mathematics, science, and physical education.

Annual reports by principals during the 1940s and into the early 1950s reveal evidence of faculty turnover, a demand for multiple preparations, and the need for school administrators to perform in the classroom—conditions that were prevalent in schools throughout Appalachian North Carolina.

Responding to the strong economic opportunities and a large black population, Catawba County had three high schools: Ridgeview in Hickory, Central High School in Newton, and Catawba Rosenwald in Catawba. The Catawba Rosenwald School, which opened in 1928, expanded into a high school in 1937. In 1940, the school earned accreditation and served all black students from the eastern part of the county. According to an article in the June 20, 1944 *Newton Enterprise,* R.K. Wright, the school's vocational instructor, led a group of his students and a bevy of men from the community to erect a school cannery, which was also available for use by local housewives. Funded by the federal government, the cannery offered a site to preserve fruits and vegetables. Principal Curtis Lewis explained that, even without access to a gymnasium, Catawba Rosenwald offered two hours of instruction in physical education and one hour in health each week. Although there was no home economics department, R.K. Wright taught four levels of agriculture. The school also had a glee club (DPI, DNE, HSPAR, Box 20).

Central High School in Newton offered two levels of band instruction, but the school had no gymnasium. Nor did it have a home economics department, according to the 1947-48 report by Phairlever Pearson (DPI, DNE, HSPAR, Box 20). In 1945, the school's basketball team used an outside dirt court for its practice sessions ("The Civil Rights Movement Comes to North Carolina," retrieved from http://www.mystatehistory.com). Ridgeview's principal,

Taft H. Broom, indicated that his school had a gymnasium with multiple showers available for boys and girls. In addition to other course offerings, the curriculum included home economics and shop (DPI, DNE, HSPAR, Box 20).

Secondary schools in the northern counties of Surry, Watauga, and Yadkin provided similar curriculum offerings, but different extracurricular activities. The J.J. Jones High School in Mount Airy provided courses in home economics, biology, physics, chemistry, English, history, physical education and health. School facilities included no laboratory for science classes. A school library was open under faculty supervision. Students published a school newspaper (DPI, DNE, HSPAR, Box 26). Later on, industrial arts and geometry were welcome additions. The students were able to participate in sports. Yadkin County High School, which had neither a gymnasium nor a lunchroom in 1947-48, according to principal B. T. McCallum, offered instruction in health, but not in physical education. Courses included history, geography, citizenship, health, government, English, science and general business (DPI, DNE, HSPAR, Box 27). Biology and algebra were added for the school year 1948-49.

At the Watauga Consolidated School in Boone, with a small high school student enrollment, Bertha M. Neal lists 1947-48 classes in English, mathematics, science and biology but no home economics or physical education classes. In her report for 1948-49, Neal cites classes in Latin, biology, English, algebra, literature, science and health. Ottie M. Folk, who filed Watauga Consolidated School's annual principal's report for 1949-50, reported that the curriculum offered courses in mathematics, English, science, literature, and citizenship. No extracurricular activities are listed (DPI, DNE, HSPAR, Box 27).

High schools in Polk County also dealt with problems inherent with small pupil enrollments. Principal W.H. Green and E.J. Barber were the only secondary instructors at Tryon Colored School in the late 1940s. One of the school's six rooms was used for high school classes. The total secondary enrollment was 17. Harold Waymon is listed as the school's single graduate in 1948. The school had no gymnasium, no student lockers or baskets, and no audio-visual equipment, but there was a daily activity period and a homeroom period. Green, a veteran teacher with 26 years of experience, taught the school's one class of home economics, and Barber, a first-year teacher, offered other classes in algebra, biology, social science, health, French and English. Barber also supervised the school lunchroom, a duty that entailed overseeing food preparation, service, and cleanup (DPI, DNE, HSPAR, Box 25).

Home economics teachers shouldered tremendous responsibility in rural high schools by being asked to exchange lesson plans with other teachers; to supervise school lunchrooms, a duty that included planning menus and shopping for food; to oversee home practice for students; and to provide lessons in other disciplines. Many were also expected to conduct adult education classes.

In the home economics section of North Carolina's Division of Vocational Education (Box 9), reports from home economics instructors for the late 1930s reveal detailed information. No home economics classes were taught at a number of schools responding to the state's demand for a report. At Elk Park High in Avery County, no home economics was offered. In 1935-36, five boys and six girls were enrolled with one teacher, Ms. W.H. Eberhardt, who had three years' experience and held a high school A certificate. The next year only eight students were enrolled in the high school. Catawba Colored High School, Central High in Newton, Negro Consolidated in Jackson County, Hudgins School in McDowell, New Hope High School in Rutherford, and Rosenwald School in Transylvania County reported the absence of home economics departments at their schools. However, each of those schools filed a report.

Schools such as Stephens-Lee, Sixth Avenue School, Tryon Colored High, Ridgeview in Hickory, Happy Plains High School, and Freedman High indicated an active home economics program. Ethel Mae Barnes, a teacher at Happy Plains High School in Alexander County, listed as projects supervising the skit "Making the Home More Livable," assisting in the production of a junior and a senior class play, and sponsoring an exhibit at the county fair. In addition, she and her students had made curtains, flower pots and had painted the tops of tables. She was relieved of any lunchroom supervision because there was none at Happy Plains.

Other teachers mentioned teaching students to repair sewing machines, to do fundamental stitches and fancy embroidery, to do laundry, to work out a budget, and to learn how to care for children. Kathleen J. McClary taught home economics to eighth and ninth graders at Walnut Cove in Stokes County, but she also taught first and second grades—quite a range. Geraldine I. Jones taught one class of home economics at Mount Airy High School in Surry County to eighth, ninth, and tenth graders, but she also taught sixth and seventh grades (DPI, Division of Vocational Education [DVE], Home Economics Section [HES], Annual Reports, Box 9).

Seven high schools in Western North Carolina filed reports for 1955-56. Hortense Potts of Carver High School in Rutherford County indicated an accumulated mileage of 1,654 miles, 35 home projects, 88 home visits, one adult class, a PTA banquet, supervision of the concession stand at athletic events, provision of meals for school athletic teams, a fashion show, lunchroom work, prom refreshments, and chairing the publicity committee as projects for that year.

Other home economics teachers listed similar undertakings. Adele Marie Miller at Ninth Avenue in Hendersonville had supervised a pre-school clinic, had organized a sewing project to make new draperies for the school auditorium, had been responsible for "football feedings," and had sponsored May Day celebration, among other projects. Miller's mileage was 3,798. Carlotta F. Haywood of Alexander County, Evelyn Williams of Buncombe, Beatrice Moore Smith of Catawba County, and Ardell Meadows, also of Catawba County, had been responsible for activities such as chairing the Christmas Seal drive, sponsoring the NHA chapter, preparing and serving luncheons for community and professional groups, sponsoring mother-daughter dinners, coordinating food units with French classes, and planning proms and homecomings. The largest mileage listed was that of Ardell Meadows at Central High in Catawba. She had traveled 4,155 miles to complete her professional commitments (DPI, DVE, HES, Annual Reports, Box 12).

Responding to School Identities

Secondary schools create identities that can be unifying forces within a community. For example, from first grade onward students obsess about the prowess of athletic teams. Mascot names depict skill, audacity, and temerity. The Reynolds High Tigers and the Stephens-Lee Bears were heroes to the both students and adults, who also identified with those teams. Thundering Mustangs of Sylva's Consolidated Colored High exemplifies a name that indicates tremendous power. Newton Central High School issued a warning with its Hornets, as did Ridgeview High with its Panthers.

While school mascots and athletic competition rally enthusiasm and excitement, schools also found other occasions to celebrate — ways that connected more directly to success in the classroom and in personal progress. Schools celebrated achievements, successes, and landmark events. In the process, the celebrations sent memorable messages about learning experiences and about school environments. As a result, the special events strengthened school connections and lessened tensions for those who faced injustices on a daily basis.

Acquiring the status that accompanied accreditation infused pride into the school's community. In 1957, Mountain View High School in Marion achieved accreditation, a source of esteem for its professional staff and for the community. However, success of earlier graduates of Hudgins High School, the previous name, inspired 1950s and 1960s students. One alumnus who achieved a lofty position as an attorney was Richard Cannon Erwin. As an accomplished member of the bar, Erwin became North Carolina's first black federal judge ("Biographical Directory of Federal Judges," retrieved from http://www.fjc.gov). In 1980, Erwin received his appointment from President Jimmy Carter. He was a member of the Winston-Salem school board, served on the North Carolina State Board of Education from 1971 to 1977, and served two terms in the North Carolina Senate. He advanced in his profession and assumed civic responsibilities. Having a student who received his basic and high school education in a segregated, unequal school offered hope that the black child's potential could indeed be maximized.

Another cause to celebrate came to Olive Hill's school community with the establishment of the Humarian Society by one of its 1965 graduates, Charles Williams. Nettie M. McIntosh, chair of the Burke County Committee for the Preservation of Black History, arranged for Williams to speak at a program in 2010. In 1997, Williams, who has a keen interest in family advocacy, founded the Save the Family Institute, which was designed to strengthen and to rebuild families. Williams founded the Humarian Society on September 4, 2009, in memory of his mother, Sadie Tucker Kincaid. The society's aim is to dismantle race by honoring only family — the family of humanity ("Morganton Library Hosts Black History Event," *The News Herald*, February 26, 2010," retrieved from http://www2.morganton.com/news).

The celebratory nature of graduations, when family and friends convene to offer hearty congratulations to young people excited by the prospects ahead, allows another path to reconciliation. At Reynolds High School in Haywood County, a 1959 graduation program, attached to Ralph H. Davis' annual report, lists eight potential graduates. Seniors participated in a formal vesper service on Sunday, May 24.

The service featured music by the school glee club with "Dear Lord and Father," "Go Down Moses," and "How Great Thou Art," the latter with a solo performance by George Simpson, Jr. The Rev. E.A. Anthony of the Jones Temple A.M.E. Zion Church in Waynesville delivered the sermon. The faculty scheduled an awards and recognition program coupled with an eighth-grade graduation for May 25. At the May 26 commencement exercises, Joyce Mills, class sponsor, presented the senior class. Rowe Henry, superintendent of Canton City Schools, presented diplomas to the graduates (DPI, DNE, HSPAR, Box 38). Graduations reflected not only the achievement of the graduates but of the professional staff and their parents.

A landmark event occurred for black students in Lenoir. An eight-month school term commenced in 1923, and academic accomplishment was recognized with the publication of an honor roll in the February 8, 1923, *Lenoir News*. The newspaper lists honor roll students of Lenoir colored school (located in the West End): Daniel Laughlin, Albert Patterson, Harry Williams, Herbert Steld, Allie Forney, Margaret Johnson, Margaret Settlemyre, Myrtle Johnson, Sarah Patterson, Cora Prophets, and Laura Williams (Hawkins, 2001).

By the mid–1930s Caldwell County and the city of Lenoir supported seventeen schools for black children and provided bus transportation into the city from Dulatown to Freedman High School at a cost of $15 monthly. North Carolina's Department of Public Instruction supplied $10, and the local board paid the remaining $5 (Hawkins, 2001). Stacy Dula recalled that students either walked to school or got up by 6 A.M. to catch a ride on one of the trucks used to transport workers to the furniture factory. Dula pointed out that a hefty walk of two or more miles remained from the factory to the school. In 1946, Lenoir resident Vernon Phillips purchased an Army truck to transport students. A high school student was hired to drive the vehicle for a monthly salary of $50. Dula himself was one of the drivers (Pearson, 1991, and Hawkins, 2001). Attending school required effort, and during the first four decades of the twentieth century officials did not normally cancel school due to bad weather. Children walked through wind, rain, or snow to attend school. Having a truck to carry them was reason to celebrate.

Freedman High alumna Victoria Howell recalls the strong cooperative spirit between school personnel and students with the community when, in 1958, a new school was constructed. Excitement coursed through the community, and civic leaders organized numerous fundraisers to support the school band. The band and glee club's performance in Lenoir's Christmas parade stimulated a sense of pride. Nostalgia marks Howell's memories of athletic events, "superior and caring teachers," school dramas, and the debutant ball sponsored by the Western North Carolina women's civic clubs. In particular, Howell treasures having had black literature included as an integral part of the school's curriculum, especially works associated with the Harlem Renaissance (personal communication, May 28, 2010). A community united to support school achievements of young people strengthens belief in the importance of secondary education.

Connecting with State Officials

Support from the state offices waned from time to time. However, school districts nearer the offices of state officials were able to claim more of their time and effort because state employees found it easier to reach those schools. Nevertheless, correspondence and regular reports prove that schools in the far Appalachian region of the state received time and attention. For example, M. Ruth Lawrence, state supervisor of Elementary Schools, traveled to Asheville in October 1948 to attend a conference with principals and Jeanes' supervisors. Her monthly report for November 1949 documented another trip to Asheville to attend the state PTA conference. Lawrence also interviewed applicants, such as Polk County teacher Mary Birdelle King, for supervisory positions (DPI, DNE, General Correspondence of the Director, July 1947 to June 1949, Box 17).

In N.C. Supervisor of Negro High Schools S.E. Duncan's May 1951 report, he mentions visits to Jackson, Macon, and Swain Counties to explore the prospect of consolidating high schools. He also visited Ninth Street (Avenue) in Hendersonville, Lincoln Heights in Wilkes, Jones High School and Sandy Level in Surry County, and Ridge Elementary and Brown Mountain Elementary in Stokes. Duncan spent several days in Western North Carolina, and in 1952 he personally conducted a workshop in elementary science at J.J. Jones School in Mount Airy and at Walnut Cove in Stokes County (DPI, DNE, GCD, Box 19). At Lincoln Heights School, Duncan made an address on resource use education. The technique involved using community resources to create learning experiences. In June 1956, Anna M. Cooke, supervisor of elementary education, delivered the commencement address at Olive Hill High School in Morganton (DPI, DNE, GCD, Box 23). The record demonstrates that as transportation improved, state officials played an ever-increasing role in the advancement of high schools in Western North Carolina. Their visits helped facilitate reconciliation.

Secondary education made more advanced learning available to students and allowed opportunities to develop social skills and to value citizenship participation. Vocational courses compelled students to learn skills for earning a living in the future. On a day-to-day basis, the community interacted with their neighborhood schools by supporting classroom activities as needed and by providing a host of fans for school competition, especially for sports. Growth also occurred beyond the classroom boundaries. School grounds provided a background for courting potential mates as the maturation of students prodded them to consider the prospect of marriage and family. Indeed, instructors in a few schools first met their future wives or husbands in that environment, which adds a further dimension to their modeling behavior for students. Students, too, discovered high schools stimulate both academic and social interaction as they matured.

Conflict did occur, but eventually debates or incidents were resolved. Perhaps the community drew strength from those experiences. However, with the success in the courts of civil rights legislation, schools that had been won with dedicated effort ceased to exist. As integration became a distinct possibility, black men and women joined the movement to determine that black students would finally have an education equal to that of white students. Their motivation was strong, but the end result of their political accomplishments did not always prove to be satisfactory.

Struggles breed tension, but progress brings reconciliation. For education, reconciliation meant that secondary schools became a certainty, first as segregated institutions and finally as integrated institutions.

11

Expectations of Education

Clear goals, strong motivation, and community cohesiveness propelled blacks to embark on the journey to achieve school integration. Aided by peer and family support, they believed in the possibility of victory on a personal level. Coupled with the desire to do well, alumni of schools educating blacks continue to advance and to enrich the lives of others while preserving the history of past struggles and victories. In modern times, the kinship and identity of African American society centers in family—immediate and extended—and in church congregations. In the past, the school was a key axis of that center. However, today's integrated school no longer functions as a vital extension of the home. It is, however, an important element in the life of the child but somewhat foreign. The journey to learning continues, but travel companions include diverse allies.

In Appalachian North Carolina, the African American endeavor for equality in education required a century to achieve, and the question still remains: Do blacks own educational equity? Black highlanders succeeded in establishing community schools as a result of resolve, patience, persistence, and willpower. Support, interaction, and scholarship also contributed to their continued success but not without setbacks. Nevertheless, thousands of black children have learned in Western North Carolina's segregated and integrated schools.

Prior to 1800, trailblazers arrived without any thoughts about schools for blacks. By the 1860s, freed slaves soon realized that education was essential to enable them to move forward. Though they faced indifference to early requests, by the twentieth century unequal segregated elementary schools abounded during a "golden" era, in which North Carolina boasted of constructing a school a day. By the 1930s and the 1940s came a drive to increase the accessibility of high schools and, by the 1950s, to desegregate schools. The journey to appropriate education covered a span of yearning, building, and protesting, from the 1860s to the 1970s.

Although frequently presented as schools with little merit, the small segregated mountain schools serving black students showcased qualities espoused as worthwhile educational practices in modern times. Small schools allowed ongoing interaction between teachers and students and increased awareness of specific student needs and the possibility of addressing those in a direct, forceful manner.

Modern educators would profit by engaging in dialogue arising from qualitative and quantitative data related to small schools. A number of advantages—individualized instruction, greater participation in extracurricular affairs, more immediate recognition for academic success, a strong sense of belonging, safety, heightened teacher morale—exist in small rural schools, as affirmed by Lorna Jimerson (August, 2006) in what she has aptly termed the "Hobbitt effect." Such qualities also characterized many segregated schools. Despite problems that existed in the past, long before access to e-mail, blogs, and the Internet brought quick solutions, educators managed to train and to inspire their pupils. Even in rural communities where communication could be severely hampered, teachers frequently discovered ways to effectively communicate with parents about their children's problems and accomplishments. No wonder there was a dominant sense of belonging; home-school interaction coupled with the interest invested in each child strengthened the student's sense of worth. Segregated schools were often havens of safety and psychological comfort.

Challenges of the Past

Many black Americans began their educational journey in furtive meetings as eager students learned the basics of reading and writing while concealing any evidence that learning might be an objective. The consequences of violating the law dwindled in importance as the possibility of learning to read and write created hope for a better life to come. Seizing upon any avenue to learn, blacks of all ages participated in clandestine lessons. White children taught slaves. Favored servants learned the basics of reading, writing and arithmetic while the educated, slave or free, sought the means to impart knowledge to others.

During the postbellum period of Reconstruction, instructors presented lessons to large congregations but primarily in regions that had sizeable black populations. However, emissaries from the North discovered mountain communities that failed to provide educational facilities for black citizens and sought to remedy that lack. In doing so they met fierce resistance. Benevolence prodded the establishment of private, religiously oriented schools. White jealousy and resentment boiled over into overtly hostile acts against private schools for black children, especially if the facilities and the programs surpassed those available for whites.

The pattern in North Carolina for educating blacks involved outlawing efforts to teach them, waging a war to free an enslaved people, establishing schools with federal and philanthropic and missionary assistance, segregating schools on the basis of race and race alone, acquiring public funds to erect buildings and hire teachers—often a one-room and one-teacher facility for each school district—and waging a battle of litigation, demonstrations, and demands to achieve integrated schools. J.G. Hollingsworth (1935) in his *History of Surry County*, confirmed that in 1900, there were eight school districts for Surry County's colored students "without even a shelter" (p. 183). Such a negligent state was also a reality for other black communities.

Three decades later, in 1933 the two most urgent needs of black schools in North Carolina were longer school terms and more and better high school facilities. Communities were "begging" for bus service to transport students to the nearest high school. In the late 1920s, Director of Negro Education N.C. Newbold suggested that money from the Rosenwald Fund be used to provide buses for school children whose homes were miles from their schools (Westin, 1966). Such buses were frequently labeled "Rosenwald" buses. In most western counties, only seven years of formal education were available for black pupils (DPI, DNE, GCD, Box 4). School terms were extended. Although not every Appalachian county had a high school, the state and the counties spent money during the 1940s and 1950s to modernize black schools.

Knowledge of increasing court action sponsored by the NAACP may have motivated leaders to build black schools that were "equal" as well as "separate" in light of impending litigation. In the late 1950s and into the 1960s, demands for equity in education, backed by court decisions, opened the doors of white schools for black students. However, after integration closed black schools, black communities gradually realized they had lost an important part of their identity and their heritage.

Success in creating elementary schools led to adding classes to provide secondary education. In a few areas, black high schools made it possible for the aspiring student to enroll nearer home rather than to relocate to attend county training schools, normal schools or private boarding schools to earn the coveted high school diploma and possible entry into a college. With the establishment of additional high schools plus more accessible and better buildings for elementary schools, the black community moved on to claim their civil rights' guarantee: equity in education. Soon the claim erupted into a clamor to desegregate schools.

White fear spawned segregation, but not until the late 1860s did law dictate separation of the races in North Carolina's public schools (Westin, 1966). Reinforcement at the federal level came with *Plessy v. Ferguson* in 1896. In rural mountain settlements with a limited number of black pupils, separate facilities meant housing a school in one room for all grade levels and hiring only one teacher. It was illegal to allow a mountain county's few Negro students to attend white schools, although both races of students would have received a social, financial, and educational benefit from that arrangement. The reality of mountain poverty persisted in white families as well as in black families; even while taking pride in their tolerance, mountain whites acquired an element of self-pride by believing there was a class even lower than their own. Almost without exception, children of North Carolina's highland region were without significant advantages. Anna Julia Cooper (1892/1988), in 1932, stated that her consuming cultural goal was to educate the underprivileged. Although not an Appalachian black, Cooper's goal was noble, but she lacked experience with the most underprivileged Americans seeking an education — those black pupils in Appalachian North Carolina. Cooper would have heartily endorsed the efforts of Appalachian teachers struggling under difficult circumstances to impart knowledge to their young pupils.

Hampered by being the poor minority in the midst of the poor majority, black communities were victims of disfranchisement. When voting did become legal, their small population could not overwhelmingly influence passage of laws to fund their children's education. However, they took pride in ownership of any building if it afforded space for a school.

Black people invested sacrificially to acquire Rosenwald funding for local schools, such as the one at Shiloh and at East Flat Rock. A Jewish American whose social consciousness was awakened from dormancy by reading two books, Julius Rosenwald experienced sympathy for "the colored race" which he attributed to his heritage in having come from a people subjected to persecution. He read *An American Citizen: The Life of William Henry Baldwin* by John Graham Brooks and *Up from Slavery* by Booker T. Washington. Baldwin's attempts to improve the economic life of the Negro and Washington's efforts to advance the cause of his race through education had a life-altering effect on Rosenwald and paved the way to construct and renovate more than 40 schoolhouses in Western North Carolina. His charitable funding improved facilities for numerous black communities and achieved a degree of interracial cooperation. Unfortunately there was no permanent or widespread success in that regard. However, despite meager economic resources, black highlanders donated money and possessions to improve schools. Western counties benefited from leadership at Raleigh's Division of Negro Education. Men such as George E. Davis, who had vacated his "black ivory tower" as professor at Biddle Memorial Institute (Johnson C. Smith University) traveled to poor black communities where his persuasive powers might convince a farmer to donate a chicken or a pig (Joshua Zeitz, "Rosenwald's Gift," *American Legacy*, Spring 2003). Whatever amount a school community raised, Rosenwald supported the project with additional funds. No gift was too small, for the combined gifts of many led to constructing new schools. The result was progress.

Poor transportation was another hurdle to conquer. School Supervisor and Principal Lucy Herring described watching the buses roll into Stephens-Lee's Asheville campus from remote hamlets. Her sympathy for the long bus ride without heat became even more pronounced once she had traveled forty rough miles to reach Burnsville. She compared her first trip there to the weekly trek by children from Yancey County:

Since there was no school near their homes, Yancey County students were allowed to attend Asheville's private Allen School circa 1961. The trip required four hours' travel in unheated buses, and after Yancey County's elementary school building was condemned, students in first through eighth grades accompanied high school students on the long trek to Asheville. Students from Yancy at Allen School, from the left, included John "Tommy" Horton, Kay Francis Griffith, Carolyn Young, John Vance Jackson, Juinata Parker, James Porter "J.P." Young, and Stevie Griffith. Allen School opened in 1887 and closed in 1974 (photograph by Juanita Wilson. Black Highlanders Collection, Hiden Ramsey Library Special Collections, University of North Carolina at Asheville).

> You know the curves you encounter going to Burnsville. I went there the first time, and I almost lost my breath going around some of those curves. Now in an unheated bus and all [those] hazardous curves in icy weather and snow, those little fellows with the older ones were transported here to Asheville High [sic].
> My classroom was on the eastside, and I could see the buses coming in from Burnsville, from Weaverville, and from all around. Now in ... communities like Canton, and out in that area, they didn't transport them; they paid tuition for them [interview by Lewis D. Silveri, Lucy Herring Oral History, August 2, 1977, Special Collections, D. Hiden Ramsey Library, UNCA].

Traveling from remote communities to attend high school classes challenged the persistence of black students. After desegregation, the controversial 1971 *Swann v. Charlotte-Mecklenburg Board of Education* decision, which mandated busing as a means to establish county white-black ratios in school classrooms, created a larger outcry than did earlier use of long bus trips to reach a segregated school destination.

Contributions of Alumni

The past had its challenges, but the present has its rewards as alumni display the same qualities — resolve, patience, persistence, and willpower — that their parents exhibited to make their children's education happen. Former students parade productivity and accomplishments from coast to coast. Representative alumni, simply a small sample, illustrate the work ethic and the milestones of representative individuals continuing on the journey to lifelong learning.

A major success story belongs to Barbara Proctor, who grew up in a "shot-gun shanty" during the 1940s in Black Mountain. She lived with her grandmother and attended Craigmont Elementary School and then Stephens-Lee High school, graduating in 1950. With a grandmother who constantly reminded her that learning counted more than looks, Proctor went on to graduate from college and eventually to own a multimillion-dollar advertising firm in Chicago. President Ronald Reagan cited her as a risk-taker with vision and ability. Proctor attributes her success to her grandmother and to the African American community in Black Mountain, which she describes as "an extended family" (Barbara Blake, January 28, 1984, "Proctor Remembers Her N.C. Beginnings," *Asheville Citizen-Times*).

Buncombe County included the two-teacher Swannanoa School, and one of its alumni, Alma Shippy, showed courage in breaking the color barrier and demonstrated compassion by setting up classes to teach deprived adults. Charity Ray attended one of the region's most humble schools, but she has a responsible administrative position in the Renfro Library at Mars Hill College. The Long Ridge school alumna is also active in supporting community projects. Such alumni offer proof that the small rural school successfully trained its students. However, blacks who were forbidden to learn to read or write demonstrated the value of home-taught principles of character and displayed learned skills in service to their masters. Although the slave George Mills had no formal education, a privilege denied his race, he demonstrated faithfulness, trustworthiness and dependability, as expected by his owner.

Attorney Gwendolyn Simmons Lucas found her education, an experience that combined segregated and integrated classrooms, more than adequate to earn a law degree at Boston University. She learned her lessons in the segregated elementary classes well. However, her initial experience as she moved to the integrated school was stressful but out of that experience came strength to deal with racial confrontations in Boston. Lucas and two other students were the first African Americans to enroll at Flat Rock Junior High School. Each of the black students were in a separate class, which resulted in loneliness. Lucas found it "really hard to fit in." Facing each class with no friendly support or interaction was difficult. However, in the midst of loneliness and isolation, Simmons discovered two white allies. "I found two friends," she said. "We misfits started hanging out together. One white friend had a brace on one foot; another was very short (personal communication, May 19, 2005). Simmons also found two teachers who were supportive and defended her when the occasion demanded it. One was Sadie Shipman and the other Lillian O. Keller. "Mrs. Keller saw me through the whole distance," Simmons said. "We [blacks] were being harassed. She calmed me down, shielded me." The harassment involved name-calling, but not physically hurtful behavior.

Later, Simmons was taunted with the "N" word while attending law school at Boston University. The unpleasant experience occurred due to mandatory busing required by *Swann*. However, Simmons had excelled in school and attending a desegregated facility simply increased her determination to learn her lessons well and to compete on an equal plane with white students.

"A teacher's words changed my life," claimed Dolores Lassiter, an Allen School alumna of the 1950s. A white missionary teacher told her class, "Nobody in the world is any better than you are." The young girl believed her teacher and the assurance of the Allen faculty that she could accomplish her dreams. Lassiter, who wanted to direct funerals in a way that would honor the deceased with dignity, followed a different path and became a mortician. Also, Allen alumna Eunice Kathleen Waymon, who was born and received her early education in

Tryon, North Carolina, in Polk County graduated from Allen High School. Later she assumed the professional name of Nina Simone and found success and celebrity as a jazz recording artist. Simone used music to support civil rights actions, but she endorsed violence as a legitimate way to protest inequities based on race (S.G. Reinhardt, "Allen High Gone but Not Forgotten," *Asheville Citizen-Times*, June 14, 1995).

The largest, and for a time the only, urban area in Appalachian North Carolina was Asheville. Graduates of Stephens-Lee High School have achieved fame and fortune. Robert Robinson was a Tuskegee Airman. Harlow Fullwood founded the Maryland foundation which bears his name through which money is funneled to support educational initiatives, among other things. Success stories about those graduates are legion, but most of them eventually moved and took their talent elsewhere. However, others remained in the Asheville area throughout their adult lives.

Lucille and Linwood Crump were a husband and wife team who personified the work ethic emphasized in elementary and secondary classrooms. The couple operated Crump's Janitorial Service in South Asheville while each worked a second job. In 1996, Crump received the Citizen of the Year Award from Asheville's NAACP for coaching youth leagues and mentoring children (P. Clark, August 17, 1996. "Local NAACP Honors Crump for Shiloh Work," *Asheville Citizen-Times*). Following Linwood's death in 2005, the Asheville City Council renamed the Shiloh Recreation Complex to honor him. Linwood had been active in establishing the complex, so the council approved calling it the Linwood Crump/Shiloh Recreation Complex and emphasized that Linwood worked closely with the children who frequented the park. Linwood Crump also volunteered to work at the concession stand and frequented meetings of the city council to ensure that the Shiloh community received due consideration when decisions were made to allocate resources, so much so that he was affectionately known as "the mayor" (Asheville City Council minutes, October 18, 2005, retrieved from http://www.cityofasheville.org/government/).

Another accomplished alumnus of a segregated school lived in Morganton, North Carolina. In 1962, John E. Fleming graduated from Olive Hill High School (personal communication, September 23, 2010). His memoir, *A Summer Remembered* (2005), alludes to his early education and to attempts by his grandfather to preserve family history. "I remember ... Olive Hill School, a modest, one-story red brick building ... that housed all twelve grades" (p. i). The school was built on land that had belonged to his family. According to Fleming's grandfather, their original ancestor brought from Africa spoke seven languages and read the Koran. The old African arranged to be returned to his homeland. Details about the man whose name was Tamishan were included in numerous lessons about family history in the Fleming household. Other lessons related to the post–Civil War activities of the Freedmen's Bureau and the establishment of Kistler Academy, founded for the black community by sympathetic whites.

Fleming also records the frustration that weighed heavily on his family's grief when a beloved relative was killed while serving in the Korean War. Fleming emphasizes that his young cousin, who had to take a seat at the back of the bus, lost his life by defending the freedoms denied him on American soil. Fleming also relates the tragic slaying of his Uncle Hilliard, who perished while attending Johnson C. Smith College in Charlotte because "there was no high school for colored in Morganton" (p. iii). As he walked on the campus, racists hurled bricks at him, killing him. Similar tragedies afflicted other black families.

As a child, Fleming had only to walk across the road to attend school. As a young adult, he pursued learning at Berea College and served as a Peace Corps volunteer in Malawi, Africa. Briefly, he worked for the United States Commission on Civil Rights, but he went on to earn advanced degrees at Howard University. He is the author of such books as *The Lengthening Shadow of Slavery* and *The Case for Affirmative Action for Blacks in Higher Education*. Perhaps his family's tradition of attempting to preserve family history influenced his choice of a career: He was the founding director of the National Afro-American Museum and Cultural Center in Wilberforce, Ohio, and chief operating officer for the National Underground Railroad Freedom Center in Cincinnati. He is the director of the International African American Museum in Charleston, South Carolina. The recipient of numerous distinguished service awards, Fleming has never returned to Morganton to live, but he refers to contact with Morganton family and friends as his life's anchor.

Surry County resident and retired educator Evelyn Scales Thompson has led a movement to document the black history of that region and has collected historical data from surrounding counties. A graduate of Mount Airy Colored High School, Thompson and others in 2000 created the African American Historical and Genealogical Society of Surry County. Her effort to create a permanent record of the black community's history resulted in preparing a book for Arcadia Press's Black America Series. A Pilot Mountain native featured in Thompson's book (2005) is the Rev. Sophia Joyce East, who successfully led two congregations. The North Carolina Conference of the Central Jurisdiction of the Methodist Church ordained the Rev. East as a deacon in 1964. In addition to rearing four children, East followed a career in church ministry. Emily Herring Wilson (1983) spotlighted Sophia East in her study *Hope and Dignity: Older Black Women of the South*.

As a child, the Rev. East did not understand why the one-room school she attended was so poorly equipped. Another hardship was the absence of a high school. "We didn't have a high school in Surry County until my oldest daughter was in the seventh grade, about 1938" (p. 181). To supplement her husband's earnings, East's mother took in washing and ironing, but with their resources her parents made sure each of their children received an elementary school education. Although East's mother was illiterate, she taught her children the difference between right and wrong, a lesson emphasized in black homes of the past. East cared for the child of her deceased sister as well as for her own children. One measure of her success is that each one completed high school, with three of them earning a college degree. East believes that race relations have improved in Surry County as a direct result of school integration, which allowed white people to learn that their black neighbors are human.

Another noteworthy representative of those students educated in black schools who moved forward was a native of Henderson County. Dr. John J. Simmons, who as a young man taught at the East Flat Rock School he had attended, later served in the military and then became a dentist. In the mid–1960s he insisted on sitting downstairs—not an area where blacks were permitted to be—in the Carolina Theater, located on Hendersonville's Main Street. He made the decision, but his niece and his nephew experienced the tense moments. Simmons believed in moving forward to claim one's rights (J. Giles, "Simmons, a Civil Rights Leader, Dies," *The Times-News*, May 14, 2004). His nephew Henry Simmons successfully manages a restaurant in Hendersonville, and his niece Gwen S. Lucas is an attorney.

Billy Martin, whose school career spanned segregation and integration, retired as a guidance counselor at McDowell High School and serves on the Marion City Council. Reba Jackson, an alumna of Hudgins High School, and her husband own a family business that combines construction and realty in Marion. Each has contributed to improving their community.

Another Hendersonville native served as vice mayor. Sam Mills, a 1925 alumnus of the high school program at Sixth Avenue School who studied at Harbison Agricultural Institute in Irmo, South Carolina, worked as shoe repairman in English Brothers Shoe Shop for 40 years and then moved on to the General Electric Company. His success in politics led to long service as a member of the Hendersonville City Council and as a member of Land of the Sky Regional Council. Mills was an active community leader and provided leadership for Henderson County's first Boy Scout troop. He also played in 1930-31 in the local city baseball league of Hendersonville. Mills received the James H. McDuffie Award for leadership and community service in 1988 (R. Smith, October 11, 1993, "Sam Mills Dead at 84," *Hendersonville Times-News*, p. 1A, and Greene, 1996).

Grahamtown High School graduate Leatrice Roberts Pearson, a retired educator engaged in writing articles for newspapers and religious publications, carries on an avid involvement in reading, a tradition practiced in her childhood home. Sitting in a room with book-lined shelves and tables piled high with reading material, she said,

> My interest in books and education began with my parents' love of reading. Although my father only completed the third grade ... he possessed the equivalent of a college degree. Our debates of the Bible and Shakespeare's plays were famous in our household. My mother was no slouch when it came to reading either. The characters from the books rivaled any actors in the soap operas on TV today. Listening to my parents discuss books ... made a lasting impression on me [personal communication, November 16, 2009].

Pearson instilled the pursuit of education in her own children, each of whom completed college. She actively defied Jim Crow practices by choosing a seat "not at the back" when she traveled. Also, she waited outside bus stations rather than using waiting rooms reserved for blacks. She refused to purchase food that would be pushed under bars to waiting black customers. "I was never that hungry," she said.

A graduate of Hudgins High School in McDowell County accepted an invitation to speak at the Mountain View High School commencement exercises as proclaimed by *The McDowell News* headline: "Former Student Addressing School's Graduating Class," (undated newspaper clipping, ca. 1963, African American Scrapbook in Vertical File, McDowell County Library, Marion, NC). The Rev. R. Logan Carson of Marion and Louisville, Kentucky, was the graduation speaker at Mountain View School, the school that replaced his alma mater, Hudgins School. Carson attended the state school for the blind, where he learned to use Braille. The sight-deprived young man graduated *magna cum laude* from Shaw University in 1957 and with honors from Hartford Seminary in Connecticut in 1960. Also, he earned a master of theology degree from Louisville Presbyterian Seminary. Carson triumphed over the limitations of his handicap and made remarkable scholastic achievements. Born fatherless, sightless and black in a world of racial discrimination, Carson's chances of achieving success were slim, but the Hudgins graduate has earned advanced degrees and served as a Christian minister.

A woman who has devoted her life to serving others, Charity C. Gambill-Gwyn, has been a lifelong resident of Alleghany County. She is employed as a funeral assistant at Grandview Memorial Funeral Home in Sparta, North Carolina. For sixteen years she served on the Alleghany County School Board and numerous additional boards. In 1994, Gambill-Gwyn received the Nancy Susan Reynolds Award for outstanding Volunteer Community Service. According to Debbie Brewer of the Northwestern Regional Library, Gambill-Gwyn has worked tirelessly to improve conditions in Alleghany County (personal communication, September 9, 2010).

William Hemphill, resident of Hudlin Gap community in Transylvania County, preserves the values inherited from his father: caring for family and working hard. Hemphill's father worked multiple jobs while being involved in his children's lives. He worked at the Ecusta Corporation, cut firewood and did plastering. Being employed at Ecusta in 1965, William Hemphill recalls little discrimination, but he was forced to use the "blacks only" bathroom. Pay was equal, and he was eventually assigned to become the first black to work on the gate, a well-paying job, but Hemphill continued to pour concrete in his off-hours. His son, William, Jr., a North Carolina Highway patrolman, said, "My parents taught me to be a good person, to go to church, to be respectful and to work hard. We don't play the race card.... If something bad happens, so many people are likely to say that happened to me because of my race or gender. We try to be honest and know that whatever things happen to us that are negative, [things will work out for us in the end]" (C.K. Knight, "Family's History Resonates with Hard Work," *The Transylvania Times,* February 1, 2007, 121/9, p. 1).

Morris Young and James Madison also indicated the strong positive role of their fathers. Madison said no other role model was needed, that his father, a man of limited education but extensive learning, supplied interest in and direction for his children's lives (personal communication, November 14, 2002). Young said,

> My father was a man who kept his word.... Every year he would have a cow and hog killed. At times, he cured his own hams. In the fall he would buy one bushel each of red and golden delicious apples— he was a great provider for his family and for others. Anyone with a need could have beef and pork.... My father has been my greatest inspiration ... I'm the man that I am because of my father. One thing I remember, even though he was not a church going man, he said, "Son, stay in the church, for there is nothing out here in this world" [personal communication, October 31, 2006].

In today's studies of African American families, much is written about an absent father and the negative effects of single parent homes. Such conditions characterized many homes during segregation. Fathers deserted their families. More often than was desirable, both parents relocated to survive economically and their children were raised by grandparents or other relatives. However, many African American homes in the past were strengthened by the maturity and wisdom of both parents, who urged their offspring to live their lives adhering to high standards and paying attention in school, which would give them the means to advance to success and prosperity.

In 2000, the North Carolina Sports Hall of Fame inducted Henry Logan as a member of its 37th class (personal communication, November 1, 2010). In 1970 Logan faced the despair of having his celebrated career cut short. Difficult times followed as he adjusted to putting his talent on the shelf. Eventually he found satisfaction in coaching young people in McDowell County as director of the Youth Recreational Center. Now living in Asheville, he continues to be involved with youth and has coached a group of 7th and 8th graders in a private school to earn championships (personal communication, November 1, 2010). Today he is admired as a man of faith who overcame a great loss and found peace in other avenues of service.

Exploitation of Racist Language

Les M. Brown, potter, writer, and former professor at Gardner-Webb University, related observations about black mountaineer life in his "The Crime of Malachia Hayden: Justice and Racial Identity in a Blue Ridge Community" (retrieved from http://www.stillhousebranch.com/malachia.htm). Brown observed that reduced contacts resulting from outmigration in North Cove, a community about twenty miles from Marion, and the closure of the black school and church in the 1930s eliminated vital support for black residents. With the "moonshining" industry thriving among enterprising white residents, the few remaining black residents had lost their net of support and fell prey to alcoholism.

Brown also cited that the white man's use of racist language deflated blacks' self-esteem and encouraged a sense of inferiority. His view is that white mountaineers were so conditioned to racial insults that they were essentially unaware of the harm wrought by their language. Brown analyzed Hayden's 1941 crime of shooting a white man, his punishment, and the implications of the crime. He acknowledged that even though racial bias was lacquered with a veneer of acceptance, the taint remained. Brown recognized that African Americans continue to deal with ingrained attitudes that result in indirect humiliation beyond the scope of public laws.

Earlier than the violent Malachia crime researched by Brown, language was a subtle weapon used to disparage the Negro. The editor of the Brevard's *Sylvan Valley News*, March 5, 1909, used patronizing language when he wrote about Jim Aiken's trip east to buy supplies for his local enterprises. The editor mentioned, in a joking manner, that the black man was Transylvania County's sole, but unofficial, representative at William Howard Taft's 1909 presidential inauguration. The editor commented in a derogatory way about how much Aiken would be paying for his overnight bed, saying that rumor indicated that Aiken slept on a cot near the inaugural site for $4 a night. Aiken was active in obtaining and in overseeing a school for black students in Brevard. An astute businessman, he frequently turned a profit. However, his death resulted from serving as a volunteer fireman. The entrepreneur was described as "a colored porter ... who knew his place" (Reed, 2004, p. 141).

Numerous examples of words resonating from hate or indifference abound. Lucy Herring, the Asheville educator, shared part of a conversation regarding the difference between race and human relations with a white minister. He described a sign he had had occasion to view frequently as he traveled to remote outposts in Western North Carolina; the words were "Nigger, don't let dark catch you here" (Lucy Herring Oral History, Special Collections, D. Hiden Ramsay Library, UNCA). William A. Reed, a long-time local resident, also confirmed having seen a similar posting. He added that once when a young man's job of unloading soft drinks took him into a Rosman restaurant in broad daylight, the owner walked outside following him with a gun in hand and refused to let him re-enter the cafe (personal communication, September 14, 2010). Unfortunately, vestiges of discrimination remain.

Emergence of Leadership

Now, more than 30 years since total school desegregation has been the backdrop for blacks moving forward in Western North Carolina, the perspective has clarified. African Americans have served as school superintendents and principals of integrated schools. They have joined the ranks of college professors. La'Ronda Long Whiteside is principal of a Rutherford County Middle School. Shelia McBee Norman is a member of the Transylvania Board of Education. Rev. Bill Whiteside serves on the Yancey County Board of Education. Thanks to the efforts of those dauntless civil rights pioneers of the past, African Americans have applied their talents into every avenue of service.

Asheville has accomplished a major coup with the election of its first black mayor, Terry Bellamy. Also the youngest person ever elected to the office, Bellamy is the product of an integrated education. While working for non-profit organizations, Bellamy became aware of needs that stimulated her desire to make a systemic difference, a desire that led her to consider politics. "For me," she said, "it was a calling. God gives the desire. I felt I was called" (personal communication, July 7, 2009).

Others influenced her ambition to succeed. John Hayes, an elder with the NAACP, educated Bellamy about past struggles that enabled her to become successful and to be aware of the significance of her actions as an African American. Her church, Tried Stone Missionary Baptist, also provides activities to increase knowledge about black heritage. During her school days, Bellamy found Eula Shaw at Asheville High School to be a most impressive teacher. "She tried to educate, not to befriend all who walked through her doors," Bellamy said. "She gave 100 percent of herself and demanded 100 percent of you."

Today Bellamy's duties lead her to pass through halls her grandmother once cleaned. She derives joy from realizing how far she has come. Unfortunately, Bellamy has experienced discrimination in her political role. "I have been belittled, and there have been negative votes to impact my efforts," she said. Realizing that civil rights remains under fire, Bellamy believes it is more important than ever for African Americans to make inroads in difficult arenas, such as politics and higher education (personal communication).

Educators such as J.H. Michael, Ethel Kennedy Mills, C.U. James and John Potts were models paving the road to integrated schools. J.T. Sapp, who had no children of his own, took an interest in the lives of his students at Swannanoa and later at Black Mountain. He challenged them to learn and supported their efforts. There were exceptions, teachers so challenged by personal dilemmas that they simply showed up, went through the motions, and drew a paycheck, but professionals striving to educate youth outnumbered the exceptions. All along the journey in towns and in rural regions, educators inspired and challenged. Also, in the majority of western counties, there were white crusaders willing to speak out for fairness in education.

Asheville's Congregational minister Frank E. Ratzell used his sermons, such as "Who Is My Brother?" and "The Fellowship of Love" to address the need to unite the races, to promote the brotherhood of all mankind, and, moved by the love of God, to reach out to help any human being regardless of his or her color. A native of Philadelphia and former newspaper writer, Ratzell moved to Asheville in 1951 and immediately spearheaded the desegregation movement. As a member of the Human Relations Council, he assisted in integrating schools, restaurants and motels (Frank E. Ratzell Papers, Special Collections, D. Hiden Ramsey Library, UNCA). In Henderson County, Mary V. Mims praised Sally Godehn, a white resident, for supporting black issues. Lucy Herring, in her oral history, praised the work in race reconciliation of Asheville Jewish physician Dr. Leon H. Fleming, who fostered human relations between the races "more than anyone else." Another white citizen who kept his promise to treat black students and their parents fairly in the courts was Judge Wilson Warlick.

When the time came for integration, parents and community leaders prepared their students for entry into the white students' world. In Asheville, leaders of the YWCA adhered to the imperative of its national charter that states: "Imperative: To thrust our collective power towards the elimination of racism, wherever it exists, by any means necessary." Endorsing the power of group action, the YWCA created a center to allow civilized group protest. Director Thelma Caldwell initiated integrated programs for black and white elementary pupils at the YWCA to promote ease in the integration of local schools. Later Caldwell started a teen program for black and white girls to encourage conversation between the races by simply having them share with one another what they enjoyed doing, as for example, visiting with friends, reading, going to movies or participating in sports (D. Maddelena, November 10, 2000). Thelma Caldwell will long be remembered for her insightful projects, which brought blacks and whites to engage in meaningful dialogue, as well as for her oversight of the merger of the black and the white YWCAs in Asheville.

Danger of Resegregation

A study of the past can be enhanced by a comparison with the present. Even in the enlightened twenty-first century hate crimes based on race do occur, and events can be interpreted as threats due to the taut wire of respect so easily broken. One widely publicized episode was the Louisiana school conflict called the Jena 6 which escalated into arrests, charges and protests resulting from school yard conflicts accented by a noose hanging from a tree. The event shows how quickly a confrontation can escalate into violent confrontation and gain national attention in an unfavorable manner. One of today's educational concerns is the existence of segregated classrooms in desegregated schools.

Does the claim that segregated education ended with the turmoil surrounding desegregating public schools in the 1960s hold true? Current academic studies reveal that black students receive a minimal education in contemporary schools (Boger, 2005). Constitutional guarantees ensure every child the right to a sound basic education, which the general public often views as learning to read, to write, and to do arithmetic. These basic competencies are a must, but other proficiencies are needed in order to function well in earning a living and in pursuing worthwhile activities, both civic and personal.

In 2008, North Carolina's Human Relations Convention addressed that growing problem. Armed with statistics from the Casey Foundation, human rights activists approached state officials to urge them to investigate the charges that discrimination in classroom placement is prevalent in North Carolina's Schools. So will it be necessary to return once again to the drawing board? Because the Appalachian section of the state continues to have a small black population, a tendency to segregate students is not as obvious as it is in eastern counties. However, it is an issue that will continue to concern those who guard the guarantees of *Brown v. Board of Education* (1954) and *Leandro v. State of North Carolina* (1997).

A basic argument of the latter case was that low-wealth rural counties received less than average tax funds but had higher than average tax rates. Such counties lacked appeal for new teachers and were handicapped in availability of supplies and materials and sued for equal funding. The court, convinced that the constitution did not assure the right to equal funding, did find, nevertheless, that each child has the right to a sound basic education and delineated the requirements. Certain characteristics of the charges of unfair practice, such as lack of materials coupled with the unequal funding, sounds like the problems confronting black segregated schools in North Carolina's mountain region in the two previous centuries.

An unfortunate aspect of the movement to resegregate is that the black race that was oppressed in recent history is again in the afflicted group. Students who are poor and black continue to need the hope cultivated by developing their minds and talents in supportive schools, an assurance that lessons well-learned bring empowerment. Positive experiences in school provide children a foundation for success in adulthood. Research indicates that those who have negative experiences struggle to succeed in the workplace and often fail. On a typical school day in North Carolina, as documented in "North Carolina: Short-Term Suspensions; Long-Term Consequences; Real Life Solutions" suspensions affect over 1600 students (*Action for Children,* February 2007, retrieved from http://www.ncchild.org/). The state's percentage of suspensions exceeds the national average by 45 percent. School suspension policies appear to target African Americans and Native Americans statewide. The peak of suspensions occurs during the ninth grade, but in 2005 there were in excess of 3300 pre-kindergarten and kindergarten students suspended. The school districts which are most likely to suspend students are North Carolina's eastern counties, where poverty rates are high, but western counties are not exempt from ethnically targeted discipline policies affecting minority populations. Suspension is upheld in the courts if students violate a school's code of conduct, but concerns of fairness and justice demand that educators reconsider local policies and practices.

The population in classes offering "softer" courses may be predominantly black and Latino. Susan Batten, former senior associate of the Annie B. Casey Foundation in Baltimore, Maryland, provided data at the 2008 North Carolina Human Relations Convention in High Point, NC. Batten believes that "policies and practices contain barriers to opportunity. The goal to improving educational prospects can be achieved through racial equity" (presentation, North Carolina Human Relations Conference, August 13, 2008).

Educational data suggests discrimination is practiced in selection related to academic tracking and magnet schools. However, "a more compelling explanation for the rise in school desegregation is the gradual waning of judicial oversight.... While many unforeseen circumstances will undoubtedly influence the future path of segregation in North Carolina's classrooms, the persistence of these trends in the first decade of the twenty-first century portends further lost ground in years to come" (Clotfelter, Ladd, Vigdor, 2005, p. 84). Because North Carolina's *Leandro* decision has established the constitutional duty of state government to provide every child the opportunity to receive a "sound basic education," the state's obligation to safeguard that opportunity is clearly mandated (*Leandro v. State of North Carolina*, 346 NC 336 [179PA96] 07/24/1997, retrieved from http://www.aoc.state.nc.us/).

Judicial oversight should be constant and allow no loopholes to block avenues for each child to achieve his or her full potential. Segregated schools should no longer exist. However, statistics provided by Clotfelter, Ladd, and Vigdor (2005) indicate modest but rising levels of segregation within the state's public schools. Possibly the journey to integrated classrooms is an ongoing process throughout the United States as well as in Western North Carolina.

In North Carolina the federally mandated requirement that schools assign highly qualified teachers to students of color and to students in the poverty level on an equal basis with their white and more affluent counterparts is not a reality. The typical black seventh grader is 54 percent more likely to have a novice teacher in mathematics than does his white counterpart and is 38 percent more likely to have a novice teacher in English than a white student (*Action for Children,* February 2007). Too often an instructor with limited professional experience begins his or her career by working with students who require greater expertise from their teachers in order to learn well. In North Carolina those students are usually poor and are frequently members of the black race. Success in the classroom challenges such students to a great extent because of deprived, underprivileged conditions in their home environments, and schools often do not address the needs of that group. Are civil rights in jeopardy when this happens?

Modern educators need to analyze local policies and procedures in a painstaking manner and determine whether change can eliminate unfairness. Education is one way to battle poverty. Any human being deserves the right to an opportunity to develop their mental ability — to maximize their learning. Education demands attention to individuals.

The high percentage of young black male incarceration, such as that explored by Michelle Alexander in *The New Jim Crow: Mass Incarceration in the Age of Colorblindess* (2010), suggests the failure of schools and families to adequately address that group's needs. It is a haunting fact that in poor urban neighborhoods three out of four young black youths are expected to do jail time.

For counties drenched in poverty, the ruling that the state owes each student a sound basic education was a victory. Making it a reality is the challenge, much as making equality in education a reality for black families in Western North Carolina was during the era of segregation. Voices squelched in the past have found a venue in moving cultural needs from the back burner to the front. The sense of pride and personal worth fostered in segregated schools is cultivated by the achievements of black Americans such as Barack Obama in the twenty-first century, but a closer look at schools in Western North Carolina reveals that the dull pain of poverty persists in many African American homes and affects classroom achievement in a negative fashion.

Educational pioneers of the past won major victories and deserve applause because their tireless efforts have brought new possibilities to all students in Appalachian North Carolina. However, the expectation that education brings empowerment continues. The educational urgency is to advance, not retreat, and the movement to improve modern schools demands courage and the power of a unified community.

APPENDIX.
HIGH SPOTS IN NEGRO HISTORY

In many segregated schools teachers instructed their pupils in black history, but rural schools were often short on material. The following was compiled from newspaper clippings by Marie McIver, Jeanes supervisor and later supervisor of elementary education in the Division of Negro Education. McIver shared such material with teachers who could then present lessons about black history to their students.

Early Africans Had High Place in Civilization
(Based on Newspaper Clippings)
Courtesy of North Carolina Archives and History, Raleigh

Trial by Jury, Iron Smelting, Stringed Musical Instruments First Developed by Africans Who Also Domesticated First Sheep, Cows and Goats

The Negro History Week Pamphlet for the 1935 celebration in February contains a summary of the African background of the colored race, according to Dr. Carter Woodson, director of the History Association.

According to Dr. Woodson, the early history of Africa is very much like that of any other continent. Just as we have learned that the Japanese, Chinese, Hindu, Assyrian, and Babylonian empires developed in Asia, and just as we have likewise surveyed the rise of Carthage, Greece, and Rome, so we find their parallels in Kumbi, Manding, Songhay, and Mossi.

African Kingdoms

Their history shows a social and political order which maintained the peace, provided for the public welfare, and promoted human progress. The people were healthy, industrious, happy, and long-lived. Their kingdoms and empires endured as long as the most successful of ancient and modern times.

In the larger organizations of kingdoms and empires in Africa we see a system of government strikingly resembling that of earlier organizations in Asia and Europe. The kings ruled with the assistance of the elders and the feudal assemblies of the people through their representatives.

Cabinets and Ministers

These rulers had a cabinet consisting of a group of ministers with carefully defined duties, and they maintained a court of the sub-vassals who ruled the smaller states of kingdoms constituting the African empires. The organization of their armies and the means of supplying the treasury by taxation did not differ widely from such methods which we observe throughout Europe and parts of Asia.

The people of Africa, like those of other parts of the world, have achieved certain things which are all but earmarked as African. It is considered exceptional to point to just one outstanding achievement for which a nation may be given solo credit. We are wont to think of the Chinese as giving the world the mariner's compass, printing, and gunpowder; of the Hindus as developing a peculiar philosophy; of the Mesopotamians as exhibiting the best architecture and government; of the Jews as teaching the unity of God and producing the Bible; and of the Phoenicians as inventing the alphabet and spreading civilization.

What Africans Developed

In the same way we may list similar achievements to the credit of the Africans. Africa first developed trial by jury as a means of assuring justice to every man in keeping with the idea of loving justice and hating iniquity. Negroes in Africa first discovered iron and with it developed the industrial arts. Africans first learned to use stringed instruments to find a new means of expression for their deep emotion. Africans first domesticated the sheep, goat and cow. Before Africans ever knew of the system of writing and printing in Europe the Vai tribe and the natives of the Cameroon produced written languages; and in our day the people of Dahomey have worked out an interesting system of writing of their own.

Bravely Defended Homes

In the passing of Africa into foreign hands, moreover, the natives were not indifferent observers. On the contrary, they bravely defended their soil. At first, the Africans followed the policy of the Romans in gradually incorporating into their kingdoms and empires the Berbers, Pouhls, Arabs, and Jews just as the Romans absorbed the Vandals, Huns, Goths, Franks, Jutes, Anglos and Saxons.

Fall of Africa

However, when this policy proved inadequate to deal with those hordes increased by large numbers of Moors and fanatical Mohammedans equipped with modern weapons, the lines of the African empires yielded and suffered destruction just as Rome did.

In the course of time came as a reorganization of certain areas on a different basis under the control of the natives weakened by the mongrel classes which had resulted; but this political organization did not have the time to develop the power of former days before the Europeans appeared upon the West Coast with their exhausting slave trade and their agencies established to penetrate the interior and dispossess the Africans.

Law Abiding

This African background offers an explanation for many things observed today among the colored people of America. The African, subjected to the strict control of chiefs, king and emperors, had the tradition of being law-abiding. To this ideal the colored man has exceptions of those charged with infractions of the law resulting from impoverishment and social repression, the colored people constitute the most law-abiding element of our population. Because of the African's keen sense of justice he could not develop otherwise abroad.

The colored man does not throw bombs; he does not start riots; he does not engage in lynching; he does not burn men at the stake. The American colored man has never assassinated a public functionary or tried to overthrow this government. Haiti, which is often cited as evidence in France, to which the former owes its beginning.

Did You Know

That the first Americans in the World War to be decorated with the French "Croix de Guerre" were two Negro soldiers, Needham Roberts and Henry Johnson?

That the largest church in the United States is Mount Olive Baptist Church in Chicago with over 10,000 members; that it has thirty-two full-time and twenty-two part-time workers?

That the only person yet living who went to the North Pole with Peary is a Negro, Matthew Henson?

That the first machine for making shoes was invented and patented by a Negro, Jan Matzoliger, of Lynn, Mass.?

That the Negro spirituals are the only original music America has contributed to the world and that they are sung by the leading musicians all over the world?

That the first person to die for American Independence in the Revolutionary War was a Negro, Crispus Attucks and that on the Boston Commons there is a monument erected to his memory?

That the first clock made in America and the first in all the world to strike the hour, was invented by a Maryland Negro, Benjamin Banneker; that he published the first almanac in his country and was the very first Negro to hold office (public) in this country?

That the first and official map to be used by the United States government of the Island of Haiti was made by the late Col. [Charles] Young, Negro author, musician, explorer, and soldier?

That William L. Dawson, thirty-five year old Negro instructor in music at Tuskegee Institute, fulfilled four years of hard work and years of constant dreaming when the Philadelphia Orchestra, conducted by Leopold Stokowski, played his first major work, "Negro Folk Symphony"?

Roland Hayes

Roland Hayes was born in Curryville, Georgia, in very humble surroundings. When he was very young, his family moved to Chattanooga, Tennessee.

Roland Hayes found work in factory where window weights were made. This was very hard work for a boy his age, but he was determined to go to school.

He finally saved enough money to go to school and worked his way to Nashville, Tennessee. He entered Fisk University and worked his way through four years. After leaving Fisk, Hayes and his mother lived in Boston. He gave recitals to earn money and studied at the New England Conservatory of Music at the same time.

It was not long before he had the opportunity to study in Europe. He is able to sing songs of foreign countries in the languages of those countries. He has been hailed, at home and abroad, as one of the greatest lyric tenors and as one of the greatest singers ever known.

Roland Hayes has made a great contribution to the world by interpreting the inner feeling of his people through song. He earns thousands of dollars during a year. People of all races and creeds are anxious to hear Roland Hayes.

When Hayes made his first appearance in Boston Symphony Hall, the whole world was astonished for he was the first Negro to appear in this famous hall. This appearance was a great success. Hayes began to give concerts to large, appreciative audiences in many parts of this country.

Harry T. Burleigh

Harry T. Burleigh was born in 1866. His father died when he was very young and the mother was faced with the responsibility of caring for the five children. As soon as they were old enough, they had to help their mother earn a living. Harry used to sell papers, and do other jobs that he could find.

While he was going to public school, it was found that he had an unusual voice. He developed a love for music and would stand out in the worst weather to listen to good music. He always worked after school in order to earn enough money to live.

Burleigh won a scholarship to the New York Conservatory of Music. His mother helped him all she could but there was still the struggle for food and clothing.

Since 1894, he has been baritone soloist in St. George's Episcopal Church, one of the largest churches in New York City. Burleigh has composed music for a large number of songs. His compositions are used by people of many races in all sections of this country and abroad.

Negro Composes First Symphony on Purely Native Rhythms

(Newspaper Clipping)

William Levi Dawson, of Tuskegee, Hands Over 537 Sheets of Music to Leopold Stokowski, Who Will Soon Put It Into Rehearsal

New York, Dec. 27 — William Levi Dawson, Negro director of the Tuskegee Choir, handed 537 sheets of music to Leopold Stolowski today, the product of four years' labor.

It was the first symphony ever composed by a Negro writing the music of his race. Stokowski and his Philadelphia Orchestra will put it in rehearsal soon.

Symphony No. 1, as Dawson calls it, will take 45 minutes to play and contains four movements—an allegro, an andante, a scherzo and finale. Through it all will appear and reappear, sometimes from wind instruments, sometimes from the strings, sometimes from one instrument and sometimes from the entire orchestra, one central theme. The theme is melancholy, a sort of wail and hymn, related to jazz in its rhythm.

"But it is not religious," Dawson said. "It is an attempt to develop Negro music, something they said again and again couldn't be developed. It is classical in the modern idiom."

Dawson wrote the music in Alabama, his native state. He was born in Anniston 31 years ago, studied in Kansas City and Topeka and played first trombone with the Chicago Civic Orchestra for four years.

He was graduated with honors from the Horner Institute of Fine Arts in Kansas City. At the graduation exercises the Kansas City Symphony Orchestra played one of his compositions.

George Washington Carver

George Washington Carver was born on a farm in Missouri. His father died when he was quite young and in some way he was separated from his mother during the Civil War. He was reared by his former master.

When he was ten years old, he went to school for a year. After this he went to Kansas where he worked in the day and studied at night for nine years. In this way he was able to complete his high school work.

He did his college work in Iowa State College, managing a laundry at the same time to earn a living. After graduation, he was made a member of the faculty.

Soon after this, Dr. Carver was called to Tuskegee where he has brought out, through experimentation, hundreds of products from the sweet potato, peanut and pecan. Thomas Edison offered him a position in his laboratory, but he preferred remaining at Tuskegee. Today he is known and honored in this and other countries.

Booker T. Washington

Booker T. Washington was born in 1859 on a plantation in Franklin, Virginia. After the Civil War, he went to Malden, West Virginia, and worked in a coal mine. He obtained his elementary education in a night school.

In some way, Booker T. Washington heard about Hampton Institute in Virginia, 500 miles away. He did not have money enough to pay his carfare, but he made his way there by begging rides and by walking. He completed his work at Hampton in three years, earning his board by working as a janitor.

He taught two years at Malden, West Virginia, his former home, then he studied eight months at Wayland Seminary in Washington, D.C. He was instructor at Hampton Institute two years.

In July 1881, in a little shanty and church, he started Tuskegee Institute, an institution that is internationally known. Booker Washington has gone down in history as one of the greatest men America has produced. He gave his life for his people.

Robert Russa Moton

Robert Russa Moton was born in Amelia County, Virginia, of slave parents. Before he was sixteen years of age he had made up his mind that he would secure an education even though there were difficulties that seemed insurmountable. He worked two years in a Surrey County lumber camp, then took the entrance examination at Hampton Institute and failed. He did not give up but worked at the saw mill in the day and went to school at night. After a year, he was admitted to the day school and completed the prescribed course in four years.

After graduation, he was made assistant commandant in charge of the male students, later he was made commandant. He served at Hampton Institute for twenty-five years. When Booker T. Washington died, Dr. Moton was chosen to succeed him as President of Tuskegee Institute. He served in this capacity twenty years, retiring recently on account of his health.

He is an outstanding educational leader and an apostle of racial good will and understanding.

BIBLIOGRAPHY

Books

Alexander, M. (2010). *The New Jim Crow: Mass Incarceration in the Age of Colorblindness.* New York: The New Press.
Allen, Sara C., ed. (1986). *The Heritage of Alexander County, North Carolina.* Winston-Salem, NC: Hunter.
Anderson, J.D. (1988). *The Education of Blacks in the South, 1860–1935.* Chapel Hill: University of North Carolina Press.
Aptheker, H., ed. (1968). *A Documentary History of the Negro People in the United States: 1960–1968.* New York: Carol.
Ascoli, P.M. (2006). *Julius Rosenwald: The Man Who Built Sears Roebuck and Advanced the Cause of Black Education in the American South.* Bloomington: Indiana University Press.
Bagwell, William. (1972). *School Desegregation in the Carolinas: Two Case Studies.* Columbia: University of South Carolina Press.
Bailey, J., and B. Lake. (2001). *The Greatest Sports Heroes of the Stephens-Lee Bears.* Alexander, NC: Land of the Sky Books.
Bailey, L.H. (2005). *Remembering Henderson County: A Legacy of Lore.* Charleston, SC: The History Press.
Bailey, L.R., ed. (1994). *The Heritage of the Toe River Valley* (Vol. 1). Marceline, MO: Walsworth.
Bennett, W., ed. (1983). *Polk County, North Carolina, History.* Spartanburg, SC: Reprint Company.
Berry, M.F. (2005). *My Face Is Black Is True: Callie House and the Struggle for Ex-slave Reparations.* New York: Alfred A. Knopf.
Blackmun, Ora (1977). *Western North Carolina, Its Mountains and Its People.* Boone, NC: Appalachian Consortium Press.
Blethen, H.T., and C.W. Wood, Jr. (1983). *From Ulster to Carolina: The Migration of the Scotch Irish to Southwestern North Carolina.* Cullowhee, NC: Western Carolina University Mountain Heritage Center.
Bogdan, S.C., and S.K. Biklen (1992). *Qualitative Research for Education: An Introduction to Theory and Methods.* Needham Heights, MA: Allyn and Bacon.
Boger, J.C. (2005). "Brown and the American South." In John Charles Boger and Gary Orfield (Eds.), *School Resegregation: Must the South Turn Back?* (pp. 304–323). Chapel Hill: University of North Carolina Press.
Brooks, J.G. (1910). *An American Citizen: Life of William Henry Baldwin, Jr.* Boston: Houghton Mifflin.
Brooks, R.L. (1996). *Integration or Separation: A Strategy in Racial Equality.* Cambridge, MA: Harvard University Press.
Brown, V.H. (1964). *E-qual-ity Education in North Carolina Among Negroes.* Raleigh, NC: Irving-Swain Press.
Bullock, H.A. (1967). *A History of Negro Education in the South from 1619 to the Present.* Cambridge, MA: Harvard University Press.
Burke County Historical Society. (1981). *The Heritage of Burke County.* Waynesville, NC: Walsworth.
Bynum, W.B., ed. (1985). *The History of Rutherford County, North Carolina.* Winston Salem, NC: Hunter.
Cabbell, E.J. (1985). "Black Invisibility and Racism in Appalachia: An Informal Survey." In W.H. Turner and E.J. Cabbell (Eds.), *Blacks in Appalachia* (pp. 3–10). Lexington: University Press of Kentucky.
Cash, W.J. (1991). *The Mind of the South.* New York: Vintage Books.
Casstevens, F.H., ed. (1981). *The Heritage of Yadkin County.* Winston-Salem, NC: Hunter.

Clinard, J.W. (1962). *Clinard Looks Back: A Collection of Stories Covering Early Days in Hickory.* Hickory, NC: Hickory Printing Company.

Clotfelter, C.T., H.F. Ladd, and J.L. Vigdor (2005). "Classroom-level Segregation and Re-segregation in North Carolina." In J.C. Boger and G. Orfield, eds., *School Resegregation: Must the South Turn Back?* (pp. 70–86). Chapel Hill: University of North Carolina Press.

Community School Plans (1924). Bulletin No. 3. Nashville, TN: The Julius Rosenwald Fund.

Connor, A.P. (2008). *Tryon: An Illustrated History.* Spartanburg, SC: The Reprint Company.

Connor, R.D.W., and C.H. Poe, eds. (1912). *The Life and Speeches of Charles Brantley Aycock.* Garden City, NY: Doubleday, Page.

Cooke, D.H. (1930). *The White Superintendent and the Negro Schools in North Carolina.* Nashville, TN: George Peabody College for Teachers.

Cooper, A.J. (1988). *A Voice from the South.* New York: Oxford University Press. (Original work published 1892).

Cooper, H. (1964). *History of Avery County, North Carolina.* Asheville, NC: Biltmore Press.

Corbitt, T., ed. (1976). *History of Development of Public Education in Watauga County, North Carolina.* Boone, NC: Bicentennial Committee.

Curtis, N.C. (1996). *Black Heritage Sites: An African American Odyssey and Finder's Guide.* Chicago: American Library Association.

Davis, L.G. (1989). *The Black Heritage in Western North Carolina.* Edited by M. Ready. Asheville: University Graphics, University of North Carolina at Asheville.

Dresslar, F.B. (1914). *Rural Schools and Grounds.* Bulletin No. 12. Washington, D.C.: United States Bureau of Education.

_____. (1915). *The Negro Rural School and Its Relation to the Community.* Bulletin 585. Washington, D.C.: United States Bureau of Education.

Du Bois, W.E.B. (1915). *The Negro.* Philadelphia: University of Pennsylvania Press.

_____. (1973). *The Education of Black People: Ten Critiques, 1906–1960.* Herbert Aptheker (Ed.). New York: Monthly Review Press.

Eller, R.D. (2008). *Uneven Ground: Appalachia Since 1945.* Lexington: University of Kentucky Press.

Embree, E.R., and J. Waxman. (1949). *Investment in People: The Story of the Julius Rosenwald Fund.* New York: Harper.

Fairclough, A. (2007). *A Class of Their Own: Black Teachers in the Segregated South.* Cambridge, MA: Belknap Press of Harvard University Press.

FitzSimons, F.L. (1976). *From the Banks of the Oklawaha* (Vol. 1). Hendersonville, NC: Golden Glow.

_____. (1998). *From the Banks of the Oklawaha* (Vol. 3). Hendersonville, NC: Golden Glow.

Fleming, J.E. *A Summer Remembered: A Memoir.* Yellow Springs, OH: Silver Maple, 2005.

Freeze, G. (1995). *The Catawbans: Crafters of a North Carolina County* (Vol. 1). Newton, NC: Catawba County Historical Association.

_____. (2002). *The Catawbans: Pioneers in Progress* (Vol. 2). Newton, NC: Catawba County Historical Association.

Gaffney, S., ed. (1984). The Heritage of Watauga County (Vol. 1). Winston-Salem, NC: Hunter.

Genovese, E.D. (1974). *Roll, Jordan, Roll: The World the Slaves Made.* New York: Pantheon Books.

Gold, B.A. (2007). *Still Separate and Unequal: Segregation and the Future of Urban School Reform.* New York: Columbia University Teachers College Press.

Goldfield, D.R. (1990). *Black, White and Southern: Race Relations and Southern Culture 1940 to the Present.* Baton Rouge: Louisiana State University Press.

Greene, G.F. (1996). *A Brief History of the Black Presence in Henderson County.* Asheville, NC: Biltmore Press.

Guillebeaux, J. (1985). "Not Just Whites in Appalachia." In W.H. Turner and E.J. Cabbell, *Blacks in Appalachia* (pp. 207–210). Lexington: University Press of Kentucky.

Hall, W.L., Jr., ed. (1998). *The Heritage of Macon County* (Vol. 2). Franklin, NC: Macon County Historical Society.

Harlan, L. (1998). *Separate and Unequal; Public School Campaigns and Racism in the Southern Seaboard States, 1901–1915.* Chapel Hill: University of North Carolina Press.

Hartsoe, D.S. (2001). *The Hill: Memories of Ridgeview Community.* High Point, NC: Marshall Group.

Haskins, J. (1998). *Separate but Not Equal: The Dream and the Struggle.* New York: Scholastic Press.

Hawkins, J.O. (2001). *The Most American Thing: A History of Education in Caldwell County, North Carolina.* Lenoir, NC: Education Foundation of Caldwell County.

Haywood County School History Book Committee. (1991). *Haywood County Schoolin': A Rich Heritage.* Haywood County, NC: Haywood County Schools.

Herring, L.S. (1983). *Strangers No More: Memoirs*. New York: Carlton Press.
Hoffschwelle, M.S. (2003). *Preserving Rosenwald Schools*. Washington, D.C.: National Trust for Historic Preservation.
Hollingsworth, J.G. (1935). *History of Surry County or Annals of Northwest North Carolina*. Greensboro, NC: W.H. Fisher.
Hoops, J. (1979). *Oral History: An Introduction for Students*. Chapel Hill: University of North Carolina Press.
Horton, J.H., T. Perdue, and J.M. Gifford. (1979). *Our Mountain Heritage: Essays on the Natural and Cultural History of Western North Carolina*. Cullowhee: North Carolina Humanities Committee and Mountain Heritage Center of Western Carolina University.
Hughes, S.A. (2006). *Black Hands in the Biscuits Not in the Classrooms*. New York: Peter Lang.
Hurmence, Belinda, ed. (1984). *My Folks Don't Want Me to Talk About Slavery*. Winston-Salem, NC: John Blair.
Inscoe, J.E. (1989). *Mountain Masters, Slavery, and the Sectional Crisis in Western North Carolina*. Knoxville: University of Tennessee Press.
_____, ed. (2001). *Appalachians and Race: The Mountain South from Slavery to Segregation*. Lexington: University Press of Kentucky.
Jackson, H.B., ed. (1983). *The Heritage of Surry County*. Winston-Salem, NC: Hunter.
Jaspin, E. (2007). *Buried in the Bitter Waters: The Hidden History of Racial Cleansing in America*. New York: Basic Books.
Jenkins, P. (1979). *A Walk Across America*. New York: Harper Collins.
Johnston, J. (1992). *McDowell County Heritage*. Marceline, MO: Walsworth.
Jones, G.A., ed. (1988). *The Heritage of Henderson County, Sequicentennial 1838–1985*. Winston-Salem, NC: Hunter.
Kilgore, T., Jr., and J.K. Ross. (1998). *A Servant's Journey: The Life and Work of Thomas Kilgore*. Valley Forge, PA: Judson Press.
Leloudis, J.L. (1996). *Schooling in the New South: Pedagogy, Self, and Society in North Carolina, 1880–1920*. Chapel Hill: University of North Carolina Press.
Litwack, L.F. (1979). *Been in the Storm So Long: The Aftermath of Slavery*. New York: Alfred A. Knopf.
_____. (1998). *Trouble in Mind: Black Southerners in the Age of Jim Crow*. New York: Alfred A. Knopf.
Lloyd, R.M., ed. (1994). *The Heritage of the Toe River Valley: Avery, Mitchell, and Yancey Counties, North Carolina* (Vol. 1). Marceline, MO: Walsworth.
Long, H.M. (1932). *Public Secondary Education for Negroes in North Carolina*. New York: Teachers College Press, Columbia University.
Lord, W.G. (1981). *Blue Ridge Parkway Guide: Rockfish Gap to Grandfather Mountain* (Vol. 2). Birmingham, AL: Menasha Ridge Press.
Madison County Heritage Committee. (1994). *Madison County Heritage Book* (Vol. 1). Waynesville, NC: Walsworth.
Marsh, Blanche, and Kenneth F. Marsh. (1961). *Historic Flat Rock: Where the Old South Lingers*. Asheville, NC: Biltmore Press.
Marshall, C., and G. Rossman. (1995). *Designing Qualitative Research* (2nd Ed.). Thousand Oaks, CA: Sage.
McDonald, V.C. (2006). *Pictorial History of the African Americans of Jackson County*. Sylva, NC: Catch the Spirit of Appalachia.
McFeely, W.S. (1991). *Frederick Douglass*. New York: W.W. Norton.
McRae, B., ed. (1987). *The Heritage of Macon County* (Vol. 1). Winston-Salem, NC: Hunter.
_____. (1998). *The Heritage of Macon County* (Vol. 2). Winston-Salem, NC: Hunter.
Medford, W.C. (1968). *The Middle History of Haywood County*. Asheville, NC: Miller Printing.
Miller, Leonard P. (1965). *Education in Buncombe County 1793–1965*. Asheville, NC: Miller Printing.
Montell, B.A., and W.L. Montell. (1982). *From Memory to History: Using Oral Sources in Local Historical Research*. Nashville, TN: American Association for State and Local History,.
Montell, W.L. (1970). *The Saga of Coe Ridge: A Study in Oral History*. Knoxville: University of Tennessee Press.
"Movement on Foot for New School House for Colored." (July 1915). From *Gleanings from the French Broad Hustler, 1914–1915*. (Vol. IV), p. 175. Available at Henderson County Historical and Genealogical Society, Hendersonville, NC.
Myrdal, G. (1944). *An American Dilemma: The Negro Problem and Modern Democracy*. New York: Harper and Row.
Newkirk, V.R. (2009). *Lynching in North Carolina: A History, 1865–1941*. Jefferson, NC: McFarland.

Ostwalt, C., and P. Pollitt. (2001). "The Salem School and Orphanage: White Missionaries, Black School." In J.C. Inscoe, ed., *Appalachians and Race: The Mountain South from Slavery to Segregation*. Lexington: University Press of Kentucky.
Patton, S.S. (1947). *The Story of Henderson County*. Asheville, NC: Miller Printing.
_____. (1957). *The Kingdom of the Happy Land*. Asheville, NC: Stephens Press.
_____. (1976). *Sketches of Polk County History*. Spartanburg, SC: Reprint Company.
Perdue, T. (1985). "Red and Black in the Southern Appalachians." In W.H. Turner and E.J. Cabbell (Eds.), *Blacks in Appalachia* (pp. 23–30). Lexington: University Press of Kentucky.
Quarles, B. (1987). *The Negro in the Making of America*. New York: Simon and Schuster.
Ready, M. (1986). *Asheville: Land of the Sky*. Northridge, CA: Windsor Publications.
Reed, B.J. (2004). *The Brevard Rosenwald School: Black Education and Community Building in a Southern Appalachian Town, 1920–1966*. Jefferson, NC: McFarland.
Richards, C.E., and K.L. Richards. (2008). *Insider Guide to North Carolina's Mountains*. Guildford, CT: Morris.
Roberson, Z.H. (1969). *Public School Education in Buncombe County, 1935–1969*. Asheville, NC: Miller.
Satterwhite, B. (1995). *A Pictorial History of Cherokee County*. Murphy, NC: Cherokee County Historical Museum.
Schwarzkopf, S.K. (1985). *A History of Mt. Mitchell and the Black Mountains: Exploration, Development, and Preservation*. Raleigh, NC: Division of Archives and History.
Shepherd, R.W., ed. (1984). *The Heritage of Ashe County, North Carolina* (Vol. 1). Winston-Salem, NC: Hunter.
Sosland, J. (1995). *A School in Every County*. Washington, D.C.: Economics and Science Planning.
Sossaman, O.L. (1988). *The Heritage of Swain County, North Carolina*. Winston-Salem, NC: Hunter.
Swain, D. (1981). *Cabins and Castles: The History and Architecture of Buncombe County, North Carolina*. Fairview, NC: Bright Mountain Books.
Tatum, B.D. (1997). *"Why Are all the Black Kids Sitting Together in the Cafeteria?" and Other Conversations About Race*. New York: Basic Books.
Thomasson, L.F. (1965). *Swain County ... Early History and Educational Development*. Asheville, NC: Miller Printing.
Thompson, E.S. (2005). *Around Surry County*. Charleston, S.C: Arcadia Press.
Trotter, J.F. (1988). *Bushwackers! The Civil War in North Carolina* (Vol. II: The Mountains). Winston-Salem, NC: John F. Blair.
Turner, W.H., and E.J. Cabbell. (1985). *Blacks in Appalachia*. Lexington: University Press of Kentucky.
Van Noppen, I.W., and J.J. Van Noppen. (1973). *Western North Carolina Since the Civil War*. Boone, NC: Appalachian Consortium Press.
Vaughn, Martha Rowe. (2005). "History" in *Around Surry County*, by Evelyn Thompson. Mount Pleasant, SC: Arcadia.
Walker, V. (1996). *Their Highest Potential: An African American School Community in the Segregated South*. Chapel Hill: University of North Carolina Press.
Ward, D.C., ed. (1981). *The Heritage of Old Buncombe County*. 2 vols. Winston-Salem, NC: Hunter.
Werner, M.R. (1939). *Julius Rosenwald: The Life of a Practical Humanitarian*. New York: Harper.
Wigginton, E. (1979). *Foxfire 5*. New York: Anchor Books.
_____, and M. Bennett. (1939). *Foxfire 8*. New York: Anchor Books.
Williams, J.A. (2002). *Appalachia: A History*. Chapel Hill: University of North Carolina Press.
Williams, M. (2001). *The History of Jackson County*. Sylva, NC: Jackson County Historical Association.
Wilson, E.H. (1983). *Hope and Dignity: Older Black Women of the South*. Philadelphia: Temple University Press.
Woodson, C.G. (1933). *The Mis-education of the Negro*. Washington, D.C.: Associated Publishers.
_____. (1968). *The Education of the Negro Prior to 1861*. New York: Arno Press.

Journal and Magazine Articles

Du Bois, W.E.B. (September 1902). "Of the Training of Black Men." *Atlantic Monthly*, 90, 289–297. Also cited by L. Hammond.
"East Meets West — Jimmy Ning & Alma Shippy." (Summer 2007). *Owl and Spade*, 27.
Hanchett, T.W. (October 1988). "The Rosenwald Schools and Black Education in North Carolina." *The North Carolina Historical Review*, 65, 387–444.
Horton, J.O. (January 2005). "'What Business Has the World with the Color of My Wife?' A Letter from Frederick." *OAH Magazine of History*, 19, 52–53.

Klotter, J.C. (March 1980). "The Black South and White Appalachia." *Journal of American History*, 66, 936–49. In Turner and Cabbell, eds. (1985). *Blacks in Appalachia*, 51–67. Lexington: University Press of Kentucky, 1985.

Krause, B.J. (1998). "We Did Move Mountains! Lucy Saunders Herring, North Carolina Jeanes Supervisor and African American Educator, 1916–1968." *The North Carolina Historical Review*, 75, 188–212.

Murray, H.M. (Spring 2002). "Adequate in Our Courtesy, Civility, Race Relations, and the Path Toward Desegregation in Jackson County, North Carolina." *Tuskegee Valley Historical Review*, 6–26.

Newbold, N.C. (November 1928). "Common Schools for Negroes in the South." *Annals of the American Academy of Political and Social Science*, 140.

Pearson, L.R. (February 2009). "Obama's Victory." *Agape-Herald* of St. Paul A.M.E. Church, Lenoir, NC.

Pollitt, Phoebe. (Summer 1993). "Learning Freely: Black Education in North Carolina After the Civil War." *Now and Then*, 10, 31–32.

Poteat, M. (May 1945). "The History of Education in McDowell County." *North Carolina Education*. Available in the archives at the Marion, NC, Board of Education.

Shumate, S. (September 1962). "The Most Unforgettable Character I've Met." *Reader's Digest*, 81.

Zeitz, J. (Spring 2003). "Rosenwald's Gift," *American Legacy*, 23–29.

Internet Sources

Action for Children. (2007). Retrieved from http://www.ncchild.org/event/simple-things-movie-benefit-screening-february-2007.

Asheville City Council Minutes. (October 18, 2005). Retrieved from http://www.cityofasheville.org/government/mayor_city_council/city_co uncil/10-18-05.htm.

"Asheville High School Riot." (n.d.). Retrieved from http://www.facebook.com/topic.php?uid=52261189486&topic=846.5

Barnwell, T. (Fall 2004). "Public School Integration in Georgia and Gwinnett County." Retrieved from http://www.mgagnon.myweb.uga.edu/students/3090/04TA3090- barnwell.htm.

"Biographical Directory of Federal Judges." (n.d.). Retrieved from http://www.fjc.gov.

Brown, L.M. (n.d.). "The Crime of Malachia Hayden: Justice and Racial Identity in a Blue Ridge Community." Retrieved from http://www.stillhousebranch.com/malachia.htm.

Bryan, James Bryan (March 31, 1964). "Parents Rally Behind NAACP." Retrieved from http://news.google.com/newspapers?id=WZYlAAAAIBAJ&sjid=vvQF AAAAIBAJ&pg=3703,1214365&dq=edmund+embury&hl=en — see.

"Carolina's First Black Ph.D. Graduate." (n.d.). Retrieved from http://www.gradschool.unc.edu/fountain/spr_01/darity.html.

"The Challenge of Civil Rights." (n.d.). Retrieved from http://www.sc.edu/library/scpc/exhibits/mcnair/civrights.html

Cheek, E.B. (1983). "Oral History of Long Ridge Students." *The Hilltop Online of Mars Hill College*. Retrieved from http://hilltop.mhc.edu/10507071/Longridgeschool/oral history.asp.

"The Civil Rights Movement Comes to North Carolina." (n.d.). Retrieved from http://www.mystatehistory.com.

Cobb, K. (June 2, 2002). "After Desegregation; Public Schools Seek New Remedies Where Race Based Orders Failed." *The Houston Chronicle*, p. A1. Retrieved from Lexis Nexis Database.

The Community Improver (July 1966). "Toward a Better Christian Education and Building of Character," Retrieved from http://toto.lib.unca.edu/findingaids/mss/housing_authority_city_ashevi lle/boxes_001_admin.com.

"Dead Bear Found Wrapped in Obama Signs: Carcass Found on Western Carolina University Campus." (October 20, 2008). Retrieved from http://www.wyff4.com/news/17764161/detail.html

Dillingham, R. (n.d.). "The Founding of Mars Hill College." Retrieved from http://www.tnphoenix.com/Rev.%20Thomas%20W.%20Ray%20and%20Mars%20Hill%20College.html

Dunne, A. (2010). "Pearsall Plan," North Carolina History Project, Raleigh: John Locke Foundation, 2010. Retrieved from http://www.northcarolinahistory.org/commentary/318/entry

"Edward Stephens." (n.d.). Retrieved from http://toto.lib.unca.edu/findingaids/mss/blackhigh/blackhigh/Biographies/stephens_e.html.

Elk Park School. (2005). "National Registry of Historic Places." Retrieved from http://www.hpo.ncdcr.gov/nr/AV0083.pdf.

"Emily Prudden 1832–1917, in Blowing Rock." (n.d.). Retrieved from http://www.stoppingpoints.com/north-carolina/sights.cgi?marker.

"Eng and Chang Bunker: The Siamese Twins." (n.d.). Retrieved from http://www.lib.unc.edu/dc/bunkers/.
Fisk University Rosenwald Fund Card File Database. Retrieved at http://rosenwald.fisk.edu/.
Good Shepherd About Us. (n.d.).Retrieved from http://www.goodshepherdtryon.org/aboutus.html.
Hennessy, John. (June 21, 2006). "Text of Hennessy's Speech." Retrieved from http://news.stanford.edu/news/2006/june21/jlhtext-062106.html.
Isaac Dickson letter of recommendation. Special Collections (September 186_). D. Hiden Ramsey Library. University of North Carolina at Asheville. Retrieved from http://www.ymicc.org/unmarked_trail/board09.html.
"Jim Crow Laws: North Carolina." (n.d.). Retrieved from http://www.jimcrowhistory.org.
Jimerson, L. (August 2006). "The Hobbitt Effect: Why Small Works in Public Schools." Arlington, VA: The Rural School and Community Trust. Retrieved from http://www.ruraled.org/user_uploads/docs/hobbitt_effect.pdf.
Journal of the Constitutional Convention of the State of North Carolina, at Its Session 1868: Electronic Edition. (n.d.). Retrieved from http://docsouth.unc.edu/nc/conv1868.html#p338.
Lankford, J. (February 18, 2004). "Exhibit to Showcase Black History." Retrieved from http://www.therecordofwilkes.com/newsa.asp?edition_number=223& pg=F.
Lewis, D. (June 17, 2010). Asheville High Riot/Facebook. Retrieved from http://ms-my.facebook.com/topic.php.
"Massive Resistance." (June 2004). *The Civil Rights Movement in Virginia.* Retrieved from http://www.vahistorical.org/civilrights/massiveresistance.htm.
Millwood, J. (2008). "God and Education." Retrieved from http://tryon1971.blogspot.com/2008_09_01_archive.html.
"Morganton Library Hosts Black History Event." (February 26, 2010). *The News Herald.* Retrieved from http://www2.morganton.com/news.
"One-Room School." (n.d.). Retrieved from *Reading 2*, http://www.nps.gov/history/nr/twhp/wwwlps/lessons/58iron/58facts2.htm.
"Pearsall Plan," (n.d.). *North Carolina History Project.* Retrieved from http://www.northcarolinahistory.org.
Poinsett, A. (October 1959). "N.C. Students Who Refuse to Go 80 Miles to School Seek to Integrate White Schools in Yancey County." *Jet*, 16 (24), 22–25. Retrieved from http://books.google.com.
"Progressive School Architecture." (n.d.). Retrieved from *Reading* 2, http://www.nps.gov/history/nr/twhp/wwwlps/lessons/58iron/58facts2.htm.
Rusher, J.R. (2003). *Until He Is Dead: Capital Punishment in the Western North Carolina History.* Retrieved from http://books.google.com/books.
Silver, J. (February 2007). "Silver Threads." Retrieved from http://homepages.rootsweb.com/~sil/south/.
"South French Broad Commencement." (July 1966). *The Community Improver*, Vol. 5. Retrieved from http://toto.lib.unca.edu/.
"Staff." (n.d.). Grandview Memorial Funeral Home Web site. Retrieved from http://www.grandviewfuneralhome.com/staff.php.
Staff Reports to United States Commission on Civil Rights. (1962). Retrieved from www.law.umaryland.edu/marshall.
The North Carolina Language and Life Project. (n.d.). Retrieved from http://www.ncsu.edu/linguistics/ncllp/.
Thomson, S.L. (March 1984). "An Invincible Schoolmarm." *Our State.* Retrieved from http://www.ncdnpe.org/documents/hhh142.pdf.
"Title VI of the Civil Rights Act of 1964." (1964). Retrieved from http://www.justice.gov.
Titus, J. "History of Allen School." (1962). Retrieved from http://toto.lib.unca.edu/findingaids/mss/blackhigh/blackhigh/allen_high _school.htm.
"Toward a Better Christian Education and Building of Character." (July 1966). Retrieved from http://toto.lib.unca.edu/findingaids/mss/housing_authority_city_ashevi lle/boxes_001_admin.com).
U.S. Census Bureau. (2000). 2000 Census. Retrieved from http://factfinder.census.gov.
"Viola Barnette Spoke Out for Education" (n.d.). Retrieved from http://hilltop.mhc.edu/012306/violabarnette.asp.
Waters, Lisa. (October 26, 2005). "Peaceful Warriors." Retrieved from http://www.mountainx.com.

Theses, Dissertations and Unpublished Manuscripts

Brown, G.C. (1940). "A History of Public Education in the City of Asheville, North Carolina." Master's thesis. University of Maryland, College Park.

Burrell, D.L. (1992). "All Quiet at the Western Front: A History of Black/White Relations at Western North Carolina University." Master's thesis. Western Carolina University.

Chujo, K. (1988). "The Black Struggle for Education in North Carolina, 1877–1900." Doctoral dissertation. Duke University.

Earp, C.B. (1979). "North Carolina Governors and Public Education, 1933–1961." Doctoral dissertation. Duke University.

Emmerich, P.O. (1998). "The Four R's: Reading, 'Riting, 'Rithmetic, and Race Relations." Doctoral dissertation. Kansas State University.

Fryar, J. (November 21, 2003). "Asheville City School Board: Efforts to Successfully Desegregate the School System." Senior thesis. University of North Carolina at Asheville. Retrieved from toto.lib.unca.edu/sr_papers/history_sr/default_UNCA_history.htm.

Hammond, L. (Fall 1999). "A Tale of Two Schools: Stephens-Lee High School and Allen High School." Unpublished doctoral project. Western Carolina University.

"History of Livingston Street School, 1920–1957" (n.d). Unpublished. On file at Asheville City Schools offices.

Holcombe, R.E. "A Desegregation Study of Public Schools in North Carolina." Doctoral dissertation. East Tennessee State University, 1985.

Horton, R.F. (1942). "Negro Life in Watauga County." Bachelor's thesis. Agricultural and Technical College of North Carolina.

Howell, V.M. "A Short History of Freedman High School." Caldwell County (NC) Heritage Museum in African American Vertical File Collection.

Ingram, M.J. (1954). "A History of Negro Education in Wilkes County, North Carolina." Master's thesis. North Carolina Agricultural and Technical College.

Leek, M. (July 2003). "History of Clay County Schools from 1850 until Present." Unpublished doctoral project in rural education. Western Carolina University. Retrieved from http://www.clayschools.org/about_us/.

Miller, J.C. (1953). "A Socio-Economic Survey of the Negro Population of Ashe County, North Carolina, with Suggestions for Utilization of This Material by the Negro School." Master's thesis. North Carolina Agricultural and Technical College.

Moses, M.I. (1989). "Universal Education for African Americans in North Carolina: A Historical Survey of the Beginning Years Through 1927." Doctoral dissertation. North Carolina State University.

Plemmons, W.H. (n.d.). "A History of the Public School System of Asheville, North Carolina." On file in the archives at Asheville City Schools offices.

Poteat, M. (May 1945). "The History of Education in McDowell County." Available in archives at McDowell County Board of Education office, Marion, NC.

Roethler, M.D. (1964). "Negro Slavery Among the Cherokee Indians, 1540–1866." Doctoral dissertation. Fordham University.

Truesdell, F.L. (1954). "The Development of Negro Education in Rutherford County, North Carolina." Master's thesis. North Carolina Agricultural and Technical College.

Westin, R.B. (1966). "The State and Segregated Schools: Negro Public Education in North Carolina, 1863–1923." Ph.D. dissertation. Duke University.

Woodside, R.E. (1952). "The Educational Development of Avery County." Thesis. Appalachian State Teachers College.

Newspaper Articles

"Affray Case Is Continued." (September 6, 1955). *Charlotte Observer*, p. 8B. Filed in African American Scrapbook, Vertical File, McDowell Public Library, Marion, NC.

Andonaras, T. (August 15, 1995). "The Castle on the Hill." *Asheville Citizen-Times*. In files at Asheville City Schools offices, Asheville, NC.

Blake, B. (January 28, 1984). "Proctor Remembers Her N.C. Beginnings." *Asheville Citizen*, p. 1. In files at Asheville City Schools offices, Asheville, NC.

"Boycott Effective at Hill Street." (August 26, 1966). *Asheville Citizen*.

Boyd, L. (August 9, 2004). "Civil Rights Pioneer, UWCA Leader Caldwell Dies at 91." *Asheville Citizen-Times*, p. 1. In files at Asheville City Schools offices, Asheville, NC.

Bryan, J. (March 31, 1964). "Parents Rally Behind NAACP in Desegregation Demand." *Tryon News*, p. 1.

Bryan, J.G. (August 19, 2009). "Brief History of Alleghany's Black Schools Listed from 1884 Until 2008." Supplement to the *Alleghany News* (Sparta, NC), p. 11.

Burgess, J. (February 29, 2004). "County's Blacks Coped with Separate Schools." *Hendersonville Times News*.

"Businesses Are Targets of Students." (October 19, 1972). *The Asheville Citizen*. In files at Asheville City Schools offices.
Capehart, J. (April 12, 2007). "Contrition for America's Curse." *Washington Post*, A 27.
Capps, J. (June 2, 1983). "A History of Asheville City Schools." *Asheville Citizen*. On file at Asheville City Schools offices, Asheville, NC.
"The City Is Now Faced with a Test of Reason." (October 2, 1969). *Asheville Citizen*. In files at Asheville City Schools offices, Asheville, NC.
Clark, P. (August 17, 1996). "Local NAACP Honors Crump for Shiloh Work." *Asheville Citizen-Times*. In files at Asheville City Schools offices, Asheville, NC.
_____. (April 29, 1999). "Stephens-Lee History Documented." *Asheville Citizen-Times*.
"Colored High School Teams Play Friday." (October 14, 1947). *Hendersonville Times News*.
"The 'Colored' People." (Fall 1992). *Black Mountain Chronicle*.
"Colored School Building Burned." (February 26, 1925). *Marion Progress*.
Conley, M. (February 21, 1996) "Before Integration Black Students Attended Hudgins, Mountain View." *McDowell News*, p. 1.
Connelly, B. (March 1, 1956). "Hearing Opens in Old Fort School Desegregation Appeal." *Charlotte Observer*, p. 2A.
"Council Promises Full Disorder Probe." (September 30, 1969). *The Asheville Times*, p. 1, Section 2. In files at Asheville City Schools offices, Asheville, NC.
"County Board Approves Carver School Closing." (August 10, 1966). *Asheville Citizen*. In files at Asheville City Schools offices, Asheville, NC.
"Countywide Curfew Remains in Effect." (October 1, 1969) *Asheville Citizen*, p. 1. On file at Old Buncombe County Genealogical Society, Asheville, NC.
Cowles, M. (August 28, 1966). "Pupils Permitted Choice of Schools." *Asheville Citizen*. In files at Asheville City Schools offices, Asheville, NC.
_____. (October 1, 1969). "Call for Changes Aired at Meeting of School Board." *Asheville Citizen*, p. 1, Section 2. In files at Asheville City Schools offices, Asheville, NC.
_____. (October 3, 1969). "Asheville Schools Open as Police Stand Guard." *Asheville Citizen*, p. 1. In files at Asheville City Schools offices, Asheville, NC.
_____. (April 11, 1972). "Livingston Street School Fate to be Known by May 1." *Asheville Citizen*. In files at Asheville City Schools offices, Asheville, NC.
"Death Toll at Catholic Hill School May Be 8 Children." (November 17, 1917). *Asheville Citizen*.
"Desegregation." File of articles from *Asheville Citizen*. Vertical File, Asheville City Schools offices, Asheville, NC.
"Education Begins Here, Sanford Tells Students." (September 27, 1962). *McDowell News*. In African American Scrapbook, Vertical File, McDowell County Public Library, Marion, NC.
"Fire Which Took the Lives of 7 Was 20 Years Ago." (November 16, 1937). *Asheville Citizen*.
"Five Negro Children Attempt Admittance at Old Fort School." (August 25, 1955). *Marion Progress*. In African American Scrapbook, Vertical File, McDowell County Public Library, Marion, NC.
"Former Student Addressing School's Graduating Class." (ca. 1963). *McDowell News*. In African American Scrapbook, Vertical File, McDowell County Library, Marion, NC.
Giles, J. (March 7, 2004). A Brick at a Time: Community's Blacks Built a Better Life in Fletcher Area. *Times News Online*. Retrieved from www.hendersonvillenews.com.
_____. (May 14, 2004). Simmons, a Civil Rights Leader, Dies. *Hendersonville Times News*.
Glanton, D. (May 22, 1977). "A Former Slave's Granddaughter Retires at Mars Hill." *Asheville Citizen*. Available in Heritage of Black Highlanders Special Collections. D. Hiden Ramsey Library, University of North Carolina at Asheville.
Gourlay, B. (August 19, 1964). "Board Assigns Negroes to 10 County Schools." *Asheville Citizen*. In files at Asheville City Schools offices, Asheville, NC.
"Hearing on Affray in Old Fort to be September 19." (September 8, 1955). *Marion Progress*. In African American Scrapbook, Vertical File, McDowell County Public Library, Marion, NC.
Hensley, Jay. (October 1, 1969). "City Police Arrest Two Militant Leaders." *Asheville Citizen*.
"High School for Negro Children Is Begun as State Board Approves." (October 3, 1932). *Lenoir News-Topic*. In African American Collection in vertical file at Caldwell Heritage Museum, Lenoir, NC.
"High School for Negro Students Is Contemplated." (1932). *Lenoir News-Topic*. In African American collection in vertical file at Caldwell Heritage Museum, Lenoir, NC.
"High Schools Must Integrate in 30 Days in Yancey Co." (September 1, 1960). *Hendersonville Times News*.
"Hill St. School Changed to Isaac Dickson Elementary." (June 21, 1991). *Asheville Citizen*.

"Hill Street School Dedicated." (February 23, 1915). *Asheville Citizen*.
Hootman, B. (May 13, 1999). "Lib Harper's Work Honored by A-B Tech." *Black Mountain News*.
_____. (March 3, 2005). "John Myra Stepp Has Important Place in Black Mountain History." *Black Mountain News*.
"Human Relations Project Is Highly Encouraging Development; Asheville Uproar Area Council on All Interracial Problems." (April 14, 1960). *Asheville Citizen*. On File at Asheville City Schools offices, Asheville, NC.
"Integration Accomplished by Jackson School Board." (August 26, 1965). *Asheville Citizen*. In files at Asheville City Schools offices, Asheville, NC.
Johnson, D., Jr. (October 25, 1950). "Dedicate School Plant: Modern Plant Now in Use by Three Counties." Hendersonville: *Western Carolina Tribune*.
Kennedy, J.P. "Valley Residents Reflect on Black History Month." (February 17, 2005). *Black Mountain News*.
Knight, C.K. (February 1, 2007). "Family's History Resonates with Hard Work." *Transylvania Times*, p. 1.
"The Long, Long Road." (December 4, 1959). Editorial in *New York Times*. Retrieved from http://news.google.com/archivesearch.
"Marion Schools Again to Follow Freedom of Choice Plan." (n.d.) *McDowell News*. In African American Scrapbook, Vertical File, McDowell County Public Library, Marion, NC.
"McDowell Board of Education Answers Petition of Negroes: No Class Space, Modern Negro School Comprise Reply to Negro Requests." (July 21, 1955). *McDowell News*. In African American Scrapbook, Vertical File, McDowell County Public Library, Marion, NC.
"McDowell School Case Stymied." (November 15, 1956). *Marion Progress*. Archived in African American Scrapbook at McDowell Public Library, Marion, NC.
Mebane, B. (October 3, 1969). "Outsiders Involved." *Asheville Citizen*. In files at Asheville City Schools offices, Asheville, NC.
Messer, J., T. Tucker, M. Forney, W. Eggleston, and R. Mitchell (n.d). "The Story of Reynolds High." *Asheville Citizen-Times*. Available in files of Wilbur Eggleston.
Metzgar, H. (February 22, 2004). "Former Slaves Founded Kingdom of Happy Land." *Hendersonville Times News*.
Miller, V.H. (Spring 1993). "The Colored People — A Salute to Diversity." *Black Mountain Chronicle*.
Mitchell, M. (March 23, 1999). "Community Remembers Educator, Leader." *Observer News Enterprise* (Newton, NC).
"Negro School Is Picketed." (n.d.). *McDowell News*. African American Scrapbook, Vertical File at McDowell County Public Library, Marion, NC.
"Negro Students Report to Old Fort School, Denied Entry." (August 25, 1955). *McDowell News*. In African American Scrapbook, Vertical File, McDowell County Public Library, Marion, NC.
"Negroes Will Fight Hill Street School Action." (June 18, 1907). *Asheville Citizen*. In files at Asheville City Schools offices, Asheville, NC.
"New Colored School Nearing Completion." (January, 18, 1915). *Asheville Citizen*.
"New Hill Street School." (March 29, 1953). *Asheville Citizen*.
"New Negro School Unit and Consolidation Set." (August 10, 1950). *McDowell News*. In African American Scrapbook, Vertical File, McDowell County Public Library, Marion, NC.
"New School (Colored on Valley St.) to be Ready Soon." (August 1, 1922). *Asheville Citizen*. In files at Asheville City Schools offices, Asheville, NC.
"9th Avenue School Status Is Uncertain." (April 7, 1965). Hendersonville *Times News*, p. 1.
"Not One Drop of Negro Blood in Grahams." (November 26, 1905). *Asheville Citizen*. On file in Special Collections, Hayden Ramsey Library, UNC–Asheville.
"Open Meeting Is Scheduled in High School Disturbance." (September 30, 1969). *Asheville Citizen*, p. 15.
Patton, Sadie D. (May 7, 1960). "Faithful Servant to Be Honored Here Saturday." *Times-News*.
"Patton Upholds Decision of Lower Court in School Case." (March 8, 1955). *McDowell News*. In African American Scrapbook in Vertical File at McDowell County Library, Marion, NC.
Peake, L. (February 2, 1994). "Breaking a Barrier: Warren Wilson Student Wrote an Important Page of History." *Asheville Citizen-Times*.
Pearson, L. (February 23, 1991). "Black Educators Persevered." *Lenoir News-Topic*.
Poteat, M. (August 9, 1928). "Schools for Colored Race Show Progress." *McDowell News* (Marion, NC).
"Principals Praised" (October 3, 1969). *Asheville Citizen*. In files at Asheville City Schools offices, Asheville, NC.
"Protesters Turn Destructive" (February 3, 1970). *Asheville Citizen*. In files at Asheville City Schools offices, Asheville, NC.

Reinhardt, S.G. (June 14, 1995). "Allen High Gone but Not Forgotten," *Asheville Citizen-Times.* In files at Asheville City Schools offices, Asheville, NC.

"Remembering the Not So Bad Old Days at Tryon Colored School" (February 3, 1995). *Tryon Daily Bulletin* 68/4, p. 1.

Robinson, H. (February 15, 1981). "Tribute to Honor Black Leaders." *Asheville Citizen.*

_____. (February 19, 1984). "Fourth Annual Awards Next Sunday." *Asheville Citizen.*

_____. (March 5, 1984). "Blacks Moving Into World of Business." *Asheville Citizen-Times.* In files at Asheville City Schools offices, Asheville, NC.

_____. (March 31, 1993). "Looking Back: A Former Educator Remembers Earlier Times, Values." *Asheville Citizen-Times.*

_____. (February 13, 1994). "Flashback: Stephens-Lee School Opened in 1923." *Asheville Citizen.* In files at Asheville City Schools offices, Asheville, NC.

_____. (March 13, 1994). "Schoolhouse Fire Claimed 7 Lives." *Asheville Citizen-Times.*

"S.C. Eleven Nips Colored Team Here." (October 17, 1947). *Hendersonville Times News.* In personal files of Patrick Gallegher.

Seitz, E. "Curfew Called After Clash: Protest Sparks Violence." (September 30, 1965). *Asheville Citizen*, 5. On File at Old Buncombe County Genealogical Society, Asheville, NC.

_____. "Schools to Reopen; Militants Enjoined." (October 2, 1969). *Asheville Citizen*, p. 1. In files at Asheville City Schools offices, Asheville, NC.

_____. "Curfew Dropped; Emergency Bans Remain in Effect." (October 3, 1969). *Asheville Citizen*, p. 1. In files at Asheville City Schools offices, Asheville, NC.

"66 Negro Pupils Applying to Attend Old Fort School." (July 18, 1975). *McDowell News.* In African American Scrapbook, Vertical File, McDowell County Public Library, Marion, NC.

Smith, R. (October 11, 1993). "Sam Mills Dead at 84." *Hendersonville Times News,* p. 1A.

Stein, H. (February 24, 1998). "A Model of Philanthropy." *Wall Street Journal.*

"Stephens-Lee Gym Dedicated." (June 6, 1941). *Asheville Times.*

"Story of Negro Who Brought Home Body of Master Recalled." (November 2, 1933). *Asheville Times.*

"Submitted Plans on Desegregation Near Approval." (July 26, 1965). *McDowell News.* In African American Scrapbook in Vertical File at McDowell County Library, Marion, NC.

"Suit Against Board of Education Is Dismissed by Judge Warlick." (July 7, 1955). *McDowell News*, 59/50. In African American Scrapbook in Vertical File at McDowell County Library, Marion, NC.

"Taylor, Beam Express Views on Segregation." (May 30, 1954). *McDowell News.*

"To Segregate Negroes Is a Minor Objective." (June 15, 1907). *Asheville Citizen.*

"Tryon Schools Must Take Embury Pupils." (June 26, 1965). *Herald Journal.* Retrieved from news.google.com/archivesearch.

"20,698 Students Register in Buncombe County Schools." (August 23, 1969). *Asheville Citizen.* In files at Asheville City Schools offices, Asheville, NC.

Warren, C.S. (February 1936). "School Notes." *Lenoir News-Topic.* On file in African American Collection in vertical file at Caldwell Heritage Museum, Lenoir, NC.

Waters, L. (October 26, 2005). "Peaceful Warriors." Retrieved from www.mountainx.com.

Williamson, M.K. (September 28, 1919). "A History of Asheville City Schools." Printed June 2, 1983, in *Asheville Citizen.*

"WNC Schools in Civil Rights Probe." (March 15, 1975). *Asheville Citizen.* On file at Asheville City Schools offices, Asheville, NC.

"Work Started Tuesday at Hudgins School; To Erect New Negro Consolidated School." (November 15, 1951). *McDowell News*, 56/18.

"Workmen Raze Hill St. School." (December 20, 1952). *Asheville Citizen.*

Law Cases and Legal Proceedings

Brown et al. v. Board of Education of Topeka et al., 347 US, 483, 74 S. Ct. 686, 691 (1954).

Brown v. Board of Education of Topeka, Kansas, 349 US, 294. 75 S. Ct. 753 (1955).

Civil Rights Act of 1964, PL 88-352, 88th Congress, H.R. 7152 (July 2, 1964).

Griffith v. Robinson, Civ. No. 1881, W.D.N.C., Oct. 28, 1963, 8 Race, Rel. L. Rep. 1433 (1963).

Griffith v. Robinson (1963). Retrieved from http://www.law.umaryland.edu/marshall/usccr/documents/cr12ed8296 4.pd).

Leandro v. State of North Carolina, 346 NC 336 (179PA96) (July 24, 1997).

Leandro v. State of North Carolina, 346 NC 336 (179PA96) 07/24/1997. Retrieved from http://www.aoc.state.nc.us/www/public/sc/opinions/1997/179-96-1.htm.

McElroy, G. (Compiler). *Sylvia Gilliland Versus Buncombe County Board of Education* 1905. Asheville, N.C.: Old Buncombe County Genealogical Society. In Special Collections, D. Hiden Ramsey Library, University of North Carolina at Asheville.

Plan for the Asheville City Schools for the Desegregation of Its School System in Compliance with Title VI of the Civil Rights Act of 1964, Adopted July 1965 by Asheville City School Board. Archived at Asheville City Schools Foundation, Asheville, NC.

Plessy v. Ferguson, 163 U.S. 537 (1896).

Swann v. Charlotte-Mecklenburg Board of Education (1971).

Proceedings of Meetings

Ashe County Board of Education Minutes, 1885–1966. On microfilm at North Carolina State Archives, Raleigh, NC.

Asheville City Board of Education Minutes 1900–1972. On file at the Asheville City Schools offices, Mountain Street, Asheville, NC.

Asheville City Board of Education Minutes 1902–1969. On file at the Asheville City Schools offices, Mountain Street, Asheville, NC.

Asheville City School Board. "Plan for the Asheville City Schools for the Desegregation of Its School System in Compliance with Title VI of the Civil Rights Act of 1964." Asheville City Schools Foundation, July 6, 1965.

Asheville School Committee Minutes 1887–1892. On file at the Asheville City Schools offices, Mountain Street, Asheville, NC.

Avery County Board of Education Minutes, 1911–1970. On microfilm at North Carolina State Archives, Raleigh, NC.

Buncombe County Board of Education Minutes 1890–1967. In storage at the Buncombe County Board of Education Offices, Asheville, NC.

Cherokee County Board of Education Minutes 1926–1965. On file at Cherokee Board of Education Offices, Murphy, NC.

Clay County Board of Education Minutes 1922–1964. On file at Clay County Board of Education Offices, Hayesville, NC.

Henderson County Board of Education Minutes 1900–1966. On file at Henderson County Board of Public Education Offices, Hendersonville, NC.

Hendersonville City Board of Education Minutes 1900–1966. On file at Henderson County Board of Public Education Offices, Hendersonville, NC.

Marion City Board of Education Minutes 1901–1966. On file at Board of Education Offices, Marion, NC.

Madison County Board of Education Minutes 1897–1967. On file at Board of Education Offices, Marshall, NC.

McDowell County Board of Education Minutes. On file at Board of Education Offices, Marion, NC.

Mitchell County Board of Education Minutes 1901–1970. On microfilm at North Carolina State Archives, Raleigh, NC.

Polk County Board of Education Minutes 1936–1969. On microfilm at North Carolina State Archives, Raleigh, NC.

Rutherford County Board of Education Minutes 1917–1964. On file at Board of Education Offices, Forest City, NC.

Surry County Board of Education Minutes 1941–1963. On microfilm at North Carolina State Archives, Raleigh, NC.

Watauga Board of Education Minutes 1885–1969. On microfilm at North Carolina State Archives, Raleigh, NC.

Wilkes County Board of Education Minutes 1885–1963. On microfilm at North Carolina State Archives, Raleigh, NC.

Yancey County Board of Education Minutes. On file at Clerk of Court Office, Yancey County Court House, Burnsville, NC.

Special Collections

Allen School Student Handbook, Collection 278. Allen High School Collection of Papers. W.L. Eury Appalachian Collection, Appalachian State University, Boone, North Carolina.

Bagwell, W. (20 February 1962). "The Pitiful State of the Negro Education in Western North Carolina,"

A. Allen Gardner Papers, 1901 Special Collections, D. Hiden Ramsay Library, University of North Carolina at Asheville.
Culpepper, L.P. (2002). *Under Their Own Vine and Fig Tree: The History of Mud Creek Baptist Church, East Flat Rock, Henderson County, North Carolina, 1867–2002*. Sylva, NC: L.P. Culpepper. Available in Special Collections, Hunter Library. Cullowhee, NC: Western Carolina University.
Department of Public Instruction. Division of Negro Education: 1921–1960. Files of the State Supervisor of Elementary Education, 1936–1961. Box 4. North Carolina State Archives, Raleigh, NC.
_____. Division of Negro Education: 1921–1960. General Correspondence of the Director. Boxes 1, 2, 4, 11, 13, 14, 15,17,18, 19, 20, 22, 23, 25, 26. North Carolina State Archives, Raleigh, NC.
_____. Division of Negro Education: 1921–1960. High School Principal's Annual Reports. Boxes 1, 6, 13, 17, 18, 19, 20, 25, 26, 27, 38. North Carolina State Archives, Raleigh, NC.
_____. Division of Negro Education: 1921–1960, Special Subject File. Boxes 1, 4, 8, 11, 13, 16, 18. North Carolina State Archives, Raleigh, NC.
_____. Division of Negro Education: 1921–1960. Elementary School Principal's Annual Reports. Box 29. North Carolina State Archives, Raleigh, NC.
_____. Division of Negro Education. Files of State Supervisor of Elementary Education, 1936–1961, Boxes 2, 3.
_____. North Carolina's Division of Vocational Education, Box 9. North Carolina State Archives, Raleigh, NC.
Edward Stephens Letter to Charles McNamee (January 20, 1892). Biltmore House Collection. Also available in Special Collections at D. Hiden Ramsey Library, University of North Carolina at Asheville.
Ferguson, G.H. (December 1962). Some Facts About the Education of Negroes in NC, 1921–60. Raleigh, NC: Department of Public Instruction, Division of Negro Education, General Correspondence of the Director, Box 1, North Carolina State Archives, Raleigh, NC.
Frank E. Ratzell Papers, Special Collections, D. Hiden Ramsay Library, University of North Carolina at Asheville.
Historical Note, Collection 278. Allen High School Collection of Papers, W.L. Eury Appalachian Collection, Appalachian State University, Boone, North Carolina.
"History of Freedman High School," *Freedman High School Student Handbook* (ca. 1962). Lenoir, NC: Caldwell County Heritage Museum African American Vertical File Collection.
Julius Rosenwald Fund Archives. Special Collections. Franklin Library. Nashville, TN: Fisk University.
Lucy Herring Oral History. August 2, 1977, Special Collections, D. Hiden Ramsey Library, University of North Carolina at Asheville.
Maddelena, D. (November 10, 2000). "Integration and the Asheville YWCA." Senior Papers, History, Special Collections, D. Hiden Ramsay Library, University of North Carolina at Asheville.
O.L. Sherrill Oral History. Special Collections, D. Hiden Ramsey Library, University of North Carolina at Asheville.
Rev. Ronald Scott, O.F.M., Franciscan: Founder of St. Anthony's School. Heritage of Black Highlanders Collection. D. Hiden Ramsey Library. University of North Carolina at Asheville.
Rosenwald Fund. Special Collections, Box 341, Fisk University, Nashville, TN.
United States Court of Appeals for the Fourth Circuit; No. 14, 497. Michael F. Keleher Collection, Special Collections, D. Hiden Ramsay Library, University of North Carolina at Asheville.
William Roland Oral History. Special Collections. D. Hiden Ramsey Library, University of North Carolina at Asheville.

Interviews and Personal Communication

Anderson, L.H. April 7, 2009.
Ashworth, N. August 13, 2010.
Bailey, L. January 18, 2006.
Blaine, B.C. March 30, 2005.
Blakley, S.D. August 3, 2009.
Bellamy, T. July 7, 2009.
Brewer, D. September 9, 2010; October 13, 2009; November 19, 2009.
Butler, W. April 23, 2009.
Carnegie, D. January 16, 2004.
Carpenter, Bobbie and Tom. May 7, 2010; August 12, 2010.
Chavis, C. April 14, 2009.
Chiles, L.R. April 26, 2007.
Crump, L. February 11, 2004; March 5, 2004.
Darity, W. November 6, 2004.
Davidson, A. June 3, 2008.
Davis, A. April 6, 2004.
Dobbins, B. April 28, 2010.
East, V. October 10, 2010.
Edwards, H.L. November 16, 2004.
Eggleston, Wilbur & LaTiece April 9, 2009 and October 3, 2010.
Ferree, E. October 27, 2010.

Fleming, J.E. September 23, 2010.
Fowler, A., with Harper, C. April 9, 2009
Freeman, G.R. March 15, 2007; March 19, 2007.
Hailey, A.M. August 21, 2002.
Hairston, E. October 30, 2010.
Hairston, G. October 30, 2010.
Harper, E.M. August 11, 2004.
Hart, S.R. September 3, 2010.
Hawkins, J. November 24, 2009; May 18–19, 25, 2010.
Haynes, E. September 9, 2007.
Henderson, M. April 21, 2009.
Howell, V. May 28, 2010.
Jones, Jill. August 7, 2007; July 24, 2010.
Kincaid, Gwyn. June 22, 2009.
Kincaid, Pat. June 22, 2009.
Knox, L. October 20, 2006; March 15, 2007.
Lamond, J. May 3, 2008
Laughter, J. March 10, 2009.
Lawson, C. November 15, 2010.
Ledbetter, G. February 1, 2005.
Littrell, Frankie T. March 30, 2009.
Logan, F. March 8, 2005.
Logan, H.L. June 11, 2010; June 22/24, 2010; November 1, 2010.
Long, D. June 17, 2010; July 8, 2010.
Lucas, G.S. May 19, 2005.
Lynch, C.H. February 25, 2005.
Lynch, Clifford. March 8, 2005.
Maney, M.A. March 30, 2007; April 4, 2007.
Martin, B. June, 18, 2010.
Martin, E. November 23, 2009; December 9, 2009.
Mauldin, G. August 12, 2009.
McMinn, A. January 18, 2004.
Mills, E.K. June 17, 1999.
Mills, J.L. March 12, 2007.
Mims, M.V. February 5, 2005.
Morrison, G. April 28, 2010.
Nicholson, M.R. February 12, 2005.
Owens, F. January 16, 2004; February 11, 2004.
Page, S. April 24, 2009.
Parkinson, O. February 25, 2005.
Payne, B. March 7, 2007.
Payne, G. November 13, 2006.
Payne, L.V. March 5, 2005.
Pearson, L.R. February 2009.
Potts, H. March 26, 2004; April 6, 2004.
Raper, S. October 24, 2002.
Ray, C. April 17, 2008.
Ray, G.C. November 28, 2007.
Reed, W.A. September 14, 2010.
Reese, S. September 4, 2010.
Rivers, G. December 1, 2005.
Robinson, H. February 18, 2009; April 8, 2009.
Roland, C.E. July 24, 2007.
Roland, Clifton. November 16, 2007.
Roland, E. September 3, 2010.
Roland, G. July 11, 2007.
Roland, P. May 23, 2007.
Rudisail, A. March 8, 2005.
Russo, D.B. August 17, 2010.
Sherrill, O.L. September 3, 2010; September 6, 2010.
Shippy, A.L. January 31, 2006.
Simmons H.S. III. February 7, 2005.
Sitton, L. February 24, 2005; March 5, 2005.
Stanley, W. September 7, 2010.
Styles, H. August 7, 2007.
Summerous, J.T. August 12, 2009
Thompson, E.S. July 29 and 30, 2010.
Trantham, B. January 16, 2006; May 8, 2006.
Weaver, J.G. April 4, 2007.
White-Carter, A. March 5, 2007.
Williams, E.J. April 28, 2010.
Williams, J. February 2, 2008.
Wilson, F. March 10, 2009.
Wilson, M. April 4, 2008.
Wykle, C. September 3, 5, 2010.
Young, M. October 13, 2006; October 31, 2006.

Letters and Reports

Asheville City Schools' Plan of Compliance with Title VI of the Civil Rights Act of 1964, on file in archives of Asheville City Schools Foundation.

Asheville High Disorder, Complete Text of Report. (September 29, 1969). Report of the Community Relations Council. Published in *Asheville Citizen*.

Ashley, S.S. (1869). "Report of the Superintendent of Public Instruction for the year 1869." Retrieved from http://docsouth.unc.edu/nc/report 1869/report1869.html).

Batten, Susan. Presentation for Annie E. Casey Foundation (August 13, 2008). *School Desegregation in North Carolina*. North Carolina Human Relations Conference. High Point, North Carolina.

Calure, Cathy, interview with Della Jackson (August 24, 1988). Taped by Polk County Historical Association. Copy on file at Polk County Public Library.

Credle, W.F. (1939) Survey Report to Cherokee County Board of Education. On file in Cherokee County School Offices, Murphy, NC.

Day, R.E. (1962). "North Carolina Report to U.S. Civil Rights Commission" in *Civil Rights U.S.A.: Public Schools: Southern States*, 59-101. Retrieved from www.law.umaryland.edu/marshall/usccr/.../cr12sch62.pdf.

Della Jackson, Presentation to Polk County Historical Association (May 5, 1987). *Schools for the Black People in Polk County*. Copy on file at Polk County Public Library.

Foulke, Stewart B. (July 1947). *Engineer's Inspection and Survey Report*. Board of Education of Henderson County, Hendersonville, North Carolina.

"Henderson County Hall of Fame for Educators Acceptance Information." In personal files of Gary Rivers, Blue Ridge Community College, Hendersonville, NC.

"History of Livingston Street School: 1920–1957" (n.d.). On file at Asheville City Schools offices in Asheville, NC.

Leona Loy, Presentation to Polk County Historical Association (March 4, 1986). *One Room Schools in Polk County*. Copy on file at Polk County Public Library.

Michael, J.H. (July 15, 1938). *Summer School Instructor's Report*. NC: Winston-Salem Teachers' College.

Neufeld, R. (October 11, 1991). Interview with Burton Street Elders. Retrieved from No. 161 at Special Collections, D. Hiden Ramsey Library, University of North Carolina at Asheville, http://toto.lib.unca.edu/collections/oralhistories.html.

Ray, McD. Superintendent's July 1, 1906 Report of Henderson County Schools, Filed with Henderson County Board of Education Minutes, Hendersonville, NC.

Reid, P.A. Letter to Each Superintendent (May 3, 1949). On file with McDowell County Board of Education Minutes, Marion, NC.

Self-Study Report of Asheville City Schools: Summary by W.P. Griffin (March 1963). On file at Asheville City Schools, Asheville, NC.

Self-Study Report of Burton Street Elementary School (March 1963). On file at Asheville City Schools, Asheville, NC.

Self-Study Report of Livingston Street School to Southern Association of Colleges and Schools (March 1963). On file at Asheville City Schools. Asheville, NC.

Self-Study Report of Lucy S. Herring School to Southern Association of Colleges and Schools (March 1963). On file at Asheville City Schools. Asheville, NC.

Self-Study Report of Shiloh Elementary School to Southern Association of Colleges and Schools (March 1963). On file at Asheville City Schools, Asheville, NC.

State Survey School Panel Report to the Boards of Education of Buncombe County and to the City of Asheville (October 1949). On file at Asheville City Schools offices and Buncombe County School Offices.

What Stands Between North Carolina Students and a Sound Basic Education? (March 2007). Action for Children North Carolina and the UNC Center for Civil Rights. Leandro Advocacy Project. Raleigh, NC. Retrieved from www.law.unc.edu/Centers.

INDEX

Numbers in *bold italics* indicate pages with photographs.

Abernathy, Christine 94
Abernethy, W.T. 72
Abrams, Amos 166
Accelerated Veterans' Classes 175
Act of 1901 70, 71
Adako School (Caldwell County) 169
Adams, Col. D.W. ***200***
Addie's Chapel 152, 201
African-American Historical and Genealogical Society of Surry County 227
An African American One Room School—Reading 2 117
Agee, James 11
Aiken, Jim 230
Airborne Ranger 55
A.J. Durner & Son 96
Alabama 68, 117, 192
Alexander, Michelle 233
Alexander County 15, 33, 99, 150, 165, 166, 167, 168, 169, 172, 216–217
Alleghany County 15, 21, 25, 30, 33, 97, 165, 167, 168, 169, 228
Alleghany County School Board 228
Allen, Marriage 177
Allen, Rev. Walter 69
Allen Home and Industrial School (Asheville) 22, 80
Allen Home School (Asheville) 22, 57, 71, 82, 156, 163, 172, 176, 177, 225, ***224***, 226
Allman, Walter 184
Alston, Robert 130
Altamont School (Avery County) 29, 95
A.M.E. Zion Methodist Church (Marion) 201
An American Citizen: The Life of William Henry Baldwin 116, 223
An American Dilemma: The Negro Problem and Modern Democracy 9
American Freedmen's Commission 21
American Friends Service Committee 25

American Missionary Association/ Society 19, 21, 96
Anders, Robert "R.G." 130
Anderson, Agnes 129
Anderson, Bob 111
Anderson, Burch 111
Anderson, Joe 139–140
Anderson, Rev. J.W. 139
Anderson, Leon H. 55
Anderson, Lloyd 111
Anderson, Meade 111
Anderson, Mrs. 127
Anderson, Mrs. S.C. 140
Anderson School (Buncombe County) 110–113
Andrews School 170
Anna T. Jeanes Foundation 19
Annie B. Casey Foundation 232
Anthony, Rev. E.A. 218
Antietam 31
Antioch School (Rutherford County) 170
Appalachian Elementary School (Watauga County) 62
Appalachian High School (Watauga County) 61, ***62***
Appalachian Regional Commission 33
Appalachian State Teachers College 166
Ararat Colored High School (Surry County) 172
Ararat School (Surry County) 171
"Architectural Styles as Applied to School Buildings" 117
Arden Colored School ***140***
Argyle 30
Arledge, J.T. 60
Arledge, Keith 53
Arney, W.W., Jr. 42
Arnold, J.A. 206
Ash Fund 116
Ashbrook, William A. 166
Ashe County 15, 29, 30, 33, 43, 123, 149, 165, 167, 168, 169
Asheland Avenue Junior High School (Asheville) 90
Asheland Avenue School (Asheville) 104, 107

Asheville, North Carolina 19, 26, 33, 43, 73
Asheville Area Council on Human Relations 25, 45
Asheville Blues 176
Asheville City School Board 43, 74, 81, 88
Asheville City Schools 44, 45, 57, 82, 169, 175
Asheville College 166
Asheville High School 36, 47, 48, 230
Asheville School Committee 74
Asheville Student Committee on Racial Equality (ASCORE) 59
Asheville Teachers College 166
Asheville Tourists 128
Ashland Avenue School 169
Ashley, Samuel S. 21, 70
Attucks, Crispus 237
Auld, Hugh 67
Auld, Sophia 67
Austin, James 148
Avery County 25, 29, 33, 95–96, 149, 166, 167, 168, 169, 192, 216
Avery's Creek 24–25
Avondale, North Carolina 211
Aycock, Charles Brantley 22, 157

Bagwell, William 25
Bailey, Johnny 176
Bailey, Louise 95
Baldwin, William Henry, Jr. 116
Ballard, David 189
Baltimore, Maryland 232
Bangs, J.H. 134
Banneker, Benjamin 237
Bannerman, Arthur H. 39
Barber, D.B. ***141***
Barber, E.J. 216
Barber Scotia Seminary (Concord, North Carolina) 72, 163
Barbour, Lottie S. 98
Barnardsville, North Carolina 110, 111, 112
Barnardsville Elementary School 112
Barnes, Ethel Mae 216
Barnes, Robert R. 49

Index

Barnett, David 163
Barnett, Herbert 163
Barnett, Viola 163
Barney Hill School (Yadkin County) 172
Bass, Dora B. 199
Bass, Guy 127, 129
Bat Cave, North Carolina 132
Batten, Susan 232
Battle, Rachel S. 91
Beal, Hugh Scott 145
Beam, Hugh 195, 200, 201
Beard, Ruby 104
Beaumont Academy (Asheville) 75
Beaver, F.M. 194–198
Bechler, Augustus 210
Bechler, Christopher 210
Bell, Allen J. 145
Bell, Ed 69
Bell, Joseph Oscar 68
Bell, Ruth 100
Bellamy, Terry 230–231
Belton, Joseph E. 175
Benedict College 94, 181
Berea College 113, 226
Bernard, S.G. *111*
Best, Addie 139
Betelle, Oscar 117, 118
Biddle Memorial Institute (Biddle University) 120, 223; *see also* Johnson C. Smith University
Big Lick School (Stanly County) 95
Birdtown, North Carolina 151
Birdtown School (Swain County) 151
Black Appalachian Commission 33
Black Codes 12, 14, 20
Black Hands in the Biscuits Not in the Classrooms 3
Black Heritage Sites: An African American Odyssey and Finder's Guide 162
Black Mountain 81, 225
Black Mountain College 40
Black Mountain Elementary School 50, 51, *105*, 169
Blacks in Appalachia 27
Blowing Rock 33
Blue Ridge Assembly Grounds 88, 190
Blue Ridge Township (Henderson County) 70
Blue-White All Star Games 176
Bobtown, North Carolina 99, 157
Bolden, Annie Mae Clark 90
Booker, A.W. 72
Boone, Daniel 27
Boone, North Carolina 33
Boone School (Watauga County) 171
Boonville School (Yadkin County) 172, 207
Bost, W.L. 19
Bostic School (Rutherford County) 170
Boston, Massachusetts 225, 237
Boston Symphony Hall 237
Boston University 55
Botts, I.A. 75

Bovian, Alsie Y. 90
Bower, R. Fred 192
Bowman, Ruby Crayton 40
Bradburn, C.W. 60
Bradshaw, George W. 71
Bradshaw, J.T. 126
Breese, V.W. 211
Brevard High School 53, 167
Brevard Rosenwald School 38, **140**, 171, 216
The Brevard Rosenwald School: Black Education and Community Building in a Southern Appalachian Town, 1920–1966 124
Brevard School (Transylvania County) 73, 95
Brewer, Debbie 228
Brickton, North Carolina 132, 165
Brickton School 102–103, **102**, 170, 186
Bridal Veil Falls 29
Bridgewater, North Carolina 153
Bridgewater School (McDowell County) 152, 170
Brigman, Louisa Burleson 113
Brigman, Nancy 111
Brim's Grove School (Stokes County) 171
Briscoe, Gibby 59
Briscoe, Manual 58, 137
Bristol School for Negroes (Ashe County) 109, 169
Britt, J.J. 80
Brittain, William C. 42
Brittian, Myrtle 129
Britton, William 27
Broad River School (Rutherford County) 170
Brooks, Carnell 188
Brooks, E.C. 22, 23
Brooks, John Graham 223
Brooks, Nathaniel 108
Broom, Taft H. 215–216
Brown, Rev. C.K. 80
Brown, Essie 194
Brown, Franklyn P. 194
Brown, H.R. 75
Brown, Les M. 229
Brown, Naomi L. 60
Brown, Pat 91
Brown, Rap 53
Brown, Shirley 47
Brown I 25, 36, 38, 40, 146, 232
Brown II 36
Brown Mountain School (Stokes County) 171, 219
Browne, F. Pickens 212
Browne, Josephine 212
Bruce Drysdale Elementary School (Henderson County) 94
Bryan, Clay 97
Bryan, James 60
Bryants School (Rutherford County) 171
Bryson, Walter 31
Bryson, William 31
Bryson City, North Carolina 150
Bryson City Rosenwald School (Swain County) 150, 171

Buck Shoals School (Rutherford County) 171
Buffalo Street School **89**
Buncombe County 9, 24, 33, 36, 49, 110, 122, 125–130, 165, 166, 168, 169, 172
Buncombe County Board of Education 24, 49, 81, 112
Buncombe County Community Relations Council 47
Buncombe Turnpike/Toll Road 30, 68
Bunker, Eng 30
Bunker, Sallie 30
Buried in the Bitter Waters: The Hidden History of Racial Cleansing in America 191
Burke County 21, 30, 33, 62–63, 99, 157, 165, 166, 168, 169, 172
Burleigh, Harry T. 237
Burnsville Colored Elementary School (Yancey County) 57, 172
Burrell, Dagan Lamont 40, 65
Burton, John 89
Burton, Lucille Pearson 46, 175
Burton Street School (Buncombe County) 89–91, 169
Bush Town School (Caldwell County) 169
Butler, Wanda 64
Butler School (Gainesville, Georgia) 147
Byers, J.W. 89
Bynum, Sarah 194
Byrd, Harry F., Sr. 38

Caldwell, Thelma 231
Caldwell County 30, 33, 99, 165, 166, 168, 169–170, 172, 208, 210, 218–219
Caldwell Heritage Museum 210, 214
Caler, Paul 145
Calicutt, Norman 195
Calure, Cathy 156
Calvary Presbyterian Church 73, 87
Cambridge University 86, 175
Camp, Cordelia 166
Candler, V.R. 155
Cane River 29
Cane River High School (Yancey County) 58
Canton, North Carolina 143, 209, 214
Capps, Julia 74
Carmichael, Stokely 53
Carnegie, Delores 126–127, 129
Caroleen, North Carolina 211
Caroleen School (Rutherford County) 171
Carolina, Ruth C. 175
Carpenter, Mattie 208
Carpenter, Tom 63
Carroll, Charles F., Jr. 36, 57, 145, 151
Carson, Emily M. **102**
Carson, John H. 206

Carson, Lionel C. 43
Carson, Lucile 97
Carson, Rev. R. Logan 228
Carson, V.E. 208
Carter, Agnes 148
Carter, Frank 79
Carter, Hargrove 113
Carter, Jimmy 218
Carver, George Washington 238
Carver Elementary School (Black Mountain) 103, **105**
Carver Elementary School (Buncombe County) 50, 51, 81
Carver High School (Rutherford County) 59, 60, **203**, 211, 217
Carver High School (Spartanburg, South Carolina) 188
Carver Optional School (Buncombe County) 51
The Case for Affirmative Action for Blacks in Higher Education 226
Cash, John 188
Cash, W.J. 18
"Castle on the Hill" 64, 174
Catawba College 157
Catawba Colored High School 216
Catawba County 15, 19, 26, 59, 72, 97–99, 157–158, 172, 193, 207, 215
Catawba River 28, 29
Catawba Rosenwald School 157, 215
Catawba View Grammar School (McDowell County) **200**
Catholic Hill 75, 79, 80
Catholic Hill School 75, 77, 80, 85–87, **86**, 174, 175
Cecelski, David C. 3
Cedar Valley School (Caldwell County) 95
Central High School (Catawba County) 72, 213, 215, 216, 217
Chalk, Victor, Jr. 47
Chambers, Beatrice 104
Chambers, Lois **151**
Chapel Hill School (Rutherford County) 171
Chapel School (Macon County) 140, **141**, 170, 202
Charles Hill's General Merchandise Store 134
Charleston, South Carolina 30
Charlotte, North Carolina 37
Chattanooga, Tennessee 237
Chavis, Clarence 177
Cheek, Edwin B. 136
Cherokee County 15, 21, 30, 33, 51–52, 63, 143, 146, 147–149, 165, 167, 168, 170
Cherokee County Board of Education 149
Cherokee Indians 27
Cherry Lane Elementary School (Alleghany County) 97, **98**, 169
Chicago, Illinois 17, 116, 225
Chicago Civic Orchestra 238
Chickasaw Tribe 27
Chigger Hill School (Clay County) 144
Church of the Good Shepherd 155

The Church Record 141
Civil Rights Act of 1866 14
Civil Rights Act of 1875 14
Civil Rights Law of 1964 40–41, 42, 51, 56, 60, 61–62, 147
Civil Rights Movement 11
Civil War 17, 19, 67
Clark, Ben 49
Clark, Miss M.G. 206
A Class of Their Own: Black Teachers in the Segregated South 3
Claxton, Philander P. 89
Clay, Henry 143
Clay, Lewis 184
Clay County 14, 21, 33, 143–147, 165, 168
Clay County Board of Education 144
Clear Creek, North Carolina 132, 165
Clear Creek Township (Henderson County) 70, 78
Clearview Colored School **77**
Clement, Mrs. G. Latta 126
Cleveland County 94
Cliffside, North Carolina 171, 211
Cliffside School (Rutherford County) 171
Clinard, J.W. 157
Clinchfield Products Corporation 192
Clingman's Dome 29
Clinkscale, Nellie 90
Clyde, Harold 52
Cobb Elementary School (Polk County) 59, 156
Cofitachequi (Lady of) 28
Colbert, Don 148
Cold Mountain 30
Coleman, Wayne 176
College of Staten Island 64
Collington, Leonard 129
Colored Children's Home (Buncombe County) 79
Columbia University 92, 175, 194
Combstown School (Surry County) 149–150, 171
Commission on Interracial Cooperation 166
Conley, A.P. 193, 194
Conley, Mike 58
Connelly Springs, Burke County 95
Connelly Springs School (Burke County) 95, 169
Conner, Anna Pack 155
Constitutional Convention of 1868 70
Cook, Mary Hansberry (Ms. Cook) 132
Cooke, Anna M. 219
Coone, Chedester 109
Coone, Estella 109
Coone, Howard 108
Coone, Odessa 108
Cooper, Anna Julia 10, 223
Cooper, Lee 198
Cooper, Vivian Cline **85**
Corbett, George C. 215

Corn, James 146
Cornelius, P.G. 136
Corner School 152
Corpening, B. Greenlee 194, 198
Corpening School 169
Couch, Ezel 69
Counts, Ulysses 212
Cowan, Daniel 108
Cowan, Mrs. 127, 128
Cowan, Robert 108
Cowart, Elah 166
Cowart, Neal 148
Cowee, North Carolina 140
Cowee School 140
Cowles, Mary 48, 51
Cox, Oddie 109–110
Cox, O.G. 110
Coxe, Franklin **154**
Coxes School **154**, 170
Coyer, Vincent **iv**
Crab Creek township (Henderson County) 70, 78
Craigmont Elementary School (Buncombe County) 225
Cranberry, North Carolina 43
Crasson, Hannah 19
Craven, J. Braxton 51
Credle, William F. 23, 120, 130, 143, 147, 151, 154, 204
Cresswell, Henry "Tippy" 95
Creston School 169
Creven and Kendall (Wilkes County) 212
The Crime of Malachia Hayden: Justice and Racial Identity in a Blue Ridge Community 229
Crisp, Will, Jr. 197
Cromer, David 60
Crosby, Zenobia 190
Crossnore School (Avery County) 113
Crowder, H.B. 184
Crown and Scepter Club 214, 215
Crum, Mable 65
Crump, Linwood 127, 226
Crump, Lucille 226
Crumpler Elementary School (Ashe County) 149, 165
Crumpler Institute (Ashe County) 169
Cullars, Charlie 93
Culpepper, Linda 130
Cundiff, E.L. "Emmett Leroy" 207–208
Cunningham, Mary Lou 103
Cunningham, Tony 187
Curryville, Georgia 237
Curtis, Nancy C. 162
Curtis, Zeb F. 80

D. Hyden Ramsey Library 128
Daily, Ruben J. 49, 50, 56, 57, 58, 60
Dalton, Charles 211
Damerson, E.P. 202
Danbury School (Stokes County) 171
Daniels, J.C. 49, 127, 129
Daniels, Lillian 127

Daniels, Virginia 64
Darby School (Wilkes County) 171
Darity, Aden Randall 131
Darity, Charles 132
Darity, Elizabeth Smith 131
Darity, Henry 101
Darity, William A. 69, 131, 181–182, 186–187
Daugherty, Charles **77**
Daugherty, Inez **77**
Davidson, Sallie Ledbetter 136
Davidson, Samuel 27
Davie County 33
Davis, Audrey 131, 132
Davis, Ben 49
Davis, Clyde, Jr. 188
Davis, Frank 60
Davis, George E. 23, 120, 121, 223
Davis, Inez 87
Davis, Col. John 68
Davis, John H. 202–204
Davis, Miss L.C. 88
Davis, Lenwood G. 125
Davis, Ralph H. 206, 209, 214, 218
Davis, Roy W. 196–197
Davis, Serepta Merritt 68
Davis Plan 202–204
Dawson, William Levi 237, 238
Day, Richard E. 43–44
Deal, Rev. John A. 141, 142
de Ayllón, Lucas Vásquez 28
Dendy, Reverend 108
Dennis, Elma R. 144, 148
Dennis, Mrs. (Jeanes Supervisor) 99
De Paul, Sister 96
de Soto, Hernando 28
DeVane, M.L. 214
Deveny, Charles 212
Dickerson, Ann Coleman 40
Dickson (Dixon), Isaac 74–75, 77, **81**, 89
Dill, Beatrice 134
Dillard, James H. 80–81
Dillingham, Linda Dale 50
Dillingham, Woodrow 112
Dirksen, Everett 40–41
Dixon, E.M. 75
Dixon, Rev. E.W. 133
Dixon, Sam 49
Dobbins, Daisy 87
Dobbins, Jean 59
Doggetts Grove School (Rutherford County) 99, 171
Dole, Alsie B. 22
Dorn, James 46
Dorn, Robert 96–97
Dougherty, B.B. 94
Dowdy, Lewis C. 109
Downs, Daisy 134
Drake, Francis 27
Dresslar, Fletcher B. 117, 118
Drexel School (Burke County) 169
Dry Hollow School (Stokes County) 171
Drysdale, Bruce 184, 185
Du Bois, W.E.B. 10, 96, 116, 158–159, 175
Dunbar, Paul Lawrence 128

Dunbar Elementary School (Rutherford County) **204**, 211–212
Duck, W.O. 59
Duckett, A.I. 87
Dudley, D.W. 129
Duke University 166
Dula, Stacy 218–219
Dulatown, North Carolina 165, 218
Dulatown School (Caldwell County) 169
Dunbar, Paul Lawrence 211
Dunbar Elementary School (Rutherford County) 211, 212
Duncan, Joseph C. 211
Duncan, S.E. 200, 219
Duncan Creek School (Rutherford County) 171
du Pont, Pierre S. 117
Durante, Spencer E. 182, 187
Dusenbury, Charles B. 73–74
Dusenbury, Paul **81**, 197
Dysartsville, North Carolina 153
Dysartsville School (McDowell County) 170

East, Rev. Sophia Joyce 227
East, Vicky **151**
East Flat Rock, North Carolina 165
East Flat Rock Colored School (Henderson County) 101, 130–136, **135**, 170, 186
East Hickory School 59
East Yancey High School 58
Eastern Woodland Tribes 27
Eberhardt, Ms. W.H. 216
Ecusta Corporation 228
Edelin, J.R. 206, 215
Edington, Arthur 92
Edison, Thomas 238
Edmund Embury School (Polk County) 60, 155, 156, 212
Edneyville, North Carolina 100, 132, 165, 193
Edneyville Colored School (Henderson County) 100–101, **101**, 170
Edneyville Township (Henderson County) 70, 78
Education in Buncombe County 1793–1965 49
Edwards, Hannah Logan 53–54, 133
Eggleston, Wilbur 214
Elementary and Secondary Education Act [ESEA], Titles I, II, and III 59
Elk Consolidated School (Avery County) 95, 149
Elk Creek Township (Watauga County) 94
Elk Park, North Carolina 22, 216
Elk Park Academy (Avery County) 165, 169
Elk Park High School (Avery County) 169, 216
Elkin School (Surry County) 171
Ellenboro, North Carolina 211
Eller, C.B. 208
Emancipation Day (January 1) 99

Emancipation Proclamation (1862 and 1863) 11, 19, 68
Embler, Mrs. W.C. 112
Embury, Edmund 155
Embury School *see* Edmund Embury School
Emory, Flossie 113
Enforcement Act of 1870 14
Enforcement Act of 1871 14
England, Emma S. **141**
English Brothers Shoe Shop 227
Ennice, North Carolina 97
Enon School (Yadkin County) 172
Ensley, Guy 112
Episcopalian Parish Schools 21
Epps, Adella L. **102**
Epps, Harold 56
Ervin, Phillip M. 59
Erwin, C.F. 214
Erwin, Clyde A. 163, 172, 173, 186, 195, 200
Erwin, H.E. 134
Erwin, Richard 196, 197
Erwin, Richard Cannon 218
Erwin, Phillip M. 59
Erwin High School 51
Etowah, North Carolina 132
Etowah Elementary School **54**, 132
Evans, Rosalind Rivers 55
Everett Farm School **140**
Everyday Foods 181

Fabrics & Dress 181
Fain's Thrift Store 48
Fairclough, Adam 3
Fairview Elementary School 51
Featherstone, Sunny **77**
Federal Writers' Project 18
Felder, Nathaniel 91
"The Fellowship of Love" 231
Ferguson, G.H. 23, 160–161, 196
Ferree, Max F. 63
Few, Janie 92
Fifteenth Amendment 14, 20
Fisher, Catherine Cowan 197
Fisk University 126, 136, 152, 237
Fisk University Rosenwald Database 126, 136, 143
Fitzsimmons, Frank L. 68
Flanagan, J.H. 183, 185
Flat Rock, North Carolina 70
Flat Rock Junior High School (Henderson County) 225
Fleming, Hilliard 226
Fleming, Mrs. I.R. 206
Fleming, Sgt. J.E. 48
Fleming, John E. 48, 226
Fleming, Dr. Leon H. 231
Flemming, Oliver W. 209
Folk, Ottie M. 216
Ford, Edna 91
Ford, Hester 75
Forest, Alma 199
Forest City, North Carolina 100, 211
Forney, Allie 218
Forney, Clyde 198
Forsyth County 33

Index

Fortune, Regina **89**
Fortune, Ruby 136
Foster, H.B. 189
Foster, Jack 125
Foster, J.M. 53
Foster, J.W. 125–126
Foules, Mary 70
Foulke, Stewart B. 134
Fourteenth Amendment 14, 20
Fourth Circuit Court of Appeals 43
Fowler, Annie 103, 135
Foxfire 5 142, 143
Foxfire 8 142–143
Francisco School (Stokes County) 171
Franklin, North Carolina 140, 141
Franklin, Virginia 238
The Franklin Press 140
Franklin School (Caldwell County) 169
Franks, Mr. 148
Frazier, Charles 30
Frazier, W.W. 141
Frederick Douglass 67
Freedman High School 170, 172, 206, 209, 210, 214, 216, 218–219
Freedman High School Herald 215
Freedman High Student Handbook 214–215
Freedmen's Bureau 19, 74, 226
Freeman, Gladys Russell 100–102, 193
Freeman, Ora Mae 191
Freeze, Gary 72, 157, 193
French Broad River 24, 29
Friends Around the World 155
Friends Here and Away 155
Friends Schools 21
Fullwood, Harlow **174**, 176, 226
Furnan Miller Store 155
Future Business Leaders of America 215
Future Teachers of America 188

Gaines, Henry 112
Gaines, Leo 47
Gainesville, Georgia 147
Gallegher, Patrick 188
Gallego, Agnes Knuckles **86**
Gambill-Gwyn, Charity C. 228
Gap Civil Elementary School (Alleghany County) 97, 169
Garrett, Alice 96
Gash, Sam 52
Gash, Thelma 53
Gaston, Rose Agnes 98
Gaston County 205
General Education Board 136–137, 161
General Electric Company 227
Georgia 26, 36, 37, 68
G.I. Outlet Store 48
Gibbs, James O. 206
Gibson Town 209
Gilliam, John 129
Gilliam, Lonnie 97
The Girl and Her Home 181
Glade Creek Elementary School (Alleghany County) 169

Glade Creek School (Transylvania County) 171
Glade Elementary School (McDowell County) 170
Glade Valley, North Carolina 97
Glassy Mountain 70
Glen Alpine 169
Glenn, Luvenia 212
Godehn, Sally 231
Godwin v Johnston County Board of Education 41
Goldfield, D.R. 12
Good Shepherd Episcopal Church (Polk County) 212
Good Shepherd Mission School (Polk County) 156, 212
Goolsby, Catherine **151**
Goss, John 191, 192, 193
Gourlay, Bruce 51
Governor's Special Advisory Committee on Education 36, 37
Graham, Charles 194
Graham County 33, 63, 146, 165–166, 168
Grahamtown High School (Rutherford County) 100, 171, 172, 206, 210–211, 228
Grahamtown School (Rutherford County) 100, 171, 172, **203**, 206, 210–211
Grandfather Mountain 29
Grandview Memorial Funeral Home 228
Granite Falls School (Caldwell County) 169
Grant, Rev. Wesley, Sr. 48
Gray, T.C. 145
Gray, Thomas **154**
Great Depression 101
Great Smoky Mountains 103
The Greatest Sports Heroes of the Stephens-Lee Bears 176
Green, Otis 80
Green, Ronald 145, 174
Green, W.H. 212, 216
Green, William 190
Green River Plantation **154**
Green River Township (Henderson County) 70, 78
Greene, Alexander 188
Greene, Joe 52
Greene, W.H. 155
Greenlee, Margaret 194
Greensboro, North Carolina 37
Greenwood, Gordon 46, 49
Gregory, John 53
Grey Eagle 75
Griffin, Geraldine 59
Griffin, Ms. H. 104
Griffin, Vickie Louise 59
Griffin, W.P. 51
Griffith, Celesta 82
Griffith, John B. 82
Griffith, Kay Francis **224**
Griffith, Stevie **224**
Griffith v. Robinson 58
Grimes, Jeffrey 24
Grimes, Lewis 24
Grimes, Marjorie 210

Gross, Joanna **77**
Gudger, H.A. 74
Gudger, Lindsey M. 88, 200
Guerrard, A.R. 130
Gunn, Mable 182

Hairston, Cora **151**
Hairston, John Neal **151**
Halback, Jackson 70
Hall, J. Fred 49
Halls, Sheriff J.Z. 75
Hamilton, John 50
Hampton Institute 238, 239
Hanchett, Thomas 123, 153, 157, 213
Handi-Skills, Inc. 64
handwriting 84, **85**
Hannon, H.H. 155
Hannon, Rachel 212
Hannon, Ruth 212
Hansberry, Mary E. (Mary H. Cook) **102**, 131
Happy Hollow (Plains) School 150, 172
Happy Land 67
Happy Plains High School (Alexander County) 172, 216–217
Happy Plains School (Alexander County) 169
Harbison Agricultural Institute 227
Harper Town School (Caldwell County) 169
Hardin, Hattie **89**
Hardin, Jim 93
Harlem Globetrotters **12**, 176
Harnett County 19
Harper, Charlotte 135
Harper, Ella Mae 125, 126, 128
Harpertown, North Carolina 165
Harris, Hazel 87
Hartford Seminary (Connecticut) 228
Hartsoe, Drusilla S. 59, 157
Haw Creek Elementary School (Buncombe County) 49–50, 51
Hawkins, W.H. 195
Hayden, Malachia 229–230
Hayes, John 231
Hayes, Roland 237
Hayesville, North Carolina 144
Hayesville Colored School (Clay County) 144, 170
Hayesville High School (Clay County) 145
Haynes, Elizabeth 103
Haywood, Carlotta F. 217
Haywood County 29, 33, 121, 165, 166, 168, 203, 206, 209
Hazard, Charity 137
Hemphill, William, Jr. 228–229
Hemphill, William, Sr. 61, 228–229
Henderson, Houston 113
Henderson, Irma 129
Henderson County 27, 28, 33, 36, 68, 70, 71, 130–136, 165, 166, 168, 175, 193, 231
Henderson County's Black Research History Committee 69, 70

Henderson County's Hall of Fame for Educators 95
Hendersonville, North Carolina 26, 31, 33, 70, 71, 73, 78
Hendersonville Board of Education 71
Hendersonville City Schools 53
Hendersonville Colored High School 170, 187
Hendersonville Graded School 78
Hendersonville High School 52, 53, 55, 185
Henkel Boarding House 98
Hennesse, Emory H. 93–94
Henrietta, North Carolina 99, 211
Henrietta School (Rutherford County) 99, 171
Henry, Curtis 198
Henry, George 149
Henry, Rowe 218
Hensley, Guy 112
Hensley, Lee 112
Henson, Matthew 236
Herbert, W.M. 144
Herring, Lucy S. 89, 129, 223–224, 230, 231
Hickerson, J.M. 97
Hickory, North Carolina 73, 98, 99
Hickory High School 59
Hicks, Lillie 111
Hicks, Paul 111
Hicks, Pearl 113
Hicks, Ruby 111
Higgins School (Yancey County) 82, 104
Hill, Sally 100, 101
Hill, Seldon 133
Hill, W.R. 119
Hill Street 79, 80
Hill Street School (Asheville) 57, *77*, 79, 80, *81*, 83, *85*, 87–88, 104, *105*, 169
The Hilltop Online 136
History and Knowing Who We Are 10
"A History of Negro Education in Wilkes County, NC" 215
History of Surry County 222
"Hobbit effect" 221
Holesclaw, Mark 93
Hollingsworth, J.G. 222
The Home Economics Omnibus 181
Home Guards 31
Home Makers Club 88
Honeycutt, A.W. 71
Hood, J.W. (James Walker) 21
Hooper's Creek Township (Henderson County) 70, 78
Hope and Dignity: Older Black Women of the South 227
Hopper, William Bessman "Bess" 143
Horn, Amanda 108, 109
Horn, Douglas 91
Horn, Haywood 91
Horne, D.A. 195, 197
Horner Institute of Fine Arts 238
Horse Shoe, North Carolina 132, 165

Horton, John "Tommy" *224*
Horton, Phin 48
Hot Springs School (Madison County) 170
Howard University 71
Howell, Effley 60
Howell, Victoria 219
Howze, Father Joseph L. 96
Hoyt, Mrs. F.S. 177
Hudgens, J.A. 134
Hudgins, Carter 209
Hudgins High School (McDowell County) 167, 170, 193, 216, 218, 228
Hudgins School (McDowell County) 82, 167, 170, 193–198, 200, 208
Hudlin Gap 228
Hudson, Mamie 92
Hudson, Mrs. 92
Hudson School (Stanly County) 95
Hughes, Langston 128
Hughes, Sherick A. 3, 5
Humarian Society 218
Humphrey, Hubert 40–41
Hunter, Alberta C. 60
Hunter, J.E. 200
Huntersville School (Yadkin County) 172
Hurmence, Belinda 18
Hutchens, A.J. 162

industrial education 96, 117, 118, 141, 158, 161, 162, 164, 175, 177, 178, 212, 213
Inez, Sister Mary 39
Ingram, Milton J., Sr. 212–213, 215
Integration 35–66, 129
Iowa Silent Reading Test 147
Iowa State College 238
Isaac Dickson Elementary School
Israel Bethel Church 19
Ivins, R.M. 71
Ivy Township (Buncombe County) 111

Jackson, Cora J. 82
Jackson, Della 156
Jackson, George 191
Jackson, John Vance *224*
Jackson, Lola M. 154
Jackson, Lorraine 186
Jackson, Mary 127
Jackson, Mildred 194
Jackson, Reba 208, 227
Jackson County 21, 33, 121, 151, 168, 173, 202–204, 219
Jackson County Consolidated School 170, 203–204, *201*
Jackson County Journal 14
Jacobs, Rabbi Robert P.
James, C.U. 49, 231
James, Wylma 129
James H. McDuffie Award 228
Jamison, Mary 87
Jaspin, Elliot 63, 191
Jeanes Fund 19, 81, 88, 99
Jeanes Supervisor 19, 208, 219, 235
Jeans, Anna T. 88
Jena 6 231

Jenkins, Ada 150
Jenkins, Rev. Albert 150
Jenkins, Lorna 194
Jenkins, Peter 148
Jensen, Henry 39
Jim Crow 12, 24, *106*, 153, 158
Jimerson, Lorna 221
J.J. Jones High School (Surry County) 213, 216, 219
J.J. Jones School (Surry County) 60, 213, 219
John F. Slater Fund 81, 116, 161
Johnson, Andrew 20
Johnson, Carl 33
Johnson, Carrie 98
Johnson, Henry 236
Johnson, Isaac 19
Johnson, James W. 128
Johnson, Lyndon B. 41
Johnson, Margaret 218
Johnson, Mayme E. 91
Johnson, Myrtle 218
Johnson C. Smith University 193, 209, 223, 226; *see also* Biddle University
Johnson School (Raleigh) 21
Johnstone, Wilkie Carpenter 96
Jolly Number Tales 155
Jones, Agnes 127
Jones, Annie Louise 194
Jones, Geraldine I. 217
Jones, Gertrude Dixon 90
Jones, Mrs. I.C. 214
Jones, J.J. 213
Jones, John 212
Jones, Lemuel 52
Jones, Leonidas H. 206, 213
Jones, Lori 148
Jones, Mary 131
Jones, Milnor 212
Jones, Monnie 108, 109, 127
Jones, Rosa LaPearl 109
Jones, Judge T.A. 79
Jones Temple AM.E. Zion Church 218
Jonesborough, Tennessee 93
Jonesville School (Yadkin County) 172
Jordan, Mr. 148
Jordon, Taft 99
Jowers, Alberta 180
Joyce, Sally *151*
Joyner, Albert 42
Joyner, J. (James)Y. 11, 23, 119
Joyner, W.T. 37
Justice, Hubert D. 57

Kansas City Symphony Orchestra 238
Kearns, Mrs. Louis 104
Keaton, Bob *200*
Kebe, Janet Battle 91
Keller, Lillian O. 225
Kelly, Elizabeth 143
Kemmer, Margaret 214
Kennedy, James T. 124, 140–143
Kennedy, John F. 41
Kepler, S.R. 74, 75
Kilgore, Jeanetta Scott 210

Kilgore, Thomas, Jr. 99–100, 210
Kilpatrick, Byrdia 97
Kincaid, Gwyn 52, 148, 149
Kincaid, Pat 52, 148, 149
Kincaid, Sadie Tucker 218
King, Martin Luther, Jr. 55
King, Mary Birdelle *154*, 219
King, Mentha 212
King, Mitchell 30–31
King, Rev. William 69
King, William Judson 68, 69
Kingdom of the Happy Land 68–69
Kingknob School (Yadkin County) 172
Kings Creek School 169
Kings Mountain City Board of Education 63
Kistler Academy 226
Korean Conflict (War) 226
Kornegay, A.D. 185
Ku Klux Klan 72

Lail, Marvin 39
Lake, Bennie *12*, 176
Land of the Sky Regional Council 227
Larabee, N.C. 172–173
Lassiter, Delores 179, 225
Laughlin, Daniel 218
Laughter, James (Jim) L. 52–53
Laurel Springs, North Carolina 97
Lawndale School (Cleveland County) 95
Lawrence, M. Ruth 72–73, 219
Leake, A. Eldridge 59
Leandro v. State of North Carolina (1997) 232
Ledbetter, Grace 53
Lee, Hester 175
Lee, Rita Hendrick *81*, 89
Lee, Walter S. 80, *81*, 175
Lee H. Edwards High School 43, 47
Leek, Mark 145
Leiceister Colored School (Buncombe County) 64
Leicester Elementary School 51, 169
The Lengthening Shadow of Slavery 226
Lennon, Madison "Doc" 176
Lenoir, Viola 143
Lenoir, North Carolina 26, 33, 165, 208, 218
Lenoir Graded School Trustees 209
Lenoir News 218
Lenoir News-Topic 210
Lenoir School, Caldwell County 95
Lewis, Curtis 215
Lewis, Ethel *151*
Lewis, T.C. 129
Lincoln Academy 72, 95, 96, 163, 172, 205
Lincoln Heights High School (Wilkes County) 97, *98*, 171, 172, 206, 210, 215, 219
Lincoln Heights School (Wilkes County) 341
Lincoln Park School (Yancey County) 57, 82

Linda Brown v. the Board of Education of Topeka, Kansas 25, 38, 55
Linville Falls 29
Lipe, Katherine 126
Lipscombe, E.H. 75
Little Richmond School (Surry County) 171
Littlejohn, Emma 101
Littlejohn, Frances 100
Littlejohn, Richard 100
Littrell, Frankie T. 112
Litwack, Leon F. 11–12, 13
Livingston, H.C. 53
Livingstone College 175
Livingstone Street School (Asheville) 48, 51, 91–92, 169
Lloyd, Charley 144
Lloyd, Jerry 146
Locust Grove School (Stokes County) 171
Logan, Fred 61, 198
Logan, Henry 9, *12*, 14, 39–40, 64–65, 176, 229
Logan, Hubert 194
Logan, Madge 198
Logan, W.E. 125
London School (Stokes County) *151*
Long, Dwight 211
Long, Hollis M. 213–214
Long, R.L. 145
"The Long, Long Road" 57
Long Ridge School 83, 136–140, *137*, 198–199, 225
Lord, Margery 92
Lord, William H. 80
Louisville Presbyterian Seminary 228
Love, Hattie 90
Love, Lillie A. 199
Love Joy Institute (Polk County) 156; *see also* Lovejoy Academy
Lovejoy Academy (Saluda, North Carolina) 96; *see also* Love Joy Institute
Lovell, John 60
Lowry, Carmen 178
Loy, Leona 156
Lucas, Gwendolyn (Gwen) Simmons 55, 225, 227
Lucy S. Herring Elementary School (Asheville) 48, 89
Lutz, J.D. 53
Lyda, Isaac 110
Lynch, Artie 134
Lynch, Clifford 103
Lytle, Gertrude *77*
Lytle, Lee Roy *77*
Lytle, Rodney *106*

Mabry, G. Woodford 162
Macon County 27, 33, 140–143, *141*, 165, 167, 168, 173, 202–204, 219
Maddelena, Daniel 44
Madison, James 229
Madison County 21, 33, 57, 136–140, 163, 165, 167, 168, 175
Madison County Board of Education 58

Maiden School (Catawba County) 157
Malawi, Africa 226
Malden, West Virginia 238
Maney, Mary Alice 113
Maney Branch 111
Manley, Albert E. *174*, 175
Maple Grove School 169
Maples, Willie 176
Marable, John 52, 187, 188, 199
Marion, North Carolina 26, 153, *194*, 229
Marion Board of Alderman 199–200
Marion City Board of Education 62, 193, 194, 195, 197
Marion City Board of Trustees 195, 199–200
Marion City Council 227
Marion Graded School 152
Marion High School 58
Marion Number 2 School 152
Marion Progress 152, 153
Markham Road (Tryon) 155
Marlow, Glen C. 53
Mars Hill College 136, 139–140, 163
Mars Hill Colored School 136, *137*, 170
Mars Hill School (Caldwell County) 170
Mars Hill School (Madison County) 136, *137*, 170
Marshall Elementary School 138
Martin, Beulah *141*
Martin, Billy 58, 64, 227
Martin, Bishop 194
Martin, Charles 198
Martin, Earl H. 189–190
Martin, Harry C. 47–48
Martin, Mamie 87
Massagee, B.B. 135–136
Massive Resistance 37
Mathes, Zetta 94
Matzoliger, Jan 236
Mauldin, C.H. 144
Mauldin, Charles 144
McAdams, Henry 148
McAlpine School (Burke County) 169
McArath, Margarite Dixon 109
McCallum, B.T. 216
McClary, Kathleen J. 217
McClelland, Isaac 148
McClelland, Lucy 148
McClelland, Texana 148
McClure, T.M. 144
McCorkle, Mae 133
McCorkle, Oliver W.H. 176, 206–207
McCormick Baseball Field 128
McCullough, David 10
McDowell, Anne 59
McDowell, Betty 59
McDowell, Mrs. Doskey Anderson 140
McDowell, Henry C. 172–173
McDowell, James 47
McDowell, Stanley 133
McDowell County Board of Commissioners 195

McDowell County Board of Education 42, 152, 199–200
McElrathe Chapel School (Burke County) 157
McFeely, William S. 67
McGlamery, Ora K. 145
McGlamery, R.L. 145
McGough, Morris L. 50
McIlwean, Walter 52
McIntosh, Nettie M. 218
McIver, Marie 235
McKee, Gertrude 204
McKissick, Floyd *174*
McKissick, G.E. 155
McMullan, Harry 36
McNair, Robert E. 38
Meadows, Ardell 217
Means, Blanche Ray 142
Mebane, Bill 48
Melton, N.A. 211
Melungeon 24
Melvin Hill School (Polk County) 156, 170
Mennonite Church 96
Metropolitan Achievement Tests 147
Metts, Van 192
Metz, Anna B. 111
Metzger, Harrison 68, 69
Meyer, O.A. 183, 185
Michael, J.H. (John Henry) 80, *81*, 87–88, 121–122, 207, 231
Michael, L.B. 88
Michael, Otis B. 97
Mill Springs School, Polk County 95
Millard, David T. 74, 75
Miller, Adele Marie 217
Miller, Helen Smith 148
Miller, James 88
Miller, John 166
Miller, Leonard P. 49
Miller, N.A. 60
Mills, Eleanor 27
Mills, Ethel Kennedy 88, 124, *140*, 140–141, 231
Mills, George 31
Mills, Joe 189
Mills, Joe L. 102–103
Mills, Joyce see Mills, Mary Joyce
Mills, Mary Joyce 181, 182, 187, 198–199, 214, 218
Mills, Sam 53, 184, 185, 199, 227–228
Mills, William 27
Mills River Township (Henderson County) 70, 78
Mims, Ernest 68
Mims, Evans K. 182
Mims, Mary Valentine (Mary V. Mims) 231
The Mind of the South 18
Mission School (Burke County) 169
Mitchell, J.T. 214
Mitchell, Monte 207
Mitchell, Samuel S. 42, 56
Mitchell County 21, 33, 72–73, 117, 165, 168, 191–193, 200

Mitchum, Earl 103
Mitchum, George 188
Mitchum, Shag 52
Mitchum, Willie 52
Montgomery, Luella 68–69
Montgomery, Robert 68–69
Montgomery, Wayne 46
Moore, Charles H. 119–120
Moore, Clarence L. 176
Moore, E.T. 59
Moore, Webb 94
Moorehead, Clarence *77*
Morehouse College 99
Morgan, J.W. 134
Morgan, William H. 166
Morganton, North Carolina 26, 33, 73
Morganton School 169
Morris, Frieda 179
Morris, Richard 95
Morris, William C. 47
Morrison, Cameron 192
Morristown, Tennessee 146, 147
Morrow, J.C. 182
Moser School 150
Moses, A.C. 204
Moses, Maryam I. 17–18
Moton, Robert Russa 238–239
Mount Airy Colored School (Surry County) 60, 150, 213, 217, 227
Mount Ararat (Surry County) 29, 149–150
Mount Guyot 29
Mount Herman Academy (Brevard) 96
Mount Jefferson 29
Mt. Mitchell 29
Mt. Moriah Baptist Church (Marion) 201
Mount Olive Baptist Church (Chicago) 236
Mountain Street School (Asheville) 48, 169
Mountain View School (McDowell County) 42, 58, 64, 208, 209, 217–218, 228
Moye, Helen Janet 197
Mud Creek Missionary Baptist Church (Henderson County) 130
Mullen, Kirsten 70
Murphy, North Carolina 145
Murphy City Schools 145, 146
My Folks Don't Want Me to Talk about Slavery 18
Myrdal, Gunnar 9

Nancy Susan Reynolds Award 60, 228
Nanney, P.D. 212
National Afro-American Museum and Cultural Center 227
National Association for the Advancement of Colored People (NAACP) 57, 58, 60, 133, 178, 222, 226, 230
National Education Association 129
National Education Association's Committee on Schoolhouse Planning and Construction 119
National Honor Society 48, 49, 188
National Trust for Historic Preservation 115
National Underground Railroad Freedom Center 227
National Youth Administration 172–173
Neal, Bertha M. 206, 210, 216
Necker, Frederick 96
Negro Consolidated School (Jackson County) 216
"Negro Education in North Carolina" 164
"Negro Folk Symphony" 237
The Negro Rural School and Its Relation to the Community 116–117
Neighborhood Youth Corps 59
Neill, John Wesley 71
Neufeld, Rob 90
New Deal Program 72, 98, 173, 179
New England Conservatory of Music 237
New Era Institutes 130
New Homemakers of America 215
New Hope School (Rutherford County) 119, 171, 172, 206, 211, 216
New Hope School (Macon County) 143
New House Elementary School (Cleveland County) 94
The New Jim Crow: Mass Incarceration of Colorblindness 233
New River 29
"New School Buildings, State of Delaware" 117
New York City 146, 237
New York Conservatory of Music 237
New York Times 57
Newbold, N.C. 23, 81, 88, 119, 122, 162, 163, 164–165, 166, 167, 172, 173, 197, 202, 207, 208, 222
Newkirk, Van R. 193
Newsome, Bessie 194
Newton, Paul 185
Newton, North Carolina 19, 72, 213
Newton Elementary School 43, 44
Newton Enterprise 215
Nicely, Allen 146
Nicely, B.M. 145
Nicely, Moody 144, 149
1964 Report to the United States Civil Rights Commission 58
1924 Community School Plans, Bulletin No. 3 118
Ning, Jimmy 39
Ninth Avenue School 52, 53, *54*, 55, 72, 101, *102*, 103, 135, 163, 179–190, *189*, 198–199, 219
Noble, C.S., Jr. 151
Nolichucky River 29
Norman, Shelia McBee 230
North Carolina 68
North Carolina Agricultural and

Technical College (A&T) 109–110, 148, 208
North Carolina Bar Association 37
North Carolina Board of Education 151
North Carolina Central University 186
North Carolina Division of Vocational Education 216
North Carolina Human Relations Convention, 2008 232
North Carolina Little Symphony Orchestra 212
North Carolina School Survey Panel's Report for Asheville and Buncombe County (1949) 82
North Carolina: Short-Term Suspensions; Long-Term Consequences; Real-Life Solutions 232
North Carolina Sports Hall of Fame 229
North Cove, North Carolina 229
North Wilkesboro, North Carolina 97
North Wilkesboro School 172
North Wilkesboro School Board 63
Northcott, J.G. 50
Northup, W.B. 80
Northwestern Regional Library 228

Oak Crest School (Yancey County) 56–57, 83
Oakland 68
Obama, Barack 10, 65
O'Brien, P.H. 192
Odd Fellows' Lodge 209
Old Fort, North Carolina 36, 41, 152, 153, 200–203, **200**
Old Fort Number 1 School 152
Old Fort Number 2 School 152
Old Fort Number 3 School 152
Old Fort Schools (McDowell County) 152, 170, **200**
Olive Hill School (Burke County) 165, 172, 205–206, 208, 218, 226–227
Oliver, Pearl Jordan 82, 91
Opportunity Corporation of Madison-Buncombe Counties 51, 64
Orangeburg massacre 38
Owen, William 184
Owen High School 51
Owens, Bill 110
Owens, Franklyn 126–127, 128, 129
Owens, M. Grace 139, 199
Owens, Rev. M.O. 197
Owl and Spade 39

Padgett, Max 212
Page, Steve 111
Parent-Teacher Association 92, 108, 118, 127–128, 155, 183, 194, 217, 219
Parham, Regina Brown 97
Parker, John J. 43
Parker, Juinata **224**
Parks Grove School (Wilkes County) 171

Paskal, Mrs. 97
Patrick County, Virginia 60
Patterson, Albert 218
Patterson, Sarah 218
Patton, George B. 42–43
Patton, Sadie Smathers 68
Patton, Capt. T.W. 79
Payne, Alonzo 188
Payne, Betty 132
Payne, Carlos 54
Payne, Curtis 54
Payne, Guy 131–132, 133
Payne, G.W. 125
Payne, Laurel Bell 100
Payne, Libby Viola 53, 54, 100, 101
Payne, M.H. 145
Payne, Mrs. R. Beatty 129
Payne, W.T. 126
Pea Ridge School 153–154, **154**, 156, 170
Peabody Fund 77
Peabody University 120
Peace Corps 226
Pead, John F. 152
Pearsall, Thomas J. 36
Pearsall Committee 36–37
Pearsall Plan 36–37, 40, 41, 49
Pearson, Edward 91
Pearson, E.W. 89, 133, 137
Pearson, Leatrice Roberts 94, 210–211, 228
Pearson, Phairlever 207, 213, 215
Pearson, Richmond 74
Pease, L.M. 177
Pee Dee River 28
Penley, James 47
Pennell, Clark 45, 47
Perdue, Theda 28
Philadelphia Orchestra 237
Phillips, Theophilus Lacy 210
Phillips, Vernon 218
Pierceson, Gertrude 148
Pierceson, Henry 148
Pigeon Street School (Haywood County) 206–207
Pilgrim, James 53, 185, 189, 193
Pilot Mountain 29
Pilot Mountain School (Surry County) 171
Pine Hall School (Stokes County) 171
Pine Swamp School (Ashe County) 169
Piney Creek, North Carolina 97
Pinnacle School (Stokes County) 171
Pipitone, John 46
Pisgah School (Surry County) 171
Plaisted, Mabel 212
Pleasant Hill Baptist Church 97
Plemmons, Jerry M. 51
Plemmons, W.H. 74
Plessy v. Ferguson 12, 14, 22, 25, 35, 223
Plumtree, North Carolina 43
Polk Central High School 60
Polk County 59–60, 62–63, 153–156, 165, 166, 168, 212, 216, 225–226

Polk County Board of Education 154
Polk County Historical Association 155, 156
Ponder, Zeno 59, 199
Pool, Parker 18
Possum Hollow (Henderson County) 69
Poteat, Mary 153
Potts, Ed 133, 134
Potts, Fred 133, 134
Potts, George 70, 130
Potts, Hortense 53, 69, 131, 133, 217
Potts, John Foster 131, **135**, 142, 231
Prathers Creek School 169
Pre-induction Training for the War Effort 187
Presbyterian Parish Schools 21
Prestonville School (Stokes County) 171
Prince, Helen 181, 182
Prince, L.B. 53
Proctor, Barbara 225
"Progressive School Architecture" 117
Prophets, Cora 218
Prudden, Emily 22, 29, 95–96
Prudden schools 22, 95–96
Public School Law of 1907 162
"Public Secondary Education for Negroes in North Carolina" 213
Pulitzer Prize 11, 67
Pupil Assignment Act of 1955 36, 41, 49
Putnam, M. 75

Quakers 19
Quarles, Benjamin 27

Rabun Gap School (Georgia) 111, 113
Ragsdale, Ella B. 148
Raleigh, North Carolina 35, 62
Ramseur, V.C. 206, 211
Ramsey, D. Hyden 201
Ramsey, Miller, Jr. 49
Randall, Hugh 52, 52
Randolph, William F. 74, 89
Ratzell, Rev. Frank E. 231
Ray, Augusta 136
Ray, Charity 138, 139, 179, 225
Ray, Elizabeth 108
Ray, Geraldine Coone 107–109, 111
Ray, Jesse 59
Ray, John 108
Ray, McD. 77–78
Reading Circle 92
Ready, Milton 30
Reagan, Ronald 225
Reconstruction 21–22
"Red and Black in the Southern Appalachians" 28
Red Brush School (Surry County) 171
Reed, William A. 230
Reid, Paul A. 36, 112
Renfro Library, Mars Hill College 225
"A Reply to Southern Slanderers: In Re to the Nigger Question" 162

Resegregation 231–233
Resource-Use Education 73
Reynolds, A.C. 125, 126
Reynolds, A.S. 92
Reynolds, L.R. 166
Reynolds, U.S. 90
Reynolds, Welton 207
Reynolds High School (Buncombe County) 51
Reynolds School (Haywood County) 64, 170, 206, 214, 217, 218
Rhett's Mill Creek 130
Rhume, Rosa 88
Rice, John Andrew 40
Rice, Thomas Dartmouth 12
Riddle, Don 112
Ridge Elementary School (Surry County) 171, 219
Ridgeview 157
Ridgeview School (HIckory) 59, 208, 215, 216, 217
Rivers, Deborah 55
Rivers, Gary 55, 95
Rivers, Ruby 55
Roberson, T.C. 50, 51, 112, 113
Roberts, Andrew 194
Roberts, E.D. 211
Roberts, James 126
Roberts, Needham 236
Robinson, E.B. 155
Robinson, Gustava 102–103, 131
Robinson, Henry T. 92, 97, 176
Robinson, Robert 226
Robinson, W.A. 161
Robinson, Willie Knuckles 175
Robinson, W.R. 180–181
Rock Creek School (Wilkes County) 171
Rock Hill School (Burke County) 157
Rock Hill School (Glen Alpine) 169
Rockefeller, John D. 136–137
Rogers, Edna 209
Rogers, Neal 145
Rogers, W.J. 94
Roland, Clifton 103–104
Roland, Patricia (Mrs. Clifton) 104
Roland, William 45, 58, 59
Ronda School (Wilkes County) 172
Roosevelt, Franklin Delano 115
Rosenwald, Julius 19, 114, 120, 122, 223
Rosenwald Fund 23, 99, 120, 121, 126, 130, 136, 144, 149, 150, 153, 154, 159, *203*, 212
Rosenwald School (Brevard) 38, *135*, *140*, 171, 216
Rosenwald School (Glen Alpine) 169
Rosenwald School (Marion) *194*
Rosenwald School (Polk County) 154, 156, 170
Rosenwald School (Swain County) *151*, 171
Rosenwald School (Wilkes County) 157
Rosenwald schools 123–159
Rosman, North Carolina 61, 230
Ross, Alma 194

Rouse, Odell Mitchum 94–95, 186
Rusher, James Thomas 192–193
Russell, Calvin 100
Russell, Dorothy 108
Russell, Mary Couch 69
Russell, Mrs. Robert 49
Russo, Denise Byrd 191–192
Rutherford, Melzo 198
Rutherford County 15, 21, 30, 33, 99–100, 166, 168, 170–171, 172, 208, 210–212
Rutherford County Middle School 230
Rutherfordton, North Carolina 26, 73, 119

St. Anthony of Padua School 96–97
St. Augustine's School 163
St. Cyprian's Church and Mission School (Macon County) 141, 142, 143
St. George's Episcopal Church (New York) 237
St. Johns School (Rutherford County) 170
St. Matthias Episcopal Church (Asheville) 142
St. Paul School (Polk County) 156
Salem Orphanage and School (Avery County) 22
Sapp, J.T. "James Thaddeus" 104, *105*, 107, 231
School Law of 1869 70
School Law of West Virginia 173
Scott, Jacqueline 129
Scott, Jeannetta Miriam (Kilgore) 99, 210
Scott, Robert W. 46
Scott, Father Ronald 96, 97
Seabrook, Pauline 127
Seawell, A.A.F. 173
Sellars, E.T. 213
separate but equal 25, 71, 73, 123, 140, 198
A Servant's Journey 99
Settlemyre, Margaret 218
Setzer, G.W. 157
Sevier County, Tennessee 29
Sewell, Shirley 136
Seymour, John S. 166
S.H. Kress and Co. 48
Sharpsburg 31
Shaw, Eula 230
Shaw University 130, 186, 228
Sherrill, O.L. 45, 46
Sherward, Ann 129
Shiloh 125, 126
Shiloh Elementary School (Buncombe County) 50, 51, 60, 126–130, 169
Shiloh School (Glen Alpine) 169
Shipman, Sadie 225
Shippy, Alma Lee 38–39, 65, 104–107, *106*, 225
Sholar, John 53
Shuford, E.L. 157
Shuford, Judge George A. 80
Sigmon, Ida 139
Siler, Jacob 27

Siler, Lucy 148
Simmons, Henry, Jr. 134, 227
Simmons, Israel, Jr. 132
Simmons, John J. 131, 133, 182, 227
Simmons, Oralene Graves 140
Simone, Nina (Waymon, Eunice Kathleen) 225–226
Simonton, Bob 157
Simpson, George, Jr. 218
Simpson, Ratherline 129
Simpson, Roy E. *154*
Simulton, Hannah 87
Sisk, William 194
Sitton, Lucy 54–55
Sixth Avenue School 52, 94, 103, 135, 167, 179, 184, 216
Skyland Institute (Watauga County) 95, 96
Slater, John F. 161
Slater Fund 81, 116, 161; *see also* John F. Slater Fund
Slave Codes 20
Smith, Beatrice Moore 217
Smith, Grace Gates 30
Smith, Mary 194
Smith, Dr. P.M. 72
Smith, Samuel L. 118, 119
Smith, Wiley 166
Smyre, John F. 98–99
Smyre's Charitable Institute 98
Snow Hill, North Carolina 72
Snyder, Reece 195
Society of Friends 19
Society of Necessity 133
Sorrell, Ellen 90
Sousanman, Miss 55
South Asheville Elementary School 169
South French Broad High School (Asheville) 45, 47, 48, 51
Southern Association of Schools and Colleges 91, 129, 178
Southern Railroad Company 91
Sparta, North Carolina 228
Spearman, Julian J. 206, 209, 212, 214
Spelman College *174*
Spindale, North Carolina 211
Spindale School (Rutherford County) 171
Springs, Louise 194
Spruce Pine, North Carolina 191, 192
Sputnik 57
Stalkup, Sally 142
Stanford University 175
Stanley, William H. 49, 61
Stanly County 63
Stanton, Edwin 19
State Board of Equalization 210
Steld, Herbert 218
Stephens, Edward 22, 86, 175
Stephens-Lee High School (Asheville) *12*, 15, 40, 43, 44, 47, 51, 56, 57, 64, *77*, 82, *86*, *106*, 146, 147, 163, 169, 172, 174–179, *174*, 216, 226
Stepp, John Myra 75

Stepp and Walker Store 134
Stepp Mountain 29
Steppe, N.F. 200, 201
Stevenson, Adlai 17
Stewart, Carrie 142, 143
Stillwell, Erle G. *102*, 182
Stokes, Lawrence C. 50
Stokes County 15, 30, 33, 60, 150, *151*, 167, 171, 208, 217
Stokowski, Leopold 237
Stoney Knoll School (Polk County) *154*, 156, 170
Story, Paul J. 195, 196–197
Stowe, Harriet Beecher 9
Stryker, Veda 178
Styles, Harriet 40
Suddreth, Belle 100–101
Suggs, D.C. 75
A Summer Remembered: A Memoir 226
Summerous, John 148
Summerous, Johnny T. 148
Summey, Oliver, Jr. 188
Supreme Court 12, 37
Surry County 26, 27, 30, 33, 60, 121, 149–150, 171, 172, 206, 207–208, 213, 216, 217, 227
Sutton, Charles 148
Swain County 33, 62–63, 150–151, *151*, 165, 168, 171, 203, 204, 219
Swain County Board of Education 151
Swalin, Benjamin F. 132
Swann, Hattie V. 88
Swann v. Charlotte-Mecklenburg Board of Education (1971) 224, 225
Swannanoa, North Carolina 51, 104, 231
Swannanoa Elementary School 51, 104–107, *105*, *106*, 169, 225
Swannanoa School (Buncombe County) 225
Swepson, Marvin 198
Sylva Consolidated School (Jackson County) 150, 217
Sylva County Training School (Jackson County) 167
Sylva High School for Negroes (Jackson County) 151
Sylvan Valley News 230
Sylvia Gilliland, et al., v. Buncombe County Board of Education and the School Committee of Avery's Creek 24

Taft, William Howard 230
Tamishan 226
Taylor, Herman L. 42, 56
Taylor, J.J. 110
Teamer, Maxine 129
Tennessee 26, 30
Tennessee Valley Authority 147
Tester, Ben 93
Texana School (Cherokee County) 142, 146, 147, 148–149, 170
Thankful Heritage 61
Thankful School (Wilkes County) 172

Their Highest Potential: An African American Community in the Segregated South 3
Third Creek School (Alexander County) 150
Thomas, C.V. 88
Thomas, J.W. 94
Thomas, Mrs. Mack 191
Thompson, Elsie 87
Thompson, Evelyn Scales 60, 150, 213, 227
Thompson, Henry 87
Thompson, Marie 131
Tillman, J.A. (Jacob Ayers) 155, 205–206
Titus, Julia 178
Toe River 29
Toliver, Frank A. 175
Tomberlin, R.A. 109
Transylvania County 33, 61, 73, 118, 124–125, 163, 166, 167, 168, 171, 175, 228, 230
Traphill School (Wilkes County) 172
Tried Stone Missionary Baptist Church (Asheville) 230
Trigg, Harold L. 181, 208
Trotter, J.F. 31
Tryon, North Carolina 212
Tryon, Polk County 154–155
Tryon City Board of Education 60, 154
Tryon Colored School 154, 155, 170, 212, 216
Tryon High School 170
Tryon Industrial Mission School 155
Tryon School 95, 170
Tschetter, Rev. Jacob 96
Tuckaseigee River 29
Turner, Cathy Rivers 55
Turner, Henry McNeal 19
Tuskegee Choir 237
Tuskegee Normal and Industrial Institute of Alabama (Tuskegee Institute) 71, 116, 237, 238, 239
Twitty, Monroe *154*
Twitty, Rena 212
Twitty, Watt *200*

Umstead, William B. 36
Union Grove School (Polk County) *154*, 156, 170
Union Mills School (Rutherford County) 171
University of North Carolina at Asheville 128
University of North Carolina at Chapel Hill 70, 166, 182, 186, 187
University of Tennessee 55
Up from Slavery: An Autobiography 116, 223
Uree School (Rutherford County) 170

Valentine, Mary Louise (Mary V. Mims) 199, 231
Valley Springs Elementary School 51

Vanderbilt, George 86, 125, 175
Vann, Cornelia 139
Vaughn, Martha Rowe 27
Vein Mountain School 170
Veterans of Foreign Wars (VFW) 103
Virginia 30, 36, 37
Virginia St. School (Surry County) 171
Voorhees College 71, 131, *135*

Wade, John 204
A Walk Across America 148
Walker, Corabelle 133
Walker, Vanessa Siddle 3
Walnut Cove School (Stokes County) 150, *151*, 167, 171, 217, 219
Walnut Cove Senior Center *151*
War Between the States 12
Warlick, Wilson 42, 56, 57, 58
Warm Springs, Georgia 115
Warner's Institute (Jonesborough, Tennessee) 93
Warren, C.S. 208
Warren Wilson College 27, 39, *106*
Warren Wilson Vocational Junior College 38, *106*
Warrior, North Carolina 165
Washington, Booker T. 114, 158–159, 162, 175, 223, 238, 239
Washington, D.C. 19, 62, 63, 146
Watauga Consolidated School 61, 62, 216, *93*
Watauga County 21, 33, 61, 92–94, *93*, 165, 167, 168, 171, 206, 216
Watauga County Board of Education 110, 210
Watauga River 29
Waters, Cleo 100
Waters, F.M. 184
Waters, Lisa 59
Waters, W.O. 135–136
Watts, R.B. 202–203
Watts Plan *141*, 202–204
Wayland Seminary (Washington, DC) 238
Waymon, Eunice Kathleen (Nina Simone) 225–226
Waymon, Harold 216
Waynesville, North Carolina 99, 121
Waynesville School 99–100, 170
Weatherford, Willis D. 88
Weaver, Alfred Fulton 46
Weaver, George E. 53
Weaver, Janice Gibson 63–64
Weaverville Colored School 51, 104, 107–109, *140*, 169
Weaverville Elementary School 51, 169
Webbs School (Rutherford County) 171
Webster's *Blue Back Speller*s 93
Wells, Helen 129
Wells, Mister 75
West, W.W. 74
West End School (Caldwell County) 170

West High School 147
Western Carolina Teachers College 166
Western Carolina University 64
Western North Carolina Sanatorium 40
Westfield School (Surry County) 171
Weston, James 129
Wheeler, Billy Edd *106*
White, Ludie Lytle 107
White, Lydia 131
White, Pauline 131
white support 19, 85, 109, 121, 139, 141, 181, 189, 209, 226, 231
White-Carter, Anita 125, 127–128
Whiteside, Rev. Bill 230
Whiteside, La'Ronda Long 230
"Who Is My Brother?" 231
Wiebe, Elizabeth 96
Wiebe, Henry 96
Wiggins, Orline 155
Wilkerson, Rodney 198
Wilkes County 21, 24, 26, 30, 33, 60–61, 62–63, 120, 156–157, 165, 166, 168, 171–172, 208, 212–213, 215
Wilkins, George 55
Williams, Allen 70
Williams, Charles 129, 218
Williams, Evelyn 217
Williams, Harry 218
Williams, John 97
Williams, Laura 218
Williams, Lucius 126
Williams, L.W. 126

Williams, Perry 69
Williams, Troy Lee *151*
Williams, Willie 134
Williamson, Lloyd 211
Willow Tree School (Burke County) 157, 169
Wilson, Miss A.R. 208
Wilson, Emily Herring 227
Wilson, Frank 64, 186, 188
Wilson, Gladys 198–199
Wilson, Mary Jane 138–139
Winston-Salem, North Carolina 37
Winston-Salem State Teachers College 94, *105*, 138, 148, 181
Withrow, Lynell 194
Wolfe, J. Harold 166
Women's Home Missionary Society of the Methodist Church 177
Wood, Carrie 129
Wood, J.H. 87
Woodfin, Mrs. L.F. 129
Woodlawn Elementary School (Wilkes County) 215
Woodson, Carter G. 10, 18, 235
Woodson, Neal 185
Woodville School (Surry County) 149–150
Woolworth Store 45
Works Project Administration 207
World Health Organization 186
World War II 213
Worley, Fred 176
Worley, H.B. 144
Worley, Harley 144
Worley, Henry 144

Worrell, Mrs. E.B. 206
Wright, R.K. 215
Wykle, Charles 46

Xuala 28

Yadkin County 21, 33, 150, 165, 167, 168, 172, 173, 207–208, 216
Yadkin County Board of Education 173
Yadkin County High School 216
Yadkin River 29
Yadkinville School (Yadkin County) 150, 172
Yancey County 21, 33, 36, 56–58, 60, 82–83, 165, 172, 175, 168, 223–224, *224*
Yancey County Board of Education 57, 58, 230
Young, Carolyn *224*
Young, Col. Charles 237
Young, Eddie 53–54, 188–189, *189*, 229
Young, Hubert 82
Young, James Porter "J.P." *224*
Young, J.E. 89–90
Young, Morris 61, 188–189, 229
Young, Robert 51
Young, Thelma 138
Young Men's Institute (YMI Center) 80, 86, 175
Youngblood, L.C. 135–136
YWCA 231

Zion Baptist Church (Murphy) 52

www.ingramcontent.com/pod-product-compliance
Lightning Source LLC
Chambersburg PA
CBHW081546300426
44116CB00015B/2772